TIME IN THE SHADOWS

TIME IN THE SHADOWS

Confinement in Counterinsurgencies

Laleh Khalili

Stanford University Press
Stanford, California

Stanford University Press
Stanford, California

Printed in the United States of America

Library of Congress Cataloging-in-Publication Data

Khalili, Laleh, author.
    Time in the shadows : confinement in counterinsurgencies / Laleh Khalili.
        pages cm
    Includes bibliographical references and index.
    ISBN 978-0-8047-7832-9 (cloth : alk. paper)—ISBN 978-0-8047-7833-6
(pbk. :   )
    1. Counterinsurgency—History.   2. Detention of persons—History.
3. Counterinsurgency—United States.   4. Detention of persons—United
States.   5. War on Terrorism, 2001-2009.   6. Counterinsurgency—Israel.
7. Detention of persons—Israel.   I. Title.
    U241.K43 2012
    355.7'1—dc23   2012022541

Designed by Bruce Lundquist

Typeset by Newgen in 10.5/15 Adobe Garamond

For May and Pablo

We've got to spend time in the shadows, in the intelligence world. A lot of what needs to be done here will have to be done quietly, without any discussion, using sources and methods that are available to our intelligence agencies if we're going to be successful. It is a mean, nasty, dangerous, dirty business out there. And we have to operate in that arena.

US Vice President Dick Cheney, September 16, 2001

CONTENTS

ACKNOWLEDGMENTS

Charles Tilly once said that one reads acknowledgments to understand where the author wants to locate herself. I hope the friends, colleagues, and strangers named here do not find it presumptuous of me to invoke their names in gratitude as I "locate" myself.

My first and greatest appreciation goes to the numerous people interviewed for this book. Many of the former detainees and prisoners cannot be named, as they fear for their lives still. Others chose to maintain anonymity for reasons of their own. I am beholden to and humbled by all of them for remembering what were often devastating memories. Among the lawyers I interviewed, I want to particularly thank Lieutenant Colonel Michael D. (Dan) Mori, who represented Guantánamo Detainee 002, David Hicks, and whose unequivocal statement—"no imperial power has ever won a counterinsurgency"—challenged me and shaped my thinking from very early on. Victoria Brittain, Walid Charara, Ghassan Makarem, Jean Makdisi, Barbara Olshansky, Jihane Sfeir, Lynn Welchman, and Steven Watt all facilitated introductions and interviews in four corners of the world with detainees, guards, and lawyers. Ali al-Qaisi and Hala Sarraf were crucial in paving the way for my interviews in Amman with former Abu Ghraib, Nama, and Cropper detainees. Muhammad Safa of Khiam Rehabilitation Center for Victims of Torture was a very helpful resource on Israeli detention in Lebanon. Without Kholoud Hussein—who helped me interview and herself interviewed many—this project would not have gotten off the ground. I also fondly remember a visit to Khiyam prison with Fadi Bardawil before Israel destroyed the prison in 2006.

I thank Richard Boylan at the US National Archives; Fabrizio Bensi at the International Committee of the Red Cross archives; Debbie Usher at the Middle East Centre Archives (St. Antony's, Oxford); Dr. Mary Curry at the US National Security Archives; and the numerous archivists of the Hoover Archives at Stanford University, UK National Archives, Liddell Hart Archives, Imperial War Museum Archives, UK National Army Museum Archives, School of Oriental and African Studies Archives, London School of Economics and Political Science Archives, India Office Records (British Library), the French Military Archives at the Vincennes, and Archives Nationales d'Outré-mer.

Without the penetrating questions and useful suggestion of first and foremost the late Charles Tilly, and later of Lisa Hajjar, Rob Dover, Jamie Spencer, Nick Toloudis, Sayres Rudy, and Rochelle Davis, my learning curve would have been much steeper. James MacDougall generously shared with me his archival documents on *centres de regroupement*. Sinan Antoon kindly allowed me to use his shimmering translation of the extraordinary poem that brings this volume to a close. Many friends and colleagues were subjected to the thankless task of having to read multiple versions of the proposal, chapters, or the whole manuscript, from the moment of inception of the idea until the completion of the manuscript. Much gratitude to As'ad AbuKhalil, Rutvica Andrijasevic, Yael Berda, Ruth Blakeley, Michaelle Browers, Kathleen Cavanaugh, Matt Craven, Muriam Davis, Rochelle Davis, David Hansen-Miller, Eric Herring, Awad Joumaa, Mark Laffey, Adrienne LeBas, James MacDougall, Peter Lagerquist, Katie Natanel, Dan Neep, Jason Neidleman, Kirstin Scheid, Jamie Spencer, Colin Starger, Anna Stavarniakis, Chris Toensing, Nick Toloudis, Charles Tripp, Leslie Vinjamuri, Bob Vitalis, and Vron Ware. I thank Paul Amar and Tarak Barkawi for their perceptive criticisms on the original proposal and am especially humbled by the patience and brilliance of Lisa Hajjar, Darryl Li, and Vijay Prashad for their excellent suggestions, readings, criticisms, questions, and generosity. All remaining mistakes are mine.

The travel to the many archives and interview sites was funded generously by the Harry Frank Guggenheim Foundation, the British Academy, University of London Central Research Fund, and the School of Oriental and African

Studies Research Fund, which supported this project when the Economic and Social Research Council found it to be "too political." I am much obliged to Lisa Anderson, Ira Katznelson, Avi Shlaim, Gary Sick, and the late Charles Tilly, who acted as referees for endless funding applications. For allowing me to present early versions of various chapters and sections of this book I am indebted to Muhammad Ali Khalidi at the Beirut Conference on Palestinian citizenship, Jean Makdisi for inviting me to Arab Feminisms Conference, Anna Stavraniakis at Sussex, Ronit Lentin at Trinity College Dublin, Shiko Behar at Manchester, Paul Amar and the Department of Politics at Bristol, Jillian Schwedler at University of Massachusetts-Amherst, Nicola Pratt then at University of East Anglia, and several panels at the Middle East Studies Association and the European University Institute's Mediterranean Conference. Some bits of various chapters have appeared in radically different form in *International Journal of Middle East Studies*, *Review of International Studies*, *Middle East Report*, and *Jadaliyya.com*, and I am grateful to the publishers and editors of those journals for allowing me to reproduce those sections. Kate Wahl at Stanford University Press has been the most extraordinary editor—professional, brilliant, timely—I have ever had the honor and pleasure of working with. I would also like to gratefully acknowledge the professionalism and brilliance of Katherine Faydash's copyediting and the patient editorship of Fran Andersen.

Kholoud Hussein, Elian Weizman, and Adrian Ruprecht were resourceful and accomplished research assistants, and their creativity and intellectual curiosity immeasurably enhanced both the material and my pleasure in working with them.

Finally, I am grateful to the women of the *Feminist Review* collective, my exceptional students and colleagues at the School of Oriental and African Studies, and more than anyone else to Clare Hemmings and David Hansen-Miller for the affection, support, and sustenance provided in all the hard times before and during the writing of this manuscript. This book is—despite its very grim subject matter—dedicated to my lovely May and Pablo, that they may grow up in a world that is, even if only a tiny bit, better than the one in which we live.

TIME IN THE SHADOWS

INTRODUCTION

In this autumn of anger, even a liberal can find his thoughts
turning to . . . torture. OK, not cattle prods or rubber
hoses, at least not here in the United States, but *something*
to jump-start the stalled investigation of the greatest crime
in American history. Couldn't we at least subject them to
psychological torture, like tapes of dying rabbits or high-
decibel rap? (The military has done that in Panama and
elsewhere.) How about truth serum, administered with a
mandatory IV? Or deportation to Saudi Arabia, land of
beheadings? (As the frustrated FBI has been threatening.)
Some people still argue that we needn't rethink any of our old
assumptions about law enforcement, but they're hopelessly
"Sept. 10"—living in a country that no longer exists. . . . Even
now, Israeli law leaves a little room for "moderate physical
pressure" in what are called "ticking time bomb" cases.

Jonathan Alter, 2001[1]

Moazzam Begg, a British citizen of South Asian origin, a devout Muslim,
and a charity worker whose specialty was Muslim war zones, was arrested
in Islamabad in February 2002 by Pakistani intelligence and handed over to
the US military; he then made his way through a number of Afghan prisons,
including Bagram Air Force Base, to the Guantánamo Bay detention center. In
his harrowing account of his carceral passage through semisecret US prisons,
Moazzam Begg conveys something of the horror and banality of the process:

I soon began to see that there nothing was consistent—except inconsistency. Nothing that was true in Bagram would necessarily be true in Guantánamo. Rules,

procedures, were different. . . . The soldier sitting guarding me meticulously recorded in the logbook every move I made. When the soldiers came on duty, they
picked up the book and began noting every detail: each time I ate, slept, used the
latrine, went for recreation and showered, read the Quran, had a medical visit, had
an interrogatory visit or made any requests or complaints—which I seldom did.[2]

The interrogatory visits were numerous and, given Begg's relative unimpor-
tance in militant circles, essentially useless. Nevertheless, he was visited by
interrogators from the CIA, the FBI, the US military, and MI5 of Britain, and
many others, "perpetually asking me the same questions, and giving me no
answers. . . . Sometimes they pleaded that they were trying to save lives, and
other times they threatened to harm mine."[3]

Abu Samer's account of his arrest, interrogation, and prolonged detention
by Israel also includes endless days of interrogations. Abu Samer, a construction worker who worked for Fatah in southern Lebanon, was arrested in June
1982, shortly after the Israeli invasion of Lebanon. He was held along with
thousands of others at the Safa Factory for four days, exposed to the sun and
the heat, and questioned daily. Thereafter he was removed to Atlit Prison inside Israel, where he was interrogated frequently: "During the interrogations,
the Israeli officer asked me if I was responsible for acts of terror. I told him,
'No, I am a civilian.' He told me, 'You are lying.'" Abu Samer was accused of
having committed acts of terror in Germany, of having been a Fatah officer,
and of having conducted operations against Israel—none of which was true.
Nevertheless, Abu Samer was held for six months and then transferred to the
Al-Ansar prison camp in southern Lebanon. There he was not interrogated
again, although he saw others being taken in for interrogations; he was released
a year later, during a prisoner exchange.[4]

Another instance of confinement is less obvious, as it has none of the
trappings of formal detention. Saleh Za-'atra, a resident of al-'Eizariya, near
Jerusalem recounts:

On 6 April 2005, we were surprised when the Israeli bulldozers, Israeli army forces
and Beit El teams, came and told us that our building is very close to the Separation Wall and that they have a decision requiring its demolition. I had not received
any written documents in this regard. Immediately, the workers who came with the
army entered our home and took the furniture out. After that the Israeli bulldozers

demolished the whole building, and all the families who were living in the building are now living in tents.[5]

The Wall, an ostensible security measure, circumscribes enclaves within the West Bank, and all of Gaza. In its aims to disrupt daily lives, choke the economy, and provide physical barriers to movement and concrete loci for monitoring and surveilling the population, it has been hugely successful. Although metaphorically Gazans have named their lot an imprisonment in an enormous open-air jail, the confinement is more real than metaphoric.

All three stories recount incarceration in the course of a liberal counterinsurgency, even as the specific forms, procedures, rules, regulations, laws, and discourses governing them are substantially different. This book is a political sociology of these forms of wartime confinement. The central contention of this book is that over the course of the twentieth century, large-scale political mobilization both in colonies and in metropolises, along with struggles to bring fairness to legal regimes that regulate warfare—in other words, liberalism in war—have led to the rise of confinement and incarceration as central tactics of counterinsurgency warfare. As direct coercion and wartime violence can accrue insupportable costs—politically, economically, and morally—new forms of control in the battlefield have had to be devised. The theoreticians of these mechanisms of containment, of confinement instead of slaughter, envisioned and advertised their tactics as more humane, as more liberal, and ultimately as techniques for socially engineering the people and places they conquered. The unmentioned axis around which much counterinsurgency revolves is that of "race" or its euphemisms "culture" and "civilization." Paradoxically, the very "humanization" of asymmetric warfare and the application of liberal precepts to its conduct have legitimated war making as political intervention.

LIBERAL WARS AND ASYMMETRIC CONFLICT

> Domination over hundreds of millions of people in the colonies by the European nations was sustained only through constant, incessant, interminable wars, which we Europeans do not regard as wars at all, since all too often they resembled

not wars, but brutal massacres, the wholesale slaughter of
unarmed peoples.

Lenin, 1917[6]

Much has been written about warfare in a liberal age, including Michael
Howard's seminal work *War and the Liberal Conscience*, in which he relates
an elegant account of how liberal distaste for warfare has paradoxically made
warfare sometimes more likely, efficient, and lethal. More recent accounts have
pointed to the ways in which liberal warfare has been constituted by law and
later by "micro-practices of liberal governance."[7] This book is about the most
significant set of micropractices exercised in liberal warfare against colonial
(or neo-imperial) subjects in places of confinement.

These micropractices are not wholly disciplinary, as they are persistently
a space in which sovereign power is exercised. At a strategic level, to deny that
liberal counterinsurgencies still serve the basic geopolitical interests of major
powers is to disavow the fundamental calculus of power that still lies at the
root of that violent culmination of politics, war. In the course of the twentieth
century, liberal asymmetric warfare has sometimes been waged in response to
revolts—where former colonies sought independence through armed struggle—
and sometimes as offensive measures or to maintain regimes of occupation, as
in Israel in Lebanon and Palestine and the United States in its War on Terror.

What distinguishes warfare by powers that claim adherence to liberal
principles is the invocation of law and legality as structuring the conduct of
war, an absolute dependence on a set of clearly defined procedures and administrative processes as means of ensuring regulatory and ethical compliance,
and finally a discourse of humanitarian intent. Where these liberal wars take
place in the context of colonialism, decolonization, or neo-imperial warfare,
a series of other characteristics emerge with some force. The most significant
is a reliance on local clients, who not only reduce the costs of rule and warfare
but also provide plausible deniability. Humanitarian discourse is supplemented
with a language that insists on the urgency of a civilizing, or democratizing, or
modernizing, or improving mandate. The tactics used in such counterinsurgencies continually slip between exemplary or performative forms of violence
meant to intimidate and more "humane" and developmental warfare intended
to persuade. Racialization of the enemy is crucial to liberal counterinsurgen-

cies, in that ultimately a racial hierarchy resolves the tensions between illiberal methods and liberal discourse, between bloody hands and honeyed tongues, between weapons of war and emancipatory hyperbole.

What I want to do in this book is to critically engage with the assertions of today's counterinsurgent theorists and practitioners, foremost among them David Petraeus, David Kilcullen, and John Nagl, that counterinsurgency is about "securing" and "protecting" the population. I shall be interrogating what security and protection have come to mean in practice. In these eminently liberal soldier-scholars' theories of warfare, the liberal imperative of security of circulation (of movement, trade, and ideas) is predicated on the security of the population "and, consequently, of those who govern it."[8] The story I tell in this book explains how liberal counterinsurgencies depend on law and administration for their continuation. This means that, even as the theoreticians and practitioners of counterinsurgency speak of Clausewitz's truism that war is the continuation of politics, in practice, counterinsurgency refuses politics, or at least transforms political conflicts and contestations, revolts and insurgencies, into technical problems to be solved. This inability to recognize the politics that defines and structures revolt means that counterinsurgency simply becomes another way to better fight a war. Yet in simply tinkering with the tactics, counterinsurgency produces its own defeat again and again, with no memory of prior losses, thus repeating the same fundamental mistakes. When a defensive George Bush distinguished between "honest critics" who "question *the way* the war is handled" and irresponsible and partisan critics who challenge the very basis of such wars, he exposed precisely this central dilemma at the heart of liberal counterinsurgencies.

THE ROLE OF DETENTION

> To win the war on terror, we must be able to detain, question, and, when appropriate, prosecute terrorists captured here in America, and on the battlefields around the world.
> *The White House, 2006*[9]

I have chosen to focus on detention and confinement as central tactics of population-centric counterinsurgency precisely because confinement lays bare the contradictions of liberal asymmetric warfare in the "Third World." The freedom of movement is an avowedly fundamental tenet of liberal rights. The extent to which liberal counterinsurgencies foreclose, limit, or entirely eradicate the freedom of movement for noncombatants crucially brings into question the tensions balanced within doctrine and the practice of such warfare. The degree of adherence of liberal powers to a set of legal—and more important, ethical—codes of practice in the detention of combatants also reveals the gaps between what is avowed and what is done.

Time in the Shadows begins with the current carceral practices used by the two major liberal counterinsurgencies of our day, the Israeli asymmetric warfare in Palestine and that of the United States in the War on Terror. The book uses a genealogical historical method to analyze the origins and development of these forms of confinement. Four categories of incarceration have taken center stage in the ongoing counterinsurgency wars in Iraq, Afghanistan, and Palestine: detention camps for combatants that are managed in industrial fashion, utilizing disciplinary forms of coercion, where extraordinary violence can occur (e.g., Abu Ghraib; Bagram Air Force Base; the Ansar camps in Lebanon, Negev, and Gaza); extraterritorial detention, which legal defenders, the Red Cross, and the press can reach only in episodic, severely circumscribed, and incomplete ways (e.g., Guantánamo Bay); invisible or proxy detention (e.g., the CIA's black sites, client states' prisons used in extraordinary rendition, prisons operated by the Israeli military's client militia in southern Lebanon); and mass confinement of civilians via enclavization of their towns and villages (e.g., Gaza for much of its time under occupation, but especially since the withdrawal of settlers from the Strip; Falluja, where after the two military assaults in 2004, the United States wrapped the whole city in barbed wire and required universal fingerprinting and iris scans of all civilians for entry and exit into the city).

These categories of coercion reflect the practices on the ground, but they also trace the varieties of power that Foucault maps in his account of the emergence and transformations of power in *Security, Territory, Population*. These forms of power are predicated on law and territory (here, extraterritorial prisons); forms of disciplinary power (here, prisoner-of-war camps); and forms of power instantiated through the security apparatuses that depend on population aggregation, statistics, demographics, and the "making" of broad population categories (here, mass incarceration of noncombatants). *Time in the Shadows* tells the stories of how this world of shadows is created. It explores the micropractices of coercion by which these forms of incarceration bring insurgent populations under control, and it explores the contrasts and connections between that far twilight realm in which sovereign violence occurs without concealment and the domestic liberal order in which the same violence is concealed in broad daylight.

Time in the Shadows argues that these illiberal practices that are so pivotal to the doctrines and functioning of counterinsurgency warfare are not exceptional occurrences in which liberal regimes "lose their way," but rather they are vital components not only in the short-term processes of warfare but more significantly in the longer-term production of the liberal order when a state expands its reach beyond its own borders. This productive aspect is a form of social engineering, which whether deliberately or as a side effect of war-fighting, remakes the worlds invaded, occupied, and controlled. As I have already written, Clausewitz has famously declared that war is continuation of politics by other means. And this is certainly true, as in the transformation of the ways in which politics has affected military action—its scope, limits, extent, and intensity. But surprisingly still, politics can also be shaped by the tactics on the field. What I want to argue is that the tactics of war—whether mass slaughter or carceral techniques—are also the condition of possibility of a politics in the metropolis. If policy makers think that war can be waged more humanely, they may choose to wage war more often.

The paradox, of course, is that the carceral regime of counterinsurgency was crafted precisely because mass slaughter as a routine colonial technique of warfare was challenged by anticolonial domestic constituencies, humanitarian monitoring and legislation, and the resistance of the colonized themselves. Many of these challengers appropriated and invoked the liberal norms that were also used by colonial and imperial powers as their justification for action in the colonies. The effect of this multisited mobilization, however, was attenuated by the expediency and efficiency of coercive methods and was filtered through a hierarchical system of racialization. In this hierarchy, for example, the white Boers were considered more worthy of humanitarian considerations than the "native" Africans who had fought alongside or were detained with them.

> Just as worrying and influential to the formation of a
> comprehensive modern COIN [counterinsurgency] doctrine
> is the fact that almost all of the better known examples of
> counterinsurgency are limited to cases where a colonial or
> postimperial government was fighting on the territory of its
> dependent (ex)colonies.
>
> *Sebastian Gorka and David Kilcullen, 2011*[10]

A 2011 issue of *Joint Forces Quarterly*, a military journal published by the National Defense University (NDU), revisits counterinsurgency in light of the diminished US operations in Iraq and a rethinking of US military activities in Afghanistan and Pakistan. It is a useful issue, as it examines problems of law and private military companies, and it includes Israeli reflections on and suggestions for US counterinsurgency. The journal also contains a significant semischolarly piece by Sebastian Gorka, a professor at NDU, and David Kilcullen, one of the foremost theoreticians of counterinsurgency in the twenty-first century. Although elsewhere in this book I examine some of the claims made in their article, here I want to cite what the authors have to say about the canonical texts of US counterinsurgency today. The authors point to the experiences of British and French militaries in Malaya, Algeria, the Philippines, Vietnam, Burma, Nicaragua, and Northern Ireland as the most analyzed small wars of the past.[11] They claim that "the Counterinsurgency data set" needs to be broadened to include revolutions (Russia, Hungarian, Iranian, Cuban) and domestic resistance and partisan warfare, such as those that took place during the Second World War in Europe. I shall reflect more on the implications of this recommendation in the conclusion. Here, however, I want to use their study to support my choice of cases to be selected here.

I have based my sites of research on the locations claimed by today's counterinsurgents—and especially the *Counterinsurgency Field Manual*—as precedents. As such, the cases to which I return most frequently are those of Malaya and Algeria. Vietnam and Northern Ireland similarly bolster my arguments. I have briefly pointed to the Burmese adventures of Major General Orde Wingate, which is presumably what the authors mean above, but Wingate is crucially significant for my argument because of his exploits in Palestine.

Further, I have included wars such as the Boer War and counterinsurgencies in Kenya, Cyprus, Aden, Madagascar, and Indochina, which are sometimes, though not often, cited by today's counterinsurgents as forebears. My intent is to show the peculiar ways in which today's US and Israeli counterinsurgencies bear the marks of their progenitors.

In choosing these cases, I have purposely limited the scope of the counterinsurgent forces to those countries that have espoused liberal reasons as the bases of their counterinsurgency actions. Although Soviet gulags and fascist concentration and extermination camps have been the subject of penetrating comparative analysis (one of the most theoretically informed and intellectually influential examples is Hannah Arendt's *The Origins of Totalitarianism*), the regularity with which liberal regimes have employed mass forms of imprisonment beyond their borders and during asymmetric warfare has been left relatively underexplored (the seminal works of Caroline Elkins and David Anderson on the Kenyan emergency are notable exceptions; the US War on Terror has also produced a vast body of literature, which primarily views these confinements through a human rights lens). What accounts for the sparseness of comparative scholarship in this area is perhaps inherent to the topic of study itself. The placement of these prisons beyond the borders of the democratic state and the tension between liberal discourses of freedom of circulation and illiberal confinement exacerbate their relative invisibility and disconnect them from the liberal orders which establish them.

Time in the Shadows draws on materials from more than a dozen archives, including those of the International Committee of the Red Cross; the US and UK National Archives; the Imperial War Museum archives; the French military archives at Vincennes; and specialist archives in London, Oxford, New York, the District of Columbia, and the Hoover Institution. It also draws on millions of pages of records released by Wikileaks or under the US Freedom of Information Act, as well as extensive interviews with former prisoners (especially those held in Guantánamo, Bagram, Abu Ghraib, and Israeli prisons in Palestine and Lebanon) and with their interrogators, guards, and attorneys, and hundreds of memoirs written by prisoners, policy makers, and soldiers over the long twentieth century.

In all, the book analyzes the ways in which liberal counterinsurgencies are situated in much broader global trends that structure transnational elite politics and ideologies of rule. It argues that the more tactics of war are represented and remade as more "humane," population-centric, and developmental, the greater the risk of such wars becoming acceptable. *Time in the Shadows* ultimately contends that these liberal forms of asymmetric warfare—saturated as they are with legal processes, administrative procedures, and an intent to co-opt and pacify intransigent populations—are also in the last instance innovations in indirect forms of rule, where coercion is not so much displaced by as dressed in the garb of hegemony.

CHAPTER I

THE FOREBEARS
Imperial and Colonial
Counterinsurgencies

> Making peace with the Indian is the primary intention of the
> prince and with it should one begin. . . . In peace the Indian
> gives vassalage and obedience, and in recognition of it does
> he give tribute to the prince, though the conquerors . . . are
> obligated . . . to indoctrinate them. . . . However, in order for
> these peaces to last, it is most important that the commander
> knows how to settle and protect them with sagacity.
>
> *Captain Bernardo de Vargas Machuca, 1599*[1]

ASYMMETRIC AND IRREGULAR WARFARE

In lectures given to a Spanish university in 1962, and published as *The Theory
of the Partisan*, Carl Schmitt traces the emergence of modern guerrilla warfare to the Spanish irregular battles against the invading Napoleonic army in
the early years of the nineteenth century. Schmitt claims that "[in] this war,
a people—a pre-bourgeois, pre-industrial, and pre-conventional nation—for
the first time confronted a modern, well-organized, regular army that had
evolved from the experiences of the French Revolution. Thereby, new horizons
of war opened, new concepts of war developed, and a new theory of war and
politics emerged."[2] Schmitt defines the four basic characteristics of the partisan as irregularity, mobility, a political aim, and telluric (i.e., tied to the soil)
character. He further claims that the Spanish war is the first modern partisan
warfare for two reasons. First is the modern nature of the Napoleonic military rather than any specific characteristic inherent to the Spanish guerrille-
ros themselves.[3] Just as important, Schmitt cites the tellurism of the Spanish

guerrilla war as inspiring the Romantic nationalism of Fichte and von Herder with their emphasis on the *heimat* (homeland). By this definitional sleight of hand, those struggles of colonized people against colonizers preceding Spanish guerrilla warfare (most obvious among them the aboriginal peoples of the Americas, but also the white settlers' partisan warfare against the European colonial powers) are erased, and the emergence of the practice and doctrine of modern irregular warfare is displaced to Europe.[4]

In fact, asymmetric warfare had long served colonial conquest, and it had even been incorporated into manuals of warfare as early as the first major wave of transoceanic colonization. In *The Military Revolution*, Geoffrey Parker tells us that after their initial catastrophic defeats in pitched battle, the natives of both North and South Americas avoided directly engaging European armies and instead resorted to guerrilla warfare. Parker quotes one New England preacher grumbling, "They doe acts of hostility without proclaiming war; they don't appear openly in the field to bid us battle"; another complains that "every swamp is a castle [or fortification] to them, knowing where to find us; but we know not where to find them."[5] Their methods of warfare did not go unnoticed by the conquerors who studied these tactics. Bernardo de Vargas Machuca's *The Indian Militia*, written at the end of the sixteenth century and quoted at the opening of this chapter, "dismissed the entire pattern of European warfare," promoted the use of search-and-destroy commando units, and advocated the training of military commanders who "knew as much about planting survival crops and curing tropical ulcers as about laying ambushes and mounting surprise attacks."[6] Simultaneously, a vast swath of legal discourse was produced to take account of the anomalous figure of the "Indian," this obstacle to conquest of the new territories in the Western Hemisphere.[7]

Asymmetric warfare was crucial to the conquest of the Americas, Africa, and Asia. In those places, asymmetry was not necessarily engendered by the numeric superiority of the colonizers, and certainly not in the early years of the conquest. In fact, in most of the colonized places, the colonizers were at first numerically inferior, sometimes dramatically so; what gave them their military advantage was their access to superior arms and often savage methods of warfare, their utilization of divide and conquer in aligning with local factions (often via economic incentives), their cunning use of treaties and laws on which they reneged unscrupulously, their immediate establishment of centralized governance regimes and institutions that codified their system of domination and that in nonsettler colonies were most successful when deployed via local intermediaries or clients, and their capacity for ruthless suppression of any resistance in war or to their new regimes of rule. All that advantage was then veiled in the cloak of "civilization" spun from the weft of law and woof of popular and expert discourse.

COLONIAL WARS OF THE NINETEENTH CENTURY

These colonial wars of conquest—fought most brutally in the second cycle of European imperial expansion in the nineteenth century—were numerous and often came at great cost to the indigenous peoples in blood, treasure, and control over their destinies. Although in a few distinct instances—and in some battles of protracted wars—the indigenous forces defeated the superior arms of the European forces, the overall picture at the end of the nineteenth century pointed to the subjugation of vast numbers of people across the globe by the European empires. Here, I briefly sketch three instances of asymmetric imperial and/or colonial warfare whose traces can be—often very transparently—detected in the subsequent doctrines and practices of the powerful states that fought those wars and where particular carceral or juridical techniques in counterinsurgency practice were innovated or consolidated. These are the French conquest of Algeria, the nascent United States' wars against Native Americans, and the alternating butcher-and-bolt and policing policies of the British Empire in the northwestern and western frontiers of India.

The French Conquest of Algeria

> I have often heard men in France whom I respect, but with whom I do not agree, find it wrong that we burn harvests, that we empty silos, and finally that we seize unarmed men, women, and children. These, in my view, are unfortunate necessities, but ones to which any people that wants to wage war on the Arabs is obliged to submit... We shall never destroy Abd el-Kader's power unless we make the position of the tribes who support him so intolerable that they abandon him.
> *Alexis de Tocqueville, 1841*[8]

> These murmurs seem to indicate that the Chamber finds my
> means too barbaric. Gentlemen, war cannot be waged in the
> spirit of philanthropy. Once you choose war as an end, you
> cannot reject any means whatever. . . . I shall always prefer
> the interests of France to an absurd philanthropy directed
> towards foreigners who decapitate those of our soldiers who
> are wounded or taken prisoners.
> *Marshal Thomas-Robert Bugeaud, 1840*[9]

Algeria was the gateway for French conquest in Africa. The subjugation of
Algeria between 1830 and 1847 is known best for its utilization of the *razzia* as
a tactic of warfare, the centrality of the military to both fighting and settlement, the establishment of an administrative and intelligence and surveillance arm—Bureaux Arabes—which recruited French Arabic speakers with
knowledge of local customs to mediate between the state and the local chiefs
or elders, France's recruitment of fighters from colonized areas into its Armée
d'Afrique from 1830 onward, and its establishment of the Foreign Legion in
1831 (whose headquarters were in Sidi Bel Abbes in Algeria until 1962).[10] Their
earlier expeditions in 1830 also established a precedent for a degree of colonial
violence that was to continue unabated until 130 years later. One of the earlier
commanders, Duc de Rovigo, "ordered summary executions on the slight-
est suspicion, showed 'unnecessary cruelty' at places like Belida—sacked in
1831—and 'swept like a destroying angel over the Metidja.'"[11] When after ten
years this brutality proved too costly and ineffective in defeating the guerrillas,
a change in direction was debated in Paris. Interestingly, Marshal Thomas-
Robert Bugeaud—who had fought under Napoléon in the Peninsular War
(1808–1814) and who had condoned plunder and rape of the Saragossan civilians
by his troops there—was originally opposed to French presence in Algeria, as
he saw it undermining France's European deterrence capabilities. But by 1836,
he had begun to see Algeria as "a useful training ground for the French army"
and a site of exile for domestic troublemakers. To conquer Algeria, however,
he believed that sufficient numbers of troops were required to "strike at the
morale of the Arabs everywhere."[12]

The solution to the problem of raising an army to conquer Algeria was
seen as settler colonization, which would allow for the generation of a colonial
economy. Bugeaud writes explicitly about the aims of military settlement: it

would shift the burden of paying for the conquest to Algeria, where taxation and trade would support further conquest. Roads built by the army would also be used for trade, and the military men could settle in fortified villages they would build through the requisition of native labor. After a year of service these men would be given leave to marry and propagate. Bugeaud advocated the devastation of the bases of Arab economy and community; he claimed there wasn't much to destroy in any case. Bugeaud asserted that the Arabs "have none of these major centres of government, population and commerce at the heart of a civilized country, nor any of those large arteries that circulate the life of civilized nations: no inland points, no major roads, no factories, no villages, nor farms; all they have are a gun and a horse."[13] For the military men to conquer and settle, they must be young and vigorous; they must have made their careers in Africa; and they must "know topography, customs, habits, and, if possible, the language of the country."[14]

Tactically, Bugeaud believed that "we must forget these orchestrated and dramatic battles that civilized people fight against one another, and realize that unconventional tactics are the soul of this war," and that the basic principles for unconventional warfare were mobility, morale, leadership and firepower.[15] To ensure the defeat of Abd al-Qadir's guerrilla force and secure the acquiescence of Arabs, Bugeaud "wanted the natives to fear the action of his troops everywhere, thus giving his army a moral prestige which in itself would result in economy in the actual application of material force."[16] Thus, the *razzia*, a tactic borrowed from the Algerians themselves but exaggerated and further brutalized, was deployed. In the French version of the *razzia* in Algeria, the French forces "chopped down fruit trees, burned settlements and crops, and seized livestock. Few of the region's numerous Arab villages escaped destruction. What once had been hillsides 'teeming with rich crops' were transformed into blackened wasteland."[17] The *razzia* served mundane functions (the plunder of crops and cattle alleviated logistical problems of supplies), strategic aims (it destroyed the local bases of the economy), provided the French with prisoners who were used as "barter to pressure the tribe in question into submission," and terrorized the population.[18] When even the *razzia* was not sufficient, an officer serving Bugeaud ordered his subordinates to "kill all the men over the age of fifteen, and put all the women and children abroad ships bound for the Marquesas Islands or elsewhere. In a word, annihilate everyone who does not crawl at our feet like dogs."[19]

Other repressive measures were disguised in civilizing intent. Bugeaud's March 6, 1841 edict relocated civilians living near settler colonies into reserved areas and required them to carry identity medallions issued by the French in order to exit their reservations—most often to work for the settlers.[20] To ensure order, Bugeaud advocated forced sedentarization of tribes, as well as a system of indirect rule, stating "that any immediate reduction of the traditional pre-rogatives of tribal aristocracies would only augment the number of the metro-pole's enemies," and putting this into effect by requiring, for example, that the settlers only acquire labor through tribal leaders.[21] The Bureaux Arabes, consisting of military officers and administrators, served as the intermediaries to the local chiefs, nominated and dismissed chiefs, inspected local popula-tions, commanded auxiliary troops, and aimed to civilize and "improve" the tribes.[22] Bugeaud recommended deportation of troublesome tribes, including noncombatants, women, and children, to Martinique, Guadeloupe, or the Marquesas Islands.[23] He gave free rein to his lieutenants, which led to his of-ficers entombing hundreds of intransigent civilians in one instance, asphyxi-ating with smoke another group numbering in the hundreds that was trapped in a cave, and being praised by Bugeaud in the bargain.[24] When Bugeaud was criticized in Paris, he resigned in disgust in 1947 and died two years later.

Bugeaud himself initially applied his counterguerrilla tactics and principles of fighting to fighting in "urban spaces and houses" against the revolutionar-ies of 1848. His ideas were later applied in a softened form made palatable for more humanitarian times, in the doctrines and practices of colonial warfare for which Marshals Gallieni and Lyautey were celebrated.

The Indian Wars of North America

> The real essence of the matter is that devastation and annihilation is the principal method of warfare that savage tribes know. Excessive humanitarian ideas should not prevent harshness against those who use harsh methods, for in being overkind to one's enemies, a commander is simply being unkind to his own people.
> *Elbridge Colby, 1927*[25]

Patrick Wolfe has famously written that in settler colonialism, "invasion is a structure, rather than an event; [and] expropriation continues as a founda-

tional characteristic of settler-colonial society."[26] Such expropriation is, however, almost never met with the acquiescence of those dispossessed. The Indian
Wars of North America began long before the United States emerged as an
independent state and continued into the twentieth century (the Battle of Bear
Valley against Yaqui Indians was fought in 1918). They attest to the continued,
variegated, and multisited struggle of Native Americans, pushed further and
further to the West through the course of several centuries by unrelenting
and brutal settlement and warfare that sometimes became exterminationist.

One such moment was the passage of the Indian Removal Act (1830), which
drove Native Americans out of the southeastern states toward the West. Before signing the act into law, President Andrew Jackson employed the soaring
vocabulary of protection and paternalism, "humanity and national honor," to
justify the dispossession. Once the act was signed, however, a far more hard-
headed language of white settlement and prosperity appeared to justify the act:

> By opening the whole territory . . . to the settlement of the whites it will incalculably
> strengthen the SW frontier and render the adjacent States strong enough to repel future
> invasions without remote aid. It will relieve the whole State of Mississippi and the west-
> ern part of Alabama of Indian occupancy, and enable those States to advance rapidly in
> population, wealth, and power. It will . . . enable [the Indians] to pursue happiness in
> their own way and under their own rude institutions . . . and [will] perhaps cause them
> gradually, under the protection of the Government and through the influence of good
> counsels, to cast off their savage habits and become an interesting, civilized, and Chris-
> tian community.[27]

What followed the passage of the act was a brutal trek through hostile territories, during which significant proportions of native tribes perished through
hunger, violence, and disease. Some tribes' members tried to elude the removals;
others, like the Seminole peoples of Florida, fought long guerrilla wars against
the US forces.[28] Not long after, they were once again subjected to settlement,
provocation, and warfare in the West. The wars almost always resulted in the
dwindling tribes cornered into ever-smaller "reservations," ostensibly set up
for their protection, often on inhospitable and infertile land, thus providing a
severely circumscribed space for monitoring and surveillance on the one hand
and freeing up maximal tracts of much-desired territory for white settlement.

The ambiguity of the role of the frontiersmen—as warriors or police—
meant that they could be found "patrolling, scouting, pursuing, and always

the endless work of building and maintaining the little forts that multiplied across the face of the West," mapping territories, building dual-use (commerce and logistics) roads, and chasing "criminals."[29]

Although the increasing professionalization of the US Army after the US Civil War meant that the military institutions began to develop self-conscious written doctrines of conventional warfare, lessons of fighting mobile irregulars with intimate knowledge of the physical terrain were passed down in vernacular or experiential fashion rather than through doctrine. Andrew Birtle points out that the US Military Academy at West Point discussed Indian wars in only one part of its curriculum, the course on law:

International law as taught at West Point approached the subject of Indian warfare in somewhat the same manner as it did the treatment of guerrillas and actively hostile civilian populations in civilized warfare. On the one hand, it maintained that the laws of war did not apply to aboriginal people—just as they did not apply to guerrillas—for the simple reason that "savages" did not abide by those laws. This meant that soldiers were free to employ the harshest measures necessary to subdue them. Yet academy textbooks also taught that principles of humanity and Christian charity demanded that soldiers employ stringent measures only when they were absolutely necessary.[30]

What was learned in the Indian Wars became the necessary, if unwritten, manual for subsequent overseas asymmetric warfare, in the Philippines, the Caribbean, and Latin America. Techniques deployed in the Indian Wars—some in use long before and continually perfected—included theories of collective responsibility, an impulse to "civilize" in order to pacify, the use of native and settler scouts and auxiliaries, the use of reservations as militarily useful spaces for concentrating and monitoring native fighters and civilians, timing the battles at night or winter to ensure lack of preparedness among Native Americans, and surprise attacks against villages to undermine the socioeconomic bases and independence of Native American communities.[31]

Many of the US military governors of the Philippines had fought and administered Native Americans, and they compared various Filipino peoples—both favorably and unfavorably—to their former charges.[32] Where in the "pacification" of the Native Americans "each tribe [had been treated] according to its particular level of cultural development," similar hierarchies—in form if not content—were applied to Filipinos on the basis of religious categories.[33] The concentration camps of the Philippines could trace their lineage to both the *reconcentrados* first used by the Spanish in Cuba in 1895–1898 and to the reservation system used in the US western frontier.[34] Filipino Scouts were modeled on the Indian Scouts.[35] Although discourses and practices were adapted to the specific contexts, a series of modularized tactics for counterinsurgency were devised that traveled from the Philippines (1898–1906) to Cuba (1906–1909), Haiti (1915–1934), the Dominican Republic (1916–1924), and Nicaragua (1927–1933), and were eventually institutionalized in the Marine Corps' *Manual of Small Wars Operations* (1935) and the seminal *Small Wars Manual* of 1940.[36] This manual was then resurrected in the Latin American counterinsurgencies of the 1980s, providing a thread that connected the Indian Wars of the nineteenth century to US asymmetric warfare in the twentieth.

Butcher and Bolt and the Sandeman System

> Sir Bindon sent orders that we were to stay in the Mamund
> Valley and lay it waste with fire and sword in vengeance. . . .
> We proceeded systematically, village by village, and we
> destroyed the houses, filled up the wells, blew down the
> towers, cut down the great shady trees, burned the crops and
> broke the reservoirs in punitive devastation. So long as the
> villages were in the plain, this was quite easy. The tribesmen
> sat on the mountains and sullenly watched the destruction
> of their homes and means of livelihood. . . . At the end of a
> fortnight the valley was a desert, and honour was satisfied.
> *Winston Churchill, 1897*[37]

In Britain's vast empire, the peoples of the frontiers, in particular in the Northwest Frontier, continued, throughout the nineteenth century and until decolonization, to resist British domination by frequently taking up arms against the attempts of the government to tax them, monitor them, or interfere in their civil affairs. Where the British had "pacified" indigenous revolt, civil authorities were eventually put into place; but the peripheries, especially in Punjab, Baluchistan, and Burma, remained under the control of military men till the very end of the empire and were the sites of chronic battles, expeditions, and punitive military measures.

At the end of the nineteenth century, the British used two distinct methods to deal with intransigent natives. In Baluchistan, the Sandeman system administered the tribes, whereas in the Northwest Frontier, the preferred strategy was the Close-Border System, which deployed "economic weapons," a gentle euphemism for a combination of collective fines and butcher and bolt.[38] As one former high-ranking British imperial officer in the Punjab (and a biographer of Sandeman) wrote, in this system, "when outrages do occur the tribe is fined . . . and when fines accumulate to an unbearable extent, the tribe is punished by a blockade, or a military expedition, only to offend again when the effect of the punishment has worn off."[39]

The blockades "kept the laborious, hard-working portion of the tribesmen from going about their lawful occasions" and aimed at "starving the tribe[s] into submission," whereas the expeditions were described by the British military as a strategy of butcher and bolt that left scorched earth, destroyed villages, and "a legacy of hatred and contempt" behind.[40] They were intended also to act as deterrence: "The point then to be decided was whether the casualties inflicted were severe enough to discourage the hotheads who were in the van of the battle, and to discredit the mullahs who were behind it."[41] Butcher and bolt did not distinguish combatants from civilians; the enemy was considered "the whole population."[42] The forces used were native irregulars, and although intelligence was considered of immense importance, the topography and particular character of social life in the frontier meant that the government of India was desperately lacking it and was least equipped to know about this region than any other in India.[43]

As part of the process of cordon and search used during the expeditions, local hostages were used. As one Northwest Frontier British officer advised other British officers in Palestine:

It might be worthwhile forming a "hostage corps" composed of the sons of hostiles. A couple of these in the front car of a convoy would discourage the use of land mines. On the Frontiers we often push the relatives of an outlaw in front of a police party when entering a house where an outlaw is suspected of hiding.[44]

These practices of punishment and deterrence continued to be used as a means of terrorizing tribes into submission as late as 1939, with Winston Churchill having participated in one such expedition in 1897 and writing about it in both his later memoirs and in *Malakand Field Force*. The Northwest Frontier had been so significant in British military practice that a substantial chapter of C. E. Callwell's *Small Wars* dedicated to "hill warfare" is primarily based on the area.[45]

The Sandeman system, in contrast, was considered the more humane alternative, a kind of "benevolent despotism" meant to "to deal with the hearts and minds of the people and not only with their fears," which even later masters of indirect rule and gurus of colonial administration such as Marshal Hubert Lyautey were to emulate.[46] Sir Robert Sandeman refined a system of proxy control in Baluchistan through a policy of "peaceful penetration" based on "knowledge and sympathy" whose object was "the gradual civilization and betterment of the tribes."[47] This policy entailed "tribal service" and "subsidized control," best summed up by Lord Curzon in a letter of appreciation as consisting

in employing the tribes as custodians of the highways and guardians of the peace in their own districts; in paying them for what they did well (and conversely fining them for transgression); in encouraging commerce and traffic by the lightening or abolition of tolls and the security of means of communication; in the protection, rather than diminution, of tribal and clan independence, subject only to the overlordship of the British *raj*; in a word, in a policy not of spasmodic and retributive interference, but of steady and unfaltering conciliation.[48]

For its enforcement, the system depended on the always present, though veiled, threat of force, including the possibility of collective fines and punishments, the use of tribal *jirgas* to mete out punishments for ordinary crimes and for transgressions against the British, the strengthening of the role of the more affluent and powerful elite in a tribe at the expense of tribal democracy, and the potential to use military violence in the last instance.[49]

When after his death attempts were made to transmit Sandeman's system to Waziristan, it failed, because, the colonial officers wrote, "owing to the democratic feeling of the race, it is often the case that the headmen, if unsupported, cannot enforce authority over the more unruly spirits." In other words, the Pashtun *maliks* (landowners) were not as powerful as those in Baluchistan; and the Mahsud tribe of Waziristan was most intractable.[50] The main reasons for failure, however, lay elsewhere: Sandeman had had a significant military presence in Baluchistan, which served to remind the tribes of the costs of noncooperation.[51] Further, a system that emphasized perpetual surveillance and massive military presence was too impractical in the geographically inhospitable and politically intransigent terrain of Waziristan.[52]

These two approaches to asymmetric warfare—unbridled force and direct control versus the use of local proxies to rule indirectly—were to be utilized again and again in some combination in the coming centuries wherever the British military faced unconventional fights.

COUNTERINSURGENCY WARFARE
IN THE LONG TWENTIETH CENTURY

As empires consolidated at the end of the nineteenth century and militaries further professionalized, and later yet, as revolt in the colonies worldwide escalated and was encountered militarily, a number of names became associated with specific doctrines of asymmetric warfare or colonial policing. By writing about these men, I do not mean to indicate that they were the *sine qua non* of policies of rule or the only innovators of military action, but in a number of instances they have become the archetypes of a particular approach or advocates of a specific solution to problems of overseas domination. They are invoked—self-consciously and argumentatively—in the debates within the transnational epistemic community of civilian and military counterinsurgents. Many of their insights and practices have been canonized not only in doctrine manuals—the French David Galula's in the 2006 US counterinsurgency manual, the British Kitson's in Britain's—but also in a more enduring fashion in embodied practices and institutional memories of men who fight. These thinkers and theoreticians of counterinsurgency can be categorized into two groups: the men who succeeded through warfare and military administration in installing or defending colonial regimes (Gallieni and Lyautey for France, Callwell and Gwynn for Britain) and the men who ultimately fought or promoted unsuccessful counterinsurgency wars against anticolonial forces (Wingate, Thompson, and Kitson for Britain; Trinquier and Galula for France; and Rostow and Vann for the United States). I have focused especially on their writings as regards confinement specifically and on questions of law and administration more broadly.

Gallieni and Lyautey

> The pirate [the rebel] is a plant which will grow only in
> certain soils, and the surest method is to make the soil
> uncongenial to him. . . . Supposing that a piece of land
> overrun by rank weeds has to be brought under tillage; it
> is not enough to extirpate these weeds; that will only mean
> starting again next day; but it is essential that, where the
> ground has been ploughed up, the conquered soil should be
> isolated, fenced, and then sowed with the good grain which
> alone will make it impervious to the tares.
>
> *General Duchemin, commander in chief of French Occupation
> Forces in Indochina, 1895*[53]

Toward the end of the nineteenth century, a new French doctrine of both warfare and postconflict rule emerged in Southeast Asia and Africa. After the brutal initial conquest of Indochina over a forty-year period and the forcible extraction of the Treaty of Protection from the Indochinese, local rebellion and resistance against colonial powers had to be dealt with both militarily and politically in such a fashion as to consolidate France's territorial gains and to ensure the circumvention of future rebellions.

In this, Colonel (later Marshal) Joseph Gallieni devised a series of new tactics and political strategies that influenced not only French colonial conquest in years to come but also counterinsurgency doctrine of the French and the United States after the Second World War. In 1892, to fight against Vietnamese guerrillas, led by De Tham in Tonkin, Gallieni adopted light mobile units and tactics of jungle warfare, abandoning Bugeaud's rapid military offensives and methods of mass brutality.[54] Gallieni was careful in surveying and mapping the areas he was to conquer, and he was adamant about securing the acquiescence, even if passive or reluctant, of the civilian population, to protect his supply lines. His pacification of the rebellious regions entailed not only his *tâche d'huile* (or oil-spot) military method, whereby areas were captured and "protected" in a gradual outwardly unfolding fashion, but also the stimulation of local markets and establishment of skeletal social infrastructure, such as schools or clinics, simultaneous with military expansion and consolidation in an area. The day-to-day administration of the area was then left to loyal local clients, as "Gallieni was a strong believer in a *politique des races*, that is, in letting the local social groups rule themselves."[55] To this end, scandalously in the eyes of French administrators, Gallieni armed loyal villagers. As Paul Rabinow recounts in his excellent *French Modern*:

> The next step in pacification was to create new needs. First, one induced the rulers and their wives to adopt European clothing; others would soon imitate them. The natives had to learn French; a well-designed educational system would produce, in one generation, a pacified and devoted population, one thoroughly open to French ideas.[56]

This ostensibly benign bout of "modernization" and developmentalism had to be enforced at the point of bayonets and using the blunt instrument of the law. The Indochina criminal code passed in the 1890s placed limits on press freedom, assemblies, elections and activism, and using the suitably vague language of "public security" and "political trouble," it provided the tools for suppressing political dissent against French rule.[57]

In 1896, Gallieni moved to Madagascar, overthrowing the Merina dynasty then ruling the island and later fighting against rebel groups in various parts of the island. His *tâche d'huile* method was consolidated here and put into effect in both military and civil domains, because in Madagascar, unlike in Tonkin, Gallieni represented unified command, required if military conquest and "civic action" were to go hand in hand. In Madagascar, Gallieni consolidated the French version of indirect rule, which became even more significant under his deputy (both in Tonkin and in Madagascar) Hubert de Lyautey. Once an area was pacified, Gallieni would set out to wholly transform the Malgache inhabitants. He did so through the appropriation of land from the local peoples (then made available cheaply to settlers) and their resettlement in new villages; the forcible acquisition of labor from the conquered natives, who were sometimes made to work their own alienated lands; and the gradual reengineering of their whole social world, including their sedentarization, transformation of their local authorities, and the enforcement of *politique des races*, or indirect rule via local chiefs.[58] In Gallieni's own formulation in 1908, the administrative hierarchies placed Europeans at the apex "to direct and survey the ensemble, while indigenous authorities [administered] the *indigènes*, collecting taxes, overseeing the execution of public work, and all other economic and administrative tasks demanded of them."[59]

Gallieni's military writings and practices of rule institutionalized a number of techniques that were to become core practices of a kind of a population-centric counterinsurgency (discussed in chapter 2): in military matters, wholesale destruction was no longer the primary or predominant means of subduing revolt. As he wrote in a famous memo to all his subordinate commanders on May 22, 1898, violence had to be held in reserve and carefully calibrated:

We must remember that unfortunately in colonial wars, the rebelliousness of the people is imposed on us all too often, but destruction should only be used in the last instance, and only as prelude to reconstruction. We must spare the country and its inhabitants, as the former shall receive our future settlers, and the latter will act as our agents and collaborators, in order to carry out our enterprises.[60]

In the conquered areas, soldiers of various imperial origins (as well as European volunteers of the Foreign Legion) provided coercive manpower.[61] Employing colonial soldiers in the wars of colonial conquest was not new to Gallieni's time and had long been utilized to keep down the costs of imperial conquest and policing, and because ostensibly white European soldiers did not have the tropical robustness of their colonial counterparts. However, by the late nineteenth century, as France itself became more democratic, conscription of citizen-soldiers could potentially "bring political influence to bear overseas."[62] Thus, to avoid the possibility of revolt by French soldiers, colonial armies were increasingly deployed in conquest.

Establishment of local proxies through whom the colonizer could rule also allowed for the appearance of independence. *Politique des races* permitted at once a dual system of control and the possibility of dividing the conquered populations for the ease of controlling them. For Gallieni the "phantom power" of the chiefs was something to which "the natives are accustomed and behind which we can manoeuvre more comfortably."[63] Aside from maintaining military control over an area, military officers acted as political overseers of the *politique des races* and were at the helm of reconstruction, managing the rebuilding (or building) of the holy trinity of roads, schools, and markets, using corvée labor if necessary.[64] If the civilizing mission was not openly discussed, a developmental agenda that saw the natives improve through better markets, education, and hygiene, was. Indeed, asymmetric warfare as "armed social work"—as described by a twenty-first-century counterinsurgent—seems to be how Gallieni saw his work as a colonial officer, although he was less coy about the power levers hidden within developmental policies.[65]

Gallieni's great protégé, Hubert Lyautey, had been his lieutenant in both Tonkin and Madagascar and went on to become the military governor and resident-general of French Morocco between 1907 and 1925. His concerns were far more administrative, and he fulfilled his dream of building "a Cecil Rhodes career" by consolidating indirect French rule in Morocco, where he established the doctrinal verity that, "since the social and political dimension of colonial conquest is as important as its military aspect, *pacification* must rely on a constant and subtle mix [*dosage*] of both coercion and consent."[66] Lyautey reinforced Gallieni's admonishment about calibrating the use of force:

The country ought not be handled with force alone. The rational method—the only one, the proper one, and also the one for which I myself was chosen rather than any-one else—is the constant interplay of force with politics.[67]

For Lyautey, the acquiescence of indigenous populations had to be secured; hence, "the answer was first force and *nettoyage* [cleanup]" and then "making administration as economical as possible, relying on local leaders, reducing effective costs, and neglecting unproductive regions."[68] In Morocco, Lyautey went native, constructing "an exoticised, cosmopolitan home," where he "loved sitting on Arab mats, drinking their strong coffee, eating their food, and adopting parts of their garb."[69] He also ordered the wholesale transfor-mation of cityscapes, building new European urban centers while annoying the French *colons* by his ostensible magnanimity toward the natives.[70] Where needed, however, the velvet glove was cast off the mailed fist. Rebellions in the mountains were subdued by tactics of siege warfare, with a particular emphasis on isolating and starving the guerrilla forces (and possible civilian collaterals).[71] In the urban centers, Lyautey preferred to rule through proxies, adapting Gallieni's *politique des races* to Morocco and calling it the "politiques des grands caïds."[72] He admonished his officers to "never forget that in every society there is a class to be governed, and a natural-born ruling class upon whom all depends. Link their interests to ours."[73] This emphasis on bolstering local chiefs' powers continues to echo through the social and political institu-tions and struggles of postcolonial states.

Callwell and Gwynn

> But when there is no king to conquer, no capital to seize,
> no organized army to overthrow, and where there are no
> celebrated strongholds to capture, and no great centres of
> population to occupy, the objective is not so easy to select.
> It is then that the regular troops are forced to resort to cattle
> lifting and village burning and that the war assumes an aspect
> which may shock the humanitarian. . . . If the enemy cannot
> be touched in his patriotism or his honour, he can be touched
> through his pocket.
> *Major General C. E. Callwell, 1906*[74]

In the 1930s handbook for British imperial officers, *Imperial Policing*, Major
General Charles Gwynn, a British officer of Irish extraction who had served
the empire in both West Africa and Sudan, usefully describes the "police duties of the Army" in the event of autochthonous revolt:

Excessive severity may antagonise [the loyal] element, add to the number of the rebels, and leave a lasting feeling of resentment and bitterness. On the other hand, the
power and resolution of the Government forces must be displayed. Anything which
can be interpreted as weakness encourages those who are sitting on the fence to keep
on good terms with the rebels.[75]

Pitched somewhere closer to civil governance, the policing action that occu-
pies Gwynn's attention occurs where the British expect to continue ruling a
population after the hostilities have been suppressed and, as such, are trying
to avoid antagonizing the civilians from whom nascent rebel or revolutionary groups can recruit members and receive logistical and moral support. The
principles Gwynn elaborates for imperial policing are fourfold: power has to
remain vested in civil authorities and the army has to remain disciplined and
loyal; force has to be the minimum necessary to get a job done (although "the
sight of cold steel has a calming effect, and the steady advance of a line of bayonets has often sufficed to disperse a mob without resort to firing"); any use
of violence has to be "firm and timely"; and the military and civilian authorities have to cooperate.[76] Further, in his postmortem of British policing action
in Waziristan in 1937, Gwynn underscores the importance of local headmen

and of economic development as a corollary to military action.[77] Even more significant, Gwynn claims

that maintenance of order by punitive action alone does not provide a solution. A firm hand undoubtedly is the first essential, but little real progress can be made till the economic condition of the country is improved and the authority of the headmen fully established. . . . Penalties may be inflicted on headmen for failure to exercise their authority, but their authority is strengthened if they can point to the benefits conferred by peaceful and prosperous conditions where roads have penetrated.[78]

Gwynn helpfully distinguishes the policing role of occupying powers from conventional warfare and even asymmetric "small wars" against irregular troops, which he defines as "deliberate campaigns with a definite military objective, but undertaken with the ultimate object of establishing civil control" and in which "[no] limitations are placed on the amount of force which can be legitimately exercised, and the Army is free to employ all the weapons the nature of the terrain permits."[79]

Perhaps this emphasis on a no-holds-barred approach to small wars is what accounts for the scorched-earth tactics of Lords Roberts and Kitchener in South Africa during the Boer War (1899–1902). The most important military document influenced by the Boer War is Major General C. E. Callwell's *Small Wars: Their Principles and Practice*, first written in 1896 and updated in 1906 with his experiences of fighting in the Boer War. The book is a veritable encyclopedia of nineteenth-century small wars, from French General Hoche's suppression of the Vendée Rebellion to the continuous wars of the Northwest Frontier. *Small Wars* was immensely influential in consolidating British Army doctrine, with the doctrine manual of 1929 summarizing parts of it under the heading of "Warfare in Undeveloped and Semi Civilised Countries."[80]

Callwell distinguishes between three classes of small wars, "campaigns of conquest or annexation, campaigns for the suppression of insurrections or lawlessness or for the settlement of conquered or annexed territory, and campaigns undertaken to wipe out an insult, to avenge a wrong, or to overthrow a dangerous enemy."[81] In a sense, the small war is fought not only for instrumental ends—facilitating settlement or acquisition of territory—but also as a performative of power, "of overawing the enemy by bold initiative and by resolute action."[82] The basic difference between regular and irregular warfare in Callwell's experience is degrees of civilization, which he distinguishes by categorizing enemies along a spectrum from "a savage race swayed by a despotic sovereign" to "independent clans" to "semi-civilised states."[83] This civilizational distinction also means that certain tactics—"committing havoc," for example—are encouraged by the imperial forces engaged in small wars that "the laws of regular warfare do not sanction."[84] Just as important is the idea that the habits and customs of the enemy are as important as their battlefield tactics.[85] If the imperial forces are learned, moral, and rational, the enemy is treacherous and capricious, and the enemy's victories depend on intuition rather than intellect.[86] A member of the "coloured races" is useless as a source of useful intelligence, "because his ideas of time, numbers, and distance are of the vaguest, even when he is trying to speak the truth."[87]

Callwell writes that tactics are crucial in small wars, because while the irregular enemy has the upper hand in strategy (with its knowledge of terrain and its ability to disappear), an imperial army can overcome their strategic handicap through tactical superiority.[88] These include what French doctrine writers later called *quadrillage* and *ratissage* (gridding a space, and raking it clear of enemy and/or logistical supplies); mobile columns in raids; the use of blockhouses and fortifications; and "punitive measures directed against [the enemy's] possessions" (because "uncivilized races attribute leniency to timidity").[89] *Small Wars* abounds with incidentally noted destroyed villages; slaughtered cattle; and whole areas laid waste by the civilized conquering armies. Callwell writes admiringly that in the French conquest of Algeria Marshal Bugeaud

perceived that he had to deal not with a hostile army but with a hostile population, that this population consisted largely of clans and tribes of fixed abode, and that to bring them to reason he must reach them through their crops, their flocks and their property.[90]

It is significant that so much of the book seems familiar from our readings of the Boer War, and so many of its admonitions and prescriptions (minus the racist language) from our contemporary counterinsurgency manuals, and yet as a US counterinsurgency guru has mentioned, in the whole hefty book, which has so much detail and so many pages dedicated to everything from hill warfare and bush warfare and infantry, mounted forces (including camel corps), and artillery, there is a single sentence about that most famous facet of British warfare against the Boers, the concentration camp.[91]

Wingate, Thompson, and Kitson

> Winning the hearts and minds of the people, and it is the minds that count, is a fine phrase but it requires a firm application of the stick as much as any dangling of the carrot. . . . Firm and seemingly unpopular measures of organization and control have to be used in order to ensure [the people's] protection and so create a situation in which they have a good chance of survival, and so of getting the carrot, if they cooperate with the government.
> *Robert Thompson, 1969*[92]

Wingate, Thompson, and Kitson, whose experiences and innovations have been fully enshrined in counterinsurgency literature, follow the tradition of Gwynn and Callwell and act as important conduits for the transmission of counterinsurgency knowledge to others; from Wingate to the Israeli military; and from Thompson to the Kennedy administration in its war in Vietnam.

Of the three, Orde Wingate (1903–1944) was the most colorful and controversial. Wingate is honored by no less than David Ben-Gurion as the *hayedid* ("the friend," in Hebrew) of the Israeli state who would have become its defense minister had he not died, and by Winston Churchill as "a man of genius who might well have become also a man of destiny."[93] A dispensationalist, committed Zionist, and eccentric (he ate onions like apples and received visitors stark naked), Wingate had served in Sudan before coming to Palestine, and he went on to fight in Ethiopia and Burma before being killed in action there. He believed the Yishuv settlers to be most loyal to empire, and he thought the Arabs "ignorant and primitive" and "liable to panic."[94] His principal invention in Palestine, the Special Night Squads, brought together British and Jewish policemen to patrol the Galilee at night during the Arab Revolt (1936–1939) and to attack Palestinian Arab villages as punishment for complicity with the revolt or "preemptively" to ensure they would not in the future. The Jewish personnel recruited into the Special Night Squads included the supernumerary police, who were drawn from the community of Jewish settlers and who were to form the kernel of the Haganah (the Yishuv's military force), as well as the

Jewish combatant members of field companies established by Yitzhak Sadeh (and included Yigal Allon and Moshe Dayan).[95] The Special Night Squads were brutally efficient, marching at nighttime, sometimes disguising themselves as Arabs; terrorizing villagers; and in some instances, as in Khirbet Lidd or Hittin, killing civilians who had stepped out to see why they were being attacked.[96] Wingate sometimes beat the villagers; at other times he humiliated them by forcing them to "smear mud and oil on their faces."[97] Sometimes, he detained the Bedouin in the middle of the night under emergency regulations and kept them in administrative detention for months thereafter.[98] The Special Night Squads were something of a model for subsequent Israeli special forces, and as Moshe Dayan wrote, "in some sense, every leader of the Israeli Army even today is a disciple of Wingate. He gave us our technique, he was the inspiration of our tactic, he was our *dynamic*."[99] The Special Night Squads were a precursor to the Chindits commandos Wingate set up in Burma, who operated clandestinely behind enemy lines. The Chindits, in turn, were the precursor to the British Special Air Service.[100]

Sir Robert Grainer Ker Thompson (1916–1992), who had been a Chindit in Burma, is a crucial figure in the Malayan Emergency (1948–1960), not necessarily because he is a major innovator of particular counterinsurgency tactics for which Malaya has come to be known, but because he is a connecting node between Wingate and Vietnam (and beyond—Thompson advised the Rhodesian government of Ian Smith on its counterinsurgency against the anticolonial guerrillas).[101] Thompson, who had served under Wingate, admired Wingate and was inspired by him; he also learned much from him about special forces operations and jungle warfare, installing just such a force, the Ferret Force, in Malaya.[102] Thompson, as secretary for Chinese affairs in Malaya, was a crucial figure in the establishment and administration of New Villages—concentration resettlements for Chinese populations suspected of supporting guerrillas—in Malaya.[103] But Thompson is most famous for deducing a set of principles of counterinsurgency from the Malayan Emergency that are still studied by Anglophone militaries. His *Defeating Communist Insurgency* summarized the five principles of counterinsurgency thus:

First principle. The government must have a clear political aim: to establish and maintain a free, independent and united country which is politically and economically stable and viable. . . .

Second principle. The government must function in accordance with law.[104]

Third principle. The government must have an overall plan.

Fourth principle. The government must give priority to defeating the political subversion, not the guerrillas.

Fifth principle. In the guerrilla phase of an insurgency, a government must secure its base areas first.[105]

Strikingly, the last principle is a kind of reversal of Gallieni's *tâche d'huile* (by placing temporal priority on securing bases), and the penultimate principle has become a crucial characteristic of population-centric counterinsurgencies, as it focuses on the civilians or the political infrastructure of revolt.

After the Malayan Emergency came to an end, Thompson was appointed by British Prime Minister Harold Macmillan to the British Advisory Mission for Vietnam (BRIAM; a six-person group of military and civilian officers with experience of the Malayan Emergency) and was seconded to Washington, DC. There, on the basis of his experience with New Villages, he became an enthusiastic founder and supporter of the strategic hamlet concept.[106] Thompson saw in strategic hamlets' reordering of peasant life in the countryside opportunities for better control over populations and resources, and more effective processes of clear and hold.

Thompson was of the opinion that force had to be calculated and calibrated. This did not mean less violence, more lenient sentencing for detainees and prisoners, or fewer deaths (even as it applied to US soldiers), but rather a more measured approach. He emphasizes "the importance of police expansion and training programme and of the establishment of a coordinated intelligence organization" to supplement militaries.[107] The language of "protection" for civilians and the first principle of isolating "the insurgent both physically and politically from the population" is present throughout Thompson's *Defeating Communist Insurgency*. Thompson highlighted information operations and the role of intelligence, the importance of feet on the ground, and constant interaction between the military and the people. Absent is any sense of the attraction of ideologies of justice, or of popular movements having a base in the population. Despite the constant invocation of politics as a weapon against insurgencies, very little thought is given to the political foundations of anticolonial or antioccupation struggle. In fact, the persistence or success of such struggle is attributed to demographics: "To put the situation bluntly, *all the people of North Vietnam had to do between 1965 and 1968 was to exist and breed.* The United States Air Force could not interrupt either of those activities."[108]

Frank Kitson, who ended his military career as commander in chief of UK Land Forces in 1985, had experience in fighting counterinsurgencies in Kenya, Malaya, Cyprus, Oman, and Northern Ireland. Kitson's thinking about counterinsurgency was not only pivotal to the development of formal UK doctrine; he, like Thompson before him, was close to the center of an epistemic community of military and political thinkers who, as he recalls about a famous RAND symposium that brought many such men together, "all spoke the same language. Probably all of us had worked out theories of counter-insurgency procedures at one time or another which we thought were unique and original. But when we came to air them, all our ideas were essentially the same."[109] The list of participants of the RAND symposium reads like a who's who of liberal counterinsurgencies: in addition to Kitson, the names of Charles Bohannan (United States, Huk Rebellion of the Philippines), Napoleon Valeriano (Philippines, Huk Rebellion), David Galula (France, Algeria), Edward Lansdale (United States, Philippines and Vietnam) jump off the page. All participants insist on instrumentalizing civilians. The political base is considered an asset, a loyal local leadership a necessity, and the job of the counterinsurgent is achieving a decisive military victory followed by securing control of areas. Although all speak about the economic and political causes of revolts, few acknowledge that social transformation can possibly be a desired outcome. For them, the goal of counterinsurgency is simply a more efficient and effective authority structure.

In a later work, Kitson attributes the emergence of popular revolt to "the changing attitude of people towards authority" and to "the development of techniques by which men can influence the thoughts and actions of men."[110] In the symposium, he puts this more bluntly:

The main cause of the Mau Mau rebellion [of Kenya] . . . was the discontent and bitterness of men such as Jomo Kenyatta, who had been educated abroad far beyond the level to which they could hope, at that time, to rise when they returned to the colony. Intensely nationalistic themselves, they incited the people to indignation and revolt over a bogus issue (they asserted, quite falsely, that land had been stolen from the Kikuyu), skilfully interweaving the movement with elements of spiritualistic cult that appealed strongly to the African natives.[111]

Kitson manages skillfully to distil a significant number of clichés and tropes of colonial counterinsurgency in one paragraph: denial of the role of settler colonialism in the dispossession of the indigenous populations, the manipulation of a population by unscrupulous leaders, the primitiveness and superstitions of this population, and the uppity native leader who gets beyond his station by being educated abroad.

Because of the range of counterinsurgencies in which Kitson served, his experiences reveal the extent to which implicit "civilizational" (if not openly racial) hierarchies structure the variation between different counterinsurgencies. Kitson is well known for having challenged internment in Northern Ireland as unproductive, for needlessly inciting the civilian population, which was "bought up in a free country," but he was avowedly comfortable with using the same tactic for native Kenyans (or indeed Cypriots), because after all the Mau Mau were, for him, associated with "all that was foul and terrible in primitive savagery."[112]

Another striking aspect of Kitson's writing is his suggestion that counterinsurgency methods and tactics can also be employed to control and suppress popular revolt domestically. Writing in the early 1970s, Kitson was deeply aware of the upheavals caused by discontent and revolt within European cities, and as such, he saw the population control measures of counterinsurgency as relevant to "a situation which was beyond the power of the police to handle," because "fumbling at this juncture might have grave consequences even to the extent of undermining confidence in the whole system of government."[113] Although his idea about importing counterinsurgency tactics into British cities runs counter to his assertion that people "brought up in a free country" should be subjected to the same harsh measures as the far enemy, nevertheless, his argument openly calls for the portability of military measures used to quell quarrelsome colonial natives and their transplantation into metropolitan policing.[114]

Trinquier and Galula

> *When a country is being subverted it is not being outfought; it is being out-administered.* Subversion is literally administration with a minus sign in front.
> *Bernard Fall, 1965*[115]

> Revolutionary war can't be waged with the Habeas Corpus.
> *Colonel Charles Lacheroy, 1957*[116]

David Galula, "the Clausewitz of Counterinsurgency," has had an extraordinary influence on US counterinsurgency doctrine. His writings of the 1960s were in fact not translated into French (his native language) until 2008, even if the experiences from which he abstracted his general theories of counterinsurgency were generated during the French suppression of the Algerian revolution.[117]

Galula's two books, the first produced under the auspices of the RAND Corporation, the second while on a fellowship at Harvard University, present a comprehensive analysis of insurgencies and prescriptions for counterinsurgency, with the former focusing on the concrete experience of antiguerrilla warfare in the Kabyle region of Algeria and the latter abstracting principles of counterinsurgency learned in battle.[118] Indeed, Galula's analysis is invoked again and again as most useful and relevant to the US counterinsurgency in Iraq. Galula sees insurgencies as endogenous events (whether communist or "bourgeois-national") that depend on a core cadre dedicated to a cause; are able to mobilize because of their "freedom from any responsibility" to maintain law and order; and "appeal to the passions of many among the millions of Moslems, a passionate race if ever there was one."[119]

Galula writes that, early on in counterinsurgencies, a judicial system that is not stripped down through emergency measures allows far too much latitude for captured dissidents and guerrillas.[120] Preemptive measures can alleviate this problem, in addition to surveillance and infiltration of the insurgents, thus "adapting the judicial system to the threat, strengthening the bureaucracy, reinforcing the police and armed forces may discourage insurgency attempts, if the counterinsurgent leadership is resolute and vigilant."[121]

Later, native experts (or French experts gone native) are needed, but they need "protection," which is provided through what can best be called a "surging" of troops throughout Algeria.[122] *Quadrillage*—or the gridding and gradual conquest of rural and urban spaces—becomes a central tactic of the French military, with the aim of "break[ing] the rebels' armed forces and then [pacifying] the population."[123] Pacification happens through finding local allies, "to identify those Moslems who were for us, to rely on them to rally the majority of the population, and together to eliminate the rebels and their militant supporters."[124] In addition to local allies, the constant presence of the French soldiers is routinized, and the population is counted, measured, monitored, placed under surveillance, punished and fined for intransigence, requisitioned for labor, and paid. Although Galula admiringly recalls a French paratrooper's purge of the Casbah in the Battle of Algiers—"Give me one hundred resolute men and I will terrorize a city like Paris"[125]—he actually focuses on acquisition of consent through persuading an ostensibly neutral civilian population through the provision of protection and security. Galula concludes with the "laws" of counterinsurgency:

The first law. The objective is the population. The population is at the same time the real terrain of the war. . . .

The second law. The support from the population is not spontaneous, and in any case must be organized. It can be obtained only through the efforts of the minority among the population that favors the counterinsurgent.

The third law. This minority will emerge, and will be followed by the majority, only if the counterinsurgent is seen as the ultimate victor. . . .

The fourth law. The population's attitude is dictated not by the intrinsic merits of the contending causes, but by the answer to these two simple questions: Which side is going to win? Which side threatens the most, and which offers the most protection?[126]

These conclusions say little about the substance of politics; rather, they emphasize technical solutions to political problems and are echoed persistently through today's counterinsurgency doctrine of the United States.

Interestingly, although Galula has been largely unknown in France, the French School of revolutionary warfare has been best represented in practice by Generals Marcel Bigeard and Jacques Massu and in theory by Colonel Charles Lacheroy (later a member of the quasi-fascist Organisation de l'Armée Secrete), General Jacques Hogard, and Colonel Roger Trinquier.[127] Of all these officers, Trinquier in particular had the greatest influence on US counterinsurgency practice in Vietnam and Latin America; his *Modern Warfare* was translated into English and taught in US military school and staff colleges while Trinquier himself corresponded extensively with the instructors at those institutions.[128] Trinquier's service in Indochina and his organization of proxy militias of Thai and Meo highlanders—something the US military emulated when fighting their own war in Vietnam—made Trinquier particularly relevant to the US Army in the 1960s.[129] Aside from having been fictionalized in Jean Lartéguy's roman à clef of French revolutionary warfare, *The Centurions*, Trinquier, Massu, and Bigeard also appear thinly disguised in Gilo Pontecorvo's remarkable film *Battle of Algiers*. After the war, Trinquier went on to help Moïse Tshombé of Katanga Province organize his military forces. In the 1990s, when the archives of the war had been declassified in France and a revision of the history of the Algerian war had begun, at least in the academy, alongside scholarly histories, Trinquier made appearances in Paul Aussaresses's memoir of the war, *The Battle of the Casbah*, and in Marie-Monique Robin's documentary film and book *Escadrons de la Mort*, about French counterinsurgency's influence on Latin American juntas.[130]

Perhaps what distinguishes the French School (and Trinquier) from Galula is the former's explicit emphasis on exogenous (read, communist) causes of insurgency and an unabashed advocacy of the use of "whatever means necessary," including disavowal of the law and norms of warfare.[131] If Galula is supremely sensitive to image and representation in fighting a counterinsurgency, then Trinquier sees the military as an instrument of raw power and does not apologize for brutality or for breaching fairness in fighting:

For the partisan and the irregular who oppose a regular army, the very fact that they violate the rules of warfare in fighting without a uniform (avoiding the risks involved) deprives them of the protection of these same rules. If taken prisoner while armed, they may be shot on the spot.[132]

Trinquier underscores propaganda and police action as central to suppression of urban revolt and breaks down these actions into a series of elements that include mass interrogation of the population, closure of neighborhoods, curfews and night arrests, the use of prison camps to accommodate large-scale detention of dissidents, and an unquestioning metropolitan government that will not criticize "the forces of order" in the colony.[133] After the suppression of the Casbah in 1958, Trinquier was involved in the fortification and sealing off of the Morice line, the martial barrier of barbed wire and watchtowers that enclosed Algeria, preventing the movement of Front de Libération Nationale (FLN) guerrillas across borders into Algeria.

In the suppression of the Casbah, Trinquier not only called on his experience of counterguerrilla warfare in Indochina but also referred to historical tactics of urban pacification. Remembering Napoléon's methods of conquest in the Rhine Valley, Trinquier, as head of the Dispositif de Protection Urbaine, "began by numbering each house and counting and identifying its inhabitants," gathering the names of inhabitants of each dwelling, cross-checking the information against that gathered from the neighbors, and applying the same methods of *quadrillage* used in rural areas to different quarters of the city.[134] He appointed loyal Muslim veterans as informers in each of these grid squares, placing the informants in the odious position of being targeted for assassination for their collaboration.[135] The extensive method of surveillance is estimated to have resulted in the detention of some 30–40 percent of all men of the Casbah, arrested at night "so that any colleagues they named under interrogation could be grabbed before the lifting of the curfew" and often subjected to torture, because in the words of Trinquier himself, the "rights of the innocent [victims of FLN operations] overrode those of the guilty."[136]

Trinquier had, like many other French officers who served in Algeria, been marked by the defeat of France at the hand of the Viet Minh in Indochina and viewed the Algerian national struggle as part of a larger communist conspiracy, eliding the FLN to the Viet Minh, to the point of calling the Algerian *fellagah* fighters "the Viet" and seeking an idea, even an ideology, that would defeat the attraction of the communist worldview.[137] Peter Paret's fascinating analysis of this search for an ideology is also reflected in Lartéguy's *The Centurions*, where one of the French officers declares, "I don't believe in God, but I feel I am bound up with Christian civilization."[138] The sense of a civilizational battle underlies what Paret calls the French military's "revolutionary change in their concept of duty and ethics as well as in their tactics."[139] While the adherents of this revolutionary vision of warfare indicate the importance of fighting a war among the people, they also call for unquestioning support of the military forces by the political echelons in the metropole. In some senses, this demand lies at the heart of varieties of stab-in-the-back stories, which insist that, although the military was victorious on the battlefield, politicians squandered the victory because of cowardice or cravenness.[140] Trinquier himself wrote that "the army, whose responsibility it is to do battle, must receive the unreserved, affectionate, and devoted support of the nation."[141] This narrative also echoes through subsequent reevaluations of the US war in Vietnam, where, the story goes, the introduction of counterinsurgency measures effectively won the war on the ground, but for the erosion of support for the US forces at home at the hand of the media and a cowardly political class.[142]

Rostow and Vann

> We can learn to prevent the emergence of the famous sea in which Mao Tse-tung taught his men to swim. This requires, of course, not merely a proper military program of deterrence, but programs of village development, communications and indoctrination.
>
> *Walt Rostow, 1961*[143]

Among the countless names associated with the US war in Vietnam , I refer to only two people whose ideas and practices have indelibly marked not only the course of that war and the narratives about it—told both contemporaneously and in retrospect—but also the language and practice of US counterinsurgency in all the decades since. If Walt Whitman Rostow's *The Stages of Economic Growth*, with its very revealing subtitle—*A Non-Communist Manifesto*—was a sort of manual of developmentalist military intervention, John Paul Vann, expansively commemorated in Neil Sheehan's *A Bright Shining Lie*, became its counterinsurgent man on the ground and iconoclast.

Rostow is unusual among advocates of asymmetric warfare in being subsequently an enthusiastic supporter of carpet bombing enemies to shape their behavior.[144] He had had a role in choosing targets for the Allied strategic bombings during the Second World War, and he was crucial in introducing guerrilla warfare and counterinsurgency to John F. Kennedy as a major tactic of war in the Third World.[145] Rostow, an economic historian who had studied seventeenth- and eighteenth-century British economic growth and who was to coin the phrase "The New Frontier" for Kennedy and become national security adviser to Lyndon Johnson, had a clearly delineated ideological program to rival Marxist political economy. In his *Stages of Growth*, he outlined a universal trajectory of development that he believed social and economic engineering could reproduce the world over. The five stages began with traditional societies, which then developed preconditions for takeoff, went through takeoff, consolidated their gains, and arrived at "the age of high consumption."[146] The magical ingredients for this trajectory were compound interest and entrepreneurship. Rostow, like all other modernization theorists, made a sharp distinction between tradition and modernity, and he saw the emergence of Third World resistance movements as "a disease of the transition" and the Third World revolutionaries as "scavengers of modernization."[147] Like so many other modernization theorists, whose viewpoints continue to shape scholarship, folk wisdom, and policy, Rostow was a liberal internationalist who saw a particular virtue in the extension of US hegemony, always envisioned as world leadership, not a new version of imperialism. For these theorists, reforms that guaranteed individual freedom, capitalism, and adherence to liberal norms would circumvent revolutions. "Nationalism" was always promoted as the bulwark against communism, even if Rostow thought that the concepts of nationalism and national sovereignty were premodern residues.[148] For Rostow, the nationalism to be encouraged through US military and economic aid was not the nationalism of Asian and African anticolonialists, "but nationalism on *our* terms: nationalism without revolution, or revolution which we would run for them—revolution, it turned out, without revolution."[149] Ultimately, Rostow saw the massive struggles throughout the Tricontinents as only adjuncts to the "Eurasian arena of power, as determined by relative stages-of-growth and of military potential," a world redeemed through the planetary spread of US-style mass consumerism.[150]

While Rostow played great-power chess in Washington, DC, another hero of today's counterinsurgents, John Paul Vann, developed his ideas and approaches in the field. Vann had been a military adviser in Vietnam in 1962, but he was forced to leave for considering the US Army hierarchy too accommodating to Vietnamese corruption and cowardice.[151] He returned to Vietnam in 1965 as an official of the US Agency for International Development. He thought the solution to Vietnamese weakness was "a strong, dynamic, ruthless, colonialist-type ambassador with the authority to relieve generals, mission chiefs and every other bastard who does not follow a stated, clear-cut policy which, in itself, at a minimum, involved the US in the hiring and firing of the Vietnamese leaders."[152] But like Rostow and other modernization theorists, he also believed that a social revolution had been in progress in Vietnam and that unless the United States learned to harness it, the communists would capture the revolution.[153] Although his program of reform and democracy included nothing about land reform or redistributive policies, he advocated US-centric ideologies about weakening central governments by calling for devolution of power from the Vietnamese government to district governors who would be closely shadowed and monitored by American military advisers.[154] He eventually became an officer of the Civil Operations and Revolutionary Development Support (CORDS) program, which was colonized by the Central Intelligence Agency (CIA) and aimed to "neutralize" the VCI, the Viet Cong Infrastructure, the euphemism for civilian supporters of guerrilla fighters. Vann believed that a CORDS adviser in a given district had to know

in detail the district's political, social, educational, and demographic structure; the local economy; the strengths and effectiveness of all components of friendly and enemy forces; the strengths and weakness of local political and military leaders; the training equipment of South Vietnamese forces (ARVN to police); the steps being taken to improve those forces; and the location of all friendly, contested, and enemy-controlled hamlets.[155]

This local knowledge was necessary to bring the local civilian populations to the side of the South Vietnamese government. Subsequent military analysts and officers frequently cite CORDS as a successful prototype of unity of command in counterinsurgency and a model to be emulated in subsequent counterinsurgencies.[156] Vann's most famous maxim is often quoted as the motto of counterinsurgency: "This is a political war and it calls for discrimination in killing. The best weapon for killing would be a knife, but I'm afraid we can't do it that way. The worst is an airplane. The next worst is artillery. Barring a knife, the best is a rifle—you know who you're killing."[157] Vann—who counted Robert Thompson and a whole raft of powerful journalists among his admirers—was, alongside Bob Komer, who ran CORDS, and General Creighton Abrams, who took Westmoreland's place, a major advocate of Vietnamization of the war, or shifting the burden of fighting to the Vietnamese security forces.[158]

It was precisely this rupture that framed—and continues to shape—the metanarrative of counterinsurgency: the story begins with a lumbering, conventional, and conservative counterinsurgent military using its firepower and technical prowess to bomb an unequal enemy into submission, all the while stoking native hostility not only with force of arms but also with naive racism. Then arrive unconventional—in both senses of the word—thinkers and military men, rebels who anger the bureaucracy around them, who, against their racist colleagues, believe that all peoples of the world deserve democracy and who look for more humane ways of acquiring local allegiances through virtuous behavior, humility, and the provision of security (and resources and social goods).[159] In his memoir of the Vietnam War, CIA operative Rufus Phillips, who had loyally worked in civic action and who admired Vann's work in the field, retold this narrative about the highest echelon of US military in Vietnam:

Abrams had moved out of Westmoreland's palatial villa into a smaller house near the MACV headquarters. He habitually wore field fatigues instead of the spit-and-polish uniform with resplendent ribbons, or sharply tailored fatigues, that most often been Westmoreland's attire. . . . . Abrams wanted to make the Vietnamese army and the local forces work, which Westmoreland never understood or was interested in. Also he wanted to humanize MACV and its command image. . . . General Abrams would also address the security of Saigon as a priority. In a very short time he would stop the rocketing through aggressive day-and-night patrolling and by the stationing of helicopter gunships in continuous night-time orbit over likely firing positions, among other tactics.[160]

Abrams was also viewed as the man who would have effectively won the war, had he not been betrayed by the journalists and politicians at home.[161]

CONCLUSION: THE ELEMENTS OF COUNTERINSURGENCY

A series of recurring themes emerges out of the liberal counterinsurgencies of the twentieth century and comes to be profoundly important in shaping the twenty-first-century thinking of the US counterinsurgents. Perhaps most striking among these themes is the idea that imperial policing should be humane, set against practices of warfare that are anything but. This constant seesawing between the idea of violently *deterring* the civilian from supporting the insurgents and the notion that these civilians would be best *persuaded* to disavow the insurgents is vastly different from the nineteenth-century counterinsurgencies in which mass slaughter, scorched-earth tactics, *razzias*, looting, rape, and destruction were commonplace instruments of asymmetric warfare.

Another recurring and related theme is the centrality of the population and the idea of counterinsurgency as either simultaneous or sequential application of military force and civic action. The population is the prize in asymmetric warfare. This emphasis also distinguishes modern counterinsurgencies from their nineteenth-century predecessors. The emergence of population as a concept of study, warfare, and manipulation emerged most apparently in the mass incarceration of civilians in a number of twentieth- and twenty-first-century counterinsurgencies, and is central to the liberal idea of warfare, both to be discussed in subsequent chapters.

If a population is an object of warfare and civic action, it has to be studied, categorized, known. The vector of civilization and barbarity become crucial not only for determining whom the counterinsurgent is fighting but also for determining how to fight and what is permitted. Savages and barbarians are less subject to the grace of law and regulated warfare than a civilized adversary. The racialization of the "native" is so prevalent and so inherent in the discourse of liberal counterinsurgency that it even emerges when the metropolitan force seeks local allies. These allies are needed to bear the brunt of the fighting—or continue it after the metropolitan force leaves—and they are needed to present the indigenous face of the counterinsurgency to both local and international publics. But despite their centrality to this type of asymmetric war, they are also subjected to the same racialization. Indeed, the "savagery" of a proxy army can be both an alibi for the metropolitan army and a tool of warfare on which it depends. Finally, the standard of civilization also comes to be important in weaving the legitimating discourse around asymmetric warfare, because a war that brings with it civilization, liberation, and emancipation is much easier to sell to a public that might be skeptical about its costs.

Given the deliberate rooting of today's US and Israeli counterinsurgency doctrines in past practice, then, it is not surprising that these themes will also appear in the fundamental texts of the militaries of the counterinsurgent forces of these two states.

CHAPTER 2

LESSONS AND BORROWINGS

The United States and Israel

Thus we should beware literal application of lessons extracted
from Vietnam, or any other past event, to present or future
problems without due regard for the specific circumstances
that surround those problems. Study of Vietnam—and of
other historical occurrences—should endeavour to gain
perspective and understanding, rather than hard and fast
lessons that might be applied too easily without proper
reflection and sufficiently rigorous analysis.

Major David Petraeus, 1986 [1]

In writing about US counterinsurgency in Vietnam in the previous chapter,
I ended with what has become a standard narrative of that war in the counterinsurgent epistemic community in the United States, whereby a lumbering
conventional army learns to fight a more cunning enemy, and where political
support at home (or lack thereof) can determine the outcome of the war, no
matter how the soldiers on the battlefield fight their asymmetric wars. This
narrative was crucial in shaping both US policy and practice in its War on Terror, but also central to the self-imagining of US counterinsurgents as engaged
in a historically informed mission.

DRINKING TEA WITH TRIBAL LEADERS: US COUNTERINSURGENCY IN THE TWENTY-FIRST CENTURY

In the eyes of the warrior, counterinsurgency calls for some
undecidedly un-warrior-like qualities such as emotional

intelligence, empathy, subtlety, sophistication, nuance and political adroitness.

Lieutenant General Sir John Kiszely, 2006 [2]

Counterinsurgency is armed social work.

David Kilcullen, 2006 [3]

The story of the transformation from a blundering conventional army to a nimble and adaptive counterinsurgent force is a powerful framing narrative. The main component of the narrative is the image of counterinsurgency as a more instinctive, intuitive form of warfare that requires charismatic leaders and a feel for what is required. The opposite of this "emotionally intelligent" form of warfare is the more rational, bureaucratized, and technologically savvy Revolution in Military Affairs (RMA), which was all the rage in the 1990s in the United States, and which was predicated on technological superiority in "surveillance, communications, and information technologies"; "employment of precision-strike capabilities"; and "network-centric warfare, rapid decisive operations, and shock and awe."[4] In the counterinsurgency narrative, however, the RMA approach was criticized for not acknowledging

the limitations of new technologies and emerging military capabilities. In particular, concepts that relied mainly on the ability to target enemy forces with long range precision munitions separated war from its political, cultural, and psychological contexts.[5]

Some of the most important thinking around this counterinsurgency narrative was based on a revisionist reading of the experience of Vietnam, advanced most eloquently by Lewis Sorley, which pitted Creighton Abrams's Civil Operations and Revolutionary Development Support (CORDS) against Westmoreland's search-and-destroy missions and conventional approach. But the new counterinsurgency doctrine also distinguished itself from enemy-centric methods, which target the guerrillas with kinetic—or lethal—force, and whose military embodiments are special operations forces. If enemy-centric counterinsurgency depends on coercive or punitive measures to deter the civilian population from supporting the unconventional forces, then population-centric counterinsurgency is meant to win over that population by "securing" and "protecting" them, as well as by providing services that would win over the population. In population-centric counterinsurgency, force is to be carefully adjusted to the particular context, though never entirely disavowed. In a sense, the new conceptualization of unconventional warfare as a spectrum with enemy- and population-centric tactics at opposite ends recalls Gwynn's categorization of small wars as distinct from policing action in which the counterinsurgent force expects to remain in place for a long time, and as such, it requires the goodwill and acquiescence of the civilian population.

This precise calibration of lethal force is most clearly set out in the US Army and Marine Corps' *Counterinsurgency Field Manual*, but also in a number of counterinsurgency classics written by soldier-scholars.[6] This new breed of military officer festooned with a doctorate is intensely aware of both time and place, history and context, in warfare, and includes such luminaries as General David Petraeus (in turn, in charge of US endeavors in Iraq and Afghanistan, the Central Command, and the Central Intelligence Agency, as well as the initiator of the *Counterinsurgency Field Manual*; he holds a PhD in international relations from Princeton), Brigadier General H. R. McMaster (known for having pacified Tal Afar in Iraq; PhD in history, University of North Carolina), retired Colonel Conrad Crane (director of the US Army Military History Institute; PhD in history, Stanford University), retired Colonel Peter Mansoor (formerly executive officer to Petraeus and founding director of the US Army and Marine Corps Counterinsurgency Center at Fort Leavenworth; PhD in military history, Ohio State University), retired Lieutenant Colonel John Nagl (former president of Center for a New American Security and current Minerva research fellow at the Naval Academy; PhD in international relations, Oxford University), retired Colonel Kalev Sepp (assistant professor at the Naval Postgraduate School; PhD in politics and history, Harvard University), and perhaps most influential, retired Lieutenant Colonel David Kilcullen (of the Australian army, former adviser to Petraeus and currently private security consultant; PhD in politics, University of New South Wales).[7]

The *Counterinsurgency Field Manual* drew on the knowledge and experience of these writers and many others besides. Conrad Crane and John Nagl were primarily responsible for the whole of the manual; Petraeus oversaw the process; and as Crane writes, the document "had a dozen primary authors, another dozen secondary authors, and 600,000 editors, because all of the Army and Marine Corps got a chance to provide their suggestions."[8] Significantly, among the authors of the *Counterinsurgency Field Manual* were human rights experts and social scientists, including a cultural anthropologist, Montgomery McFate, who had written her doctoral thesis on British counterinsurgency in Northern Ireland and who had advocated strongly for gathering ethnographic intelligence in wars where "holistic, total understanding of local culture" is a significant determinant of military action.[9] As another coauthor of the manual wrote elsewhere:

In counterinsurgency, the first mission of the intelligence agencies is to understand the context of the conflict, which means collecting information about the whole society, understanding local conditions, monitoring public opinion, and analyzing social and political relationships and networks. And that is just the start. The next step is to find the insurgent and try to understand his organization. . . . The kind of intelligence analyst needed in counterinsurgency is essentially a foreign area officer, someone who speaks the language fluently, has studied the country and the region in depth, and understands the societal context of official and unofficial networks.[10]

The involvement of liberal human rights practitioners in the drafting of the *Counterinsurgency Field Manual* has meant that population-centric counterinsurgency is now considered a progressive form of warfare by many liberal interventionists in the European and North American capitals.[11] The *Counterinsurgency Field Manual* became so famous that although it was available online from US military websites, the University of Chicago Press decided to publish it as a book. The introduction to the published edition of the manual is written by Sarah Sewall, former director of the Carr Center for Human Rights Policy at Harvard University, who was also involved in drafting the manual.[12] The emphasis by the human rights and humanitarian theorists is always on the language of "protection," on winning hearts and minds (now a cliché), the "restraint" of the population-centric method, even its "political correctness."[13]

What makes the *Counterinsurgency Field Manual* and the writings of aforementioned counterinsurgents ostensible repositories of progressive intent and liberal thinking is also what distinguishes population-centric counterinsurgency from both conventional warfare and enemy-centric counterinsurgency. Conventional warfare requires the counterpositioning of opposing armies with both forces "striving into touch to avoid tactical surprise"; by contrast, guerrillas "might be a vapour," and their weapons are "speed and time" rather than firepower.[14] The manual calls for an undoing of the doctrine of overwhelming force and for transforming the military into the kind of modernizing instrument of social engineering that could build schools and clinics as easily as fighting, all the while seeking to transform bureaucratic, centralized, and rational political-military structures into decentralized, porous structures that admit civilians, social scientists, private military operatives, and local actors.[15]

The ghostly presence in all this is Mao's dictum that to achieve best results, guerrilla leadership must strengthen "the relationship that should exist between the people and the troops. The former may be likened to water, the latter to the fish who inhabit it."[16] The emphasis on the relationship with civilian populations and the tactics used to "drain the pond" and sever this connection is what distinguishes enemy-centric and population-centric counterinsurgencies, as they are today categorized by the US military. The former is the attempt to kinetically (i.e., via the use of maximal firepower) defeat the guerrillas and kill them, and to use punitive measures to deter the civilian population from supporting the guerrillas; the latter is about persuading civilians that they can be best protected by the counterinsurgent army, thus literally starving irregular combatants of vital support, including shelter, food, and medical supplies.[17]

David Kilcullen's *The Accidental Guerrilla* and the articles preceding it argue precisely this point. Kilcullen's first widely read piece was an essay published in *Military Review* and self-consciously modeled after T. E. Lawrence's "Twenty-Seven Articles," providing advice on mobilizing guerrillas. Kilcullen's "Twenty-Eight Articles" lays out detailed guidance for company commanders in counterinsurgencies. Some of his recommendations have to do with everyday operations of the military, interagency cooperation, knowledge of the locale, diagnosis of the "problem" or motivations for insurgency, and the like. The heart of the article, however, is concerned with the interactions between counterinsurgents and civilians, and the meaning of hearts and minds:

"Hearts" means persuading people their best interests are served by your success; "Minds" means convincing them that you can protect them, and that resisting you is pointless. Note that neither concept has to do with whether people like you. Calculated self-interest, not emotion, is what counts.[18]

The article emphasizes the importance of building relations with and using local populations, including community leaders, nongovernmental agencies, and security forces. For Kilcullen, counterinsurgency is "armed social work," and it depends not only on the fighting abilities of the invading and occupying military but also, especially, on performing for local and international audiences, presenting a "unified narrative" that can counter nationalist sentiments, and "coopting neutral or friendly women, through targeted social and economic programs."[19] In *The Accidental Guerrilla*, Kilcullen presents a series of concrete cases—Iraq, Afghanistan, Pakistan, Thailand, Indonesia, and even Europe—via which he argues that insurgents work through provoking their opponents to act, intimidating the local population to prevent them from cooperating with the counterinsurgents, and prolonging the conflict to "exhaust their opponents' resources."[20] Kilcullen applies a medical model to the "pathology" of insurgency, whereby "the accidental guerrilla syndrome" is a disease that follows a cycle of infection, contagion, intervention, and rejection.[21] The accidental guerrillas are the ostensibly neutral civilians who "become accidental guerrillas, fighting alongside extremist forces not because they support *takfiri* ideology but because they oppose outside interference in their affairs."[22] Some of this statement rings true—particularly the resistance of populations against foreign occupiers; but Kilcullen goes on to propose what has become a counterinsurgency truism:

Counterinsurgency theory, as well as field observation, suggests that a minority of the population will support the government come what may, and another minority will back the Taliban under any circumstance, but the majority of Afghans simply want security, peace, and prosperity and will swing to support the side that appears most likely to prevail and to meet these needs, and that most closely aligns with their primary group identity.[23]

Kilcullen is rephrasing a "basic tenet of the exercise of political power" put forward by David Galula, who is regularly declared to be the forefather of US counterinsurgency effort today. Galula writes, "In any situation, whatever the cause, there will be an active minority for the cause, a neutral majority, and an active minority against the cause. The technique of power consists in relying on the favourable minority in order to rally the neutral majority and to neutralize or eliminate the hostile minority."[24] Aside from the fact that Kilcullen very much veils and minimizes the latter portion of the formula, his entire book seems to pivot on this Machiavellian understanding of politics.

The Galula-Kilcullen thesis finds its academic counterpart in Stathis Kaly-vas's much-vaunted *The Logic of Violence in Civil War*.[25] Interestingly, rather than calling a counterinsurgency operation by that name, Kalyvas uses the conceptual framework of a civil war, thus fundamentally obscuring the most important element of a counterinsurgency: the asymmetry of power between governmental or occupying security forces and guerrilla groups. In his sophis-ticated, extensively sourced, and multimethod book, the central case is the 1940s Greek state's suppression of the communist insurgency. To emphasize the "civil war" element, Kalyvas doesn't really tell us that the United States provided the counterinsurgent government with $467 million in aid, a "flood of arms and equipment" and a corps of military advisors under the auspices of the Truman Doctrine.[26] Like Galula and Kilcullen, Kalyvas sees two methods that can win over a neutral population: deterrence through intimidation and persuasion through protection. Kalyvas's central contention, like that of Kil-cullen, is that civilian support for either side is neither ideological (based on what he calls a master narrative) nor even political (or macrofoundational). Kalyvas argues instead that in asymmetric warfare civilians can be detached from such broader considerations, acting as more or less autonomous, ratio-nal monads. This leads to his argument that the "control [of the population by a given side] is increasingly likely to shape collaboration because political actors who enjoy substantial territorial control can protect civilians who live in that territory."[27] In other words, whoever dominates in a given battlespace also manages to win over the population. Although convincing in its argument for the transformative effects of violence and its insistence that a population's allegiances may remain dynamic throughout the period of fighting, Kalyvas transforms violence itself into the raison d'être of most conflicts and, by fo-cusing solely on violence, evacuates the motivations of actors of memory and history, or mobilizing ideas about politics, power, and justice (except insofar as these things can be used instrumentally by either side).[28]

The process by which the "protection" of a population can work is complex and, Kilcullen suggests, requires a root-and-branch transformation of both military and political practice. The *Counterinsurgency Field Manual* lays out the operational and tactical steps taken in the field, including integration of civilian and military activities, the judicious and extensive use of intelligence (defined not only as operational intelligence but also as social, economic, and political information about the people among whom the counterinsurgent is to operate), the use of information operations, population control, provision of essential services and economic development, the ensuring of good governance, and development of the local security forces.[29] Kilcullen's suggestions are much broader, strategic, and macropolitical. He suggests developing a new disciplinary approach to this new form of conflict, based not on International Relations but on anthropology, which he defines as "the study of social roles, groups, status, institutions, and relations within human population groups, often in nonelite, non-state-based frameworks."[30] To better address the new "environment" of warfare, Kilcullen wants the imbalance between military and nonmilitary capabilities of the United States remedied, development and diplomacy organizations expanded, and US soft power reinforced. In a sense, Kilcullen would like to see what Michel Foucault has called sovereign power, or "the power over life and death," give way to a panoply of disciplinary forms of power, including "cultural and ethnographic intelligence, social systems analysis, information operations, early-entry or high-threat humanitarian or governance teams, field negotiation and mediation teams, biometric reconnaissance, and a variety of other strategically useful capabilities."[31] But even here, sovereign power, the power to yield indiscriminate violence, has to be kept in reserve. As John Nagl said only half jokingly on *The Daily Show*, counterinsurgency means, "Be polite, be professional, be prepared to kill."[32]

Nagl himself has been crucial to providing the historical parallels to bolster the case for population-centric counterinsurgency. In what has become an unquestioned verity in counterinsurgency community, the British suppression of communist guerrilla warfare in Malaya (1948–1960) is presented as the touchstone of all post–Second World War counterinsurgencies.[33] What makes it so is that the guerrillas were militarily defeated, the civilian Chinese squatter population was deterred from supporting the guerrillas, and the regime that came to replace imperial British rule was decidedly friendly to British interests. The suppression of the Malayan counterinsurgency required the declaration of a state of emergency and the flooding of Malaya with British military units from the rest of the empire. A three-pronged process was put into place to suppress the revolt. In the cities, emergency regulations were used to silence critics (particularly of Chinese extraction) and to send significant numbers of potential "agitators" to detention camps; tens of thousands of troublemaking

Chinese residents were also deported.[34] Military units were sent into the jungle to fight the guerrillas; they were aided in this by trackers from other parts of the empire. Perhaps most significant, an ambitious social engineering plan was put into place to sever the connection between the civilians and the guerrillas: a mass resettlement of five hundred thousand squatters into New Villages and some six hundred thousand laborers into "controlled areas"—still near the tin mines and rubber plantations to ensure a steady supply of labor, but with these compounds surrounded by barbed wire and guard towers, accessible via military checkpoints and heavily monitored.[35] Food denial operations rationed the amount of victuals the residents of the New Villages received and controlled areas to ensure that they did not pass on any food to the guerrillas.[36]

Nagl attributes the success of Malayan counterinsurgency to this resettlement of the civilians, which he admiringly attributes to the British colonial officials giving "strategic directions" to the campaign.[37] In addition, Nagl views the lessons of the Malayan counterinsurgency as the decentralization of antiguerrilla military action, the "protection" of civilians, extensive use of the Special Branch and gathering of intelligence, and information operations, all guaranteed by the British military's flexibility and capacity for organizational learning and strategic thinking by the leadership.[38] Extraordinarily, Nagl sees the New Villages as benign institutions, "more than concentration camps" hosting village cooperatives and "even Boy Scout Troops."[39] They are the very emblem of population-centric counterinsurgency, the symbols of protection provided to uncertain civilians, and Nagl admiringly cites Harold Briggs, the British Army's director of operations in Malaya:

The problem of clearing Communist banditry from Malaya was similar to that of eradicating malaria from a country. Flit guns and mosquito nets, in the form of military and police, though some very local security if continuously maintained, effected no permanent cure. Such a permanent cure entails the closing of all breeding areas. In this case the breeding areas of the Communists were the isolated squatter areas.[40]

Alongside the more immediate tactics of population control, two broader long-term strategies, the hardening of both lateral boundaries between "ethnic" groups and the vertical power relations within presumed or existing social agglomerations (e.g., tribes, clans, neighborhoods, castes), define counterinsurgency practice across the twentieth and twenty-first centuries. These require the conceptual reification of local (or native) political structures and relations to a mosaic of tribes (or communities or castes) that can be fixed in time, bought off, rearranged, or manipulated to fit the military and political requirements of the counterinsurgent power. Here, the reification, petrifaction, and universalization of fluid and complex social relations into tribes make the impenetrable and inscrutable native legible to colonial eyes. In a much-cited and much-praised document, Major Jim Grant of the US Army Special Forces describes the political landscape of Afghanistan as being

constituted of tribes. Not individuals, not Western-style citizens—but tribes and tribesmen. . . . [T]ribes understand protection. Tribes are organized and run to ensure the security of the tribe. Not only physical security, but revenue and land protection. But most important of all is preservation of the tribal name and reputation. . . . When honor is at stake, tribal members stop at nothing to preserve their tribe's integrity and "face." [T]ribes understand power. How many guns do we have? How many warriors can I put in the field? Can I protect my tribe? Can I attack others who threaten my tribe? Can I back my words or decisions up with the ability to come down the valley and kill you? Can I keep you from killing me? Lastly, tribes understand projection. Tribes have no "strategic goals" in the Western sense. Their diplomatic, informational, military, and economic (DIME) priorities are almost without exception in reference to other tribes.[41]

Officials in the United States take Gant so seriously that this "Lawrence of Afghanistan" has been sent there to implement his vision of tribal control.[42] The same faith in the explanatory power of tribes also underpinned the US Surge in Iraq, even if that policy came with considerably more window dressing about "hearts and minds."[43] There, a famous PowerPoint presentation by US Army Captain Patriquin (later killed in action) showed stick-figure tribal "sheiks" who have "been leading the people of this area for approximately 14,000 years. In spite of many, many conquering Armies trying to remove him, this man and his family have been involved in the politics here since recorded time began." Patriquin recommended drinking tea with the sheik to convince him to incorporate his militia into the police force, which performs the local tasks of counterinsurgency.[44] In both places, the images of US commanders having endless cups of tea with local "tribal" leaders have become the absurd staple of news items about the "progress" of counterinsurgency in Iraq or Afghanistan.

What is striking about the current US counterinsurgency doctrine and practice is the practitioners' intense awareness of historical experiences and the invocation of past cases as bases for learning. Tom Ricks, the great popularizer of US counterinsurgency in Iraq, was instrumental in having David Galula's *Pacification in Algeria* declassified and his *Counterinsurgency Warfare* reissued.[45] Ricks has also read the British counterinsurgency forebears and saw the pre-counterinsurgency US tactics as violating "at least three" of the very rules set by Charles Gwynn in his *Imperial Policing*: "Civil power must be in charge, civilian and military authorities must cooperate relentlessly, action must be firm and timely, but when force is required it should be used minimally."[46] *The Gamble*, which covers the years 2006 to 2009, by contrast, is the story of how the US military in Iraq began to embrace counterinsurgency and obey the rules of imperial policing. In Ricks's account, two of the most significant early steps in the counterinsurgency effort were, first, to recognize Iraq's "tribal" character and, second, to prize open any fissures in the hostile opposition's ranks. With regard to the former, he writes of the "insight" of a US general who idolized the British imperial officer Gertrude Bell to the effect that "tribal society makes up the tectonic plates in Iraq on which everything rests."[47] Ricks writes of the commander of US military forces in Ramadi and his Arabic-speaking right-hand officer (the aforementioned Captain Patriquin) whose approach to co-opting the structures of power in the area was to separate the "tribes" from the insurgents: "Together they tried to sort out who was a real sheik, with big *wasta*, or influence and who was a lightweight."[48] In turn, this tribal chieftain was paid money and given some autonomy of action to have him and his followers challenge insurgent groups. In this, the US military officers were following an edict of the *Counterinsurgency Field Manual*, to "remain alert for signs of divisions within an insurgent movement," as "rifts between insurgent leaders, if identified, can be exploited."[49]

If the *Counterinsurgency Field Manual* draws on Galula's experience in Algeria and Thompson's in Malaya, then it defines the arc of evolution of modern counterinsurgency as passing through the rupture point of the Second World War and the rise of nationalism. In its historical panorama, the manual refers to the Vietnamese struggle, CORDS, Ireland (and Northern Ireland), the Napoleonic war against Spanish guerrilla forces, Algeria, the Chinese Civil War, Malaya, and of course—again and again—Iraq. Notably, despite paying the

usual tributes to context, history, and culture, the case studies are stripped of
their historical specificity and transformed into modular lessons—or "historical tropes"—about how to manage conflicts against nonstate guerrilla forces.[50]
The *Counterinsurgency Field Manual* shows its awareness of the media problem
and speaks of the importance of information operations. The manual specifies
that there are four audiences for the counterinsurgency action: "the population, the insurgents, the counterinsurgent force, and regional and international
audiences."[51] This awareness of an external audience that can scupper military
action is so important that when Edward Luttwak called for "out-terrorising
the insurgents,"[52] a gathering of "American, British, German, and French doctrine writers unanimously rejected such an approach, based on international
law, *the realities of the current media environment*, and a shared conviction that
such an approach is counterproductive."[53]

Narrative and performative aspects of counterinsurgency are at the very
heart of two much-hailed books, Rupert Smith's *The Utility of Force* and T. X.
Hammes's *The Sling and the Stone*. Smith, a retired British general who had
commanded the North Atlantic Treaty Organization's peacekeeping forces in
the Balkans, describes the evolution of warfare from Napoléon and Clausewitz
to Israel—with detours through countries from Bosnia to Zimbabwe—and
avers that "war as cognitively known to most non-combatants, war as battle
in a field between men and machinery, war as a massive deciding event in a
dispute in international affairs: such war no longer exists."[54] Instead, today's
conflict takes the shape of "war amongst the people," where "the people in the
streets and houses and fields—all the people anywhere—are the battlefield."[55]
To succeed in such wars, plans must be made well and ends must be well considered; the military must act as a police force, using violence minimally and
establishing courts of law, and in the field such wars are "conducted best as
an intelligence and information operation, not as one of manoeuvre and attrition."[56] This means that the media matters greatly:

To link the actions in theatre to the context and to exploit them to the next act there is
a need to capture the story—to which end a "narrator" is necessary, one who explains
to the audience what has happened, its significance and where events might lead.[57]

The Sling and the Stone, whose cover image is a well-known picture of a
Palestinian boy throwing a rock at an Israeli tank, argues that the predominant

form of warfare today is fourth-generation warfare, which mobilizes political, economic, social, and military networks and can last for decades.[58] The
book examines Mao, Vietnam, Nicaragua's Sandinistas, both Palestinian Intifadas, al-Qaeda, Iraq, and the "tribal networks" of Afghanistan to conclude
that because the enemy is not hampered by "an entrenched bureaucracy," it
can use everything from commercial satellite imagery to worldwide weather
reports and news items to generate data on the US military, use the Web to
send coded messages or transfer funds, and manipulate the media to "attack
the US center of gravity: our political will."[59]

On the battlefield, as explicated in the *Counterinsurgency Field Manual* and
in much of the writing about population-centric counterinsurgency, what becomes crucial is the clear-hold-build pattern first explicated in Gallieni's "oil
spot" approach, which requires the "clearing" of an area "by destroying, capturing, or forcing the withdrawal of insurgent combatants. This task is most
effectively initiated by a . . . cordon-and-search operation."[60] Once an area
has been secured, security forces are established to hold it, and the information operation phase kicks in. The final phase is "building support and protecting the population," whereby in addition to maintaining regular patrols,
a series of tasks "that provide an overt and direct benefit for the community"
are performed. These tasks include everything from clearing rubbish from the
streets to digging wells and building schools, and perhaps most important,
"preparing and building an indigenous local security force," including "local
paramilitary security forces."[61] These security forces are considered the *sine
qua non* of nation building, whose consolidation and ability to challenge insurgencies is the necessary prerequisite to the "host nation" providing services
to the populace to deter them from revolt. Development of such a security
force is so significant that an entire chapter (of eight) is dedicated to it in the
manual. Significantly, these developmental strategies are also accompanied by
population control measures that begin with conducting censuses and issuing
identity cards and that develop into curfews, pass systems, and checkpoints.

Counterinsurgents have addressed criticisms of the extensive prescriptions
of these doctrines by claiming that counterinsurgency doctrine and practice is essentially a series of tactics and techniques needed to implement the
commands—and strategic vision—of civilian leaders and the political classes.
Critics from within the establishment have pointed out that in the absence of

a strategic vision, counterinsurgency tactics have come to stand in for strategy, or even policy. My criticism is of a different order. I argue here and throughout the book that military tactics do not arise in a vacuum or operate independently of social relations. They may be technical solutions to problems brought about by political incompetence or venality, but they are technical solutions shaped by the political exigencies and ethos of the time, and by the zeitgeist. These tactics and techniques, as will become clear here, make and transform places, peoples, and social relations. They affect politics in direct and indirect ways: directly where they transform the political and social landscapes of invaded and occupied countries and peoples; indirectly, because their availability and their claim to virtue and humanity authorize their usage by politicians and demand support from publics in ways that mass slaughter or brutalism would not. In a sense, strategies and tactics are mutually constituted: a strategy is devised not independently but on the basis of the possibility and desirability of tactics used to implement it.

In some ways, the focus of today's US counterinsurgency on the everyday processes and procedures of governmentality and the unquestioned commonsense framing devices of stability, security, protection, and development or nation building, and eventually elections and democracy, point to the remarkable persistence of modernization theory in which socially and politically engineering defective or incomplete polities is thought to eventuate in their redemption as liberal democracies of a sort. These celebratory projections of US managerial prowess—whether with oil spots or accounting ledgers— represent population-centric counterinsurgency as a particularly capacious vessel for an ostensibly humanitarian agenda that relies far more on pliant proxies (whether in political or in security positions) than on gung-ho occupying forces, depends on scientific or ethnographic knowledge of the peoples who are to be made legible to the state, and ultimately refuses the possibility of political sentiments among the civilian populations of conquered countries.

BREAKING BONES, BREAKING DOWN DOORS: CONTEMPORARY ISRAELI COUNTERINSURGENCY

> As long as there is a spark of hope that [the Palestinians] can
> get rid of us, they will not sell these hopes, not for any kind of

sweet words or tasty morsels, because they are not a rabble but
a nation, perhaps somewhat tattered, but still living. A living
people makes such enormous concessions on such fateful
questions only when there is no hope left. Only when not a
single breach is visible in the iron wall, only then do extreme
groups lose their sway, and influence transfers to moderate
groups. Only then would these moderate groups come to us
with proposals for mutual concessions.
Ze'ev Jabotinsky, 1923[62]

Let the individual know that he has something to lose. His
home can be blown up, his bus licence can be taken away, he
can be deported from the region; or the contrary: he can exist
with dignity, make money, exploit other Arabs, and travel in
[his] bus.
Moshe Dayan, 1967[63]

The US military theorists who advocate population-centric counterinsurgencies view their doctrine as diametrically opposed to Israeli counterinsurgency
in the Occupied Palestinian Territories (OPT), which they describe as "kinetic
[i.e., more focused on killing power] and enemy-centric," aimed primarily at
deterring Palestinian civilians from supporting the guerrilla or insurgent forces
by making this support costly in property and lives lost to assassination, bombing, and especially through punitive mass detention.[64] In this, although Israel
has been a site of innovation in counterinsurgency techniques, in a significant
number of instances, it has, in fact, inherited, adapted, and refined techniques
of control from its British predecessor and other counterinsurgent militaries.[65]
These techniques have aided the Israeli conquest, consolidation of domination
over, and subjugation of Palestinian civilian populations.

One of the most notable characteristics of Israeli counterinsurgency has
been the extent to which tactics and operations have developed in an ad hoc,
and therefore flexible, fashion but always within the framework of overwhelming military superiority and victory achieved in a short time frame. Following
this has been the centrality of counterinsurgency in transforming the Israeli
military into a constabulary force. All this has resulted in the embedding of

counterinsurgency techniques in the practices of the state, both historically and institutionally.[66] Here, interestingly, this inseparability means that what is proposed as the overall philosophy of war-fighting—overwhelming force and speedy war-fighting—is also a political imperative. A settler-colonial form of warfare depends on destroying both the military and the social capabilities of the adversary at any cost, where the expulsion or destruction of the enemy is considered a more desirable alternative to having to rule the subjugated population directly. One finds the military imperative succinctly summarized in this way:

[Israel's] doctrine of defense obligates us to seek quick military decisions with the aim of concluding wars in their early stages, while inflicting painful defeats on the enemy and eliminating significant parts of enemy forces and conquering parts of enemy territory. Eliminating a military force means destroying its organization and denying it the capability to function according to its designated purpose. Destroying a force . . . removes the direct and immediate threat to our existence, and therefore this is clearly and important and "useful" military objective.[67]

Notably, the military imperative seems to suit the fundamental exigencies of settler colonialism that, in the case of Israel, is so well articulated in the writings of an early revisionist Zionist Ze'ev Jabotinsky.[68] Jabotinsky is most famous for his essay "The Iron Wall," in which he calls for an "iron wall of Jewish bayonets" that would so utterly encircle the Arabs and drive them to abjection, that when "there is no hope left" they would be forced to make massive concessions, acceding to their own subjugation.[69] This neat convergence between political aims and military imperatives is of course born not simply of a plan but also is developed through a series of historical developments, where the emergence of a Zionist, and later Israeli, fighting force depended on British know-how; where the parameters of such fighting were set by British legal practices; and where strategic military decisions were predicated on the zero-sum calculus that always lies at the heart of settler-colonialism: it is them or us.

Given this fusion of counterinsurgency techniques and political practice, it is not surprising, then, that counterinsurgency tactics deployed in times of occupation have been, for example, applied to Palestinian citizens within Israel during peacetime—or that the legal mechanisms regulating Palestinian lives were those originally devised as part of British emergency measures in

Palestine. Many of Israel's emergency regulations and laws are originally the British laws that were adopted wholesale in 1948 upon the birth of the state.[70] For example, the rules under which Palestinians are held in "administrative detention" without trial are only marginally modified versions of the punitive detention laws that the British used in the 1930s.[71] Along with techniques of collective punishment, the laws were first applied to Palestinians remaining within the border of the nascent state of Israel, and later to the Palestinian populations of the OPT.[72] From 1948 to 1966, the period of Israel's military administration of Palestinians remaining within the 1949 Armistice (or Green) Line, the counterinsurgency methods of control were used as preemptive measures:

> The decision to enforce the restrictions on movement (Article 109), police supervision (Article 110), administrative detention (Article 111), curfew (Article 124), closed areas and travel permits (Article 125), and weapons licenses (Article 137) was left to the military governor, who could impose them, under Article 108, at any time he considered it necessary "for securing the public safety, the defense of Israel, the maintenance of public order, or the suppression of mutiny, rebellion, or riot."[73]

Military administrators applied collective punishment to whole communities inside the Green Line to neutralize even the mildest of intransigence.[74] Curfews were used extensively, and in one notorious instance in 1956, forty-one villagers from Kafr Qasim (sixteen of them younger than the age of seventeen) who were returning from their fields after a curfew that had been announced only hours before, and of which they were not aware, were killed en masse.[75] Temporary residence cards were made compulsory not only to obtain work permits but also to secure one's place of residence and travel passes necessary for leaving that place, thus allowing the Israeli state and military to keep track of all Palestinian "trouble-makers."[76] Divide-and-rule methods were deployed whereby the Israeli military recruited members of Druze, Circassian, and Bedouin communities to police other Palestinians.[77] Sweeps and detentions were deployed both to demonstratively keep Palestinians in their place and to gather up yet more Palestinians to be expelled.[78] Even after military administration was rescinded, administrative detention of Palestinian citizens of Israel continued.[79]

Since 1967, and especially with the two Palestinian Intifadas (1987–1991 and after 2000), the counterinsurgency methods of the Israeli state, and in particular its use of collective punishment against civilians as deterrence, have become more kinetic in practice.[80] Mass detentions without trial have been used so extensively—in particular during the Palestinian Intifadas—that nearly half of all Palestinian men in the OPT have been detained at one time or another.[81] Laws—including some 2,500 military regulations for Palestinians in the OPT—have served military power, and almost all detainees have been tried through military courts.[82] In many instances, detainees have been simply deported.[83] Curfews and closures have been frequently used as methods of control; for example, in 1988, during the First Intifada, 1,600 curfews were imposed throughout the OPT and the "number of curfew days exceeded 'normal' ones."[84] The Israeli state has used house demolitions in Jerusalem, ostensibly for city planning purposes, and in the OPT as a form of collective punishment against families of Palestinian combatants.[85]

In 2002–2003, during the Second Intifada, intensely restrictive internal closure rules facilitated Israeli military control over the movement of civilians in the West Bank, detention of tens of thousands of civilians, and continued expropriation of their land.[86] During military operations, the Israeli military has extensively used hostages and human shields, even after Israeli courts have explicitly ruled against that practice.[87] In gathering intelligence, Israel has used both "pseudo-gangs"—or Israeli military or intelligence personnel dressed as Arabs—and local collaborators.[88] In addition, disruption of the everyday life of ordinary Palestinians not only was used punitively but also was routinized as part of military operations. As a commander testified in court:

The mission is to try to upset the equilibrium of the neighborhood, village, or particular location, to get information . . . or to cause a hostile entity inside the village to make mistakes as a result or in reaction to actions of our forces, and thus disrupt his activity and expose it. The acts of disruption can be done at a number of levels. The first is entering the village. Jeeps speed to the entrance of the village. Sometimes, just entering the village disrupts the perpetrator. The second way is to use pressure, throwing stun grenades, breaking into a number of houses or institutions in the village, arresting residents, seizing areas on rooftops, and the like. . . . We will detain, interrogate and use suitable pressure on every person to get to the one terrorist. Of all the means of pressure that we use, the vast majority are against persons who are not involved. This is true of the checkpoints, of combing whole neighborhoods, and also of questioning passersby. . . . There is a difference between going to a village where there isn't a threat and you don't suspect anything, and going on a mission given you, where aggressiveness toward every one of the residents in the village is common.[89]

One of Israel's most significant counterinsurgency techniques has been its population control measures via massive restrictions on movement of civilians, thus rendering those civilians visible to the state. This tactic is discussed at greater length in chapter 6. As a corollary to the mass detention techniques, settlements are also used as strategic weapons. Frontier settlements in Israel have always been intended to compensate for "lack of strategic depth" in projected conventional warfare against neighboring countries' militaries, and they have "prevent[ed], as far as possible, fixed boundaries being imposed on the National Home, and expand[ed] the territory of the Jewish State." They also have served very specific counterinsurgency functions.[90] But in the counterinsurgency against Palestinians in the OPT, these settlements, often perched on a hill above a Palestinian village or town or straddling a strategically significant route, informally police Palestinians, and ensure the round-the-clock presence of a punitive force within a stone's throw of Palestinian habitation.[91]

One of the most striking features of Israeli counterinsurgency has been the edifice of "morality" that holds up punitive military actions. A great deal is written on the "ethics" of Israeli action in the OPT by military philosophers and ethicists, most of whom still serve as reserve officers in the Israeli military. In much of this writing, the categorization of persons as "terrorists" allows a discursive and legal maneuver whereby a person so described is excluded both from the laws of war and from ordinary criminal policing. These ethicists reject the priority of the noncombatant enemy in asymmetric warfare. Their argument invokes citizenship and empathy, but only insofar as the Israeli military is considered:

A combatant is a citizen in uniform. In Israel, quite often he is a conscript or on reserve duty. His blood is as red and thick as that of citizens who are not in uniform. His life is as precious as the life of anyone else. . . . The state ought to have a compelling reason for jeopardizing a citizen's life, whether or not he or she is in uniform. The fact that persons involved in terror are depicted as noncombatants is not a reason for jeopardizing the combatant's life in their pursuit.[92]

This particular discursive transformation gives the ethicist—and the citizen combatant he envisions—the license to attack civilians (who are never called by that name but are always referred to as noncombatants), as long as they are not specifically intending to attack civilians. Thus, intentionality becomes the only standard by which the death of a bystander is measured: "Where the state does not have effective control of the vicinity, it does not have to shoulder responsibility for the fact that persons who are involved in terror operate in the vicinity of persons who are not. Injury to bystanders is not intended."[93]

This insistence on intentionality (rather than consequences) stems not only from a liberal understanding of the ethics of political acts but also from the manner in which Israeli military activity—as all Israeli political activity—is imbued with the rhetoric of legal legitimacy, where such intentionality matters in law. The self-representation of Israel as a liberal democracy is contingent on the claim of legality of both Israeli counterinsurgency techniques and the everyday administrative processes of its military occupation of the West Bank, Gaza, and East Jerusalem. Further, the long history of bureaucratization of military control of Palestinians—both inside and outside the Green Line—have meant that the law plays a central role in shaping the contours and defining the limits of what is militarily permissible. When questions of detention and imprisonment in counterinsurgency are addressed, the apparatuses of the law, legislation, the courts, and legal contention all end up mattering a great deal. Thus, we have a defining tension of Israeli counterinsurgency: on the one hand, the military requirement of decisive, destructive, and precipitate military assault on adversaries who are by definition already occupied and significantly weaker; on the other hand, a liberal insistence that such assault is, must be, legitimate.[94]

CONCLUSION

The counterinsurgency practices of the US and Israeli militaries differ in obvious ways, for obvious reasons. Whereas the US operates far from its own territories, and its intents are ostensibly not territorial, the Israeli military's operational space is literally inseparable from its unbounded, flexibly bordered territory, and Israel itself is decidedly engaged in a zero-sum struggle over dominion of lands held by Palestinians (and in the case of Golan, Syrians). That the Israeli military has largely become a constabulary force distinguishes it from the US military, whose training and orientation, despite its huge role in policing the world, has been geared toward conventional warfare.

In other ways, however, the two counterinsurgencies have significant parallels. The two powers converge on their use of overwhelming force alongside a discourse of legality. In both cases, the law has been innovatively interpreted and deployed to allow a fairly unfettered freedom of action for the military. Both militaries have borrowed and learned significantly from previous colonial counterinsurgencies, especially from the asymmetric or small wars of the British Empire. In both countries' current counterinsurgencies, the war in the shadows has been fought in spaces of confinement, and in fact, the regime of enclavization devised by the Israeli military and political elites has been exemplary in its persistent and expansive umbrella of surveillance; techniques of repression and information gathering; and its careful recruitment of law, procedure, and knowledge in the service of territorial control and security. In both instances, pliant proxies have also been necessary for reducing the cost of domination, whether these proxies are "tribal" elders or long-discredited "nationalist" leaders.

CHAPTER 3

FROM ISLAND PRISONS TO GUANTÁNAMO BAY

The law should be used as just another weapon in the government's arsenal, and in this case it becomes little more than a propaganda cover for the disposal of unwanted members of the public. For this to happen efficiently the activities of the legal services have to be tied to the war effort in as discreet a way as possible.

Frank Kitson, 1971[1]

In his famous speech calling on Congress to pass the Military Commissions Act in 2006, George W. Bush delineated one of the reasons the act was needed: "The men and women who protect us should not have to fear lawsuits filed by terrorists because they're doing their jobs."[2] Indeed, with the centrality of legal discourse to humanitarian intervention, many proponents of liberal military activism have spoken derisively of "lawfare," or the use of legal means as a weapon of war by which a weaker actor seeks advantage over its asymmetrically superior enemy.[3] But within the same discourse of liberal warfare, the rule of law has become central to the plans of the US War on Terror in Iraq, Afghanistan, and other places where the United States has operated its detention centers. The US counterinsurgency and stability operations field manuals explicitly state that counterinsurgency is primarily aimed to restore order and the rule of law.[4] Even the same officer who had disparaged lawfare now argues that "the new counterinsurgency doctrine also emphasizes that lawfare is more than just something adversaries seek to use against law-abiding societies; it is a resource that democratic militaries can—and should—employ *affirmatively.*"[5] Despite its contested meaning and utilization, the rule of law and adherence to law are invoked as the talismans that justify wars, define the boundaries of detention and interrogation, and dictate procedures.

Whether adherence to law is construed as national or transnational obligations, whether law is defined as constitutional, statutory, regulatory, or conceived through common practice, in peace or war, the constancy of law is the trope through which liberal practice produces itself. In the liberal way of war, law—international or domestic; military or civil; legislated, regulated, interpreted, or challenged in court—makes, unmakes, and shapes counterinsurgency detentions in complex and often dialectical ways. As a discourse and practice that establishes boundaries of actions and defines who has the power and "right" to wield violence, law is present in carceral counterinsurgency in breach, or in full force, or in self-contravention, and sometimes in all of those simultaneously. The certitude and density of legal discourse, the conventions of repetition and precedent, the insistence on the stability of rules and procedures in legal practice—all these conceal the extraordinary ancestries invoked and conjure legitimacy out of atrocity.

Law works, alongside other practices and procedures, to produce variegated spaces, hierarchies of places to which law applies in excess, or applies partially, or applies not at all. The concept of jurisdiction, so central to the notion of lawmaking, is itself a mechanism for regulating status and hierarchies, even if application, interpretation, and implementation render such a thing as a consistent, indivisible, and regulated jurisdiction largely a fiction of liberal rule. Anomalous zones created in law, by law, outside of it, or in an indeterminate unstable space bordering it show the margins—so often invisible—that can be extended to accommodate emergency situations.[6] A series of legal techniques operate in these fictive or concrete liminal legal spaces that allow for the differential application of law in line with contours of power. These legal techniques define categories of people to whom laws apply or not, categories of people who have the "right" to carry the law, and significantly, they define spaces through and within the law where detainees are made invisible and inaudible to law. What I argue here is that contrary to claims that places like the Guantánamo Bay detention center are lawless or legal black holes, their very creation and reproduction has been steeped in legal argument and definition. Even though some say that law stops at the water's edge, I argue that legal arguments carry on, defining processes and procedures, and contextualizing these indeterminate places in a body of precedent and legal definition.[7] Against Schmitt's vision of imperial spaces as places where law does not apply and Agamben's notion of legally indistinguishable zones of inclusion and exclusion, and in slight modification of Nasser Hussain's analysis of the emergency in a colonial setting, I argue that liberal empires and conquering powers create *ostensibly* lawless places through a conscious and deliberate legal process of temporarily and functionally setting aside one body of law and adopting another, or in rarer and more extreme instances, replacing legal procedures with administrative procedures.[8] The exalted place of law in liberal empires is what distinguishes them from illiberal ones. Law is supposed to not only provide legitimacy but also to circumvent arbitrariness and caprice. But in situations structured by racialized hierarchies, law can simply become another malleable tool, "another weapon in the government's arsenal."[9] Perhaps the main difference is that the elision between law and power in liberal regimes is not total, and as such, contestation can sometimes make a difference. My argument, then, is not that these rules and procedures or alternate bodies of law cannot protect the conquered, the colonial, or the powerless (they sometimes do), but rather that they provide an instrument of legitimation—albeit imperfect, incomplete, unstable, and fiercely contested—alongside military power.

What I aim to do in this chapter is to examine extraterritorial detention—in islands or outside of borders of a counterinsurgent state—and to elucidate the ways in which these places are defined in law. In other words, I scrutinize how *jurisdiction* is defined in discourse, text, and practice of law to make territories conform to bodies of law and the manner in which legal discourse is used to create variegated spaces in which law is applied differentially. I also examine the specters of colonialism that lurk in the most banal convention of legal arguments about counterinsurgency detention, the use of precedent. When conjugating jurisdiction to precedent, a whole series of descriptive, practical, and normative characteristics are conferred upon a given place where law is intended to apply in ways that bolster the might of the powerful within the boundaries of liberal decency.

CAPRICIOUS JURISDICTIONS: THE BANISHED

> "This is how things stand," said the officer. "I have been
> appointed judge here in the penal colony. . . . The principle

on which I base my decisions is: guilt is always beyond
doubt."

Franz Kafka, 1919[10]

European legal corpus has long used banishment and exile as tools for the
control of territories that European countries have held as colonies. The fact of
their control over multiple continents gave the European powers the ability to
send undesirables—criminal or political—from one colony to the other. Islands
were particularly useful in this regard: their watery surroundings provided a
natural barrier against escape, and their geological boundedness provided an
easier setting for establishing control measures over prison populations. Such
remote islands could also help shield convicts from outside scrutiny. The relative invisibility and inaccessibility of islands allowed administrators of penal
colonies extraordinary latitude in instituting punitive regimes of control, surveillance, labor extraction, punishment, and racialization on their convicts.[11]

Islands have long been designated as sites of punitive exile and forced labor.
The most famous of all convict colonies, those of Australia, were established
as places of "great and salutary dread," used to preempt through terror the
possibility of crime or insurrection.[12] Although modern island penal colonies
were originally intended for those prisoners defined as "ordinary criminals"
and domestic political outcasts—"philosophers, foreigners, actors, astrolo-
gers, and Jews"—banished to far-flung places from the metropolis, with the
emergence of concerted anticolonial struggles in the colonies themselves, island prisons began to receive vast contingents of revolutionaries, rebels, and
insurgents.[13] The French used Guiana, New Caledonia, and smaller islands
elsewhere as penal colonies. Algeria itself had been used as the site of prisons
for French convicts in mid-nineteenth century.[14] After the 1871–1872 revolt of
the Kabyle in Algeria, 212 of the rebel leaders were tried in Constantine, Algeria, and although most were imprisoned in France itself, 89 were deported
to New Caledonia, where they were joined by Communards deported from
Paris. Although the Communards were amnestied in 1870, the deported Algerian Arabs were granted amnesty only in 1895, and they received permission to return to Algeria only after 1904.[15] Toward the end of the nineteenth
century, deposed Indochinese kings were sent to Algeria, Réunion, French
Guiana, and New Caledonia.[16]

The British used a number of islands near their various imperial holdings as such penal reserves. The most dreaded of these were the Andaman Islands in the Indian Ocean, but smaller islands near Australia (especially the Norfolk Islands), the Indian Ocean islands of the Seychelles and Mauritius, the island of Malta, and the Bermudas were also used as prisons for political exiles at other times.[17] The Andaman Islands became particularly well known toward the end of the nineteenth century as increasing numbers of Indian mutineers, insurgents, and militant nationalists were shipped there.[18] The prisons on many of these islands were former garrisons or purpose built; but during counterinsurgencies, ad hoc prisoner-of-war camps were set up on the far-flung islands. For example, during the Boer War, twenty-four thousand Boers were sent to fourteen prisoner-of-war camps in India, six camps in Bermuda, five in Ceylon (Sri Lanka), and two on the island of St. Helena, already famous for Napoléon Bonaparte's banishment there.[19] In South Africa itself, Robben Island, where Nelson Mandela and other antiapartheid activists were imprisoned in the twentieth century, had served as a penal colony since the seventeenth century.[20]

Britain's use of banishment during two revolts in Palestine—by the Palestinian Arabs in 1936–1939 and by the Yishuv (Palestine's Jewish community) militants in 1946–1948—is instructive. During the Arab Revolt that began in 1936, Britain reinforced old and enacted new emergency regulations that severely expanded the police powers of the British mandatory government in Palestine and circumscribed the legal avenues on the rebels. The Emergency Regulations of 1936 and the Palestine (Defence) Order in Council of 1937 permitted collective punishments of fines and house destructions, significantly loosened the burden of evidence, legalized unannounced punitive searches, and expanded death-penalty sentencing.[21] Accounts of military courts that convicted Arab rebels, often with dubious evidence, rarely represented by lawyers, and executed within forty-eight hours for owning a gun, abound in archives and memoirs.[22]

By 1937, the British had detained a number of the leaders of the revolt and banished them to Seychelles without trial. Seychelles was chosen because it was geographically distant, culturally far from Arab concerns, and by then an established destination for banishment both by the British and the French who had been the island's overlords before the British. In the case of the

Palestinians, the Colonial Office commanded the governor of Seychelles to amend the law specifically to allow any reference to political prisoners there to include those from "any territory in respect of which a mandate on behalf of the League of Nations has been accepted by his Majesty," thus including the banished detainees in the category of prisoners to whom little legal recourse was available.[23] A few days later, the Colonial Office wrote to the Seychelles government, "If you feel that the powers conferred by [the aforementioned detention] Ordinance are insufficient to enable you to exercise the strict degree of surveillance which is necessary, the Secretary of State would wish you to report it and to make proposals for the extension of your power."[24]

When astute deportees (who included lawyers) moved to bring a libel action against a Seychellois newspaper that had called them terrorists, the governor and the Colonial Office scrambled to prevent such legal action. In a remarkably forthright note, the Colonial Office wrote, "Our policy in deporting these men to the Seychelles was 'to keep them out of sight, out of mind' for a time, and this policy will surely be defeated if they [the detainees] were able to push to extreme limits a libel action which would probably provide them with an excellent opportunity of ventilating their views on the illegality and inequity of their detention."[25] These detainees were held for years, some even until after the Second World War.[26] Seychelles was used for so long and so often to house Palestinian anticolonial leaders that a British diplomat in Egypt told the Colonial Office in 1946 that the island had become "traditionally associated in the Middle East with nationalist martyrs."[27] In protest against the clandestine transportation of further Palestinian detainees through Egypt to Seychelles, the same diplomat wrote that "to bring these people through Egypt in secret in an internationally illegal way is likely to involve us in considerable trouble with Egyptian local authorities seeing what has happened. It is most undesirable that in the midst of all our troubles here such justifiable provocation should be given to Egyptian nationalism already on the edge."[28] There is a sense in which legality and illegality mattered for the British as performative elements in the theater of political contestation.

Emergency Laws and Banishment

The interconnection of law and politics was an unquestioned assumption of the officials corresponding with one another in the metropole and in colonial centers. Political acts had to be justified with reference to law, and laws had to be hastily drawn up or amended to provide the necessary framework—however ad hoc—for contentious political action. What permitted this ramshackle and cursory conjuring of a dubious legal corpus was first that the colonies had such ambiguous jurisdictional status (Seychelles law was considered sovereign in that island, even if its text and terms were commanded from London) and second that the subjects of the law were themselves of dubious standing—a colonial subject was rarely a citizen in domestic law, or considered civilized enough to be recognized in international law.[29] The geographic dispersion of empire further allowed the consolidation of a spectrum of places to which various laws applied, or not, on the basis of the constructed notions of jurisdiction and legal access. Political prisoners who could not be brought to trial—because of political sensitivities or lack of evidence—or could not be sent to places from which they had originally been banished could also not be held in "the United Kingdom or any other British territory where special legislation for the detention of such persons does not exist" because of the "possibility of their instituting habeas corpus proceedings."[30] Although a habeas corpus writ could be brought in the United Kingdom, Seychelles' colonial status precluded habeas protection to the same people detained there. Even there, however, law had to be drafted to suspend habeas rights. Even better than Seychelles, which was officially a British colony, were places over which the British had de facto control, but whose status was not legally clear: one possible site of detention considered was the island of Kamaran off the coast of Aden, which the British had occupied during the First World War but over which they had not formally declared possession. As the Colonial Office wrote, Kamaran was "administered by Aden but whose territorial status has never been defined since 1919—it is not British territory, thus there would be no difficulties" with the law. The problem there, however, was that the island was "much too much a place of Arab interest to be a suitable detention camp for these renegade Arabs."[31]

The same considerations were also in operation when the British banished more than four hundred Jewish militants belonging to the extremist Irgun and Lehi groups between 1946 and 1948. If widespread slaughter of popular Arab leaders and rebels had been an option in the mid-1930s (with the elite, Western-educated, Arab leadership being sent into exile), the option was not open to the British in their suppression of Jewish militants. Aside from the

European origins of many of these militants, which made them more "us" than "them," the slaughter of Europe's Jews in the Shoah in the intervening years made executions or counterinsurgency assassinations (which had been used widely in the Arab Revolt ten years earlier) unacceptable. Detention and the removal of the militants from Palestine became the primary instrument of suppression of the militant Jewish groups in the late 1940s. Between 1944 and July 1948 (when the detainees were allowed to move to the nascent state of Israel), some 439 persons were detained in prison camps in Sudan, Eritrea, and Kenya.[32] In addition to inaccessibility, the variation in legal regimes was another incentive in holding the prisoners in places whose laws did not allow habeas corpus writs to be lodged. Although they had been arrested and originally detained in Palestine, once removed to East Africa, they were outside the legal domain of the British in Palestine. General Alan Cunningham, the British high commissioner in Palestine, told a petitioning Jewish delegation that "once these detainees have left Palestine I have no legal jurisdiction over them."[33] Here, rather than jurisdictional ambiguity, fragmentariness of imperial jurisdiction was deployed to prevent the possibility of appeal to law.[34]

In addition to problematic jurisdictions, the personal status of the prisoners was also uncertain. "What" a detainee was considered was as important as "where" he was located. Once deported to East Africa, the major issue the detainees had to contend with was the indeterminacy of their status, which gave the British the latitude they needed to apply whatever body of law they found most amenable. One former detainee recounted in his memoir, "I was a prisoner of war, a status for which we fought and demanded. But the British refused to recognise us as an army at war and sent the best of our boys to the gallows as common criminals."[35] This was also the complaint that the International Committee of the Red Cross (ICRC), when it was finally allowed to visit the prison camps, conveyed to the British government. The ICRC representative, a Mr. Munier, reported that the detainees' gravest concern was their status. They had been told that they had been detained under section 15b of the Emergency Regulations of Palestine (but they also pointed out that section 15b only allowed for twelve months of detention, whereas some of the detainees had been held since 1944).[36] The detainees had also been told that they were detained under section 17 of the same law, which allowed for the deportation of detainees. They were sometimes called prisoners of war by a commanding officer who had inspected the camps. As the ICRC representative wrote, "There is apparently no definition whatever regarding duration or limit of the period of detention. Many detainees appear to have been over five years in prison or in a concentration camp."[37] This very ambiguity foreclosed the recourse to law for the detainees, and the law itself was consistently said to set the parameters, boundaries, and agendas of detention. The conjugation of practical inaccessibility and legal anomaly (but not illegality or absence of law) was to prove an effective means of denying the adversary the ability to fight, then, in subsequent British counterinsurgencies, and most famously in the United States' extraterritorial detention centers at Guantánamo Bay and elsewhere.[38]

HISTORIES EMBEDDED IN PRECEDENTS: GUANTÁNAMO NAVAL BASE

> In the Tryal of Persons accused for Crimes against the State, the Method is much more short and commendable: the Judge first sends to sound the Disposition of those in Power, after which he can easily hang or save a Criminal, strictly preserving all due Forms of Law.
> *Jonathan Swift, 1742*[39]

> The law must accord the Executive substantial authority to apprehend and detain those who pose a real danger to our security.
> *Anthony Kennedy, US Supreme Court Justice, 2008*[40]

The Guantánamo Bay detention camp is liberal carceral confinement taken to its logical conclusion. Procedural excess and an intricately constructed legal edifice characterize the detention space there. In a sense, the detention center in Guantánamo is the physical embodiment of the panopticon nightmare. Earlier versions of the holding pens in Guantánamo were camps built to hold Haitian asylum seekers and Cuban "excludables" and were essentially cages, open to the elements, and to surveillance.[41] The subsequent prisons modeled on the supermax prisons in the mainland United States are the concrete manifestations of another form of discipline—an attempt at isolation and total and invasive control. The interrogation rooms at Guantánamo are yet another kind of theater of power: of the uses of body to intimidate; to make known who is in power; and, more mundanely, to extract "mosaic" information (quotidian "intelligence" about everyday habits and practices that allows the construction of a broad sociopolitical picture about the detainees). The whole complex, and the worldwide network of lawyers, legal scholars, advocates, military judges and prosecutors, human rights activists, and news reporters, attests to something else again: a space of legal dispute. Not of lawlessness, as it is claimed again and again, but of excess of law, rules, procedures, legal performances made by the government to legitimate control, and contested by those who seek to subject the detainees there to an alternate regime of legality. At Guantánamo Bay, there is no "deficit of lawyers or legal analysis" but a kind of palimpsest of what may prove expedient for the government.[42] Or as Karen Greenberg has written about the birth of the detention center there, "rather than a state of limbo being created out of a policy void, administration lawyers had for-mulated a policy embracing limbo as its primary characteristic. There was to be no policy. That was the policy."[43]

Law here calls upon precedent, of convention, and of new or borrowed or reanimated legal conceptions (e.g., unlawful enemy combatants and military commissions) to allow detention. International law—invoked by the activist lawyers representing the detainees—is there and is not there, because even when used, itself introduces in subtle ways the very hierarchies and privileges written into its ancestry.

The corpus of laws constantly crafted, legislated, argued, defended, and implemented by the US government have an ad hoc quality, and incremen-tally codify the arbitrary practices already established. But this makes them no less a legal set of discourses and practices.[44] This is of course not new; law was always at the forefront of imperial conquest, acting as the distinguishing standard between the civilized and the barbarian, the spectacle of the court designed to educate the natives,[45] the people Rudyard Kipling identified as "the lesser breed without the law."As a perceptive critical legal scholar reminds us, empire itself "is a *legal* construct—not only encumbered by international law, but also partly constituted by it."[46] It is the shadow spaces of this com-plex legal terrain that is so harshly illuminated in the glare of Guantánamo Bay court cases.

The Other Anomalous Bodies in Guantánamo Bay Naval Base

> The island was a large city divided into neighborhoods—
> McCalla and Bulkeley, each with its own purpose. Imagine
> a town where everyone who lived there was bonded, not by
> blood, but by a secret mission. The Joint Task Force (JTF)—
> the unification of all military forces: Army, Air Force, Navy,
> Marines, and the elitist Coast Guard, who prided themselves as
> the most superior—composed this governmentally engineered
> extended family. Here, everybody was a piece of a whole, like
> body limbs, completely incapable of functioning alone.
>
> *Nikòl Payen, 2002 [1992]*[47]

Long before the orange-suited, goggled, shackled, bound, kneeling prisoners in
the cages of Camp X-Ray—with its weed-strewn gravel ground—became the
staple image of the post-9/11 detention center at Guantánamo Bay, the naval
base had hosted persons whose presence and status there can be described as
"anomalous."[48]

The base, located in a harbor in the southeastern corner of Cuba, was first
occupied by the United States in the Spanish-American War in 1898, and the
United States extracted a perpetual lease from the Cuban government in 1903.
The sedimented history of the conquest, and of the unequal terms that guaranteed eternal US control over the strategically significant bit of land and harbor, should include the Platt Amendment of 1903, which not only spelled out
the terms of the lease in perpetuity, guaranteeing the liminal condition of the
base, but also set the stage for unrestrained US interference in Cuban affairs
to "protect" the base's "independence," giving the US government "the right
to intervene" at will to maintain not only Cuba's attachment to the United
States but also its sanitation, legal geography (control over the Isle of Pines,
for example), and, of course, its commerce.[49]

An official history of the Guantánamo Bay naval base tells us that the base's
civilian workers between its inception and the Second World War hailed from
Cuba, Jamaica, India, China, Malta, and Spain, and by 1953, the number of
mostly Cuban and Jamaican workers had increased to three thousand.[50] After Fidel Castro came to power in Cuba, the number of Cuban workers was
massively depleted, as more than two thousand were dismissed (in retaliation

against Castro ordering the water to the base to be cut, as he considered it illegally occupied).[51] To replace the Cuban base workers, the US Navy established contracts with the Jamaican government. As a rich history of civilian workers on the base tells us, the unambiguous benefits of such a contract with the Jamaican government included the efficiency of negotiating with a single overarching authority that was very amenable to the US terms. The US Navy "could also conduct the vast majority of labor relations out of the public spotlight . . . [and] could also easily eliminate any worker opposition by not renewing an individual's contract."[52] Invisibility was already proving profitable to the US forces occupying the Cuban land.

The kind of total spatial control a military base provides became even more beneficial to the United States with the Haitian refugee crisis in 1991. There, tens of thousands of Haitian refugees were kept in cages surrounded by barbed wire, under the haze of stigma of AIDS, in conditions that still shock. A judge deciding a case described the place as follows:

They live in camps surrounded by razor barbed wire. They tie plastic garbage bags to the sides of the building to keep the rain out. They sleep on cots and hang sheets to create some semblance of privacy. They are guarded by the military and are not permitted to leave the camp, except under military escort. The Haitian detainees have been subjected to predawn military sweeps as they sleep by as many as 400 soldiers dressed in full riot gear. They are confined like prisoners and are subject to detention in the brig without a hearing for camp rule infractions.[53]

Michael Ratner, a lawyer who represented the Haitians (and later defended detainees of the War on Terror), added: "For 14 months they have used portable toilets that are rarely cleaned, that are filled with feces and urine. The camp is bleak—no grass, hardscrabble ground and temporary wooden barracks on concrete slabs. Within those 'homes' 15 to 20 Haitians are huddled with only sheets hanging from the rafters. Rain, vermin and rats are the other occupants."[54] A Kreyòl-to-English translator's account of her stay in the base includes stories of bored US guards punishing small children for their mischief by marching them up and down endlessly; of malnourished, despairing children; and of barbed-wire medical quarantines for "infectious" asylum seekers and their healthy relatives who refused to be separated from their loved ones.[55] But though the physical conditions of the detained asylum seekers are as shocking—if not more so—than that of the War on Terror detainees, the legal and political circumstances seem eerily familiar, and the US government invokes exactly the same legal precedents to keep the asylum seekers out of the continental United States and incarcerated in the naval base. The US government denied access to the camps to the press, denied the asylum seekers access to attorneys, denied their right to due process, and disavowed its own sovereignty over the base.

Although up to 1991 the status of the base was compared to the Panama Canal Zone and other territories in which the United States "exercised the powers of sovereignty while nominal sovereignty lay elsewhere," the desultory refugee camps on the base became laboratories in which technologies of control, and legal arguments for incarceration, were first tested.[56] The precedents used to support the continued detention of the asylum-seekers included *Johnson v. Eisentrager* and *United States v. Verdugo-Urquidez*, the first of which denied habeas corpus to German spies and the latter of which justified an early illegal (or euphemistically, "informal") rendition of a Mexican citizen wanted for drug offenses. These precedents, discussed below, also became pivotal to the major Guantánamo detention cases argued in front of the US Supreme Court after the commencement of the War on Terror.

Ratner's account of the struggle for the release of the Haitian refugees detained in Guantánamo gives the reader an acute sensation of déjà vu, and Ratner himself presciently tells us that the government was very hesitant to allow the refugees due process or access to attorneys because "it was worried not just about the present case, but about future cases."[57] In his article, Ratner insists that without the concurrent political mobilization of the public by legal representatives of the refugees and queer rights and Haitian activists, the judges would not have been aware of the complexities of the situation, and the US immigration authorities would not have actually screened the refugees as required by the judiciary.[58] This sense of a public contestation over law was as important in determining the outcome of legal cases as the arguments made in formal court settings. This was to prove as critical in the War on Terror detention cases as well.

Unlawful Combatants

> When combatants and non-combatants are practically
> identical among a people, and savage or semi-savage peoples
> take advantage of this identity to effect ruses, surprises, and

massacres on the "regular" enemies, commanders must attack
their problems in entirely different ways from those in which
they proceed against Western peoples. When a war is between
"regular" troops and what are termed "irregular" troops the
mind must approach differently all matters of strategy and
tactics, and, necessarily also, matters of rules of war.

Elbridge Colby, 1927[59]

One of the former guards at Guantánamo Bay talks about

the use of the term "detainee." We were told it had to be detainee. If it's a prisoner,
then they are a Prisoner of War, and subject to entirely different laws. . . . Because
they are called detainees, they don't get trials and there is no code for how they're
treated. It's semantics, and we need to pay attention to those; they're important.[60]

Among the most contentious issues in War on Terror detentions has been
the indeterminacy of the applicable regime of law under which persons could
be incarcerated, interrogations could be conducted mostly out of view of
monitoring, and trials could be held. Somewhere in the liminal zone between
criminal law and the collation of customs and treaties that make the corpus of
the international laws of war, thousands of detainees have been held under an
ad hoc legal regime that would on the one hand give maximum strategic flexibility to the US government and, on the other hand, make the detainees as
inaccessible, unapproachable, and indefensible as possible. The indeterminacy
of the legal regime is in essence an act of strategic creation of interstitial spaces
in which the terrorist can be both criminal and prisoner of war (or neither),
depending on what is expedient for the government.[61]

This flexibility is maintained not only through the liminality of the legal
space in which a detainee moves but also through the very categorization of
the detainee within that space.[62] This flexibility in legal categories is created
through both the creation of categories themselves and a strategic vacillation
between different regimes of law that facilitate the process of categorization.
For example, because international laws did not readily yield a liminal category of a combatant who could still be tried and condemned to death, the
Geneva Conventions and the Conventions against Torture had to be set aside
to allow domestic laws to provide such flexibility. This was not as difficult as
it seems. John Yoo, the author of many of the complex legal memoranda that

authorized so many of the different detention aspects of the War on Terror, had built a career on insisting that international laws and treaties simply do not have the same authority as domestic US law, unless and until incorporated in the latter. On everything from international tribunals and international intelligence gathering to war powers and the use of force, Yoo has written historically grounded disavowals of international adjudication and an insistence on not simply a decisionist executive but a decisionism that is profoundly, historically, and constitutionally enshrined in US law.[63] The events of September 11, 2001, and the ensuing War on Terror have only consolidated these views and brought them into the realm of policy.[64] This view is confirmed by an eventual case brought by Jose Padilla against John Yoo, in which the Ninth Circuit Court of Appeals granted Yoo immunity because,

although it has been clearly established for decades that torture of an American citizen violates the Constitution, and we assume without deciding that Padilla's alleged treatment rose to the level of torture, that such treatment was torture was not clearly established in 2001–03.[65]

As the most politically astute lawyer in the Office of Legal Counsel, Yoo transformed into legal policy his particular vision of how laws applied or did not. Because article 17 of the Geneva Conventions does not allow for interrogations or trials, the Geneva Conventions had to be sidelined to allow for a category of detainee that could be interrogated or tried.[66] A complex ten-page draft memo by John Yoo and Robert Delahunty suspended the treaty obligations of the United States under the Geneva Conventions and argued that customary international law does not bind the president. Their argument was not arbitrary but rather appealed to domestic law, stating that because the War Crimes Act "does not criminalize all breaches of the Geneva Conventions," the domestic act applies to the situation of detainees rather than the treaty obligations that form the basis of the Geneva Conventions.[67] In the subsequent and final version of the memo, however, even the War Crimes Act is said not to apply to the detainees; rather, the detainees are legally placed under presidential authority in an emergency. A gamut of legal arguments and precedents are then invoked to substantiate this decision.[68] Accordingly, the order issued by George W. Bush that suspended the Geneva Conventions' applicability following this legal advice established the "unlawful combatant" category, stating that unlawful combatants do not "qualify as prisoners of war" and vaguely referring to "applicable laws" under which they were to be held.[69]

This flexibility to reject international laws of war has been bolstered by a rich and layered body of legal argument, from which necessary precedents for establishing categories of prisoners can be drawn. The case that defined the category of unlawful combatant was *Ex parte Quirin*:

Lawful combatants are subject to capture and detention as prisoners of war by opposing military forces. Unlawful combatants are likewise subject to capture and detention, but in addition they are subject to trial and punishment by military tribunals for acts which render their belligerency unlawful.[70]

In that case, German saboteurs were arrested and tried in 1942 and sentenced to death. The Supreme Court, in a case that even conservative Justice Antonin Scalia has called "not this Court's finest hour," decided that the saboteurs could be tried and executed rather than held in detention, as is often the case with prisoners of war.[71]

The new categories of persons and detainees depended not only on these legal inventions and resurrections but also on "mundane" legal classifications present in everyday conduct, such as citizenship and residency.[72] Here, the status of citizen, of permanent resident, or of nonresident noncitizen aliens became decisive in determining the extent to which detainees could be concealed, where they could be kept and for how long, to what treatment they could be subjected, and the extent to which criminal due process could be denied or proffered to them. An "ascending hierarchies of rights," acknowledged by even the liberal members of the Supreme Court, was constantly in operation in determining the fate of US detainees.[73] This ascending hierarchy of rights, and the special privileges reserved for citizens, is so powerful that in denying relief to Maher Arar, a Canadian citizen rendered for a year of unspeakable torture to Syria by the US government, the appeals court opined:

Whether or not the present litigation is motivated by considerations of geopolitics rather than personal harm, we think that as a general matter *the danger of foreign citizens' using the courts* in situations such as this to obstruct the foreign policy of our government is sufficiently acute that we must leave to Congress the judgment whether a damage remedy should exist.

Of course, the irony was that the judges were not stating a new opinion but rather invoking a precedent set by (and directly quoting) former appeals court judge Antonin Scalia, in a case that sought remedy for noncitizen victims of the Nicaraguan Contras some decades earlier.[74]

The creation of a third way—an indeterminate space in which sovereign power could choose between the legal regimes most expedient and flexible for its rule—is neither historically nor geographically new. The state of Israel had in 2002 passed an illegal combatant law that claimed to draw on international humanitarian law and was scrupulous in its claim of legality. Before that, "Israel appears to accord the Lebanese detainees [abducted in occupied Lebanon] no particular status under the laws of war. It is as if the detainees are without status of any kind."[75] The administrative detention laws and the legal regime of occupation forged precisely to deal with Palestinians had already provided fertile ground for this sort of liminal legal reasoning.

Historically, it is also noteworthy that the legal categories to which habeas corpus applied often dissipated under the conditions of empire, with overlapping, or alternative, or abbreviated versions of metropolitan law in operation in the colonies.[76] The empire insisted on law operating as a means of creating order, as a way of instilling "the spirit of industry," as a civilizing tool, but imperial law also created whole communities to whom different standards of punishment and treatment applied, and an incomplete, partial, or variegated implementation of the law became another method by which hierarchies could be reinforced.[77] This culminated in the "civil death" of the banished, which placed them ostensibly outside the law, even if their condition and categorization were also legally defined.[78]

The standard liberal interpretations of the Geneva Conventions view it as protecting national civilians on a battlefield.[79] However, not now, or ever historically, have the people on the battlefields been unambiguously civilian or clearly combatant; nor have the categories of "national" been so easy to imagine as the universal vector, given the newness of the universal nation-state form, the innumerable populations that do not fit it, and the increasing movements of people—as refugees, travelers, foreign "neutrals," formal combatants, tradespeople, and guerrillas—across the battlespace. "Foreign fighters" are yet another category to be added to this list of people with ambiguous or nonexistent access to the privilege of combat or protection of the law. Further, in a civil war, the Geneva Conventions are said not to apply in the way they would in an international war, and as such in Iraq, reclassifying an ongoing war from "occupation" to "civil war" has allowed the United States to override the protections afforded foreigners there and has underwritten large-scale rendition of those foreign fighters from Iraq.[80]

The celebrations of international law and the Geneva Conventions occlude the vector of civilization at the heart of the conventions. Dividing humanity "into three concentric zones or sphere—that of civilized humanity, of barbarous humanity and that of savage humanity" on the basis of "peculiarities of race or stages of development" had long been incorporated into the European understanding of how law was to apply to different "nations" and "races."[81] Such categorization provided the basis of deciding not only which states to recognize as worthy of sitting at the table of nations but even which would be considered *necessarily* subject to invasion and occupation by a higher civilization:

The Barbary States were never recognized by European nations; and the conquest of Algeria by France was not regarded as a violation of international law. It was an act of discipline which the bystander was entitled to exercise in the absence of police. . . . Had Algeria come to respect the rights of life and property, its history would not have permanently deprived it of the right to recognition.[82]

In the laws of war, such division between the civilized and the savage and barbarian were also institutionalized in the very body of law itself, as the various conventions originally only regulated warfare between civilized European nations.[83] Colonial wars were excluded from such regulations, and arguments about brutalities of Germans in Southwest Africa or Belgians in Congo were, if discussed at all, marginalist debates for specialists.[84] As scholars have shown, the racialized view of a hierarchy of humanity was even entrenched among those who enthusiastically supported the application of the laws of war to the colonized; they could agree that the "savages" may need to be considered in law, but they had "little doubt that 'savages' they were."[85] Even later, in 1947, as the British delegation sincerely argued for other nations to sign Common Article 3 of the Geneva Conventions, their colonial security officers wanted to ensure that their colonial subjects were not regulated or protected by the convention.[86] Later the British argued that the conventions also did not apply to insurgents, as the counterinsurgencies overseas were "internal" wars, as late even as the Mau Mau Revolt of the Gikuyu peoples in Kenya.[87] As one critical legal scholar points out, "The guerrilla under the Geneva Conventions remains what he has always been: an outlaw," but it must be noted that the law itself creates the category of the "outlaw."[88]

Passing laws regulating colonial counterinsurgencies has been so difficult that when Third World countries finally prevailed in passing the Additional Protocols—which made wars of decolonization subject to regulation and gave some recognition to guerrillas—the protocols were met with vehement contempt and disavowal from the more vociferously expansionist quarters of the US neoconservative legal community. For example, the coolly argued article by three Federalist Society lawyers on illegal combatants serenely glosses over the Additional Protocols; leapfrogs retroactively over the 1949 Geneva Conventions; and harks back to a more innocent colonial time, when colonized and occupied people could be categorized as unlawful combatants subject to the will and the law of the occupying colonizer.[89] Or in his discussion of the diplomatic conferences in the 1970s that led to the adoption of the Additional Protocols that recognized guerrilla warfare, Douglas Feith accuses the participants of "malign perverseness" and the protocols of being in effect "a pro-terrorist treaty masquerading as humanitarian law."[90] The same Douglas Feith would serve in the same administration whose lawyers went to such length to restore the colonial exclusions and hierarchies of humanity, through their "unlawful combatant" classification and even more through the arcane and complex set of overlapping personal jurisdictions that make the application of law an exercise in extraordinary discretion.

Military Commissions

> A precisely similar condition of things existed in 1862, when nearly four hundred Indian warriors, taken prisoners by the forces under my command, were tried and the greater number condemned to death by a Military Commission ordered by me upon charges and specifications preferred by myself.
> *Colonel Henry Sibley, 1863*[91]

Another historical recovery reanimated in War on Terror detentions has been the military commission. Long before the Uniform Code of Military

Justice was adopted by the US military in 1950, the US military had used military commissions alongside courts-martial to try and convict enemies, saboteurs, and traitors, even if military commissions—unlike courts-martial—have been legally ambiguous institutions.

Military commissions had been used in the war against the Seminoles (1818) to punish British citizens who aided the Native Americans, in the Mexican War (1847) to try civilians who were thought to have committed war crimes, and again during the US Civil War. The Union side used the commissions to supplant civilian criminal courts in the South, as the territory under Northern occupation was in essence under martial law. As an extraordinary history of the military commissions tells us, "The Supreme Court in 1857 confirmed that the President had the authority to establish such tribunals, but lower courts held that trial by these military commissions could continue only while military necessity demanded it and only during actual hostilities."[92] Military commissions were enshrined in the Lieber Code, the set of regulations drawn up by the jurist Francis Lieber; the code guided Union action in the Civil War and was later incorporated into the Hague Conventions. Article 13 of the code clarified the distinction between courts-martial and military commissions as the difference between laws legislated by Congress and those adjudicated in the corpus of common law. "Military offenses which do not come within the statute" or did not fall "within the 'Rules and Articles of War'" were tried by military commissions.[93]

After the Civil War, military commissions were used most spectacularly in small wars against Native Americans. Carol Chomsky's account of the Dakota military commissions in which nearly four hundred members of the Dakota tribe were brought before the court, and of whom forty were executed, points to the incongruity and oddity of the practice:

The Dakota were tried, not in a state or federal criminal court, but before a military commission. They were convicted, not for the crime of murder, but for killings committed in warfare. The official review was conducted, not by an appellate court, but by the President of the United States. Many wars took place between Americans and members of the Indian nations, but in no others did the United States apply criminal sanctions to punish those defeated in war.[94]

She might add that the Dakota, because of their ostensible sovereignty, were considered noncitizens and combatants (albeit irregular), and as such, the com-

mission broke with past practice of trying citizen civilians. The reason the Dakota had not been considered legitimate belligerents not only was the broader
interest of the settler community to appropriate their lands (which they did,
as the Dakota communities were forced into reservations) but also because of
a hierarchy of civilization that saw the "savagery" of the native as the basis of
denying him the privilege of being counted a prisoner of war. Military commissions did this by severely punishing the rebels with minimal due process.

The use of military commission in the Civil War was written into law
by Congress, which gave commanders in the field authorization to "execute
sentences imposed by military commissions upon guerrillas for violation of
the laws and customs of war."[95] However, as Chomsky points out, the commissions were considered subject to the same rules and regulations as ordinary courts-martial but with the expediency required in times of war. In
the twentieth century, military commissions were most famously used in
the case of eight German saboteurs, combatants captured in civilian clothes.
A summary trial sentenced the majority to execution, and the verdict was
confirmed by the Supreme Court in *Ex parte Quirin*. The case also famously
distinguished these combatants as "unlawful," thus carving out new territories in the bodies of law and jurisdiction that allowed the state maximum
strategic flexibility.[96]

Although William Barr (the attorney general in the George H. W. Bush
administration) had contemplated using military commissions to try the suspects in the bombing of Pan Am flight 103 over Lockerbie, Scotland, the most
recent time it was actually resurrected was very shortly after September 11.[97]
On an executive order issued on November 13, 2001, George W. Bush declared:

Given the danger to the safety of the United States and the nature of international
terrorism, and to the extent provided by and under this order, I find consistent with
section 836 of title 10, United States Code, that it is not practicable to apply in military commissions under this order the principles of law and the rules of evidence generally recognized in the trial of criminal cases in the United States district courts.[98]

Only days before, conservative lawyers had laid out the case for such tribunals, precisely because of the lack of transparency the commission afforded.
They argued that commissions could be conducted quickly without disclosing
"sensitive intelligence material" and without the same due-process protections
that the Constitution guaranteed in "Article III, the Fourth, Fifth, Sixth, and

Fourteenth Amendments, as well as those articulated in various judicial decisions interpreting those constitutional provisions."[99]

When lawyers for the detainees at the Guantánamo Bay naval base tried to question the legality of military commissions in *Hamdan v. Rumsfeld*, the US government invoked *Ex parte Quirin*.[100] Although the court in *Hamdan* decided against the executive's decision to hold military commissions and declared that military commissions had not been authorized by Congress, the actual opinion was far more concerned with the fidelity of the process to a set of preestablished procedures, to the formal rituals of justice, and to the clear delineation of the duties of the branches. Absent in the issued opinions were any substantive concerns that may arise when the most powerful state in the world holds hundreds of men in detention thousands of miles from their homes or the battlefield with minimal access or oversight by monitors, the press, or the public. The variation in opinion seemed to concern the extent to which a detainee can be bound to and by law and the state, and about extending the empire of the law, rather than a question of justice. The liberal judges seemed to be more exercised by the perceived slight to the rule of the judiciary in what reads like a jealous guarding of the judiciary's domain; one of the justices ends his concurring opinion by taunting Bush: "Nothing prevents the President from returning to Congress to seek the authority he believes necessary."[101]

George W. Bush did just that. In 2006, the US Congress passed the Military Commissions Act, which circumscribed detainee access to the Geneva Conventions; suspended due-process rights afforded in criminal trials; severely abbreviated the requirement of giving notice to the detainee for his or her trial; foreclosed the provisions of a court-martial for speedy trial, self-incrimination, and pretrial investigation; and most extraordinarily decreed that "no court, justice, or judge shall have jurisdiction to hear or consider an application for a writ of habeas corpus" for such unlawful enemy combatants.[102] When the act was amended in 2009, the admission of coerced and hearsay evidence was restricted and access to attorneys expanded, but other provisions were left untouched.[103] In a sense, the military commission became a legal institution, fashioned by democratic representatives of US citizen: a startling instance of the violence that makes and preserves law in a mutually constitutive relationship.[104] This is confirmed as much, when in their 2011 *en banc* decision against Salim Hamdan, the military commission invokes its Seminole War precedents, and although it "takes no comfort in the historical context in which these events occurred," it nevertheless sees it as "an embryonic effort" to bring into the domain of law the violence of conquest.[105]

The military commission thus provided a mechanism for making detainees invisible even as the ritual of trial gave the small handful brought to court a severely circumscribed and surveilled platform from which to speak. Judicial proceduralism is one way in which the detainees are prevented from speaking about their torture; for example, various minor demands of detainees are granted so as to prevent having them testify to their torture in pretrial motions.[106] A major feature of the main Guantánamo courtroom (there are two) is the soundproof glass barrier segregating the audience from the participants, "so that the only way an observer can hear what is going on is through headphones with a forty-second delay"; this allows the military to enforce the rule whereby "detainees are forbidden from speaking about their torture."[107] As David Cole writes, "the US cannot compel the detainees themselves not to speak of the unspeakable. The only way it can keep them from telling their stories is by keeping them detained, behind bars, behind glass, silenced."[108] Just as important, the attorneys who have represented the detainees have had to go through rigorous background checks, have to apply for classified security clearance to see documents relevant to their clients, and as a condition of access to the detainees have their legal documents, including the notes of their meetings with their clients, monitored by the Department of Defense in a warehouse in northern Virginia.[109] Where usually the performative of justice allows the accused to speak for him- or herself, in a military commission the detainees' voices are smothered.

Precedents and Legal Progenitors

> It is a Maxim among these Lawyers that whatever has been done before, may legally be done again: and therefore they take Special Care to record all the decisions formerly made against common Justice, and the general Reason of Mankind. These, under the name of *Precedents*, they produce as Authorities to justify the most iniquitous Opinions; and the judges never fail of directing accordingly.
> *Jonathan Swift, 1742*[110]

The most striking characteristic of the legal edifice around counterinsurgency incarcerations is the perpetual return of the repressed, of the histories of colonialism and domination being read into the present through precedents, even when those precedents are invoked by liberal judges in the cause of granting the detainees rights the government wants denied.[111]

Certainly, the arguments put forward by the Office of Legal Counsel, in defending the new legal procedures pertaining to the detainees, already openly declaimed their histories. In giving the White House the ability to deploy the military domestically, John Yoo invoked the US suppression of Native Americans and the insurgents of the Boxer Rebellion; in other instances, broad discretion of the executive to declare martial law in conquered colonies was cited.[112] In another memo that legally circumscribes the application of Geneva Conventions to Taliban and al-Qaeda operatives, John Yoo refers to the examples of French and British suspensions in their counterinsurgencies in Algeria and Kenya, respectively.[113] In yet another memo, John Yoo mentions that in the 1967 War, because of exigencies of war, Israel refused the ICRC access to prisoners of war, and given the particularities of the circumstances, this was justified and eminently useful to emulate.[114]

The rooting of the War on Terror's legal parentage in colonial counterinsurgencies is not surprising when it appears in the legal reasoning of the proponents of the War on Terror, including those who built its legal edifice. More vexing are the precedents claimed by liberal Supreme Court judges for the decisions they have taken to ostensibly protect civil rights in times of heightened calls for security. In a sense the invocation of past empires, hypersovereignty and decisionism writes into the liberal opinions the "racist, illiberal ideology" of the precedents that legitimate today's legal opinion.[115] The very use of precedent is a discursive positioning of present juridical text in the context of a tradition with such depth and breath as to provide by its sheer volume, repetition, and familiarity the justifications we require today of our legal reasoning. The density and stickiness of these precedents work in favor of maintaining structures of power as they are, no matter how unjust or historically anachronistic those precedents may be. It is true that legal texts are open to interpretation and contestation, and the use of precedent is precisely supposed to invoke differing interpretative intents, but to accept that ultimately, judges are not insulated from the zeitgeist or from political pressures is to recognize that the contingency of interpretation sways it toward the arguments of power.

Tracing the precedents in Supreme Court cases pertaining to War on Terror detentions reveals a fundamental dependence on a palimpsest of laws that consolidated US hemispheric domination in the Americas, the Pacific, and the Caribbean, from the Monroe Doctrine and the Platt Amendment through the War on Drugs and the bloody indirect counterinsurgencies in Central America.[116] In the first category of precedents are those cases arising in wartime and concentrating sovereign power—the power over life and death—in the hands of the executive. In the second category are a broad range of cases dealing with such questions as "Does the constitution follow the flag?" "Can habeas corpus be applied to foreign citizens who may or may not have been abducted overseas?" "Can habeas corpus be applied or suspended in places with de facto but not de jure US sovereignty?" and finally, "Is the US responsible for atrocities committed by its clients overseas?"

In wartime cases, the executive does its best to advance its aims without further adjudication by the judiciary, and as much as possible without contentious oversight by the legislature (although the latter is more often than not amenable, when "security" is invoked). The case of *Hamdi v. Rumsfeld*, stands out: Yaser Esam Hamdi was a US citizen declared an unlawful combatant and held in Guantánamo and later in a naval brig in South Carolina, where his lawyers petitioned for habeas corpus. When the case reached the Supreme Court, both the majority and the dissenters invoked *Youngstown Sheet & Tube Co. v. Sawyer* (1952), a Korean War case in which President Harry Truman seized a steel plan to prevent a strike by steelworkers there. As the *Youngstown* case notes and arguments show, the executive (represented by the secretary of commerce, Charles Sawyer) could have invoked a series of extant laws that would have allowed it to do precisely the same thing, but it foreshortened such activity in the interest of expediency. In that case, the Supreme Court confirmed a district court injunction barring the president from seizing the plant. The particular event is of interest, because the Court made its decision simply on the basis of the executive's short-circuiting of accepted procedures. Had Truman been more patient, he could have invoked legislation itself against the steelworkers, but the Court ruled that liberal decorum could not allow the president to brazenly jettison procedure. The text of the case is of great interest as well, because although the majority opinion denied the executive unlimited power, a much-cited concurring opinion by one of the justices, Robert Jackson, set out a series of criteria blurring the boundaries between the executive and the legislature—"Presidential powers are not fixed but fluctuate depending upon their disjunction or conjunction with those of Congress"—and presciently pointed to a Congress that out of "inertia, indifference or quiescence" can allow the president the latitude he needs to exercise his power. When the *Hamdi* judges invoke *Youngstown*, both the majority and Justice Thomas dissenting confirm the "broad powers [vested] in military commanders engaged in day-to-day fighting in a theater of war." In the end, although the Court ruled in *Hamdi* that the US government could not hold detainees without due process, it also confirmed that the minimum requirement for such due process was remarkably low and at best procedural rather than substantive, best embodied in the Combatant Status Review Tribunals.

The other executive power cases central to the Supreme Court are invoked as precedent in *El-Masri v. United States*. Khaled El-Masri was a German citizen of Lebanese origin who, traveling in Macedonia, was mistaken for a wanted Islamist, arrested, rendered to Afghanistan, and released some months later, several weeks after his CIA captors had discovered that he was not the wanted man. El-Masri's case was thrown out by the Fourth Circuit Court of Appeals, on the basis of the government's invocation of state secrets. Here, the appeals court judges called on several cases, but two in particular are of note. In the first, *United States v. Reynolds*, families of three civilian engineers who had been killed in a military plane crash sued the government, but they were prevented from finding out the cause of the crash because the government invoked state secrets. When decades later the case material was declassified, it was discovered that much of what had been classified as state secret would have embarrassed the government by showing incompetence and faulty maintenance as the root of the problem and would not have revealed information of importance to "national security."[117] The second case used as precedent was *United States v. Nixon*, in which the Court ruled that state secrets did not protect President Richard Nixon from having to provide recordings of his conversations to a Watergate special prosecutor. As Nixon's attorney stated to the court, "The President wants me to argue that he is as powerful a monarch as Louis XIV, only four years at a time, and is not subject to the processes of any court in the land except the court of impeachment." The Court refused to accept the absolutism of sovereign power in the hands of Nixon. Of course, between the *Reynolds* case and *El-Masri*, the body of decisions in favor of state secrets had considerable thickened, tipping the balance in favor of the US government.

When in the *El-Masri* case the appeals court cited *Reynolds*, it ignored the history of the case, in which state-secrets privilege had protected the government from embarrassment. Even more strikingly, *Nixon* was turned on its head, its substance wholly eviscerated, to provide the judges with the following justification for denying El-Masri any relief:

In *United States v. Nixon*, the Court further articulated the [state secrets] doctrine's constitutional dimension, observing that the state secrets privilege provides exceptionally strong protection because it concerns "areas of Article II duties [in which] the courts have traditionally shown the utmost deference to Presidential responsibilities." . . . The *Nixon* Court went on to recognize that, to the extent an executive claim of privilege "relates to the effective discharge of a President's powers, it is constitutionally based."

The ostensible interpretive freedom of using precedents here allowed a complete reversal of what a case may have "meant," but in favor of executive power.

Just as important to the wartime category of cases were those in which the executive or the military chose to detain their adversaries. The two cases most often cited as precedent here were *Ex parte Quirin* and *Johnson v. Eisentrager*, but the circumstances in which *Ex parte Endo* and *Korematsu v. United States* are cited are also noteworthy. I have already written about *Quirin* in my interrogation of the military commissions. *Johnson v. Eisentrager* brings other war stories to bear that are in their own way instructive. In that case, after the surrender of Germany in the Second World War, a US military commission in China convicted twenty-one German officers of war crimes and moved them to a prison on a US military base in Germany. When the prisoners petitioned the Court for habeas corpus, the court essentially ruled that it had no jurisdiction over the case. But it also ruled that because the men were not citizens, and had not been captured on US soil, and because their transportation to stand in front of a US court "would require allocation of shipping space, guarding personnel, billeting and rations" and would damage the prestige of military commanders at a sensitive time, "the Court sought to balance the constraints of military occupation with constitutional necessities."[118] Again, here, the court deferred to the executive, by refusing to afford the enemy prisoners privileges that would place "the litigation weapon in unrestrained enemy hands." Even more important, careful juridical categorization of places and persons bound them to one form of law and not another, thus allowing the government maximum expediency. Indeed, the process of categorization was at the very heart of the opinion delivered in the case. Although Justice Robert Jackson lauded US law for having "come a long way" from a "public and private slaughter, cruelty and plunder," nevertheless, he wanted recognition that

even by the most magnanimous view, our law does not abolish inherent distinctions recognized throughout the civilized world between citizens and aliens, nor between aliens of friendly and of enemy allegiance, nor between resident enemy aliens who have submitted themselves to our laws and non-resident enemy aliens who at all times have remained with, and adhered to, enemy governments.

The uses of *Ex parte Endo* and *Korematsu* are both far more dubious. Both cases arose out of US internment of US citizens and residents of Japanese origin during the Second World War. In *Korematsu*, Justice Hugo Black had ruled that because "an immediate segregation of the disloyal from the loyal" among the Japanese was not possible, all could indeed be interned and excluded from their homes, then declared closed "military zones."[119] Further, the Court's ruling sanctioned detention by noting that "the power to exclude includes the power to do it by force if necessary. And any forcible measure must necessarily entail some degree of detention or restraint whatever method of removal is selected."[120] But the Court's opinion, as a later scholar comments, "remains strangely enigmatic about the governing standard of review of military orders that impact the civil and constitutional rights of American citizens. He never says which standard of review a court should use in assessing the constitutionality of the military order."[121] Further, *Korematsu* places maximal discretion in the hands of the military.[122] It is precisely this ambiguity and the deference shown the executive that make *Korematsu* useful as a precedent for the government strategy of maximum executive convenience and flexibility. On the same day that *Korematsu* gave the government the ability to exclude Japanese from their homes, in *Ex parte Endo* it ruled that Mitsuye Endo as a "loyal and law-abiding citizen" could not be detained in a War Relocation Authority Center by military authorities. It is notable that the practical effect of the conjunction of the two cases (i.e., the continued legality of exclusion from the West Coast with the declaration that "loyal" Americans of Japanese descent could not be detained in relocation centers) was that the magnanimity of the *Endo* ruling remained wholly theoretical: the detainees in the relocation centers could not leave even if they were granted permission to do so by the Court. Their livelihoods, homes, and earning capabilities were all tied up to their West Coast existence, which had been expropriated by the state. Their apprehension about being perceived as traitors in unfamiliar places in the United States and the lack of employment meant that many had to remain in the relocation centers until the end of the war.[123]

Outside of wartime precedents, the second body of law that is invoked in Guantánamo and rendition cases includes former legal opinions about instances in which the US projection of power worldwide—but particularly in the Western Hemisphere and in the Pacific—was contested in court. These cases arose out of the extracontinental expansion of the United States to establish naval and coaling stations throughout the oceans. One of the most influential texts of the time in the United States was Alfred Thayer Mahan's *The Influence of Sea Power upon History*, a narrative of the ways in which naval sea power could be deployed to ensure national supremacy. Mahan argued for "a suitable base upon the frontier, in this case the seaboard . . . and an organized military force, in this case a fleet, of size and quality adequate to the proposed operations."[124] Mahan's ideas were central in the Spanish War conquest of a chain of islands in the Caribbean and the Pacific, in an age of imperial rivalry, in which European states and the United States competed to colonize far reaches of the world to achieve imperial prestige, exploitation of rich natural resources, and international dominance as "policeman as well as triumphant businessman" of world politics.[125] But conquest brought with it a series of controversies fundamental to the structuring of empires and subject to juridical challenge: What does US territorial possession entail in law, administration, and procedure? How are jurisdictions defined, and how do they equate or overlap with spaces that are controlled and governed by the US government? What categorical rights are granted in law to the persons occupying such spaces when they are not citizens? And what categories of personhood do such spaces create?

The most famous cases, which have not been set aside and are still in effect, are the series of Supreme Court cases decided between 1901 and 1922, known collectively as the *Insular Cases*.[126] These cases emerged out of the contestation over what it meant for the US military to invade, conquer, and administer islands in its periphery, whether in the Caribbean or in the Pacific. The earlier cases (*De Lima v. Bidwell*; *Goetze v. United States*; *Fourteen Diamond Rings v. United States*; *Downes v. Bidwell*; *Dooley v. United States*; *Armstrong v. United States*; *Huus v. New York and Porto Rico Steamship Co.*) determined whether these possessions should be considered "foreign" or "domestic" with respect to determining the applicability of tariffs and duties. The response was that they were betwixt and between: *De Lima* ruled that they were not foreign, but *Downes* determined that they were not domestic. In deciding the ambiguous and liminal position of such islands, they were "domestic for one purpose and foreign for another," even if this was precisely what the Court's opinion repudiated.[127] The complex overlapping opinions listed above and concerning Puerto Rico, Guam, Hawaii, and the Philippines—then direct targets of US colonization—created intricate legal categories that allowed the United States "to take control over territory while avoiding many of the responsibilities that sovereignty implies," and thus such imprecise and ambiguous territorial concepts as appurtenance, rather than of possession or dominion, were deployed to allow US expansion into the islands.[128]

This complexity was further reinforced when the status of the people occupying the islands came into question. In a series of subsequent cases the Supreme Court decided whether in these interstitial spaces, the people conquered and owing allegiance to the United States could be tried by jury consistent with the Fifth and Sixth Amendments of the US Constitution (*Dorr v. United States, Balzac v. Porto Rico, Hawaii v. Mankichi, Kepner v. United States, Dowdell v. United States*, and *Ocampo v. United States*); whether they were resident aliens or US nationals (*Gonzalez v. Williams*); and how far their rights resembled those of the nationals not from an insular possession. Race and the extent of "civilization" of the inhabitants of the insular possessions were at the crux of the cases, even if not always explicitly stipulated.[129]

In reading the texts of these opinions, which deal with whether tariffs should be applied to goods brought in from Puerto Rico or the Philippines, one meanders through explicit histories of insurrection and revolt and a veritable chronology of US colonial counterinsurgencies. For example, in *14 Diamonds*, a US citizen served in the volunteer army that invaded Luzon in the Philippines and brought back with him to the United States diamonds that he had bought there. When challenged to pay customs for the diamonds, he took his case to the courts, where the Supreme Court decided that for the purposes of the case, the Philippines resembled Puerto Rico, whereby for the application of tariffs, it should have been considered "domestic." But the text of the opinion records the insurrection of the Filipino population:

The Philippines thereby ceased, in the language of the treaty, "to be Spanish." Ceasing to be Spanish, they ceased to be foreign country. They came under the complete and absolute sovereignty and dominion of the United States, and so became territory of the United States over which civil government could be established. The result was the same although there was no stipulation that the native inhabitants should be incorporated into the body politic, and none securing to them the right to choose their nationality. Their allegiance became due to the United States, and they became entitled to its protection.

The fact that there were insurrections against [Spain], or that uncivilized tribes may have defied her will, did not affect the validity of her title. She granted the islands to the United States, and the grantee, in accepting them took nothing less than the whole grant. If those in insurrection against Spain continued in insurrection against the United States, the legal title and possession of the latter remained unaffected.

We do not understand that it is claimed that, in carrying on the pending hostilities, the government is seeking to subjugate the people of a foreign country, but, on the contrary, that it is preserving order and suppressing insurrection in the territory of the United States. It follows that the possession of the United States is adequate possession under legal title, and this cannot be asserted for one purpose and denied for another. We dismiss the suggested distinction as untenable.

In some ways, the subsequent projection of US power in Latin America and its juridical legitimation continue the application and extension of the original *Insular Cases*. A respected judge of the US First Circuit Court of Appeals, Juan Torruella, argues as much when he includes among the progeny of the *Insular Cases* the landmark *United States v. Verdugo-Urquidez*, in which the Supreme Court held that the constitutional limits on searches and seizures did not apply to a Mexican citizen living in Mexico, whereas the United States had de facto authority to conduct such searches.[130] The opinion in *Verdugo-Urquidez*, written by Chief Justice Rehnquist, directly references *Balzac v. Porto Rico*, which limited the access of Puerto Ricans to the same constitutional protections US citizens enjoy on the basis of incommensurable civilizational differences between Puerto Ricans and (white) citizens. Fascinatingly, the case is dependent on both a distinction between "people" and "persons" as those covered under US law and those who are not, as well as their territorial location.[131] Rehnquist wrote that "it is not open to us in light of the Insular Cases to endorse the view that every constitutional provision applies wherever the United States Government exercises its power." In his concurring opinion in *Verdugo-Urquidez*, Justice Kennedy—who called upon the *Insular Cases* again some twenty years later (discussed below)—wrote, "Just as the Constitution in the Insular Cases did not require Congress to implement all constitutional guarantees in its territories because of their 'wholly dissimilar traditions and institutions,' the Constitution does not require United States agents to obtain a warrant when searching the foreign home of a nonresident alien."

It is the contextual familiarity of the *Insular Cases* and their progeny that makes them such appropriate—if deeply disturbing—precedents for the War on Terror cases. Of course the concept of liminal juridical spaces is ideally suited to conservative Supreme Court justices, who invoke the idea of interstitial insular possessions as justification for ruling against expansion of rights to detainees held in Guantánamo Bay. For example, in his dissent in *Hamdi v. Rumsfeld*, Justice Scalia directly invokes the suspension of habeas corpus in both the Philippines and Hawaii via the Philippine Civil Government Act (1902) and the Hawaii Organic Act (1900), and he considers the circumscription of rights and bodies justified "in case of rebellion or invasion (or threat thereof)."

The liberal Justice Stevens who writes the Court's opinion in *Rasul v. Bush* invokes *In re Yamashita*, a case involving a Japanese prisoner of war captured in the Philippines during the Second World War, when the archipelago was still an insular possession of the United States. He does so to instantiate the right of captives there to habeas corpus, but in so doing, he also recognises the ability of the United States to hold such interstitial spaces as "insular possessions" with their colonial regimes of rights. Similarly, in *Boumediene v. Bush*, which grants the courts the right to review the habeas corpus petitions of accused in military commissions, Justice Kennedy turns to the *Insular Cases* to argue that they provided a framework for adjudicating habeas cases in the War on Terror. Strikingly, Kennedy lets pass with implicit approval a quote from *Downes* in which the incommensurability of "race, habits, laws and customs of the people, and . . . differences of soil, climate and production" is cited as reason enough for the variable and incomplete application of the Constitution to these interstitial spaces.

The analogical use and reinterpretation of precedent is so flexible as to allow circumscribed extraterritorial application of constitutional protections in *Verdugo-Urquidez* and expansion of such protection in *Boumediene*. Even where such protection is afforded, however, what remains unspoken, invisible, elided, but crucial to the constitution of US power is the extent to which it can be exercised extraterritorially in an incomplete way enshrined in the law. Even when well-meaning liberal justices expand habeas corpus to detainees held in Guantánamo Bay in the teeth of fierce US government opposition, they do so by invoking and confirming the conditions of possibility of US imperial control over others' territories.

LAW, JURISDICTION, CATEGORIZING SUBJECTS

> Gentlemen, the title of America to the island of Luzon is better than the title we had to Louisiana. It rests upon a more just foundation than the title we had to Texas. It rests upon the sure foundation of international law, and the surer foundation of high duty in the family of nations and to the cause of humanity.
> *Elihu Root, 1899*[132]

> Our strength as a nation state will continue to be challenged by those who employ a strategy of the weak using international fora, judicial processes, and terrorism.
> *US Department of Defense, 2005*[133]

In January 2002, not too long after the abandoned and weed-strewn Camp X-Ray had been brought out of retirement to hold the War on Terror detainees in Guantánamo Bay naval base, a liberal lawyer and professor at Harvard

University, Alan Dershowitz, famously called for torture warrants in a newspaper article. In the piece, Dershowitz argued:

The "third degree" is all too common, not only on TV shows such as "NYPD Blue," but in the back rooms of real police station houses. No democracy, other than Israel, has ever employed torture within the law. Until quite recently, Israel recognized the power of its security agencies to employ what it euphemistically called "moderate physical pressure" to elicit information from terrorists about continuing threats. . . .

An application for a torture warrant would have to be based on the absolute need to obtain immediate information in order to save lives coupled with probable cause that the suspect had such information and is unwilling to reveal it.

The suspect would be given immunity from prosecution based on information elicited by the torture. The warrant would limit the torture to nonlethal means, such as sterile needles, being inserted beneath the nails to cause excruciating pain without endangering life.[134]

Although the passing of years and the preponderance of hideous opinions issuing from Dershowitz have dulled the initial shock this piece produced, there is a kind of honesty to the recognition that indeed law can—and so often does—act as an alibi for violence and that the state of emergency that does sanction torture is constituted in law.[135] But it is reductive to imagine that law is only an alibi for power. Indeed, what makes law such a subject of contestation is its elasticity.[136] That the US Department of Defense would consider the cases brought on behalf of War on Terror detainees as direct instruments of warfare against the United States, explicitly put on par with terrorism (as in the epigraph above), or that the Israeli state considers itself a target of lawfare when subjected to lawsuits by victims of its counterinsurgency, indicates the extent to which this arena of contestation can also be a space in which power is at least made visible, if not always successfully challenged.

Because, in the end, law is not the neutral, objective, and eternally transcendent embodiment of justice. This "almost salvific belief in [laws'] capacity to conjure up equitable, just, ethically founded, pacific polities" is disputed in the very history of international law, and in the ways in which sovereignty, territory, and jurisdiction are constituted in law.[137] The original founders and fathers of international law had themselves been implicated in imperial conquest, and the very structures of law were steeped in the racial hierarchies and desire for conquest that made Europe the master of so many continents.[138] Francisco de Vitoria, for example, defined the American Indians' title to land as incomplete and their sovereignty subject to their unlimited acceptance of Spanish proselytization and trade, with their capacity for self-determination and protection from despoliation in war always already impaired by their cultural inferiority.[139] Hugo Grotius, cited reverently as the founding theorizer of international law, had developed his treatise on the laws of the sea in the context of Dutch East India Company forcing open trade routes in Southeast Asia and of natural "justice" legitimating the conquest of the Indies.[140] The contingency and historicity of law and its saturation with power relations has meant that when war is subjected to the "technical guidelines," adherence to which renders a war "legal," its violence is not eradicated but rather channeled, monitored, and regulated, and vast discretionary powers are left to the states through such conceptual alibis as "military necessity."[141]

Laws convey not just a set of rulings but also imaginaries of territories as jurisdictions, the contours of rule (how the law gets implemented), and the subjects of the law—who is the population to whom the law applies, whom the law interpellates (the police's "Hey, you there" of Althusser), who is punished (or spared or ignored or excluded), who can sidestep the law, who is the law. Conventions that allow for palimpsests of precedent to read into present juridical rulings the histories and techniques and categories of colonial pasts unwittingly absorb these pasts into the present. To contest the law is a heroic attempt to battle the weight of a whole history of juridical decision making.

First, territories and jurisdictions. Much has been written about the relationship between spaces and laws.[142] Jurisdiction is a relatively modern "governmental technique" that transforms space "into an empty vessel for governmental power" and more often than not, "property" of the state (or conqueror).[143] In the latter instance the liberal notion of private ownership of property was transposed unto international law, where territories, those complex spaces in which people live, imagine their lives, and fight over, were conceptualized as "the space within which the state exercised absolute competence, a procedural space of jurisdiction."[144] In international law, this transformation occurred in particular through the process of colonial expropriation, where for example Native American land in the Western Hemisphere was parceled into "titles," with the ownership, propagation, and settled use of land being how the savage was distinguished from the civilized.[145] Thus a place like Guantánamo can be subject to US law, considered a de facto "possession," where law applies in an uneven, unpredictable, and arbitrary way. The jurisdictional status of Guantánamo itself is defined through a series of precedents that rely on the continued legitimacy of the US colonization of Caribbean and Pacific islands.

Just as important as jurisdiction are the categories of persons who make laws, who challenge them, who are subject to them. In Anglo-Saxon law, habeas corpus is envisioned as the "synecdoche for modern liberal ideals."[146] Yet the history of habeas shows that it was originally intended not as an emancipatory concept but as the prerogative of the king.[147] The transnational applications of habeas occurred in the context of imperial conquest, where "the bonds of allegiance stretched as the king's subjects moved. The law concerned with habeas corpus thus marked a potentially huge zone of allegiance and royal obligation."[148] As habeas attached to bodies, each body subjected to it could, would, become "a floating island of sovereignty," and the claim to habeas could be a way of stretching the king's (or the US government's) sovereignty to conquered and contested spaces.[149]

In international law, the categorization of persons has happened through the standard of civilization. Even where the barbarian is not at the gate, the privilege and priority given the states and their combatants in law, and in laws of war in particular, has meant that a process of sorting divides humanity into those who can be spared and those who can be subject to sovereign violence. The very processes of sorting—of making captives "unlawful combatants" and subjecting judgment to procedures outside civilian or military corpus of law—is nevertheless legally elaborated. There is no lawlessness, but an excess of laws in conjugation with power.

CHAPTER 4

INVISIBLE PRISONERS, PROXY-RUN PRISONS

From Khiyam to Rendition

In fact, we are confronted with opposing and mutually contradictory necessities: on the one hand we are well aware that it is essential to preserve the native character of the canton chief and to make use of the traditional feudal spirit which still survives in him; on the other hand the very fact of colonization forces us to shape him to our administrative outlook. . . . Should the traditional authority of the canton chief be restored? . . . We could certainly reconstitute a décor of pomp and ceremony around them, but we should not be able to re-create the soul of their ancient authority.

Robert Delavignette, 1946 [1]

Do not try to do too much with your own hands.

T. E. Lawrence, quoted by David Petraeus, 2006 [2]

The US Department of Defense files for 765 Guantánamo Bay detainees run anywhere from one page to fifteen pages of dense, single-spaced text. The longer they are, the more clinical their accounts seem, supported as they are with a thicket of footnotes referring to enigmatic documents with strings of letters and numbers. The files for Abu Zubayda and Khalid Shaykh Muhammad, two of the best-known "high-value detainees," include detailed records of the travels and activities of the men, and they were apparently substantiated and verified by other detainees, or by other documents, including the 9/11 Commission Report, Foreign Broadcast Information Service (FBIS) transcripts of foreign news, and various other sources.[3] Neither document mentions the waterboarding to which the two were subjected. Abu Zubayda's file does not include any information about his preexisting mental illness—nor does it indicate where he was held between March 2002, when he was arrested, and September 2006, when he was moved to Guantánamo. Abu Zubayda is said to be "moderately compliant," and his handful of "disciplinary infarctions involve meal refusal." Khalid Shaykh Muhammad's file includes a substantial sketch of his family members who are also involved with al-Qaeda, an account of his "masterminding" various attacks against the United States, and his global web of agents. It also includes an intriguing footnote on his retained property after his arrest: "The Casio model F-91W watch is linked to al-Qaida and radical Islamic terrorist improvised explosive devices." But the file says nothing about where he was held between his capture in 2003 and his transfer to Guantánamo in 2006.

Among the leaked files, files for fourteen known detainees are missing. The most curious is that of Yaser Esam Hamdi, a US citizen of Saudi origin, who was one of eighty prisoners who survived the prison revolt and massacre at Afghanistan's Qala Jangi fort in November 2001. Hamdi was transferred to Guantánamo Bay in January 2002 and, when it was discovered that he was a US citizen, to a navy brig in Norfolk, Virginia, in April 2002. A petition for habeas corpus brought by his father finally reached the Supreme Court in 2004, and the Court rejected the US government's appeal to hold Hamdi indefinitely without trial. He was then stripped of his citizenship and deported to Saudi Arabia. His file is missing.

Also excluded is the file of Ibn al-Shaykh al-Libi, known from early on to have been the source of the rumor—presented as fact—that an al-Qaeda representative had met with Saddam Husayn's intelligence agents in the Czech Republic. His file is missing, because he never spent any time at all at Guantánamo. What we do know about his whereabouts is shadowy and relayed at several removes, but it seems that from the moment of his arrest in 2001 in Afghanistan, he was held at the Kandahar airport; later moved to the prison ship USS *Bataan*; possibly held in CIA prisons in European countries; rendered for torture to Egypt, Mauritania, Morocco, and Jordan; and held thereafter in CIA "black" prisons in Afghanistan. Finally, in 2006, he was sent back to Libya, where startled Human Rights Watch representatives saw him briefly in the prison yard at the notorious Abu Salim jail, and just as the lawyers for Abu Zubayda were hoping to contact him to verify where his story and Abu Zubayda's intersected, Al-Libi was said to have "committed suicide" in prison.[4]

The maps these detentions draw are not limited to the United States, the territories it controls, or the battlespaces in which it has situated its military. Rather, the story of these detainees is one of alliances, mobilized to keep detainees invisible and to extend the period during which they can be interrogated. The smooth functioning of imperium has always been an impossibly difficult desideratum. The costs of direct military and administrative presence are often prohibitive, and it is sometimes easy to find local allies—even if not permanently loyal—who will, in return for the favor of authority, power, or gain, do the bidding of imperial masters, at least for a while and until the possibility of independent power proves too irresistible. Nevertheless, indirect control by a client is often touted not only as less costly—in lives, political cachet, and economic terms—but also as a convenient alibi when the squalid exercise of violence is called for.

The deployment of colonial armies has been a notably effective method not only for defraying costs of military conquest, an "economy of force," but also for spreading any blame that is to be apportioned in the aftermath of asymmetric wars.[5] The British used their colonial armies—and especially the Indian Army—not only in a variety of small wars but also in the killing fields of the First and Second World Wars.[6] The King's African Rifles were involved in suppressing the Mau Mau insurgency in Kenya, and the British used Gikuyu loyalists to guard besieged Gikuyu settlements and reservations.[7] Although a comprehensive history of the experience of *harkis* is yet to be written, we know that the Muslim Algerians who collaborated with the French Army in Algeria are another instance of indigenous forces veiling the brutality of the colonial encounter.[8]

Since the end of the Second World War, another use of proxies has entailed the arming and training of African, Asian, and Latin American militaries by Europe and the United States.[9] Robert Kaplan, an enthusiastic promoter of US imperialism, writes, "Imperialism was less about conquest than about the training of local armies. Reliance on American techniques and weapons systems, and the relationship established between American officers and their Third World protégés, helped give the US the access it needed around the globe."[10] And a counterinsurgent theorist points out that such training allows "intervening forces to leverage relatively small numbers of their own forces to dramatically increase the counterinsurgency effectiveness of indigenous forces."[11] Between 1990 and 2002, the United States trained some 100,000 foreign soldiers and policemen in the United States and in 150 countries around the world.[12] This number had accelerated to such an extent after September 11, 2001, that in 2007 alone, "74,300 students from 151 countries participated in training, total value of which is approximately $506.8 million."[13] This number did not include the security forces in Afghanistan and Iraq being trained by the US and its allies.[14] In 2008, the United States had trained nearly 130,000 Iraqi police personnel, military men, and special operations forces (for a total to date of nearly 650,000).[15] In Afghanistan, the United States and Germany had trained around 60,000 Afghan police officers between 2002 and 2006, and the number of Afghan National Army soldiers trained in 2008 was around 50,000.[16] The US counterinsurgency and stability operations have a significant element of foreign security training, and the US military has established an umbrella organization, the Joint Center for International Security Force Assistance, to assist in the training of Iraqi, Afghan, and other police and military.[17]

These numbers and statistics, however, point to military and police forces trained by the US military, and not the Afghan and Iraqi—and other—security forces that have aided the programs of much more shadowy intelligence agencies, such as the CIA.[18] Nor do we have a clear picture of exactly how many other kinds of proxies—those who work for private military contractors—perform such services for the US military or for the various intelligence agencies. As the *Washington Post* investigative reporter Dana Priest points out, "an alternative geography" of privatized intelligence work exists "that is hidden from public view, lacking in thorough oversight," and whose sheer size is staggering: "out of 854,000 people with top-secret clearances, 265,000 are contractors."[19] The "deniability" of the work these contractors do, Blackwater foremost among them, is often marketed as "a big plus."[20] The politics of intelligence requires demarcating a space that cannot be reached by the press, or by monitors and activists.

The creation of zones of invisibility—always challenged, often eventually discovered—is at the heart of detentions in shadows. Below, I discuss first the prisons managed by proxies and how such torture by proxy is excused by racialized and gendered languages. I end with a discussion of invisible prisons operated by the CIA itself.

PROXY-HELD PRISONS: KHIYAM AND SALT PIT

> All that was required, in his [Moshe Dayan's] view, was to find [a Lebanese] officer, even if he was only a major, and to win him over or buy him so that he might agree to proclaim himself the saviour of the Maronite population. Then the Israeli army would enter Lebanon, occupy such areas as it could, and establish a Christian government in alliance with Israel. The area south of the Litani would be annexed to Israel once and for all, and all would go well.
>
> *Moshe Sharett's diary entry, 1955*[21]

Suleiman Ramadan, a twenty-year-old Hizbullah operative, was detained by the South Lebanese Army (SLA) and the Israeli military in 1985 in the Lebanese territory occupied by Israel and designated a "security zone." When he was finally released from the Khiyam detention center in 2000, he had been the longest-serving detainee there. He was held incommunicado in a darkened room for the first three years, and without trial for the duration; his leg was amputated after an injury he had sustained during his arrest grew gangrenous, and he was tortured extensively during the early years of his detention.[22] Mustafa Tawbeh was arrested by the SLA in 1997 and tortured with electric shocks; he ended up in the local hospital. Ten days after his arrest, the SLA also detained his son, Ali Tawbeh, to pressure his father to cooperate with his interrogators. Ali was also subjected to electric shocks by his SLA interrogators.[23] Rabah Abu Fa'wur had been sixteen and visiting family members in the South when the Israeli military detained him in 1998 and handed him over to the SLA for interrogation and detention in Khiyam.[24]

Khiyam prison, destroyed by Israeli bombing in its 2006 assault on Lebanon, had between 1985 and 2000 been relegated to an ambiguous place of shadows. Located at the SLA headquarters in the town of Al-Khiyam (itself the heart of the "security zone"), it was invisible to outside monitoring (the International Committee of the Red Cross [ICRC] did not have permission to visit the detention center for much of its operational duration), and was hidden in plain view, in a jurisdictional and juridical no-man's-land, not quite a terra nullius, but not one that the effective occupier, Israel, would claim as its own. Israel disavowed its relationship to the SLA in a letter to Amnesty International, even if Israeli intelligence headquarters had been located in or near SLA headquarters in Khiyam or Marjayun.[25]

Khiyam detainees included Lebanese and Palestinian militants, village and town residents who were thought to have sheltered or have knowledge of Hizbullah and other antioccupation organizations (including the communists and pan-Syrian nationalists), and elderly or adolescent hostages held to pressure their relatives (such as Raba Sharur, arrested at the age of twelve and detained for twelve months, and Soha Bechara's elderly mother and uncle, held briefly and interrogated).[26] Additionally, youths who refused to be conscripted into the SLA, or villagers who did not pay the "tax" demanded by the SLA, could similarly be detained. What was significant about these detainees was the extent to which they were useful as hostages, either as a means of pressuring other detainees to speak or as tokens of exchange for captured Israeli military personnel (foremost among them the downed pilot Ron Arad).[27] Some had been interrogated in Israel, others in Khiyam, and yet others in different interrogation centers before being sent to Khiyam. Some were initially interrogated in Khiyam and then sent to Israel for detention in secret facilities (see below). Khiyam was probably the most important node in the carceral complex built by Israel and SLA in the jurisdictionally complex territories that traversed the boundaries between Israel and its "security zone" in Lebanon.[28]

The Khiyam prison had been built by the French in 1933, during their mandatory rule, to serve as their southern military headquarters and barracks, and it served the same function for the Lebanese Army after 1943. The stables of the compound were transformed into prison cells by the SLA militia, which took over the site in 1978 from the Lebanese Army and transformed it into its headquarters.[29] Between 1984 and 1985, Khiyam was used primarily as an interrogation center, with the detainees being removed after interrogations to the Israeli-held Ansar prisoner-of-war camp in Southern Lebanon or to the Atlit prison in Israel (in contravention of the Geneva Conventions to which Israel claims to adhere). With the closing of Ansar in 1985, this practice ceased and Khiyam became both interrogation and detention center.[30] Physically, the Khiyam compound consisted of three areas (for detention, interrogation, and

SLA commanders' quarters), and the detention area was in turn divided into five numbered sections (with section 1 holding detainees being interrogated and section 4 housing female detainees). Section 1 included "at least four isolation cells measuring less than one by one metre; six cells measuring less than two by two metres; and seven or eight cells measuring two by one-and-a-half metres which sometimes were so overcrowded to earn the section the additional name of 'Cemetery Prison.'"[31]

Khiyam was notorious for the tortures meted out with impunity to the detainees upon arrival and during interrogation and for its horrifying conditions of incarceration. Before the ICRC monitors were allowed to visit the prison in 1995, a box named the "chicken coop" was used to hold detainees that needed to be "softened up" for interrogation or be punished for noncooperation. The chicken coop measured fifty centimeters by fifty centimeters with a height of seventy centimeters (or twenty inches by twenty inches by twenty-eight inches), where detainees were forced to fold their bodies for three to four hours at a time with their head buried between raised knees.[32] Detainees were beaten and subjected to electric shocks on extremities, nipples, and genitals; alternated drenching in hot and freezing water; hanging by the elbows with their wrists shackled behind the back (*balanco*); and beating on the soles of the feet with cables or studded whips (*falaqa*).[33] Women and men were regularly threatened with rape, and some men were sodomized with wooden batons.[34] When held in isolation during interrogations, detainees could be denied meals or would have their right wrist shackled to their right ankle to prevent them from standing up.[35] Pious Muslim women were violently unveiled, and devout men were force-fed alcoholic drinks.[36]

Being released into general detention after interrogation was no respite. When informed that her formal interrogations had come to an end, Soha Bechara recalls that her interrogator told her, "There is no reason to celebrate. Now you'll learn what it's like to be dead."[37] The conditions of the cells between 1988 and 1995, the period during which the ICRC and families had no access to Khiyam, were particularly horrendous. Cells were small, overcrowded, damp, intensely cold in the winter, and unbearably hot in the summer; they had no running water and until 1995 no toilets or beds, nor even, in most instances, mattresses.[38] Discarded oil drums were used as the receptacle for the prisoners' feces and urine; because of overcrowding prisoners had to sleep head to toe with their heads near to the pail.[39] Until 1995, prisoners did not receive any reading or writing material, no proper health care (painkillers were begrudgingly given for all ailments), and women prisoners were not allocated sanitary napkins or change of clothes (male prisoners had a standard issue blue uniform also used in Israeli prisons and detention centers).[40] When families were allowed visits (before 1988 and after 1995), permission had to be obtained from Israeli authorities in the town of Khiyam, from the SLA headquarters in the town of Marjayun, and finally from Israeli intelligence housed in the same headquarters.[41] Between 1988 and 1995, however, if family members saw one another at Khiyam, it was during interrogations. The Khiyam detention center had a dual command structure for much of its existence, with a prison director overseeing and conducting interrogations and a military commander of the prison, who was in charge of the guards and other military personnel at the detention center.[42] In 1992, Amnesty International reported that Khiyam hosted "nine interrogators, working in shifts under the supervision of the prison director," as well as two units of thirteen male guards each and two units of three women each who worked two-day shifts guarding men's and women's postinterrogation sections, respectively.[43] Many of the guards were known to the detainees, as they resided in the same or neighboring villages.

Proxy militaries are curious things.[44] On the one hand, they mimic the command structures and rituals and habits of a sovereign army and many of their members have learned their military skills through having served in sovereign armies. On the other hand, their legal and sovereign position is anything but certain. They carry with them the delegated authority of their masters, but they are loudly declared to be independent patriots. Their demands, interests, practices, and ideologies do not leave their masters unscathed. Whether they are particularly incompetent in military action, or notably efficient in extracting the resources they need, if they are brutal or violent, nevertheless, they occupy a liminal zone, almost always hidden in shadows, which gives them and their masters a certain amount of cover. The SLA had originally been set up as Major Sa'ad Haddad's Free Lebanon Army in Southern Lebanon by the Israeli military in an eerily accurate (down to Haddad's rank), though ultimately unsuccessful, realization of Moshe Dayan's plan for control over Lebanon via a proxy.[45] Sa'ad Haddad's army was joined by a handful of smaller proxy militias and village "defense" units. These proxies on the one hand lowered the immediate cost of occupation in Southern Lebanon and on the other hand allowed Israel both "plausible deniability" and the ability to disavow formal territorial occupation, which would entail legal obligations. In the authoritative narrative of the Israeli journalist Beatte Hamizrachi (who eventually became the press liaison for Sa'ad Haddad's militia and whose husband, Yoram Hamizrachi, was the Israeli military intelligence liaison to the group), as early as 1975, the Israeli military had specifically established a unit for liaison with proxy militias in Southern Lebanon. The unit, first called ADAL (in Hebrew, Ezor Drom Levanon), and eventually succeeded by Liaison Unit for Lebanon, set the goals for the various ally-proxies and wielded a great deal of power within the Israeli military. Hamizrachi writes, "ADAL orders were *always* carried out" even when Haddad's men didn't listen to Haddad himself.[46] The ADAL officers were often Arabic speakers, and sometimes they belonged to Israel's Druze or Mizrahi communities. One of the earliest and most influential was Colonel Fuad, the nom de guerre of Binyamin Ben-Eliezer (an Israeli officer of Iraqi origin) who was an architect of Israeli invasion of Lebanon in 1982 and was to become the Labor Party leader briefly in 2001–2002.[47] The ADAL officers spent so much time in Southern Lebanon that they were directly involved in many of the military operations there, making them "the de facto commanders of the Lebanese in the field," who in turn wore uniforms issued by the Israeli military.[48]

Although Beirut—"cleansed" of Palestinians and under the control of Israel's Maronite allies (especially Phalange and Lebanese Forces led by Jumayyil)—was the long-sought prize of Israeli politics, Southern Lebanon was nevertheless important in Israel's strategic calculus. To consolidate its control there, between 1975 and 1982, Israeli policy in Southern Lebanon had two facets. The first, the "good fence" policy, recognizable as belonging to population-centric counterinsurgency, was primarily aimed at the Maronite villages of the South, and it provided them with civil aid, health care, and other social goods. The second facet of the policy was classic divide and rule, intended to isolate Maronite villages from their Muslim neighbors, by providing the former with resources while harassing the latter. Recruiting young men into the Maronite militias, further, was made possible by the fissures within the Lebanese Army and the release of thousands of unemployed, demobilized, and armed soldiers into the villages.[49] The loyalty of village elites was further secured by methods bordering on blackmail. For example, local elders were photographed with Israeli soldiers against a background of Israeli flags, their encounter recorded for Israeli media, as Saʿad Haddad confirmed, "in order to incriminate them, to force them to fully cooperate with us and with Israel."[50] Both Haddad's militia and Lahad's army were primarily Maronite Christian, and those Shiʿa and Druze from the South who served did so in subordinate positions, rarely being promoted in rank.[51] This guaranteed the continuation of Israel's conscious *divide et impera* policy.

After Haddad died of cancer in 1984, following Dani Shamʿun's recommendation, Israel selected a retired Lebanese Army general, Antoine Lahad, to lead the rechristened South Lebanese Army.[52] In 1985, when Israel ostensibly withdrew from main population centers and cities of Lebanon, it consolidated its buffer zone and placed the SLA in charge of "protection" duties, under the "advisory" supervision of several hundred Israeli officers and other ranks.[53] At the same time, a series of counterinsurgency measures were put into place intended to win over the local population to cooperation with the Israelis and their proxies. Every SLA soldier on the front lines would receive a substantial salary of US$500–$600 per month, as well as one permit per family to work in Israel.[54] Years before the withdrawal, Israel was "reported to be arranging visas and asylum for SLA security commanders in countries like Canada to protect them from reprisals by their fellow Lebanese."[55] Antoine Lahad carried an Israeli passport long before the Israeli withdrawal from Lebanon in 2000.[56] Lahad transformed the security zone into his own fiefdom. He operated monopolies on Israeli goods, banned petrol arriving from Lebanon into the zone, and imported Israeli petrol at an estimated profit of US$7,000 per day. He and his main officers levied taxes on all products leaving or entering the security zone. ʿAql Hashim, his feared western sector commander, also raised taxes, with which he built himself a villa in his village of Dibl.[57] Hashim had also been the head of Mabat intelligence, established by Shin Bet in 1989.[58]

Shin Bet, or the General Security Service (GSS), is one of Israel's three main intelligence services (along with Mossad and the Israeli military's Aman), whose specific duties have included infiltration and pacification of Palestinian groups both inside the Green Line and in occupied West Bank and Gaza. Unusually, Shin Bet was called on to become involved outside the borders of Israel and Palestine, in Southern Lebanon, first with information gathering

in Palestinian refugee camps, in the immediate aftermath of the Israeli invasion in June 1982, and later in countering the rising insurgency in the South
against continued Israeli occupation. There, Shin Bet "set about trying to reproduce the West Bank-Gaza model of informers, agents, safe houses and interrogation facilities."[59] Many informants were enterprising hashish smugglers,
whose access to their market in Israel was guaranteed by the travel and work
permits they received from Shin Bet.[60] Others were coerced or blackmailed
into cooperation. The Shin Bet men, all of whom assumed Arabic aliases
in interrogations, were in direct competition with the military intelligence
Aman, and "Aman officers who tried to strengthen their ties with the Shiites
claimed that the GSS used especially aggressive methods of interrogation on
Shiite detainees."[61] Institutional rivalry was to beleaguer the relationships and
operations of various Israeli security agencies, as often occurs in situations of
occupation, with various organizations often working at cross-purposes, badly
communicating with one another, and contradicting one another's analyses
and recommendations.

At Khiam and other SLA detention and interrogation facilities, Shin Bet
officers trained the Lebanese interrogators and at least until 1992 were present
during sensitive interrogations in those facilities.[62] The same Shin Bet interrogators often worked on the same prisoners in both sides of the border, although
in Israel they used the threat of the brutality of Khiam to intimidate prisoners.[63] Hajjeh Rasmiyeh recounted that in her interrogation in an unknown
center in Israel before she was sent to Khiam, her interrogator told her, "Do
you know what Khiam prison is? There they'll rape you and do horrible
things to you."[64] At Khiam, a clear hierarchy existed: Shin Bet interrogators
were in charge, and the SLA men conducted the routine violence.[65] Amnesty
recounts the presence of a plain-clothes Israeli, deferentially called "the Shaykh"
by the SLA men, and without whose authorization the SLA could or would
not do anything.[66] Several of my interviewees also described the presence of
Israeli interrogators, most of whom spoke fluent Arabic with Hebrew accents.
They also recounted the contempt with which the Israelis held the SLA men:

The Israelis despised the Lahad fighters so much they even surprised us. For example, when the Israeli officers were interrogating us they would say, "Will you confess
or shall I bring the Lebanese dogs to interrogate you?" Another time, Jean Homsi,

Abu Nabil, was standing there when this Israeli officer Yaki came and tried to nego-
tiate with us to stop our hunger strike. We told him, we don't believe you. Abu Nabil
made us promises and he didn't keep them. He said contemptuously, in front of Abu
Nabil himself, I am not Abu Nabil. I am Yaki.[67]

The salaries of the SLA men came from Israel, and the southern Lebanese
who agreed to work for Shin Bet as informants received a monthly salary of
$1,000.[68] This "purchased loyalty," however, meant that the informants were
not exactly reliable even if they were numerous. Their "intelligence" led to
the arrest of many whose detention was more indicative of their usefulness as
hostages than it was of their actual involvement in antioccupation insurgency.
Suleiman Ramadan, Mustafa and Ali Tawbeh, and Rabah Abu Fa'wur, whose
detention stories I related at the beginning of this chapter, were not necessarily (or in fact at all) fearsome Hizbullah operatives, yet most had been held at
Khiyam without trial in an unreachable and invisible limbo, which for Suleiman Ramadan lasted fourteen years.

In April 1999, Ramadan, the Tawbehs, and Abu Fa'wur, along with Israel's Center for the Defense of the Individual (HaMoked) and Association
for Civil Rights in Israel, petitioned the Israeli Supreme Court to compel the
Israeli minister of defense to release the men. Shortly after the petition was
launched, the Tawbehs were released. Abu Fa'wur and Ramadan had to wait
until the villagers of Khiyam broke through the doors of the notorious prison
after Israeli withdrawal from Lebanon in May 2000, before they could be free.

Their case was significant not because it was unique—HaMoked had brought
several such petitions to the Israeli Supreme Court—but because it elicited
an affidavit from the head of the Operational Division of the Israeli military,
General Dan Halutz, on the precise nature of the relationship between the
Israeli military and the South Lebanese Army.[69] The affidavit, which Human
Rights Watch, in ironic understatement, has described as "carefully worded,"
delineates the scope of empirical and judicial responsibility, accountability, and
degree of territorial control of the Israeli military vis-à-vis its proxy, the SLA.[70]

The affidavit deploys a series of legal discursive strategies to forge its argument: the invocation of precedent, an ostensibly precise language outlin-
ing "verifiable" facts, and the ability to reinterpret "verifiable" facts in ways
propitious to the aims of the state of Israel. Dan Halutz's main purpose in

his affidavit is to deny any Israeli responsibility for the actions of the SLA in Southern Lebanon. To do so, he must establish that Southern Lebanon is under Lebanese sovereign rule (even if this is devolved to the SLA) and that the SLA acts independently of the Israeli military. Thus, any form of Israeli territorial or personnel control must be disavowed. Some of the efforts to do this are so inchoate or casuistic as to be comical: Israel does not maintain "military bases" in Southern Lebanon but "military outposts" (para. 22); the SLA soldiers in the "security zone" outnumber Israeli soldiers (para. 24), thus showing SLA's primacy; and "IDF [Israeli Defense Forces] forces hardly ever search villages in the Security Zone, and do not perform activities that are designed to restrict the movement of Lebanese residents. Actions of searching villages are almost exclusively performed by the SLA" (para. 25). Even the Israeli military's un-restricted ability to build military bypass roads in Southern Lebanon is seen precisely as a sign of Israel's lack of military control there: because the roads are built to avoid using Lebanese villages, and because this resembles the by-pass roads built in post-Oslo West Bank and Gaza by the Israeli military, this "testifies to the absence of effective control by the IDF in the populated terri-tory of settlements in South Lebanon" (para. 27).

As for the SLA personnel, Halutz admits that "the State of Israel assists the SLA, among other ways, through financing, weapons and maintenance," past training of its soldiers in Israeli bases, and current "professional training for SLA soldiers, such as in the field of navigation" (para. 40). Halutz goes on to say that the SLA "coordinates its activity" with the Israeli military, but the SLA's indiscriminate shooting against civilians shows Israeli military's "lack of effective control" (para. 28). As for Israeli influence over Khiyam, the detention center holds people "who are not citizens of residents of Israel" (para. 7), "IDF soldiers or other Israelis are not routinely present in the al-Khiam facility, and they do not administer it, nor do they conduct interrogations there" (para. 6). Halutz insists that Khiyam was fully under SLA command, although "more than 18 months ago the SLA, at Israel's request, stopped the Red Cross visits and family visits at the facility" (para. 45), and the "Israeli security forces bring their position on the issue of the release of the detainees to the attention of the SLA" (para. 44). Israel does not control the prison, even if "GSS [General Security Services, or Shin Bet] personnel cooperate with members of the SLA, and even assist them by means of professional guidance and training, [and] hold meetings several times annually with SLA interrogators at the al-Khiam prison" (para. 51); and regardless of the fact that "information from the interrogations in al-Khiam is transferred by the SLA to Israeli security forces [and] certain detainees under interrogation are examined by means of polygraph by the Israeli side" (para. 52). Further, once the *Ramadan* petition revealed to the Israeli military that the salaries of SLA operatives and interrogators were being paid directly by the Israeli military, Halutz claimed, "It was decided to cease the direct payment of salaries to members of the SLA who serve in al-Khiam, and that will be done starting from the next salary," routing the lump-sum payments through the SLA headquarters instead (para. 54).

Halutz's insistence on defining—so seemingly precisely—the legal boundaries and definitions of what constituted effective control over a given territory is noteworthy. The law here was not something to be avoided or circumvented. Halutz's (or his lawyers') reference to "Regulation 42 of the auxiliary regulations of the Hague Convention of 1907," which defines the parameters of belligerent occupation, recognized applicability of international customary law. As Lisa Hajjar has written, "Israeli officials have always taken international law very seriously."[71] Halutz's tortured prose uses the law precisely to abdicate any responsibility for the occupied "security zone" in Southern Lebanon.

In addition to international law, Halutz's invocation of precedent, explicitly acknowledges the domestic legal edifice within whose bounds he claims the Israeli military is operating. This precedent was the petition for habeas corpus brought by Tanyus Assaf and Elias Nasrallah against the state of Israel in 1998.[72] Assaf and Nasrallah had been detained by the SLA in Khiyam, and their attorney, Rafi Masalha, had petitioned the court for their release. The Israeli Supreme Court judges decided that, although the SLA had arrested the men in consultation with Israeli military officials, nevertheless, SLA men were not Israeli civil servants or military officers over whom the court could have jurisdiction, and in response to the petitioners' claim that Israel is an occupying force, as no legal infrastructure (including affidavit) is provided, "without expressing any opinion on this question . . . there is no basis for the court's intervention in this case."[73] The use of this precedent is interesting because a case that was decided not on its merits but rather on the incompleteness of its documentation is cited as an authoritative guideline for subsequent juridical decision making. Even more significant, the very same case, *Assaf v. State of*

Israel, is cited ten years later in *Boumediene v. Bush* (itself also a habeas corpus petition on behalf of Guantánamo detainees). In the 2008 amicus brief filed by experts in Israeli military law, the *Assaf* case is invoked alongside a number of other cases as a shining example of the justness of the Israeli court, where access "is never refused simply because of the personal status or geographical location of the petitioner."[74] The substance of the case is wholly elided.

The insistence that Israel was and is operating within the bounds of recognized law is central to the military operations that the state undertakes. This declared adherence to law is so central to the claims of Israel as a righteous occupier that it is proudly advertised in two volumes prominently displayed on the website of the Israeli Ministry of Foreign Affairs. The two volumes of *Judgements of the Israel Supreme Court: Fighting Terrorism Within the Law* cover the years 1997–2005 and a number of cases brought by legal activists pertaining to detention, interrogation, military operations, and collective punishment. Again and again within the texts of the decision, Israeli Supreme Court judges declare their strict adherence to the law. The feted Aharon Barak boasts in the foreword that the law "is how we distinguish ourselves from the terrorists themselves. They act against the law, by violating and trampling it, while in its war against terrorism, a democratic state acts within the framework of the law and according to the law."[75] No mention is made of the flexibility of the law, or the ease with which proxies allow the law to be bypassed.

But Israel is not the only power that uses the alibi provided by a proxy to detain unwanted and troublesome insurgents in counterinsurgencies; it is not even the most egregious. That honor goes to the United States, whose asymmetric warfare in far-flung places has all too frequently depended on the existence of amenable proxies—both military and civilian—to provide plausible deniability when necessary.[76] The official operator of the Phoenix Program (discussed in chapter 5) was ostensibly the South Vietnamese government. Latin American jailers during the military era had been trained by the United States, but they were the ones responsible for what happened during detentions and interrogations (even if US interrogators were present). The War on Terror, however, provided the broadest display of the use of proxies anywhere. Not only did the US military rely on foreign and domestic mercenaries and private military corporations; it also could not operate in its covert and overt fighting—in Iraq, Afghanistan, Yemen, Pakistan, Somalia, and elsewhere—without the logistical support and cover provided by the local regimes.

Detention, however, remained a hierarchical operation. The most important prisoners were kept by the United States, but the rest of the detainees were numerous and militarily insignificant and as such could be handled by proxies. In the most notorious instance of proxy detention in the War on Terror, however, any rational or economic calculation about detainees was simply subordinated to the intense desire for revenge against foreign fighters. There was little or no outcry when a prison riot by Taliban and foreign fighters detained by the brutal Northern Alliance warlord Abd-al-Rashid Dostum resulted in the death of all but eighty-nine detainees out of six hundred; Dostum's men flooded a basement cell in which detainees—including John Walker Lindh—were taking shelter first with diesel fuel which was set on fire, and later with freezing water, which drowned many of the injured detainees.[77] The US and UK Special Forces happily aided the destruction of the Qala Jangi prison by fighting alongside Dostum's men, and in many instances by calling in air strikes to bomb the garrison prison with several five-hundred-pound precision-guided bombs (a two-thousand-pound daisycutter actually fell on the Northern Alliance position, killing between thirty and fifty of Dostum's men). Aside from the intransigence of the detainees, what had triggered the full fury of the Coalition forces had been the killing of a CIA agent, Mike Spann, in the early hours of the prison riot. Amnesty International was the only transnational human rights organization to call for an investigation of the massacre of prisoners at Qala Jangi.[78]

Even more horrifying had been the "death-by-container" of unknown thousands of Taliban prisoners at the end of November 2001, again at the hand of Dostum's men, and possibly with the knowledge of US Special Forces.[79] After the Qala Jangi debacle and subsequent surrender of Taliban forces at Mazar-e-Sharif, Dostum's commanders ordered freight container after freight container to be filled with Taliban detainees to be transported from Mazar-e-Sharif to Sheberghan prison in Dasht-e-Leyli. The containers had no ventilation, air-conditioning, or waste system. The number of detainees in each container was so numerous—hundreds per each container—that their bodies were piled on top of one another. Unless the detainees succeeded in creating makeshift ventilation holes in the containers, the great majority of those trapped inside died of suffocation. Even when they had air to breathe, many died of thirst. After twenty-four hours without water, survivors spoke of having "licked and chewed each other's skin to stay alive." The survivors mentioned that "the agony in the containers was intensified because they were tied up. This appears to have been a fate reserved for Pakistani—and perhaps other non-Afghan—prisoners." The US special operations forces were aware of the process but "were more focused at the time on prison security, and preventing an uprising such as the bloody outbreak that had happened days earlier in the prison fort at Qala Jangi."[80]

Although both the FBI and the State Department noted the occurrence of this particular massacre, US officials prevented any investigation because Dostum "was on the payroll of the CIA and his militia worked closely with United States Special Forces in 2001."[81] Even the United Nations spoke of the "political sensitivity" and the fear of "instability and ethnic tensions" that the matter might have generated.[82] In the end, although the forensic scientists of Physicians for Human Rights performed a preliminary investigation of the Dasht-e-Leyli mass grave and found evidence of atrocities wholly consistent with the survivors' accounts, no international investigation of the event ever occurred, and news stories about the event itself were overtaken by stories of US detention centers in Afghanistan and later at Guantánamo Bay.[83]

In Iraq, noninterference with violence wielded by the interim Iraqi state was institutionalized in military fragmentary order (or FRAGO), brought to light by Wikileaks in October 2010. As one of the leaked reports indicated, "per MNCI [Multi-National Coalition-Iraq] FRAGO 242, only an initial report will be made for apparent LOAC [Laws of Armed Conflict] violations by or against allied military or civilian personnel not involving us forces personnel. No further investigation will be required unless directed by HHQ [higher headquarters]."[84] The FRAGO was issued in June 2004 and was modified by a subsequent order, FRAGO 039 issued on April 29, 2005, which required that Iraqi-on-Iraqi abuse "be reported through operational channels"; however "provided the initial report confirms US forces were not involved in the detainee abuse, no further investigation will be conducted unless directed by HHQ."[85] Other reports released in the same cache included the use of the following torture on detainees: "strappado stress position, whereby his hands were bound/shacked and he was suspended from the ceiling; the use of blunt objects (i.e. pipes) to beat him on the back and legs; and the use of electric drills to bore holes in his legs"; applying electric shocks; burning with cigarettes; and being urinated upon.[86] Among the former detainees I interviewed, Abu Uthman recounted his time at the Jadriyya prison (in 2005) operated by the Iraqi interior ministry, where he was beaten with cables and rods, had his fingernails extracted, and was subjected to "Palestinian" hangings (in which the detainee's hands are tied behind his back and hung from a hook, often resulting in dislocated shoulders) combined with beatings on the soles of his feet. Abu Uthman also recounted how the US military, which had arrested him and handed him to the Interior Ministry, eventually transferred him from Jadriyya to Abu Ghraib.[87]

The US forces were far more directly involved in the Afghan Salt Pit prison, operated by proxies for the CIA, where a number of ghost prisoners kidnapped in Afghanistan, Iraq, Pakistan, Europe, and Africa (most famously Khaled El-Masri, who was abducted in Macedonia) were held for months on end. A *Washington Post* investigation showed that the CIA preferred the Salt Pit to be a "host-nation facility," and although it paid for its construction and maintenance, and although its Afghan guards were vetted by the CIA itself, the prison was considered client-run.[88] When a CIA supervisor allowed a naked Afghan detainee named Gul Rahman to freeze to death (and ordered his body buried in an unmarked grave), the CIA argued that "it was the Afghans who had run the prison on foreign property, so the CIA had no legal liability and the US government no jurisdiction." The Department of Justice declined to prosecute, and the responsible CIA officer was subsequently promoted.[89]

RACE AND GENDER AT THE SEAM OF ENCOUNTER

The use of proxies was useful not only because of the legal ambiguities of jurisdiction and accountability but also because it reinforced certain civilizational hierarchies in which the proxies' brutality reinforced the humane superiority of their patrons. In 1938 mandatory Palestine, when British members of Palestine Police shot a detainee, the Colonial Office blamed the war crime on the Arab officers of the Palestine Police because, they claimed, the British Tommy "is incapable of perpetrating [these] hideous barbarities."[90] The French General Jacque Massu had similarly blamed the torture inflicted in Indochina on the

Vietnamese interpreters and on their "ancient methods," which supposedly included the water cure.[91] A recent article similarly places blame for atrocities committed in the British counterinsurgency in Kenya on the King's African Rifles, manned by African recruits and officered by white settlers, claiming that the "KAR regiments would certainly not be expected to exhibit the same cultural mores as a British regiment."[92] After the massive devastation of Falluja in 2004, a *Washington Post* article stated without any apparent irony that "American ideals that were among the justifications for the 2003 invasion, such as promoting democracy and human rights, are giving way to values drawn from Iraq's traditions and tribal culture, such as respect, fear and brutality."[93]

In the Israeli invasion of Lebanon, referring to the brutalities committed by both the Israeli military and the SLA in Lebanon, Rafi Malka, head of Shin Bet's Operations Branch, claimed, "Lebanon gave us Lebanonization, levantinization. . . . In order to stay sane and stay alive, you had to do things that were unacceptable. The Shin Bet was no exception. It was a struggle in a wild west and people paid with their lives if they tried to behave according to accepted standards. The general impact was not good, to put it mildly."[94] Thus, cultural contagion, a transmission of barbarity from the lesser people to the more superior Israelis, was blamed for criminal coercion. The idea of Levantinization in the military fed on fears of Arab hordes running through Israeli political discourse. David Ben-Gurion himself had succinctly put forward the dominant view: "We do not want Israelis to become Arabs. We are duty bound to fight against the spirit of the Levant, which corrupts individuals and societies."[95] As a confidential report to the American Jewish Committee stated in 1962, "Among more sophisticated Westernized groups [in Israel], prejudice takes a semi-cultural form, as the word 'black' is replaced by 'Levantine.' 'Levantinism' is regarded as a threat to national existence, and the fear is expressed that 'Levantinization' will 'drag Israel down to the level of Arab countries.'"[96] Thus, not only legal liability but also existential causation for brutality was passed on to clients.

Racialization of the proxy is not the sole mean of producing hierarchies of rule at the seam of encounter between imperial officials and their clients. Gender is also weaponized to create docile clients, or at the very least to displace failure onto these clients.[97] Recounting a failed mission in Iraq, a commander of the 1st Marine Regiment thus effeminized Iraqi police officers and Civil

Defense Corps troops who fled the battle: "When are these people going to discover their manhood and stand and fight with us to save their city?"[98] Videos circulating online show a marine officer screaming at Iraqi security trainees, labeling them a "bunch of women," "pussies," and "cowards," "too much of a fucking woman to die for [your] country." When an Iraqi sneers at him, the marine in typically macho fashion challenges him to "[go] out back and have his little ass be beaten."[99]

This constant creation of an abject and conquered feminine client to be controlled, taught and civilized by the masculine master itself, operates not only at the corporeal level but at the metaphorical level too. "Imperial conquest [is seen] as a natural expression of masculinity" which, taken to its logical conclusion, implies that conquered populations in this asymmetrical dyad become owned, penetrated, feminine.[100] The metaimagery of gendered asymmetry is then again telescoped onto human bodies, and the "oversexed native" client who lacks courage, independence, and moral vigor—all masculine virtues—comes to bear the burden of imperial failures.[101] Again and again one encounters the disgust imperial officials express toward the "deviant" practices of men whom they secretly do not believe are competent enough or advanced enough or civilized enough to do the bidding of their masters. A particularly revealing account from a former US military man stationed in Afghanistan contains all the relevant tropes:

Homosexuality was pervasive among the Afghans, especially the Pashtuns in the south. Even when they weren't overtly engaged in acts of sex, they would cling to each other, hold each other's hand, and generally cavort in ways that would astonish Westerners and repulse soldiers. Some of the marines would laugh incredulously. Others would be moved to violent reactions. In one case, Fitzgerald watched a gigantic marine march furiously toward two coupled Afghans and pick them up and toss them in different directions like dogs, yelling the whole time in English the Afghans couldn't understand. The "female" of the two scurried away. The dominant male was sort of indignant and flipped his scarf over his shoulder and walked off.[102]

The Pashtun client is thus dehumanized—"dogs"—and effeminized because his homosociality "repulses" the US military men. The vocabulary reinforces the masculine-feminine dichotomy: a "gigantic marine" symbolizes uncorrupted American masculinity, whereas the "indignant" Pashtun "flips" his "scarf" over a shoulder, as a petulant teenage girl would in exasperation. Thus, the ally-client-proxy, even in his allegiance and loyalty, is made monstrous and abnormal.

This process of humiliation is intended to reinforce the perceived superiority of the US forces in personal encounters. But the use of proxies and clients can also be facilitated through interstate relations, as they have been in extraordinary rendition.

RENDERING DETAINEES TO CLIENT STATES: "TORTURE BY PROXY"[103]

> If you want a serious interrogation, you send a prisoner to Jordan. If you want them to be tortured, you send them to Syria. If you want someone to disappear—never to see them again—you send them to Egypt.
> *Robert Baer, 2002*[104]

> Egyptian jails are full of guys missing toenails and fingernails. It's crude, but highly effective, although we could never condone it publicly. The Egyptians and Jordanians are not that squeamish.
> *Vincent Cannistraro, 2002*[105]

On a January morning, Francisco Toscanino was abducted by Uruguayan policemen in Montevideo; gagged, bound, and blindfolded; and transported via a "circuitous route" to the Uruguay-Brazil border. There, Brazilian agents took custody of him; he was denied consultation with attorneys, the Italian consulate, or his family. Eventually transported to Brasilia, he was held for seventeen days, during which he was interrogated by Brazilian officials in the presence of US government agents, and he was tortured in ways "reminiscent of the horror stories told by our military men who returned from Korea and China." He was deprived of sleep and denied food; he was "forced to walk up and down a hallway for seven or eight hours at a time. When he could no longer stand he was kicked and beaten but all in a manner contrived to punish without scarring. When he would not answer, his fingers were pinched with metal pliers. Alcohol was flushed into his eyes and nose and other fluids

. . . were forced up his anal passage." The case documents add, "Throughout this entire period the United States government and the United States Attorney for the Eastern District of New York prosecuting this case was aware of the interrogation and did in fact receive reports as to its progress." Toscanino was then drugged by both Brazilian and US agents, placed on a plane unconscious, and transported to the United States to be prosecuted. "The government prosecutor neither affirmed nor denied these allegations but claimed they were immaterial to the district court's power to proceed."[106] Toscanino's abduction was not one of the hundreds of post-9/11 extraordinary renditions, but it occurred in January 1973, nearly thirty years before September 11, 2001. Toscanino was not a detainee in the War on Terror but a captive of the War on Drugs; the US agents involved in his interrogation did not belong to the CIA but to the DEA; and his transportation terminated not in a secret labyrinth but in the US prison system and eventually in a court case that on appeal led to his release.

Toscanino's abduction—outside the framework of extradition treaties and with the cooperation of Uruguayan policemen—has been labeled "informal" or "irregular" rendition, used for decades by the United States to capture those wanted for criminal offenses (often having to do with drugs charges) or accused of "terrorism."[107] In an official 1997 document, the FBI claims that irregular rendition "has deep historical roots," tracing it back to the abduction in Alexandria, Egypt, of John Surratt, a conspirator in the assassination of Abraham Lincoln. Thus, the historical narrative that legitimates the use of such a legal "device" begins with a character whose deed would be universally reviled and the invocation of whose crime would inevitably elide a discussion of the legality of the means by which he was brought to court.

Rendition had become a significant weapon in the arsenal of various US presidents, although doubts about its use persisted, for example, when the Carter administration did not give FBI authorization for renditions. But the process was legalized when in June 1989, George H. W. Bush's lawyer in the Office of Legal Counsel, William P. Barr, submitted a legal opinion that established a new policy, "the President's snatch authority," thereby empowering the FBI and other US law enforcement agencies to kidnap "fugitives from US law" without the consent of the countries in which the abduction occurs.[108] In November 1989, a companion opinion submitted by Barr conferred the same authority on the US military, paving the way for the kidnapping of the Panamanian Manuel Noriega and his rendition to the United States.[109] All these irregular or informal renditions eventually ended in court in the United States.

The Toscanino case is often invoked in scholarly legal debates as the possible exception to a US legal doctrine that essentially gives the executive the authority to abduct people at will and bring them to the United States.[110] Toscanino is notable for its use of third country—Brazil, under the military rule of the junta—as an intermediate interrogation (and torture) station, where the impunity of the Brazilian regime was utilized to extract information via illegal means and in ways the US agents could not have done so in the United States itself. This form of third-country rendition was first devised in the classified National Security Directive 77, issued by George H. W. Bush in 1993.[111] This authorization was used "dozens" of times to abduct militant Islamists in Africa, Southeast and Central Asia, and the Balkans; some were rendered to the United States, and many were sent to Egypt or Jordan, where they were interrogated, tortured, or put to death.[112] Michael Scheuer, former head of the CIA's Bin Laden unit, recounted, "It served American purposes to get these people arrested, and Egyptian purposes to get these people back, where they could be interrogated."[113] One of the more notorious precedents for the post-9/11 extraordinary renditions is the 1998 kidnapping of five Egyptian Islamists suspected of planning an attack against a US embassy. The five were arrested by the CIA and the Albanian police in Tirana and were beaten and interrogated in Albania before being rendered to Egypt, where all were tortured with electricity, hanged from the ceiling, and beaten, and in the end most were executed (some without trial).[114]

The Bush directive was confirmed by Bill Clinton, who in December 1999 signed a Memorandum of Notification "giving the CIA broader authority to use foreign proxies to detain Bin Ladin lieutenants, without having to transfer them to US custody."[115] In subsequent testimony to the Congress, CIA Director George Tenet testified to a total of seventy renditions, "including 'two dozen' between July 1998 and 2000."[116] Michael Scheuer insists on the legality of the process, and he cites the phalanx of lawyers involved in the planning and execution of international renditions: "Every suspect who was apprehended had been convicted in absentia. Before a suspect was captured, a dossier was prepared containing the equivalent of a rap sheet. The CIA's legal counsel signed off on every proposed operation."[117] Before 2001, although the complex extraordinary rendition process was not as heavily utilized as it was afterward, nevertheless, the help of "dozens of foreign intelligence services" was required to detain "suspected radicals, minimally to keep them off the streets, but also in the hope of gaining confessions or intimidating them into aborting planned attacks."[118] Intimidation was partially outsourced, because allied Mukhabarat servicers "particularly those outside the West, can operate more freely in accordance with laws and procedures often less restrictive than those of liberal democracies."[119]

After September 11, 2001, the gloves were off. As one official involved in rendition told *Washington Post*, "We don't kick the [expletive] out of them. We send them to other countries so they can kick the [expletive] out of them."[120] One of the higher-profile victims of the kicking was Maher Arar, a Canadian citizen who was arrested in September 2002 as he was transiting through the United States; he was told that he was inadmissible to the United States on the suspicion of terrorist activities. When a severely injured child soldier, held in Guantánamo and interrogated more than forty times, falsely claimed to have seen Arar in Afghanistan, Arar was rendered to Syria (his country of origin), where a confession to involvement in terrorist activities was extracted from him under torture in the fearsome Far' Filastin prison.[121] Even Human Rights Watch, which submitted an affidavit on Arar's behalf to the official Canadian Commission, eventually convened to investigate Arar's rendition, admitted that "Maher Arar's case may have been a rendition within *a lawful procedure*, given that it appears he was removed from the United States after being placed in expedited immigration proceedings."[122] Just as noteworthy was the fact that Arar was rendered not to a client or an ally but to a member of the so-called axis of evil, Syria, with whom the United States had only the frostiest of diplomatic relations.

A more ironic case is that of Abdel Hakim Belhaj, a leading member of the Libyan Islamic Fighting Group, who, along with his pregnant wife, Fatima Bouchar, was kidnapped in Malaysia in 2004, taken to a black site in Thailand, and rendered to Libya via the US base at Diego Garcia, to be interrogated under torture and detained for six years. British and US intelligence personnel were involved in both his rendition and his interrogations in Libya. Two weeks after Belhaj's rendition to Libya, the British prime minister Tony Blair visited Tripoli and embraced Qaddhafi, celebrating his return to the fold. What makes Belhaj's case unique is that during the NATO intervention in Libya in 2011, Belhaj was one of the opposition leaders who worked with NATO, two of whose member nations had planned and implemented his rendition, to overthrow Qaddhafi.[123] After the Libyan opposition entered Tripoli, in the offices of Qaddhafi's foreign minister and former intelligence chief, Moussa Koussa, an investigator for Human Rights Watch found a file that contained correspondence from the CIA and the British MI6 to the Libyan intelligence services. According to the *Guardian*,

One fax from Mark Allen, then head of counter-terrorism at MI6, congratulated Koussa on the "safe arrival" of Belhaj—"the least we could do for you and for Libya"—and referred to an "amusing" request by the CIA that anything the dissident said under interrogation should be passed first to them. "I know I did not pay for the air cargo," Allen says: but after all, the intelligence that led to the couple's rendition was British.[124]

A certain grotesque decorousness seems to be at work here: most prisoners (though certainly not all) are rendered to their "home" countries, even if they have sought asylum elsewhere precisely because their home countries were not so welcoming. Maher Arar was rendered to Syria; Abu Umar (Usama Nasr), an Italian-Egyptian cleric, and Ahmad Agiza and Muhammad Al-Zeri, two Egyptian asylum seekers in Sweden, were kidnapped by the CIA in Milan and Stockholm, respectively, and were rendered to Egypt, where they remain.[125] In other cases, however, when such deals are not possible, other allies are happy to provide necessary services, as was Morocco providing torture for rendered detainees, most prominent among them Binyam Mohamed, an Ethiopian permanent resident of Britain, kidnapped in Karachi and rendered to Morocco.[126] In the early stages of his interrogation by Americans in Pakistan, Mohamed was told, "The law has been changed. There are no lawyers. You can co-operate with us the easy way, or the hard way. If you don't talk to us, you're going to Jordan. We can't do what we want here, the Pakistanis can't do exactly what we want them to do. The Arabs will deal with you."[127] To the roll call of Arab rendition destinations should now be added East African allies of the United States who have also been implicated in such rendition.[128]

The combination of invisibility and deniability make this kind of detention ideal when secret services wish to perform interrogations that under ordinary circumstances would be considered illegal. No arrest warrant is issued; the process by which a person is detained and transferred to the country in which he or she is ultimately held (and likely tortured) is at best opaque. In the last instance, the curtain of state secrets can drop on any kind of investigation or court case pursuing such detentions, as it has done with the case Binyam Mohamed and other rendered prisoners brought against the airline that helped in their rendition to the countries in which they were tortured.[129] In any case, law is not the equitable instrument of justice but the basis of legitimation of power. This becomes most clear in an essay written by John Yoo, formerly of the Office of Legal Counsel in the Bush administration's Department of Justice. In an argument for the legality of "transferring prisoners" to third countries, Yoo cites past legislation and even the history of Great Britain, and through an intricately woven web of argument and legal invocation, he insists that the fate of prisoners of war is in the hand of the sovereign to dispose of however he or she wishes. Nowhere do sovereigns—or executives—act as they personally please, but rather their very sovereign power is authorized by the law.[130] The irony of course is that the transfer of these detainees to countries in which they are tortured occurs on the basis of treaties of alliance and verbal assurances of various sorts which anti-internationalists such as Yoo view with contempt.

Yoo's thinking was translated into a raft of legal memoranda from the Office of Legal Counsel that argued that because the detainees cannot be "removed" ("removal" being what is done to those on US territory) or "extradited" (extradition being what happens when a treaty or agreement exists between two countries), they can be "rendered."[131] Extraordinary volumes of law and reams of historical precedent are cited, and clever legal categories are used to euphemize the process by which prisoners are made invisible. By comparing rendition to everyday instruments of crime control (removals and extraditions), rendition is laundered.

Another notable character of rendition is the breadth of international collaboration in intelligence and counterintelligence.[132] Although US intelligence services have long had cooperative relations with allies, such liaisons have exponentially expanded after September 11.[133] The FBI now has "legal attaches" in various embassies facilitating the process of extradition, and the

CIA has established joint intelligence centers in Europe, the Middle East, and Asia, and it has a multinational center in Paris, Alliance Base, to which intelligence officers from Britain, France, Germany, Canada, and Australia contribute. These centers organize and institutionalize intelligence liaisons; they provide equipment and training in intelligence and special operations tactics. "Foreign countries send officers to the CIA's training school for weeks-long courses in counterterrorism operations and analysis."[134] In addition to routine liaisons, the intelligence services of the United States' European, Asian, and Middle Eastern allies have been involved in detention or kidnapping operations and in managing black sites. A report by Amnesty International states, "European agents [have been involved in] interrogating, or sending questions to be used in interrogating, victims of rendition in places where the detainees faced a real risk of torture or other ill-treatment, and keeping the whereabouts of such detainees concealed from their families."[135] On the one hand, the US State Department (or its European counterparts) issue reports condemning torture committed by their allies and secure "diplomatic assurances" for rendered detainees, and on the other hand, as former CIA director Porter Goss testified to Congress, "once [these detainees] are out of our control, there's only so much we can do."[136] The institutional wink-wink-nudge-nudge goes so far that an Arab diplomat representing one of these destination countries said that the CIA did not really keep track of these detainees, "because then you would know what's going on. . . . It's really more like 'Don't ask, don't tell.'"[137] One might add, "don't see or let be seen." Beyond the services of reliable allies, counterinsurgency detentions also occasionally require the holding of prisoners oneself, to secure information or to retain them as bargaining chips. Here, the regime of invisibility is even more insuperable.

A REGIME OF INVISIBILITY: FACILITY 1391 AND BLACK SITES

> Police intervention in public spaces does not consist primarily in the interpellation of demonstrators, but in the breaking up of demonstrations. The police is not that law interpellating individuals (as in Althusser's "Hey, you there!"). . . . It is, first of all, a reminder of the obviousness of what there is, or rather, of what there isn't: "*Move along! There is nothing to see*

here!" The police says that *there is nothing to see on a road, that
there is nothing to do but move along.* . . . . Politics, in contrast,
consists in transforming this space of "moving-along" into
a space for the appearance of a subject: i.e., the people, the
workers, the citizens: *It consists in refiguring the space, of what
there is to do there, what is to be seen or named therein.*
Jacques Rancière, 2001[138]

Given the excess of information so easily available to us today, disappearing
detainees requires producing an impregnable regime of invisibility through
legal compartmentalization, spatial emplacement, and active secrecy.[139] As
Jacques Rancière has written, today, the antipolitics of policing have replaced
participation and contestation with a neutered space from which the political
subject is expelled—*"Move along! There is nothing to see here!"* The regime of
invisibility in wartime that relegates detainees to invisibility and inaudibility
in the name of security is the logical conclusion of such expulsion. This invisibility conveys a kind of finality, in which even capricious jurisdiction is not
present, because if a detainee cannot be found, seen, heard, known, or legally
represented, then that detainee simply cannot exist. The invisibility guarantees
a de facto stripping of a detainee of legal personhood. Paradoxically, in a liberal
counterinsurgency, the space of invisibility is not wholly lawless. After all, the
interrogators, the detainees, the special operations forces, all carry with them
the delegated authority of the state, and the possibility of discovery always
places these invisible domains in the liminal space between a classified security law and relatively more recognized and open place of legal contestation.
Here I analyze the regimes of invisibility created in Facility 1391 in Israel and
the black sites employed by the United States in its War on Terror.

Muhammad Al-Budayr recounts his stint at "Sarafand" prison:

The walls were black, and there was a weak lamp in the middle of the ceiling. During the interrogations, they make sure you don't sleep. They come for you every half
hour, and they say "carry your mattress, pillow and the blanket and move to another
dungeon." There are many dungeons; so automatically every half an hour we carry
our things and move from one dungeon to another, and if anyone tries to sleep, they
have these big speakers which play white noise and they focus these speakers on the
prisoners. . . . The detainees who don't cooperate are placed in small solitary cells;

they are about 80 cm by 80 cm, with red walls and claustrophobic like a closed coffin. I was only in that cell for a very short time. But there were others who were there for days.[140]

The intelligence gathered at this prison was mostly of the "mosaic" variety, understood as "disparate items of information, though individually of limited or no utility to their possessor, [which] can take on added significance when combined with other items of information."[141] Al-Budayr recounted:

They wanted to know personal things about me from the moment I was born until the moment of my arrest. They wanted to know where I had studied, and worked. How I liked the Hizbullah; my circle of relations, my friends and relatives. They wanted to know about the people who lived in my village, their habits, their politics, their relationships. They wanted to know the geographic area that I was living in, for example this house belongs to whom, this bit of land belongs to whom.[142]

Al-Budayr differed from many of the other people who had been held at "Sarafand," in that he was tried for his membership in Hizbullah and later held in known prisons in Israel, including those in Ashkelon, Beersheba, and Nafha, from which he was released in 2001 in a prisoner exchange between Hizbullah and Israel.

Although prisoners of war are not to be tried during the war itself, in 1971 the Israeli Knesset passed legislation that made "security" offenses liable to trial in Israel.[143] Some detainees were tried by secret military courts, sentenced, and then kept for a decade or longer after their sentence had been served.[144] Many prisoners held in "Sarafand" never saw a trial. During their interrogation, they were invariably held in solitary confinement and did not know where they were; many could not meet with ICRC delegates or lawyers. When they asked about their location, they were told, variously, "you are on the moon," "an army (AMAN) interrogation facility," "a submarine," or "Southern Lebanon" (presumably to frighten the prisoners with the possibility of being captives of SLA); most often they were told they were in "Sarafand," or were categorically refused any information.[145] Ha'aretz reported that "most maps of Israel also do not cite the facility, though on a few maps of the Nature and National Parks Protection Authority, it is marked by means of a letter, with no further explanation. There is no sign on the main road directing the curious to the camp."[146] The prison camp was baptized "Facility 1391" on April 16, 2002, long after it was first established, and it is located somewhere on a military base in Israel. The name "Sarafand" began appearing in the testimonies of detained Lebanese prisoners as early as 1986 (e.g., that of Bilal Dakrub, collected by Human Rights Watch).[147] A HaMoked petition mentions the late naming date and points out that before the interrogation center was declared a military prison in 2002 (during the Second Intifada), "for a prolonged period of time, the facility was used illegally by unknown bodies; the very existence of the facility and the actions taking place there were concealed over time."[148] The interrogators belonged to IDF human intelligence or to the Shin Bet, and the guards wore army uniforms. If—sometimes after years—detainees were allowed to meet ICRC delegates or attorneys, the meeting took place outside the facility. The camp had a double fence guarded by attack dogs and patrolling jeeps, and it was constructed around a "large concrete structure, dating from the British Mandate period, when it was used by the British police."[149]

The prison was so secret that even though it has—at least according to the Israeli authorities—not been used since 2006, the Israeli advocate general refuses to investigate allegations of torture there or to allow visits by human rights monitors.[150] Some have speculated that 1391 is the base for an Israeli military intelligence unit (named Unit 504) in charge of gathering human intelligence through handling of agents in the Occupied Territories.[151] Secrecy also allowed Facility 1391 to be used for torture during interrogations and for holding Lebanese detainees as hostages. According to an Israeli state attorney, the facility "is not used as a routine detention facility, but is intended, generally, for special cases and for detainees who are not residents of the territories. The primary purpose of the facility is 'an interrogation facility' in those special cases, and as a rule it is not intended as a 'detention facility' for persons whose interrogation has been completed."[152]

Perhaps the most famous prisoner of 1391 was Mustafa Dirani, a high-ranking officer in the security apparatus of the Lebanese Amal militia, who was kidnapped from his home in Southern Lebanon in 1994 by the Israelis and held as a bargaining chip to exchange for the captured Israeli pilot Ron Arad. When Dirani was finally allowed to see a lawyer and ICRC representatives in 2001, he brought a suit against the Israeli government in which he recounted how he "had been raped and tortured in detention to extract information from him about the whereabouts of Mr. Arad. According to the lawyer, Mr. Dirani was beaten, violently shaken, raped by a soldier brought in specifically for this purpose, sodomized by the head of the interrogation team [using a baton], deprived of sleep and at one point forced to wear diapers after being fed laxatives."[153] Dirani also testified that his interrogator, Captain George, "identified himself as the 'Director of the Mighty Torture Department.'"[154] His account was confirmed by other interrogators.[155] Captain George denied the charge of rape, "except to confirm that one soldier had been sent into the prisoner's cell wearing only underwear to threaten him with a sexual act."[156] Captain George was later sacked from the intelligence unit, and the courts have refused to dismiss the case, even as Dirani was released in a prisoner exchange in 2004.[157]

Even more important than information extraction, however, was the function of the facility as a secret place to hold "bargaining chips." One such bargaining chip was twenty-year old Hashem Fahaf, kidnapped by the Israeli military in 1989 as he was visiting Shaykh Abd-Al-Karim Ubayd, a Hizbullah cleric also kidnapped on that day. Fahaf was held in Facility 1391 and later in Ramleh prison for a total of eleven years while Israel continued denying that he was even being held in Israel. In April 2000, Fahaf was ordered released by the Israeli Supreme Court along with eighteen other bargaining chips, two of whom had been kidnapped when they had been sixteen and seventeen years of age, and another of whom, a relative of Mustafa Dirani, had developed catatonic schizophrenia in Facility 1391.[158] Notably, in 1997, in an earlier case of Lebanese detainees suing for release, the court had ruled that holding them as bargaining chips was justified.[159] However, in the intervening years, criticisms of the ruling had been so fierce, particularly focusing on the hypocrisy of the ostensibly liberal judge Aharon Barak's defense of the practice, that when the court had to rule on the matter again in 2000, it reversed its initial decision.[160] Those High Court judges who opposed the release of the detainees refused the label of "bargaining chips" while ingeniously categorizing the men held in limbo as "*quasi* prisoners of war."[161] Once the reversal occurred, the Israeli state scrambled to ensure that Mustafa Dirani and Abd-al-Karim Ubayd could be kept incarcerated in Israel. Thus, it introduced a bill in the Knesset that moved the fate of such prisoners from the courts to the Defense Ministry.[162] The bill was argued for two years, and Ariel Sharon, who became prime minister in 2001, heavily lobbied for it; the bill was enacted in 2002 as the Internment of Unlawful Combatants Law. The law suspended article 4 of the Third Geneva Convention, essentially giving the chief of the general staff the ability to order the incarceration of a detainee if he has "cause to believe that a person being held by the State authorities is an unlawful combatant and that his release will harm State security" where the person crosses the threshold of lawfulness by having "directly or indirectly" committed hostile acts against Israel.[163] The job of monitoring, inspection, and maintenance of the condition of these detainees was left to the Israeli military, and the military was also given authorization to try the unlawful combatants as it saw fit.

By contrast, the use of prisoners as bargaining chips was not as significant in the CIA's black sites. The sheer power and reach and the vast web of alliances of US intelligence meant that it simply did not require such a negotiating tool. The secret prisons created by the CIA differed substantially from the detention center at Guantánamo Bay, as the latter was subject to visitations by representatives of ICRC and had been brought within the US jurisdiction via a series of legal challenges. The CIA had received extraordinary authority via a still-classified Presidential Finding issued on September 17, 2001, which allowed it to easily circumvent congressional or any other kind of monitoring.[164]

In the early months of the War on Terror, the CIA had operated a detention center within the military-run complex of Guantánamo Bay, but with the Supreme Court ruling in *Rasul v. Bush*, the CIA hurriedly relocated its prison to places where habeas corpus could not reach. The CIA required "total isolation, total secrecy, and total control"; even the threadbare guarantees provided to Guantánamo detainees were too generous for its interrogators.[165] As Jose Rodriguez, the CIA official responsible for destroying recordings of torture in black sites, would write in his long and aggressive apologia for CIA torture, these sites were used precisely because the CIA feared that the detainees would hire lawyers who would then circumvent the ability of the CIA to obtain information through torture.[166] The CIA also planned to keep the detainees on ships, never harboring at a port, perpetually in international waters, out of the reach of courts, camera lenses, and questions. A former CIA official anonymously told Jane Mayer, "It was going to be like the Flying Dutchman—they'd sail forever," and mentioned that the CIA had used merchant marine vessels for such secret missions.[167] Investigations by human rights organizations revealed that the US military had also used such ships—including the USS *Bataan* and USS *Peleliu*—as floating prisons.[168] The detention center at Bagram Air Force Base in Afghanistan, managed by the US military, has remained outside the reach of habeas corpus. The CIA had its own detention block at Bagram. As a former soldier recounted:

They built high walls around the detainee center. I figured, "Well, yeah, they're terrorists. You don't want them seeing out. You want to contain them, deny them any information that they could use to escape." Later on, I realized it was also so we couldn't see in.[169]

The *New York Times* had already reported that, at the request of the CIA, the US military had kept some detainees "off the rolls" at Abu Ghraib and other US military detention centers in Iraq, so as to prevent visits by the ICRC and to allow the CIA maximum flexibility to move the detainees to wherever they wished, including third countries.[170] A frustrated General Taguba wrote of how the agency held "ghost detainees" in a separate block at Abu Ghraib "without accounting for them, knowing their identities, or even the reason for their detention."[171]

The special treatment of the detainees had already been approved in a legal opinions issued by the Office of Legal Counsel, where, for example, insurgents of non-Iraqi origin were said to fall outside of all Geneva Convention protections.[172] In any case, even where the Geneva Conventions were said to apply, in the field, officers invoked "military necessity" to delay or deny detainee access to the ICRC.[173] In at least one instance, a detainee was removed to indefinite detention: the detainee, an operative of the Iraqi Ansar al-Islam group, had been transported out of Iraq for questioning, but once he was designated an Iraqi unlawful combatant, he was sent to Camp Cropper, where he was questioned once by military intelligence but remained in detention there for months thereafter—he was not registered as a detainee there, seemingly "lost" and forgotten.[174] Among other ghost detainees at Abu Ghraib were two Iraqi generals, Manadel al-Jamadi and Abd Hamed Mowhush, who both died under interrogation and whose homicide would not have come to light without the scandal at Abu Ghraib.[175] Camp Nama, the base of operations for the shadowy Task Force 6-26 (whose name changed with some frequency), was the site of a "black room" in which all manner of torture took place.[176]

In addition to the CIA sites located at the heart of inaccessible military bases—very similar to Facility 1391 in its military-intelligence liaison—the agency also maintained a number of secret prisons throughout the world where high-value detainees were kept for years before being finally transferred to Guantánamo in 2006. What particularly distinguishes the black sites is the massive effort at keeping them, their structure, their working, their processes, and their location invisible. Although the Bush administration claimed that the black sites were no longer functional after 2006, we know that as recently as 2011 such black sites have continued to exist offshore and onboard US naval vessels or in inaccessible reaches of Afghanistan or Somalia. Rendition to third countries has similarly continued.[177]

A CIA background paper on the black sites laid out in clinical detail—and with a level of cool detachment that shocks—the conditions not only of interrogation but also of the actual holding cells. The document clearly conjugates the conditions of incarceration to the process of information extraction by stating that while "detention conditions are not interrogation techniques . . . they have an impact on the detainee undergoing interrogation"; it helpfully delineates a regime of white noise ("not to exceed 79 decibels") and constant light. The document chillingly continues:

The HVD [high-value detainee] is typically reduced to a baseline, dependent state using the three interrogation techniques discussed below in combination. Establishing this baseline state is important to demonstrate to the HVD that he has no control over basic human needs. The baseline state also creates in the detainee a mindset in which he learns to perceive and value his personal welfare, comfort, and immediate needs more than the information he is protecting.[178]

This baseline was achieved not only through interrogation techniques perfected over decades but also through the production of a constantly surveilled panopticon-like space.[179] In testimonies to the investigator for the Council of Europe, former detainees recounted the baleful presence of surveillance cameras, "positioned so that in every inch of the cell they would be observed," and of microphones hidden in the walls that recorded their every breath.[180] The cells were completely anonymous and artificially lit twenty-four hours a day. Time could be measured only by the allocation of food or the announcement of times of prayer. The guards, as if playacting in a bizarre Hollywood thriller, "were covered in black from head to toe—Muhammad Bashmilah [a black-site detainee] described them as 'ninjas'—and communicated only by hand gestures."[181]

In the cocoon of invisibility the black sites afforded, the highest-value detainee, Khalid Shaykh Muhammad, would be waterboarded at least 183 times; his seven- and nine-year-old sons had been taken hostage at a black site, and their whereabouts remain unknown.[182] Abu Zubayda, who had apparently been providing information to the FBI, was nevertheless subjected to torture despite evidence of a preexisting mental illness.[183] Ibn Al-Shaykh al-Libi gave false testimony under torture about the connection between Iraq and al-Qaeda, which was subsequently used in Colin Powell's speech to the United Nations.[184] Ramzi Bin Al-Shibh, a "mastermind" of the September 11 bombings, and Mustafa al-Hawsawi, the "paymaster" for the attack, became so mentally ill with severe schizophrenic disorders that their capacity to stand trial has been questioned.[185]

Extraordinarily, the CIA Inspector General's report on the interrogation techniques in black sites takes great pains to show that the techniques used were all approved by the lawyers at both the CIA and the Department of Justice (DOJ).[186] A heavily redacted paragraph manages to convey to readers that the statutory basis of the CIA's ability to interrogate is the 1947 National Security Act.[187] The concern with legality went so far that videotapes of Abu Zubayda's torture were watched by a CIA lawyer to "assure compliance with the August 2002 DOJ opinion. . . . He reported there was no deviation from DOJ guidance."[188] When they discovered that methods had been used that had not been specified in the DOJ guidelines, the matter was referred to the DOJ, which chose not to prosecute.[189] The videotapes of the torture have disappeared.

That this shadow world of detention could go undetected for as long as it has, and that the locations of the black sites remain largely unidentified, attests to the extent to which US alliances were mobilized in the service of secrecy. The British were happy to cede de facto sovereignty and territorial control over the Chagos Archipelago in the Indian Ocean to the United States in the 1970s; the United States subsequently expelled the residents and used the island of Diego Garcia as a secret detention center decades later.[190] The US military bases in Germany—at least in Mannheim—have been used for the detention of high-value detainees.[191] Morocco and Yemen have both provided facilities operated and controlled by the CIA.[192] A Council of Europe investigation with access to CIA sources reported that a facility in Udon Thani in Thailand was the first black site in the War on Terror and the first site of detention for Ramzi Bin al-Shibh and Abu Zubayda. A Thai Air Force base near the facility had been a Vietnam War deployment base for the US Air Force and the forward operating base of Air America, a CIA-controlled civilian airline used in the "secret war" on Laos and Vietnam. As a former CIA operative told the Council of Europe investigator, "In Thailand, it was a case of 'you stick with what you know.'"[193] But the two countries on which the same investigation primarily focused were two of the closest allies of the United States in "new Europe," Romania and Poland. Poland had been a member of NATO, and Romania an "aspirant," facilitating the process of rendition and detention through "blanket overflight clearance for US military flights, access to airfields, and increased security for US facilities."[194]

Romania joined the network of black sites in 2003, and the sites there remained in operation at least until 2005. The Council of Europe investigation found that the United States chose to work with military intelligence in Romania "because the military 'cover' provided guarantees of secrecy under the NATO framework."[195] Accession to NATO required that "the policies a member state adopts regarding security of information should govern all kinds of sensitive information, in all parts of government"; that information is super-classified; and that "centralization of responsibility and strong coordination" is a prerequisite for joining NATO.[196] Two elements in the Council of Europe investigation are noteworthy. First is the importance of extrainstitutional personal relationships between the security forces that allowed for the development of such sites. As one US source told the investigators, "If your men on the ground have a very good personal relationship with the men in the partner service, that means a lot."[197] But as important was the development of a formal bilateral agreement in which the ally received compensation and aid for improvement of their military facilities—runways, barracks, and new military hardware—in return for territorial access and control.[198] The process by which such bilateral agreements were reached is also significant. Most started as informal agreements between "friends" with whom security forces had personal relationships and were formalized only years later. This incremental method and the gradual thickening of relations allowed for scrutiny to be avoided, as no given moment stands out for an oversight body to investigate the terms of a relationship, and often such oversight bodies are faced with a fait accompli.[199]

In Poland, invisibility was similarly guaranteed by formal bilateral agreements developed over years of interaction and support. The United States had access to the Stare Kiejkuty military base in Poland, and Poland provided both physical security and a "buffer zone" around the base to shield the activities there. The United States' chosen institutional partner in Poland was the Military Information Service (Wojskowe Służby Informacyjne, or WSI), which wholly circumvented civilian oversight and utilized the WSI penetration of civilian agencies to provide such support to CIA as, for example, short-circuiting Polish Border Guard, Polish Customs, and flight-control procedures and processes.[200] What allowed the WSI this level of secrecy and power was that it had emerged "'virtually unscathed' from post-Communism reform processes designed at achieving democratic oversight."[201]

Thus, a regime of secrecy and invisibility is created through formal and institutional procedures, treaty agreements, and informal cooperation that should be open to scrutiny, accountable to oversight, and politically transparent, but that were precisely not, because the border crossings of the relationship make it difficult for any national body to monitor.

CONCLUSION: INDIRECT POWER AND INVISIBILITY

The construction of a regime of invisibility in the age of liberal empire requires the scaffolding of law, treaty, and a system of classification and control, not only of persons but also of information about them. It is notable that the system of extraordinary rendition and the creation of black sites would be most enthusiastically pursued under an administration that "classified [documents] at twice the rate of the previous administration."[202]

Law was not absent from the process, and despite the insistence of international lawyers, both domestic US legal reasoning and international treaties underpinned the processes of abduction, transportation, and occultation of the detainees. Bush himself was alive to this contention, and in the famous press conference in which he admitted to the existence of the black sites he insisted on their legality: "This program has been subject to multiple legal reviews by the Department of Justice and CIA lawyers; they've determined it complied with our laws. This program has received strict oversight by the CIA's Inspector General."[203] The cooperation of US allies was secured through bilateral treaties, and in the case of NATO allies, the secrecy of detention practices was guaranteed by the very process of accession to NATO.

Where allies' prisons and detention centers served as holding cells for US detainees, proxies provided the mechanisms of concealment and denial. As I have written elsewhere, the use of proxies transforms spaces of war into interstitial landscapes of uncertainty and complexity in which who may act and who may be held responsible for that action is not always apparent.[204] A proxy may be a private military corporation, or an informal militia, or even most effectively an ostensibly sovereign state's formal military or secret services. Precisely because of the asymmetric proxy relations in which a powerful state dictates the terms of action to the less powerful violence workers, such proxies serve to extend and deepen the domination and control of the powerful state. This, of course, does not happen without contestation, or clashes of interests, or the attempt of the proxy to make a more advantageous bargain, but in the end, legal argument can absolve the ruling military of institutional responsibility (while assigning criminal liability to individual officers).[205] As such, a proxy is a useful cloak, a kind of alibi that allows coercive state institutions to maintain their legal innocence.

CHAPTER 5

BANAL PROCEDURES
OF DETENTION
Abu Ghraib and Its Ancestors

In Vietnam, about nine Viet Cong guerrillas were killed for
each one captured. In Iraq, about one insurgent is killed for
every three captured.

Bing West, 2008[1]

Because internment is, at its best, population engagement.

Major General Doug Stone, 2008[2]

The three tableaux that follow illuminate tensions that inhere to "regular"
detentions in asymmetric warfare. These stories exemplify the transformation of a military-political act—the confinement of the enemy—into a set of
minutely delineated procedures that require no skill or thinking on the part
of the soldiers involved. They show the presence a missionary zeal for improving and reforming detainees; and they illustrate the eruption of violence and
torture not simply as bad behavior on the part of a few ignorant "bad apples,"
but through a systematic leakage of violence across boundaries of legality.

The US Department of the Army issued a memorandum on February 19,
2007, shortly after the announcement of the "Surge" that put into place the
population-centric doctrines of General David Petraeus. The document, released by Wikileaks in 2011, concerns procedures in the event of detainee death
in Camp Bucca (the largest US detention facility in Iraq) and is an archetype
of managerial communication.[3] It bristles with acronyms (SOP, SIR, TIF,
CID, OAFME, BATS, PAD, NDRC, and so on) and form numbers—"death
certificate (DO 2064), Hospital Report of Death (DA 3894), and statement of

medical examination (DA 2173)." The directions are exhaustively described in a kind of bureaucratic dialect: utterly rational, functionally useful, clinically precise, and terrifyingly inhumane. For example, one particular paragraph reads: "Within 30 minutes of death, the remains will be scanned in Bio-metric Automated Toolset Systems (BATS) to verify the detainee's identity, by TIF processing section. The first 30 minutes are key to positive ID due to the body decomposing process."[4] The body of the dead detainee appears only ephemerally throughout the memorandum (it is mentioned around a dozen times in a five-page memo). Instead, the rest of the document is infinitesimally concerned with filling the right forms, entering the right data into digital repositories, and informing the correct personnel.

The second tableau is sketched in a 2009 *Military Review* article by three serving officers.[5] The article about "behavior modification" in US detention camps in Iraq focuses on the work of US Marine Major General (Reserves) Douglas Stone, a soldier-scholar with a PhD in public administration and a civilian career in management, primarily as chief executive officer of three different software companies. The reason his personal curriculum vitae is relevant is because

> Major General Stone is as atypical a leader of detention operations as his strategy is to the world of detention operations. He is a Marine, often touted as the service most willing to embrace small wars, filling a traditional Army position. He is a reservist rather than active duty officer. Having spent many years running successful businesses, he is a thinker with a doctorate in public administration.[6]

Stone is considered atypical because between May 2007 and June 2008 he put into place a program of education and behavior modification as the head of Task Force 134, assigned the job of detainee operations in Iraq. Brown, Goepner, and Clark describe how Stone's program of reeducation required detainees to join "the moderates' camp" by a process of "awakening" from extremism, marginalizing extremists through education, and participating in Internment Facility Reconciliation Center activities, which include religious instructions by Muslim imams opposed to violent resistance.[7] As the authors usefully summarize: "Camp Bucca, Iraq, has a proactive counterinsurgency strategy for detention operations. The strategy identifies detainees who no longer pose imperative threats, then educates and trains them, and subsequently releases them to return to their homes as 'moderate missiles of the mind' who can marginalize extremists."[8]

The last of these stories is the most familiar: detention and subjection to torture and humiliation in Abu Ghraib. Shaykh Abd-al-Sattar Abd-al-Jabbar was the imam of a mosque where US forces found weapons that he claims were used by the mosque guards. Shortly after the US invasion of Iraq, the shaykh was arrested alongside his two teenage sons (sixteen and eighteen years of age), and only his wife's tearful pleading stopped the US forces from also arresting his eleven-year-old son. Because his neighbor had refused to allow the US forces inside, he was also arrested. They were all sent to Abu Ghraib, where the shaykh himself was kept in the "hard site" and subjected to attacks by dogs, forced nudity, and other forms of torture of sexual nature that he did not feel comfortable talking about. He was incarcerated for eighteen months without charge, after which he was released. The conditions of his detention are now well known, more than anything else because of the large body of investigative journalism around the torture at Abu Ghraib and a leaked report by the International Committee of the Red Cross (ICRC), and because of classified investigations by Major General Antonio Taguba and by Lieutenant General Anthony Jones and Major General George Fay, which were leaked to journalists.[9]

These tableaux exemplify a number of tensions in detainee operations. On the one hand, the requirements of discipline and the combined Taylorization and bureaucratization of the military has meant that the US military operates with reams of complex documents that break down the procedures of detention into infinitesimal elements concatenated together to make a process and, in so doing, to eliminate the need for the soldiers to make on-the-spot decisions about vulnerable detainees. In the War on Terror, these highly regimented standard operating procedures have systematically incorporated elements of torture and abuse, imported from the most sterile, regimented, surveilled, and monitored detention center of all, Guantánamo Bay.[10]

The other tension is evident in the story of Doug Stone and his plan of "counterinsurgency inside the wire." Doug Stone, the urbane businessman described by one reporter as sporting a haircut that resembles that of Gordon Gecko (of the film *Wall Street*), "a businessman's coif that suggests money or power or both," reads the Qur'an to understand the Iraqi detainees and implements a plan of education in which detainees undergo "enlightenment, deprogramming and de-radicalization sessions," in what sounds like a dystopian program of behavior control.[11] Here, (pseudo)scientific psychological methods are transformed into a liberal program of "improvement" that evacuates the process of detention and indeed the motivation and lives of the detainees of any politics. This program of improvement that I describe below changes the prisons into spaces of mutual suspicion, recrimination, and denunciation, and it operates on the basis of categorizing detainees and offering them a hierarchy of privileges in return for their political about-face.

These tensions echo the three broad categories of power relations that Michel Foucault has sketched in his Collège de France lectures *Security, Territory, Population*. There, Foucault distinguishes between the law that permits or prohibits disciplinary techniques "within the domain of surveillance, diagnosis, and the possible, transformation of individuals" and the praxis of security, which is dependent on a calculus of probability and cost and is therefore entirely tied to a quantitative conceptualization of political problems.[12] Counterinsurgency detention camps of liberal powers gain their traction and suppleness precisely through a constant juggling of these different mechanisms of power.

Historically, the purpose of detention in conventional warfare has been to warehouse soldiers and officers, and to "disable enemy combatants from participation in combat, not to punish or rehabilitate them."[13] In counterinsurgencies, in contrast, these camps confine not only suspected enemy combatants but also vast numbers of noncombatants swept in on "mop-up operations," which are significant elements of asymmetric warfare. Detention in asymmetric warfare is also a mechanism for extraction of information, acquisition of hostages (usually families of suspected or wanted combatants), and spectacular performances of sovereign power. Such prison camps are often visible, even if located in "out of the way" sites. They are at once orderly and violent. The spaces of detentions camps and complex registration procedures classify the detainees in discrete categories subjected to varying treatment on the basis of detainee intransigence or malleability. The procedures and categories are deeply interrelated, as any variation in procedures—internally or in comparison with conventional warfare—is attributed to the breadth of different categories of detainees in counterinsurgencies.

In this chapter, I examine how detainees in unconventional warfare are categorized along spectrums that are intended to facilitate "understanding" them but also to use them more functionally and efficiently. I also scrutinize the Taylorized bureaucracy of detention; the proceduralism of interrogation processes aimed to produce disembodiment of torture; the liberal will to "improve" and reeducate detainees; and the processes of representation, presentation, and recording that make these detainees objects of counterinsurgency knowledge.

THE SPECTRUM OF DETENTION

> Generally, the guerrilla in insurgent wars is considered a violator of municipal law, or a common criminal, and while US forces must accord any prisoners or internees humane treatment by US regulations, care must be exercised to prevent enhancing the status of the guerrilla force to that of a recognized belligerent power.
> *Counterguerrilla Operations Field Manual, 1967*[14]

> In reference to the Global War on Terror there is an additional classification of detainees who, through their own conduct, are not entitled to the privileges and protection of the Geneva Conventions. These personnel, when detained, are classified as enemy combatants. Although they do not fall under the provisions of the Geneva Convention, they are still entitled to be treated humanely, subject to military necessity, consistent with the principles of GC. . . . Enemy combatants may be identified into the following sub-categories:
> (a) Low Level Enemy Combatant (LLEC).
> (b) High Value Detainee (HVD).
> (c) Criminal Detainee.
> (d) High Value Criminal (HVC).
> (e) Security Detainee.
> *Joint Doctrine for Detainee Operations (draft), 2005*[15]

As with other control mechanisms, the creation and enforcement of categories of people is central to deciding where to place detainees along a spectrum from "dangerous" to "relatively harmless." One banal reason for the process is the regulation of costs: confining the latter category does not require the same intensity of guarding or interrogation; less skilled personnel can be assigned to their maintenance in less sophisticated spaces, often tented camps. The question of cost becomes particularly urgent when, as in the US war in Iraq, the detainee population is enormous and when a counterinsurgency tactic such as "the Surge" causes a doubling of detainee numbers.[16] Statistics indicate that after the Surge had begun in 2007, the number of detainees held in US custody in Camps Bucca and Cropper rose to 25,600, of whom only 10–15 percent were ever brought to trial. By then the average duration of detention was 333 days, and around 1,500 (5 percent of all detainees) had been held without charge for more than three years.[17] That the Iraqi camps were much more exposed to news reporting and monitoring explains why at the Bagram detention center in Afghanistan, some detainees had been held for six or seven years without charge.[18]

In conventional prisoner-of-war camps, prisoners are generally categorized as combatant prisoners of war, subject to "combatant immunity" and the protection of articles 4 and 5 of the Geneva Conventions, retained persons (usually medical personnel), and civilian internees who are usually considered protected persons and are kept in separate places.[19] In counterinsurgency confinement, however, these distinctions are blurred and indeed increasingly finer gradations and categories of detainees are introduced, whose treatment is dictated by their usefulness and—as population-centric counterinsurgency takes hold—by their ability to "improve."

Such processes were used by the French in both Indochina and Algeria. In the former, the French established rehabilitation camps (*le camp de la liberté*) in 1953 for Viet Minh guerrillas, where prisoners were categorized according to their "political permeability" and subjected to indoctrination. If these prisoners "grew politically reliable," they were given leave from detention to try to influence others.[20] In Algeria, the process was far more formalized, and three different places of overt detention (as the French also operated secret sites of confinement and torture) held three different categories of prisoners. Ordinary prisoner-of-war camps operated fairly close to the norms of conventional warfare. Beyond uniformed detainees, those arrested were fed to *camps de triage et de transit* and *camps d'hébergement*. The screening and transit camps were holding places for detainees picked up in large-scale sweeps. There the detainees were screened and interrogated to determine the extent of their political commitments and malleability, and they were assigned to one of the three informal administrative categories, "reducibles," "irreducibles," and "innocents." The "innocents" were released, and the "irreducibles" were kept under close monitoring, possibly leading to eventual trials.[21] The more ambiguous category of "reducibles" would be sent to a *camp d'hébergement* (i.e., accommodation camp), where they were subjected to *l'action psychologique*, to be redeemed from their revolutionary intransigence.[22] As one eyewitness recounted to the ICRC: "An inmate leaves the Centers of Transit to be released, to be transferred to a *[c]entres d'hébergement*, or to be slaughtered."[23] "Special sections" in the *centres d'hébergement* held men and women who resisted "psychological action" and refused to help the French in their search for information or detainee reform.[24] A service order commanded that psychological action "should aim at their recruitment in the ranks of the *harkas* (indigenous paramilitaries) or the troops, or their use as instructors in the psychological action carried out in the *douars* (villages)."[25]

In the US war in Vietnam, detainees included North Vietnamese Army soldiers captured as prisoners of war, Viet Cong guerrillas captured in battle who were then interrogated and eventually handed to the South Vietnamese forces, and a third group that allowed for a great deal of operational latitude.[26] This third category was the VCI (Viet Cong infrastructure), or the civilian supporters of the guerrillas, who through euphemistic renaming and reduction to acronym were semantically transformed from a broad class of persons (most of whom were ordinary villagers) to objects of coercive confinement and assassination in the Phoenix (Phung Hoang) Program. Phoenix was first launched by Civil Operations and Revolutionary Development Support (CORDS), a hybrid body composed of CIA, US Agency for International Development, and US military personnel in 1967, and it was consolidated under the CIA's William Colby. Where interrogated, the detainees were considered "human data banks," with information generated through the snowballing of arrests and the accumulation of information gained through interrogations. Despite the fact that more than eighty thousand Vietnamese were "neutralized," of whom twenty-six thousand had been killed, in remembering Phoenix, one former US interrogator lamented, "The major fault of the Phoenix dragnet was that the holes in the net were too big."[27]

The Phoenix Program officers divided the nebulous and faceless VCI into three administrative, rather than judicial, subcategories. Category A included leading members of the People's Revolutionary Party; Category B encompassed "other VCI members who held important but not leading positions." The subcategory whose breadth allowed detention of just about anybody in a hamlet comprised

(a) rank and file guerrillas; (b) rank and file members of front organizations; (c) soldiers and members of organized VC/NVA military units; (d) persons who pay taxes to the VC; (e) persons who perform miscellaneous tasks for the VC; (f) members of the populace in the VC-controlled areas.[28]

The forty-page Phoenix Program Green Book then provided a detailed breakdown of VCI categories and helpfully provided this guidance at the outset: "Final classification authority lies with the Province Security Committee; however, listing of the categories in the Green Book should aid materially in targeting and reporting."[29] Strikingly, although the Green Book lists hundreds of different VCI executive positions listed under categories A and B, 40 percent of all those detained were actually category C, or unimportant, detainees.[30] The detainees who were not released were either tried (around 5 percent were ever put on trial) or kept in administrative detention, which the CIA described as similar to emergency measures in Malaya, Kenya, and the Philippines.[31]

In the US War on Terror, the categories of detainees were expanded even further. In addition to the ordinary prisoners of war, subject to protection under articles 4 and 5 of the Third Geneva Convention, new categories were introduced on an ad hoc basis.[32] These included unlawful enemy combatants, ghost detainees, high-value detainees, and security detainees (who included not just civilians caught at the scene of a battle but also families of wanted people, practically held hostage). If there was no certainty as to what category a person belonged to, a new interim category, "persons under US control (PUCs)" created an official interstitial space, "a bureaucratic blank spot where prisoners could reside temporarily without entering any official database or numbering system.

We could keep them in this temporary status—designated by a new number beginning with T— for up to fourteen days, giving us time to make a call."[33]

Even once a prisoner was categorized, it was not entirely clear what corpus of rules, regulations, and procedures applied to him or her. Douglas Feith finessed the definition of prisoners of war in Afghanistan in this way: "Deciding that the Conventions governed the war with the Taliban was not the same thing as deciding that Taliban detainees were entitled to prisoner-of-war (POW) status."[34] Within each of the categories, still, treatment could also vary. A so-called high-value detainee could be protected by the provisions of the Third Geneva Convention or could be designated "unlawful." People could move between categories, and could be even physically moved from confinement in camps located in Iraq to Afghanistan (and vice versa) or to Guantánamo or to a country involved in rendition. Detention categories seemed to vary from one arena of battle to the other, and the treatment of detainees across different arenas even for people categorized under the same label differed substantially. This meant that although the formal and legalistic naming processes ("unlawful enemy combatant," "high-value detainee," and even the already-familiar "enemy prisoner of war") made confinement seem controlled and well managed, in reality the process was highly arbitrary.[35] After population-centric counterinsurgency was put into place, the informal categories of "reconcilable" and "irreconcilable" were introduced, echoing the aforementioned French categories in Algeria—"reducible" and "irreducible."[36]

Whether these categorizations are formally enshrined in doctrine and field manuals or are informally enforced, they nevertheless function to compartmentalize detainees and to allow for maximal surveillance of those considered unsalvageable or dangerous. "Dangerous" detainees are isolated during drawn-out interrogation processes and even sometimes during their regular detention to allow for the extraction of any information they may have or to prevent them from mobilizing or inciting other detainees. Such things as food have been regulated: in the early months of the invasion of Iraq, "proper" prisoners of war received two meals a day, whereas those not considered legal combatants received only one.[37]

Soldiers, military police, and interrogators themselves also created vernacular categories to account for the liminal spaces opening in the seam between formal procedures and new directives, old—and internationally recognized—categories of detainees, and new classifications. These vernacular categories, "brought-ins" in Israel's Ansar detention camp in Lebanon (1982–1985) and "fifty-meter detainees" (all persons detained within 50 meters of an attack on US forces), were at best descriptive categories that did not give any indication of where or how a person was to be placed in the highly compartmentalized set of procedures.[38] This explosive tension between numerous and amorphous categories and an impulse to compulsively and infinitesimally define procedures, all in an environment that sanctioned racialization of the enemy, meant that many counterinsurgent foot soldiers often transgressed the bounds of ethical behavior with their confined charges.

PROCESSING DETAINEES

> Its specific nature . . . develops the more perfectly the more bureaucracy is "dehumanized," the more completely it succeeds in eliminating from official business love, hatred, and all purely personal, irrational, and emotional elements which escape calculation. This is the specific nature of bureaucracy and its specific virtue.
>
> *Max Weber, 1909*[39]

> The American soldier today is a part of a great machine which we call military organization; a machine in which, as by electrical converters, the policy of government is transformed into the strategy of the general, into the tactics of the field and into the action of the man behind the gun. Through that machine he is fed, clothed, transported and armed, equipped and housed.
>
> *Elihu Root, 1899*[40]

The arrest and incarceration of an enemy in war, particularly when this enemy is not distinguished and distanced by uniform and rank and the rituals of the battlefield, can be a disconcertingly intimate affair, with all the affect, vulnerability, and brutality that such intimacy can generate. As if echoing Max Weber's description of bureaucracies, the processing of detainees is bureaucra-

tized to such an extraordinary extent that it is evacuated of emotion, spontaneous reasoning, and the possibility of personalizing the relationship between
the prisoners and their captors. This maximal attempt at bureaucratization—
through proceduralism, appeals to law, and a codification of ethical rules
of behavior—is also intended to enforce military discipline and to channel
aggression, anger, and brutality into areas in which such affect is deemed not
only legal but also useful.

Bureaucratization through formalization of institutions and procedures
in the military (as in other state institutions) had already been well under
way by the end of the nineteenth century in France, Britain, and the United
States, though following different paths and logics and at different speeds. In
the United States, the bureaucratization of the military followed a peculiarly
American style. This occurred partially because Elihu Root, the secretary of
war (1899–1904) under Presidents William McKinley and Theodor Roosevelt,
reorganized the army, professionalizing and bureaucratizing the institution in
line with the managerial edicts of Frederick Taylor, and in conscious confor-
mity with nascent ideas about rationalizing bureaucracies.[41] This meant that
not only the businesses that fed the military but also the military itself adopted
formulas of management and procedure advanced by Taylor.[42]

Although Taylor himself has fallen out of fashion, many of the specific
procedures he advanced survive, especially his recommendation of breaking
down processes into discrete tasks that would allow for the measurement,
analysis, optimization, and ultimately control of human actions, as if humans
were "physical objects."[43] The military under Root's leadership self-consciously
adopted the philosophy of scientific management, but the partisans of the philosophy themselves likened their ideas to those already used in large organizations, such as the army.[44] This constant traveling of management styles in
and out of the military has left its mark on the military: even as Taylorism is
forgotten, its remnants—the division of processes into discrete tasks, the insistence on the "science" of management, and the shifting up of responsibility to
those who manage—survive, irretrievably interwoven with military culture.[45]

Procedures and processes around confinement have been developed not
solely on the basis of this bureaucratization but also with reference to the
development and codification of ethics and laws around war-fighting. As
some military officers have argued in reflecting on the process of Taylorist

bureaucratization, "the tendency of institutional demands to override ethical considerations" means that the more procedures are minutely defined in a top-down fashion, the less ethical autonomy the officers and soldiers have.[46] The aim of rationalizing bureaucracy is to subtract affect and spontaneous reasoning from the process, to shift responsibility away from those who act, and to allow for "a discharge of business according to *calculable rules* and 'without regard to persons.'"[47] The very formalism of bureaucracy, as Karl Marx pointed out long ago, thus evacuates the procedures so defined of any content, effacing both politics and ethics.[48]

This tension means that despite the best attempts to regulate and discipline soldierly behavior in that intimate space of capture and confinement, violence can erupt in ways that should be predicted but that often are not, especially if the very procedures and processes are in upheaval, or if ad hoc amendments and additions are being made. Further, the emphasis on proceduralism often does not account for cruelties as a result of incompetence. For example, in the Paul Cazelles detention camp in Algeria in 1957, the lists of detainees included "many who were not present but had either escaped or become victims of 'work in the woods' (slang for summary execution)" and conversely did not include detainees that were in fact in the camp. To allow for the numbers to meet the needs or bureaucratic accounting, random arrests were made to fill the vacant places.[49] This same sort of bureaucratic incompetence was also present in Abu Ghraib prison in Iraq, where many of those who were detained, at least in the early months of capture in 2003, were not recorded in official records, either through omission or, in the case of "ghost detainees," commission.[50] The US Army's provost marshal general would say in 2005 that in Iraq, "roughly 65,000 people have been screened for possible detention, and about 30,000 of those were entered into the system, at least briefly, and assigned internment serial numbers."[51]

A lack of resources can also undermine the procedures. In Iraq, the massive sweeps of populations and neighborhoods, conducted at night, would result in large numbers of detainees "being delivered to collection points only wearing night clothes or underclothes. SGT Jose Garcia, assigned to the Abu Ghraib Detainee Assessment Board, estimated that 85%–90% of the detainees were of no intelligence value based upon board interviews and debriefings of detainees." Nevertheless, to process these detainees, "already scarce interrogator and analyst resources were pulled from interrogation operations to identify and screen increasing numbers of personnel whose capture documentation was incomplete or missing. Complicated and unresponsive release procedures ensured that these detainees stayed at Abu Ghraib—even though most had no value."[52]

In addition to incompetence and scarce resources, the overlapping of procedures, regulations, and laws—or conversely, gaps between areas covered by these—could result in violence, arbitrariness, and ultimately torture. For example, the CIA high-value-detainee program was "extraordinarily compartmentalized in order to maximize secrecy."[53] This compartmentalization meant that different personnel followed procedures and legal instructions differently. This provided bureaucratic alibis where the responsibility for obeying a procedure ultimate rested nowhere, because it was unclear who was in charge and because the procedures, however minutely described, ultimately left soldiers who could not see their discrete acts of torture as anything but an infinitesimal and unimportant "task" among many.

The process of compartmentalization was sometimes implemented spatially. For example, all detention camps in the cases included here specifically separated guerrilla officers from ordinary combatants, and they often also distinguished between civilians and guerrillas. In some cases, for example in Israel's Ansar detention camp in Lebanon, the subsequent Ansar II in Gaza, and Ketzi'ot (Ansar III) in the Negev desert, one particular block would be reserved for "trouble-makers" or for "intellectuals and lawyers" removed from "the harder cases."[54] In all instances, the massive camps were divided into different blocks, separated with large sand berms, barbed wire, and sentry towers.[55] The various US bricks-and-mortar prison sites in Iraq and Afghanistan were so quickly filled with prisoners that eventually tented camps, and later more permanent barrack-like structures, were erected. Everywhere, the design of the camps aided categorization and control.

Even if the camps were meant to be cautionary tales for the population, they were in practice shielded from outsiders. In Lebanon, the Israeli forces blocked all roads leading to Ansar.[56] Ketzi'ot was "almost perfectly isolated from the rest of Israel."[57] Abu Ghraib was isolated not only spatially but also through its history and memory of horror. To the guards and wardens, however, the prisoners were to be supremely visible, so as to "enable ringleaders to be readily identified and isolated."[58] This happened through the subdivision of the camp under the watchful eyes of guards in closely placed sentry towers but also through disciplinary practices such as daily headcounts, informants inside the camps, and punitive interrogations.[59] At Ketzi'ot, a "chicken house" for trouble-makers was a "walled-in enclosure of concrete and barbed wire" that was surrounded by a "screen of black netting" to capture messages sent wrapped around rocks from one block to another.[60]

Prisoners' ability to ingeniously overcome surveillance through "faxed" letters sent as notes tied around the rocks, and through autonomous organization within the blocks, is not the sole factor undermining disciplinary control (in its Foucauldian sense). These camps—even Guantánamo—are far from sterile panopticons. The sheer number of prisoners can make monitoring more difficult. Lack of hygiene, generated because of inadequate preparation, can be transformed into modes of punishment that are far from disciplinary. For example, a former guard at Ketzi'ot writes, "the latrines—one latrine for every thirty prisoners—weren't dug deeply enough into the desert floor, on the faulty assumption that the army would be able to crush the Intifada before the Palestinians drowned the desert in shit."[61] The shit-encrusted prison tents and prison cells were means of coercive punishment.[62]

It is noteworthy that when population-centric counterinsurgency was said to have replaced the earlier enemy-centric small wars, procedures were supposed to have become more humane, rational, and less bureaucratic. However, the degree of bureaucratic control does not give any indication of how humane treatment can be. Detainees in Guantánamo Bay are subjected to the most detailed procedures and processes, and yet the ostensibly sterile and controlled environment of that camp is debilitating and abusive.

Procedures of Registration and Confinement

> America could win the war if they just applied the exact
> process that you're putting in detention to the rest of the
> entire nation.
> *Tariq Hashimi, 2008*[63]

The procedures delineating detainee capture, registration, confinement, and eventual release are all imbued with this inherent tension. After capture, procedures dictate that the detainees are photographed, their fingerprints (and eventually iris scans) recorded, and their names entered into a registry. This process is familiar from counterinsurgency after counterinsurgency, where detention records become a source of information for data mining and for keeping track of populations. In the US War on Terror, as in previous counterinsurgencies, sometimes informal methods of determining the extent of "guilt" of the detainees are used. General Doug Stone explained that in screening evaluations in Iraq, "If [the detainee] has a beard, it's a data point," recalling the Malayan "callus index," whereby a detainee's noncallused hand could indicate that the person wasn't a "regular" peasant.[64] There is also a performative aspect to the process of registration. A British military officer who had fought the counterinsurgency in Aden recounts, "Each suspect was photographed with a Polaroid camera and finger-printed and this, although it did not result directly in the conviction of a single terrorist through civil proceedings, helped dominate the area and cow our enemies and potential enemies."[65]

The process of confinement itself can be profoundly controlled via minute procedures, only if the environment is sterile and the number of detainees not overwhelming. As such, although Guantánamo Bay is the site of extraordinary proceduralism, Abu Ghraib—or at least the tented mass detention camp therein—has been less subject to intensive monitoring and bureaucratic control. Although in most instances, different procedures (with different intensity) are in place, the same site of confinement can exhibit different regimes of control. The tented camp at Abu Ghraib, for example, was minimally monitored, whereas the "hard site" was under constant surveillance and control. The detainees at Guantánamo Bay and the US Navy brigs in South Carolina were the most closely monitored and controlled. In Guantánamo, detainees were "weighed and fingerprinted, swabbed for DNA, clipped for hair samples, and given a plastic bracelet embossed with their identification information."[66] They were given Individual Service Numbers, which were the only means of identifying some prisoners, of whose identity the Pentagon was unsure.[67] The camp's military administrators compulsively issued orders on everything from the behavior and manners of the guards and medical staff to what the detainees could and could not do. Some members of the staff felt that the uncontrollable proliferation of written orders was a "strategy of using memos to mitigate the overpowering sense that things were out of [their] control."[68] The more regimented the regime seemed to be, the more it hinted at the fragility of its foundations.

By 2004, Guantánamo had had two substantial documents delineating standard operating procedures. The main difference between the two documents, issued in 2003 and 2004, respectively, was the inclusion of extensive sections on mental health, self-harm, and military commissions in the latter.[69] The two documents exhaustively detail the procedures for in-processing, the use of force, operations in various parts of the detention camp, "detainee behavioral management," and a vast array of other operations. The language of the documents is prosaic even—especially—when the content is far from mundane. For example, the section on the ICRC in both versions lists four permitted visitation levels:

a. No Access: No contact of any kind with the ICRC. This includes the delivery of ICRC mail.

b. Restricted: ICRC is allowed to ask the detainee about health and welfare only. No prolonged questions.

c. Unrestricted: ICRC is allowed full access to talk to the detainee.

d. Visual: Access is restricted to visual inspection of the detainee's physical condition. No form of communication is permitted. No delivery of ICRC mail.[70]

The section on disciplinary procedures is even more shocking in its banality. A detainee's infraction is judged against a tabulated "list of offenses." The document advises that, should the exact offense not appear in the table, "a similar offense or an offense of equal severity" should be found. Then, the particular detainee's record is examined to find his or her previous record of punishment. A second table, "Detainee Movement and Discipline Matrix" is used to "cross-reference the category of most severe offense with the number of days between the current offense and the previous offense," to decide where to move the detainee and for how long.[71] The section goes on for much longer, listing all the other possible variations. Superficially, this degree of detailed proceduralism should encourage the guards and wardens to act according to preestablished rules, and the intimate process of punishment—after all, the detainee has to be physically removed from his or her cell to some punishment unit—is evacuated of possible emotion. But a further examination shows how such a facade of bureaucratic rationalism, this ostensible iron cage, is in fact perforated throughout with fissures through which affect and spontaneous decision making irrupts. "Offenses" are subjectively measured against one another, and their severity is subjectively determined. The process of removing the detainee from one place to another places bodies and emotions in collision with one another. Records of past behavior do not speak of the mental or physical condition of a particular detainee being punished. The bureaucratic prose conceals the brutality of the process of punishment.

Another form of punishment used in Guantánamo (and other detention camps of the War on Terror) has been food control. The document mentions matter-of-factly that if the detainee "removes the ID bracelet, he will not be fed until another is made for him."[72] The section titled "Loss of Hot Meals" indicates that the number of days an infraction has resulted in this punishment should be recorded in the "duty logs," and a "DD form 508" (a record of disciplinary action) is left in the detainee's file on the block and another copy kept in the detention operation center.[73]

The lawyers who eventually won the right to represent Guantánamo Bay detainees describe how much these procedures restrict their ability to meet with their clients. Before proceduralism became the norm, the lawyers "had been able to take advantage of the lack of formal procedures governing attorney-client visits. But more lawyers meant more rules," and perversely, more rules meant fewer visiting hours and far more rigid and stringent guidelines delineating interactions.[74]

The same degree of (seeming) control is also exercised elsewhere. In the case of Yaser Esam Hamdi, the US citizen of Saudi origin who was held in the brig, the officer in charge of the brig wrote an email, dated April 17, 2002, to clarify the degree and rationale for denying the detainee access to a soccer ball or a checkerboard: "We want to stay identical with JTF-160 [Joint Task Force, 160; Guantánamo Bay detention task force]. At JTF-160, detainees have their hands shackled and their feet free, and they are permitted to exercise in a fenced area by themselves, for 15–20 minutes, twice a week. There are no soccer balls." The same officer writes that the chaplain "is there to provide spiritual advice, not to become a buddy and provide recreation." In response to Hamdi's request to call his family, the officer writes, "Bad idea to set US Navy personnel up as liaisons to Al Quaeda [sic] family members."[75] The emails in all their banality and ordinariness are revealing. Even the most mundane requests are policed, disciplined, reviewed, and approved (or more often, denied). Secretary of

Defense Donald Rumsfeld seems to be directly involved in determining whether or not the detainees receive visitors, any visitors at all, including a chaplain, an ICRC representative, or legal counsel, and in deciding the degree of monitoring and withholding of correspondence, including official legal correspondence. As the emails proceed, the gentler and more accommodating tone of the direct warden (the commander of Navy Brig Norfolk) is slowly disciplined into the same bureaucratic language of her higher-up.

The same sort of proceduralism applied to detention and rendition on US or European soil. In the case of the Canadian citizen of Syrian extraction Maher Arar, he was detained while transiting through New York. Arar was whisked away from the airport—according to procedures—and after a brief detention was sent to be tortured by the Syrian regime for a year. Because both the US Immigration and Naturalization Service (INS) and the FBI had been involved in the detention (as well as the CIA behind the scenes), when Arar's attorneys tried to reach him, they were told, "Mr. Arar was still in New York (although he was not) and the FBI did not know when he was getting out—it was an INS matter, he said."[76] Meanwhile, the INS had constructed a dossier of official documents against Arar, whose very bureaucratic banality concealed the feebleness of their case. The INS removal order stated:

On October 1, 2002, Mr. Arar was served with all unclassified documents that the INS was relying on in initiating proceedings for his removal. These documents included: 1) an executed I-147 notice saying that Mr. Arar had five days to provide a written response to the allegations and charge of inadmissibility; 2) an attachment to the I-147 alleging Mr. Arar to be a member of an organization that had been designated by the Secretary of State as a Foreign Terrorist Organization (al-Qaeda) and charging Mr. Arar with inadmissibility under the *Immigration and Naturalization Act*; 3) a publication issued by the U.S. State Department listing al-Qaeda as a Foreign Terrorist Organization; and 4) a publication relating to free legal service provided in the New York area.[77]

The flurry of documents and publications again acted as a bureaucratic alibi for what was a disruptive, cruel, and illegal detention.

At Abu Ghraib and other detention camps in Iraq this degree of proceduralism was most relevant at the points of encounter between the detainees and their captors. These were in-processing, interrogation, and release. After the population-centric turn that occurred with the Surge in Iraq, precisely these moments of encounter were streamlined, the number of points at which the detainees encountered their captors (through vocational and indoctrination classes) was expanded, and these moments of encounter were transformed into instruments not only of persuasion but also of data gathering.

Before the reforms, more than 65 percent of detainees had been innocent (as a Coalition Provisional Authority official wrote, "Many people who should be let go are spending long periods in detention without reason") and entanglement in the red tape, the very registration of the detainees, meant that "it was almost impossible to extricate them."[78] After the reforms, Doug Stone described the initial screening interview by a Muslim imam who helped evaluate the religious beliefs of the detainees:

[The aim of] a lot of initial assessments [is] to understand who we've got and what their orientation towards religion, their skill, their education, their morale and motivation of what got them here. We are assigning them to certain theater internment facilities based on, you know, what our assessment is of being able to take them from, if they are on the extremist end or just under the unemployment end, to kind of get them modeled back and bend them back to our will.[79]

The data collected were used as the bases of psychological profiles and family demographic studies, which provided necessary intelligence as to what the detainees' circumstances were.[80] Knowledge was to make detention not only more humane but also more effective as a counterinsurgency measure in which detainees were transformed and improved.

At the point of release, after the reform, Doug Stone invoked a 1957 Iraqi law on the basis of which detainees "slated for release [would] go before an Iraqi judge and take an oath to keep the peace. With deceit an obvious concern, the military required detainees to select guarantors who would be legally liable for their conduct."[81] The release process itself included ritual celebratory elements, indicating a rite of passage. In the period between screening and release, the new procedures required extensive exposure to both religious reform and vocational training, and a process of "improvement" to facilitate "reentry" into the Iraqi society as allies of the United States, not its enemy.

Interrogation: Intelligence and Performance

> The abuses at Abu Ghraib are unforgivable not just because
> they were cruel, but because they set us back. The more a
> prisoner hates America, the harder he will be to break.
> *"Chris Mackey," 2004*[82]

> Since detentions are the basis for good intelligence obtained
> by interrogation, and wide-scale detention can only be carried
> out when there is genuine control of the territory, only
> such control will provide the flexibility to activate complete
> networks to follow up partial information from a lead that is
> not totally clear...
> *Major General Yaakov Amidror, 2008*[83]

Much has been written about the torture of detainees in Afghanistan, Iraq, and Guantánamo Bay (and elsewhere) not only by the interrogators but also by military police or wardens as a means of "softening up" the detainees. My intent here, however, is not to specifically address the horrors of torture but to discuss the more banal and quotidian aspects of interrogation, which through proceduralism evacuate the infliction of pain of its abhorrence.

From the very moment of capture, procedures for interrogation—ostensibly cool, rational, and bureaucratic—aim to use affect, through prolonging the shock of capture for the detainees, to extract information from them. One interrogator would describe the steps to ensure the protraction of the captives' anxiety "without breaking the Geneva Convention's prohibition on coercion":

As perfunctory handling as you can possibly muster. Rough handling but never beating up. Like big, burly—two MPs [military police] for every prisoner, picking up each prisoner by his armpits, because . . . they're actually quite physically small, picking him up by his armpits and moving him over to the next station and standing him up. That was part of the— I encouraged that. I thought that had a positive effect.[84]

The Department of Justice's Office of Legal Counsel specifically and minutely examines and documents these procedures and adds sanguinely:

The procedures [the high-value detainee (HVD)] is subjected to are precise, quiet, and almost clinical; and no one is mistreating him. While each HVD is different, the rendition and reception process generally creates significant apprehension in the HVD because of the enormity and suddenness of the change in environment, the uncertainty about what will happen next and the potential dread an HVD might have of US custody.[85]

The feminist scholar Carol Cohn has interrogated how the gendered "technostrategic" language of nuclear bombing "cleanses" horrors and transforms death into life through the use of abstraction, acronyms, metaphors, and euphemisms.[86] Here, the bureaucratically banal language of HVDs and clinically precise procedures deplete the act of arrest and the anxiety of uncertainty of their meaning. If dread is invoked, it is intended as a rational instrument of information extraction. Physical and psychological torture, wrapped in procedure and arcane legalese, become ordinary. What is notable about the prevalence of torture in the War on Terror is not that it could have emerged but how it could not have emerged, given the extent to which lawyers, psychologists, interrogators, and military and intelligence officials enshrined it in bureaucratic procedures, memoranda, and processes.

Intelligence gathering in a counterinsurgency collates not only tactical information but also strategic data about the structures of people's lives, politics, societies, and economics; the mode of operation of intelligence gathering should—according to established normative discourses—prevent backlash. There are of course institutional disagreements over methods of interrogation and the immediate or strategic applicability of such information.[87] For example, during the Malayan Emergency, a memorandum by the Colonial Office argued:

The bulk of our reliable information is obtained not from agents or police friends or contacts but instead from corpses, prisoners of war and captured documents. This process builds up an interesting academic or even strategic picture. It would be most useful in fighting regular troops in formal battle, but it is of much less value against a mobile, intelligent and localised guerrilla force. The provision of more "live" as opposed to "blown" or "dead" information must be the task of the Police Force.[88]

By contrast, the great majority of detainees captured in the early stages of the War on Terror would be grilled again and again for tactical information, even long after they had been detained and after any such information would have expired. To maximize this form of information extraction, an assembly-line model of interrogation was established.[89] An account of 2003–2004 detention practices in Iraq describes this:

> The interrogators worked in shifts. . . . At this US facility in Iraq [Camp Nama], interrogations were based on a Henry Ford model. Each interrogator had a specialization and operated as if he were on an assembly line. This technique was more complex (it involves several individuals) and brutal (interrogators take turns, allowing the abuse to continue unabated). . . . It is an evolved, mechanized Monstering.[90]

The process of interrogation in the US military and in the CIA converged at more or less the same point through at least three different routes. In the case of the CIA, a long history of interrogation practices in a variety of covert settings and a series of interrogation manuals, many of which are formally expired, allowed for a reintroduction of interrogation methods long considered abhorrent and banned through legislation and congressional monitoring.[91] Vice President Dick Cheney had specifically "searched the CIA's archives to see what worked in the past. He was particularly impressed with the Vietnam War-era Phoenix Program."[92] But the CIA also had other manuals it had used in past counterinsurgencies. The "KUBARK Manual" of 1963 foreshadows subsequent methods of torture and lists coercive techniques as follows: "arrest, detention, deprivation of sensory stimuli through solitary confinement or similar methods, threats and fear, debility, pain, heightened suggestibility and hypnosis, narcosis, and induced regression."[93] The "Human Resource Exploitation Manual" of 1983, which was used to train Honduran and other Latin American interrogators, draws both on the "KUBARK Manual" and on military interrogation manuals generated during the Vietnam War. The original document, which has a long section on coercive techniques, states, "We will be discussing two types of techniques, coercive and non-coercive. While we do not stress the use of coercive techniques, we do want to make you aware of them." The sentence is edited by hand to read, "While we deplore the use of coercive techniques, we do want to make you aware of them so that you may avoid them."[94] The same hand also changes "The questioner should be careful to manipulate the subject's environment to disrupt patterns" to "Another coercive techniques is to manipulate the subject's environment to disrupt patterns."[95] The newer, gentler version simply changes the verb from active to passive, without changing the meaning: a procedurally detailed method of creating terror through arbitrariness and uncertainty becomes a fact of life. The doer and the done-to disappear from the sentence. This language sketches an environment of supreme control. The manual defines control as "the capacity to cause or change certain types of human behavior by implying or using physical or psychological means to induce compliance. Compliance may be voluntary or involuntary. Control can rarely be established without control of the environment. By controlling the subject's physical environment, we will be able to control his psychological state of mind."[96] A total disciplining of the person allows for extraction of information. Involuntary compliance becomes just a step in a process of information extraction. What we imagine is the sterile space of the lab, not the filthy torture chamber stained with urine, blood, and shit.

The second route to convergence is via an inversion of military training exercises, intended to harden US special operations forces against capture. In this, the US military drew on its own history to enhance its repertoire of interrogation techniques. Here, the reference point was not the military's own interrogation methods but rather the methods taught in the Survival, Evasion, Resistance, and Escape (SERE) training program, which prepares US military personnel for possible capture and torture by enemies. The SERE program, originally known as the Communist Interrogation Model, drew on the experience of US military personnel captured by the enemy in the Korean War and devised a series of techniques—including forced nudity, stress-and-duress positions, and waterboarding—into a tool to inoculate US soldiers tortured by the enemy. The reverse engineering of SERE techniques of torture was central to the military's interrogation repertoire in the War on Terror.[97] The former chief of "Interrogation Control Element" at Guantánamo Bay testified at an internal investigation that his predecessor had "arranged for SERE instructors to teach their techniques to the interrogators at GTMO. The instructors did give some briefings to the Joint Interrogation Group (JIG) interrogators."[98] Although he claims that he chose not to use the SERE methods, his actual testimony (as with scores of other such testimonies enclosed with the investigation) indicates that indeed the SERE techniques had been used.

The third route was more informal and involved specialized detention task forces in various battlefields, where CIA operatives and military intelligence officers worked together. Here, the actions and processes of one bled into the other. For example, Task Force 121 (previously Task Forces 5 and 20, and later, Task Force 6-26) operated at Camp Nama and was a hybrid task force of special operations forces troops from the Joint Special Operations Command; "CIA officers, FBI agents and special operations forces from other countries also worked closely with the task force."[99] Although subsequent investigation of their actions—heavily redacted on declassification—listed five techniques familiar from SERE training ("sleep management," "stress position," "dietary manipulation," "environmental manipulation," and "yelling/loud music"), the report itself more or less whitewashed the actions and mildly indicated that the policy documents needed to be changed.[100]

The proceduralization of torture is on display in the interrogation transcripts of Mohammad al-Qahtani, detainee number 063 at Guantánamo Bay.[101] Al-Qahtani was interrogated continuously for fifty days, during which he was allowed to sleep only in four-hour blocks every twenty hours, if that. On the third day, al-Qahtani, who was on hunger strike, was given several bags of fluid intravenously and prevented from using the lavatory. The logs report impassively that the "detainee goes in his pants" while his interrogation continued. By the fourth day, he had to be forced to stand every fifteen minutes to keep awake. After the first week, he had painfully swollen limbs and had been compelled to exercise, been given an enema, and forced to have intravenous fluids. In the second week, after his beard and hair were forcibly shaven and he was disoriented by being moved between different interrogation rooms while hooded, the interrogators used "Pride and Ego Down, Fear Up Harsh and Invasion of Space by a Female." By then, he was severely dehydrated and his heart rate had dropped to thirty-five beats per minute. After he was revived in the hospital, he was returned to the interrogation room. In the third week, the regime of interrogations, forced listening to loud music or white noise, forced intravenous feeding, and the aforementioned interrogation methods continued.

By the fourth week, after more forced shaving, loud music, and struggles over food and drink, the interrogators leashed al-Qahtani and forced him to perform dog tricks. And "a towel was placed on the detainee's head like a burka with his face exposed and the interrogator proceeded to give the detainee dance lessons." In the fifth week, al-Qahtani was subjected to yet more crushingly similar assaults while told that his mother and sisters were whores: "At this point of the discussion I was forehead to forehead with the detainee and he stated that he would rather be beaten with an electrical wire than to have me constantly in his personal space. Also, he stated that he would rather die at my hands than to be subjected to my invasion of his personal space. He stated that this is unbearable to him, my being in his personal space." He was recorded as weeping on a number of occasions. By the sixth week, he was denied the right to pray unless he "gives something up"; he had cold water thrown at him, had been questioned continuously, had been subjected to white noise, had been forced to strip in front of women, and had been straddled by a woman interrogator. In the seventh week, the forced sleeplessness continued, as did the repetitious questioning, struggles over eating and drinking, and al-Qahtani's weeping. Four years later, agents of the Pentagon's Criminal Investigation Task Force told MSNBC that al-Qahtani could not be tried because of "what was done to him." Al-Qahtani is still held in Guantánamo.

Al-Qahtani's interrogation logs are extraordinary, not only because of the horror emerging out of the impassivity of the language of the person recording the process but also because of their very tedious banality. The use of culturally calibrated abuses, the refusal to believe that al-Qahtani may be ignorant of the requested knowledge rather than cunningly evasive about it, the bureaucratic conscientiousness with which every exercise break and lavatory trip is recorded—all are prosaically familiar and yet malevolently innovative. The interrogators treated al-Qahtani as a conniving enemy whose slow-motion mental breakdown is taken to be a performance and further proof of his familiarity with the Manchester Document, with which al-Qaeda operatives are said to be instructed in resisting interrogation. In the isolation of Guantánamo, US military intelligence officers have all the time and legal sanction in the world to do as they please to detainee 063. Al-Qahtani and others do not have access to lawyers, they are not charged with any crime, and they are held indefinitely. What the log does is to simply draw a veil on this horror and transform the process by which a man is humiliated, made to piss his pants, and nearly lose his mind into a neatly logged record of information extraction. Because the tortures do not leave physical marks on his body, his pain and suffering and the culpability of his interrogators in generating it are effaced.

In his meditation on torture, Talal Asad points to "the scrupulous concern of a liberal-democratic state with calibrating the amount of pain that is legally allowable."[102] It is this constant calibration of pain, finally, that legitimates the exercise of torture. Asad himself cites the Israeli Landau Commission, which censured "torture" but authorized "moderate physical and psychological pressure."[103] The United States in the War on Terror has taken this process of measurement of pain to its absurd conclusion. It is now well known that the memorandum authored by the Office of Legal Counsel delineating permissible interrogation techniques set the boundaries of measurable pain in this way: "physical pain amounting to torture must be equivalent in intensity to the pain accompanying serious physical injury, such as organ failure, impairment of bodily function, or even death."[104] Less well known is a subsequent memorandum written for the CIA's counsel, John Rizzo, in which the process of carefully measuring doses of pain is further described and justified. Here, "severe physical injury" is said to equate to that caused by "severe beatings with weapons such as clubs: and the burning of prisoners."[105] The memorandum further pontificates that for the procedures to be classified as torture, "such procedures must be *calculated* to produce this effect." However, the legal document goes on, because in these instances the intent of the infliction of anguish is to generate fear and get a response, rather than to cause imminent death, such procedures are considered legal.[106] The memorandum continues in the same prosaic language of legalism and bureaucracy:

Although the waterboard constitutes a threat of imminent death, prolonged mental harm must nonetheless result to violate the statutory prohibition all infliction of severe mental pain or suffering. . . . Based on your research into the use of these methods at the SERE school and consultation with others with expertise in the field of psychology and interrogation, you do not anticipate that any prolonged mental harm would result from the use of the waterboard. Indeed, you have advised us that the relief is almost immediate when the cloth is removed from the nose and mouth. In the absence of prolonged mental harm, no severe mental pain or suffering would have been inflicted, and the use of these procedures would not constitute torture within the meaning of the statute.[107]

Thus, the condition of possibility of torture is the question of intent. The document goes on to absolve the interrogator of any responsibility for inflicting torture on the basis that the interrogator lacks "requisite specific intent" if he or she "has a good faith belief that that the procedures he will apply, separately or together, would not result in prolonged mental harm."[108]

Procedures, insistence on intent rather than consequences, careful mea-surement and calibration of pain, and professionalization of the infliction of anguish at once conjugate liberal intent with military necessity.[109] Again and again, procedures—scientific, sterile, clinical—aim to modify behaviors, to distance from emotion and affect, to give meaning and reason to the admin-istration of physical and psychological violence. Again and again, calibration and measurement are made to substitute for a consideration of what it means to torture and to be tortured.

After the Abu Ghraib images came to light, there was a scramble to disavow torture, to cleanse the interrogations. As with humanization of detention con-ditions, new studies insisted on also humanizing interrogations, with many of the voices supporting these coming from inside the military itself. The product was an edited volume produced by the National Defense Intelligence College in December 2006 that examined "the science and art" of interrogations. Among its authors were psychologists, military interrogators, and experts in conflict management. The volume cautiously insists on rejecting physical violence as a means of extracting information, instead focusing on more humane methods. The two most relevant articles here are by academic experts in "negotiations" who have taught at management schools and have been ombudsmen in busi-nesses. Here, *humanization* means transforming the relationship between the interrogator and the captive into a negotiation. Even here, the power asym-metry between the two is effaced; it is positively turned on its head—one of the articles is written by an expert who has worked on "sources of power for people in negotiations who are traditionally seen 'not to have any power.'"[110] I do recognize that the document intends to politely subvert the notion that the US forces can and should torture, and it does so out of noble intentions. But I also think it is remarkable that in such a process, again, the ideas used are bureaucratic and procedural ones, here, those directly tied to business. As with valorization of Taylor in early twentieth century, today we acclaim new business concepts in negotiation and management as the solution to torture.

IMPROVING AND REEDUCATING DETAINEES

> Despotism is a legitimate mode of government in dealing
> with barbarians, provided the end be their improvement.
> *John Stuart Mill, 1859*[111]

With the capacity to hold more than 21,000 detainees, Camp
Bucca is the largest internment facility currently supporting
Operation Iraqi Freedom. Camp Bucca leaders and soldiers
are working to modify the behavior of detainees so that when
they reenter Iraqi society, they are no longer threats to the
Iraqi government and coalition forces but rather agents of
change for the future of Iraq.
Colonel James Brown, Lieutenant Colonel Erik Goepner, and
Captain James Clark, 2009[112]

Beyond more humane interrogation methods, the one element of confinement
that distinguishes liberal counterinsurgencies from their illiberal counterparts
is the will to improve in the former.[113] The programs of improvement point to
a paternalism that hopes that security is achieved not through "total and passive" obedience but rather through educating the native so that they consent
to being occupied or governed by a more enlightened force.[114] Programs of
improvement are about technical solutions to political problems; what makes
this depoliticization particularly effective is that it also acts as a mechanism of
containing rebellion and maintaining the status quo.[115] In counterinsurgency
confinement, to not submit to improvement can mark a prisoner as a "hard case."

The emergence of programs of improvement or "counterinsurgency inside
the wire" in Iraq was marked by the appointment of General Doug Stone,
already discussed in the introduction to this chapter, to reform US detention
processes. All the adulatory narratives describing Stone mention his graduate
degree from the Stanford Graduate School of Business and his success as a
businessman. Many also mention his enlightened need to "understand" the
"Islamic mind" through studying the Qur'an.[116] His agenda of reform included
segregation of "hard cases" from "moderate prisoners," provision of vocational
training, and, most important, its "true center of gravity, a moderate exegesis
of the Qur'an to encourage debate and refute extremist arguments."[117] Stone
hired sixty imams for the "religious enlightenment courses" vetted for the tilt
of their political and religious opinion, some two hundred teachers and trainers to teach literacy and vocations, and psychiatrists and counselors to monitor
the "progress" of the detainees.[118] Therapeutic approaches were advanced.[119]
Short courses were offered on "how you control anger, the oath of peace, the
sacredness of life and property."[120] Were Foucault to write his *Discipline and*

Punish for the US occupation in Iraq, the Stone era would neatly track to the disciplinary mode of confinement, with its reformist methods, its broad reach, and its training and therapeutic approach.

In addition to training, Stone set out to make use of "traditional" disciplinary structures such as tribes and families. The ostensibly tribal "Iraqi cultural operating codes, such as shame and honor and patronage" were activated to encourage detainees to improve themselves. This attachment was concretized further through the exchange of money and obligation. To be released, a detainee had to "secure a guarantor, often a tribal leader, to assume responsibility for their post-release conduct." The program was lauded by its proponents for "capitalizing" on family bonds by encouraging family visitations to constrain possible radicalism in detainees.[121] Stone himself described the other side of paternalistically encouraging family bonds: reforming detainees meant that not only the detainees themselves but also "the detainees' web of relatives, friends, and tribesmen who were directly affected by their internment and who, by some estimates, included a half-million Iraqis" could also be transformed.[122] Detention became a means of disciplining vast numbers through the familial conduit.[123] What was not mentioned is that the tribe was a concept reinvented in the process of occupation, or even more astonishingly, "prior to detention, more than 70 percent of detainees were not fastidious mosque-goers; in fact, 36 percent had never even set foot in one."[124] Thus, religion and tribe were introduced in places where they were not prominent, as a means of control and discipline.

Although the program is presented as innovative—and it may be within the context of the War on Terror—it in fact in many ways follows methods put into place in previous counterinsurgencies. I have already written about how its categorization of detainees into "reconcilable" and "irreconcilable" mirrors the French classification of Algerian detainees as "reducible" and "irreducible." There are also other similarities. For example, "social action" that included "resolving family problems resulting from detention" was at least on paper part of an attempt to reform the detention process in Algeria.[125] The same French document mentions the processes of segregation inside the camps and a long rehabilitation process that required detainees to renounce their beliefs and attend film screenings and lessons. The humaneness of such reeducation was of course more a matter of performance, as in one instance, a detainee who refused to attend an educational screening was handcuffed, beaten, and placed in solitary confinement.[126]

The British, however, were the masters of rehabilitation. The detention camps of Malaya were to be one of the sites of such programs, and their model was the British-sponsored Greek counterinsurgency against the communists in the 1940s.[127] In that earlier Greek project, held on the island of Makronisos, the prisoner had to successfully complete a series of stages to be declared reeducated:

First sign the declaration. Second fill in a questionnaire . . . and make a confession. Thirdly write three letters to the Local Police, the Nomarch of his town and the press and finally give a lecture to the remainder of the camp. . . . As the man carries out each of these stages his treatment improves. For instance on signing the declaration and making a confession he gets cigarettes. Thus a man awaiting trial receives worse treatment than his fellow prisoner if he is unwilling to provide the prosecution with the evidence for his own conviction.[128]

The process did not simply occur through the allocation of rewards for good behavior. Rather, "a certain amount of rough treatment" was considered beneficial in inducing "respect for the power of the institutions which the Communist Party is seeking to overthrow."[129] Much like Stone's program, the "redemption" was viewed as a mechanism not only to "persuade" other inmates to also redeem themselves but also to proselytize to "polluted" Greeks on the outside.[130]

The Taiping Rehabilitation Centre was established in Malaya in 1949 explicitly based on the Makronisos model. Police Interrogation Units classified detainees as "black" (irredeemable) or "grey" (open to reeducation).[131] The high commissioner of Malaya, Sir Henry Gurney, argued in 1949:

The process of isolation of the "hard core" can only be permanently successful if some alternative object of affiliation, stronger than the bandits and at the same time inspiring greater fear, can be introduced to which the floating Chinese can attach themselves.[132]

Enormous numbers of the "hard core" were deported to China, whereas for the "greys," the process of affiliation was facilitated through training and "improvement" at the Taiping Rehabilitation Centre. The center provided vocational training and literacy to the general population who had been segregated from the hard-core detainees among them. Welfare was provided to the families of the detainees who were considered moderate.[133] After rehabilitation the detainees were reintegrated with the help of the accommodationist Malayan Chinese Association.

The same method, transplanted to Kenya, produced the "pipeline" that also depended on classificatory segregation, "improvement," and the augmentation of the program of reform through the whole "community."[134] Caroline Elkins points out that even if the government had genuinely supported rehabilitation rather than summary punishment, financial and staffing constraints and the extant process of mass detention circumvented the possibility of rehabilitation.[135] In Kenya, race was much more of an issue, where even the most liberal of the white governing class could ask, "Courses in civics, training in carpentry, can they reclaim these self-condemned people?"[136] I discuss the ways in which racialization ultimately attenuates the liberal impulse in chapter 7.

MANAGEMENT AND BUREAUCRACY IN COUNTERINSURGENCY DETENTIONS

> One might want to say that the generalization of an
> "enterprise form" to *all* forms of conduct—to the conduct
> of organisations hitherto seen as being non-economic, to the
> conduct of government and to the conduct of individuals
> themselves—constitutes the essential characteristic of this
> style of government.
> *Graham Burchell, 1993*[137]

In their tour de force on the transformation of capitalism, Luc Boltanski and Eve Chiapello trace the emergence in the 1990s of a new managerial language that disavowed the Taylorist model of production, instead venerating autonomy, flexibility, "decentralization, meritocracy, and management by objective" as the new spirit of the age.[138] This new spirit co-opted the tradition of 1968 rebellions against militarized hierarchies, against bureaucracies, and against "authority" and "petty tyranny."[139] The cross-pollination of military and managerial discourse has been so far reaching that one can similarly trace such a transformation in the emergence of counterinsurgency discourse, particularly in the United States. In this discourse, rigid and unthinking military confinements are replaced by a softer, more enterprising method of incarceration in which detention is about social engineering. The emergence of this managerial narrative produces a multilayered system in which the new will to improve coexists with the proceduralism that is immanent to all bureaucracies.

What both the proceduralist and the improving notions of confinement have in common is the transformation of the political process of dissent, of the intimately embodied and therefore—as feminists have taught us—political processes of interrogation into categories without content, technical processes evacuated of political contestation, of a series of moral injunctions ossified in rules that proliferate to such an extent that they erase themselves in the act of proliferation. As Bob Komer would write, what Vietnam needed was "effective . . . public administration."[140] What matters is policy, not politics.

In both notions, data matters. Metrics have always been important to the bureaucratic ethos. They were central to Rostow's ideas about Vietnam, and they were privileged by the Coalition Provisional Authority over qualitative data, which was considered "messy, imprecise, and imperfect."[141] The French General Staff's secret service was aptly called the Statistical Section, and every Israeli counterinsurgency has also been an act of collecting data.[142] The bureaucratic spirit resided in the personnel who saw in authorized procedures a carte blanche for actions ordinarily considered beyond the pale. As one observer of the staff at Guantánamo Bay would astutely remark, "people saw themselves as doing their job, fighting the war on terror, and not questioning what they were doing and not being able to see what they were doing."[143]

We know already about the habituation, the rationality, the evacuation of emotion and affect, the extensive taxonomies bureaucracies are supposed to produce.[144] Weber has already told us about the impersonality of bureaucracy, its being a "power machine," its hording of its secrets.[145] But Weber has ignored the tension in this. A power machine is not affectless, and the hording of secrets can produce very personal forms of exercise of power.[146] As we have seen, the ostensible impersonality of procedures of interrogation has authorized the brutality of the interrogators. Perhaps a CIA officer musing on this process indicates the way in which streamlining of such torture becomes normalized most pithily: "Brutalization becomes bureaucratized. . . . I mean, were there career paths in this now? What are the criteria for evaluation and promotion? That's how bureaucracies work."[147]

The process of improving prisoners and calibrating the force they are subjected to is not innocent either. If the sweeps and screening processes are humanized, it is with an instrumental result in mind. Doug Stone, who himself invokes the centrality of his business and entrepreneurial experience, mentions the importance of "practical problem-solving and initiative," or the new spirit of the age in shaping policies toward detainees.[148] Listening to the detainees facilitates gathering of necessary data points. Training them, preaching to them, and incorporating them into invented traditions of tribalism and religious piety all permit a more hegemonic process of social engineering. Foucault has written that "the apparatuses of security . . . have the constant tendency to expand; they are centrifugal. New elements are constantly being integrated: production, psychology, behavior, the ways of doing things of producers, buyers, consumers, importers and exporters, and the world market. Security therefore involves organizing, or anyway allowing the development of ever-wider circuits."[149] The ever-wider circuits of liberal detention, the effects of "COIN inside the wire," are meant to be felt in households and streets and neighborhoods everywhere.

CHAPTER 6

FROM CONCENTRATION CAMPS OF THE BOER WAR TO PALESTINIAN ENCLAVES

The main problem in the Strip now is how to reduce the [population] density of the Strip, not that of the camps. A way must be found of moving part of the population of the Strip to other places. The second problem that requires attention is that of dismembering the Strip, for, with its population of nearly half a million, the Strip must not be allowed to remain a single political, administrative and economic unit. Soon we shall see Jewish settlements in the Strip, which will help to merge it with Israel.

Amos Haddad, 1972[1]

The retired British general Rupert Smith introduces his reflections on the utility of force by writing that "war as a battle in a field between men and machinery, war as a massive deciding event in a dispute in international affairs" no longer exists; that with the advent of nuclear weapons the paradigm of "industrial war" began its slow but decisive decline; and that today "there are no secluded battlefields" and "people in the streets and houses and fields—all the people, anywhere—are the battlefield."[2] Although the idea that population-centric warfare is a twentieth-century "paradigm shift" neatly fits a myth of progress and of humanitarianization of warfare, in fact, the idea that the population is central to warfare, that the control of the population can not only determine the outcome of the battle but also should decide the means of fighting it, has long been a component of colonial warfare and "tribal" management.

In this regard, the will to improve the native is central and requires intimate knowledge of the native.

Where colonial powers, best exemplified by the likes of Gwynn and Gallieni, have reflected on what must remain after the last bullet is fired—a population that is amenable to the idea of rule, or at least subdued enough not to rebel—a more calibrated approach to violence and an emphasis on both discursive and practical means to persuade the population become central to warfare. These two concepts, in fact, become axiomatic: first is the idea of "protection" of civilians (which often means mass removals, resettlement, and sometimes internment); second is a concurrent notion that the population as a whole will be administered, controlled, and, if need be, punished. In an article about the "deep fight" in counterinsurgencies, two US officers approvingly cite US methods in the conquest of the Philippines, where "the Army used 'attraction' and 'chastisement' in the insurgent deep areas by combining deliberate civic action such as road construction, education, and improvement of local security forces with the occupation of villages and raids against key leaders."[3]

Methods of population control have differed in settler colonial counterinsurgencies, and they have entailed expulsion, encirclement, or suppression of the indigenous inhabitants, and ultimately their expropriation. Land and territory (and emphatically not the indigenous population) have continued to be the prize in settler colonialism, and as such, violence has always been used more swiftly, punitively, and ferociously. If "improvement" has at all appeared in the settler-colonial discourse and the practice of population control, it has essentially been as a euphemism for making acquiescent and legible populations. Below, I discuss the development of mass incarceration, as well as both the technologies of punishment and the knowledge apparatus required for its functioning.

PUNISHMENT AS PROTECTION: CUBA, THE PHILIPPINES, AND SOUTH AFRICA

> I take so large a command for the purpose of thoroughly searching each ravine, valley, and mountain peak for insurgents and for food, expecting to destroy everything I find outside of

towns, all able-bodied men will be killed or captured. Old men, women, and children will be sent to towns.
Brigadier General Franklin Bell, 1901[4]

The only exception to the general principle of the binding force of the rules of warfare is in the case of reprisals, which constitute retaliation against a belligerent for illegitimate acts of warfare by the members of his armed forces or of his own nationals.
The Hague Convention, 1907

The Spanish, British, and US militaries first used concentration camps in Cuba, South Africa, and the Philippines as "protective" measures for civilian populations. These were the first instances in which the vocabulary of protection was used to effect mass incarceration of civilians, and almost immediately and inevitably, "protective" methods were reconfigured as punitive instruments.

Concentration camps were originally conceived as mechanisms for removing the civilians from a battlefield, the entirety of the countryside, thus allowing maximum firepower to the conquering European armies. In Cuba, the Spanish general Valeriano Weyler ordered his first *reconcentración* as early as his arrival in 1896, and in the course of a year he uprooted half a million Cubans from their villages and resettled them in appallingly administered camps in areas under Spanish control.[5] Although the Spanish Army did provide meager rations, "enough to prolong the suffering," more than one hundred thousand *reconcentrados* died from starvation or disease.[6] When two years later the order of *reconcentración* was revoked, the countryside had been devastated, and the *reconcentrados* were in such pitiful shape that they could not easily be deconcentrated. Weyler's original orders justified the action on the basis of the necessity of "protecting" the population, even if that meant incarcerating this population in forbidding patches of land surrounded by barbed wire and trenches.[7]

Almost concurrently, in the Boer War in South Africa, the British Lord Kitchener, fresh from his slaughter of thirty thousand Sudanese, sought a new approach to defeating the Boer guerrillas who "refused to fight a pitched battle." Kitchener decided to organize his small war on two fronts: first, flushing out the guerrillas in military drives "organized like a sporting shoot," and second, sweeping "the country bare of everything that could give sustenance to the guerrillas, not only horses, but cattle, sheep, women, and children."[8] To accomplish the latter, the British Army adopted a policy of scorched earth, destroying crops, slaughtering livestock, and looting and incinerating farms and villages. Boer civilians, given that they were of European descent, could not be put to machine gun as easily as the racialized enemies of other colonial wars. Dozens of tented concentration camps were erected to house Boer women and children, with separate concentration camps for black Africans. Not only was the civilian support for guerrillas thus removed, but also as one camp commander wrote, the camps were viewed as places for the collection of intelligence, and "many farmers latterly came in for protection and gave valuable information."[9] Here, as before, the language of protection was invoked, and the internees were designated "refugees" residing in the camps voluntarily.[10] The children were even provided education, though the intent was to inculcate the pupils with the superiority of the English language, "race," and culture.[11] Over the course of the war, nearly twenty-eight thousand Boer women and children and more than fourteen thousand black Africans perished, although the exact number of the latter is uncertain, as neither the British military nor the philanthropic women who monitored the camps were concerned with enumerating the black internees and casualties or recording their plight.[12]

In its conquest of the Philippines, after the conflagration of guerrilla warfare, the United States, which had loudly decried the Spanish *reconcentración*, issued a legal edict ordering the *reconcentración* of Filipino civilians. The order read:

In Provinces which are infested to such an extent with ladrones [bandits] that . . . it is not possible with the available police force to provide protection to such barrios, it shall be within the power of the Governor-General . . . to order that the residents of such outlying barrios be temporarily brought within stated limits of the . . . municipality, there to remain until the necessity for such order ceases to exist.[13]

The *reconcentrados* of the Philippines became means of depriving the guerrillas of rice (all of which was confiscated or destroyed by the US Army) and recruits, as well as circumscribing the movement of civilians.[14] Perhaps more significant, the measures were intended to coerce the population into not supporting the nationalist guerrillas. As one circular order clearly explained:

To combat such a population it is necessary to make the state of war as insupportable as possible; and there is no more efficacious way to accomplishing this than by keeping the minds of the people in such a state of anxiety and apprehension that living under such conditions will soon become unbearable.[15]

It is estimated that between 200,000 and 250,000 civilians perished in the US war on the Philippines, primarily from starvation and disease, although the exact number of casualties of *reconcentración* is unknown.[16] Only a few years later, the US military was to use *reconcentración* in its small wars in the Dominican Republic (interventions in 1903, 1904, and 1914; occupied by the United States from 1916 until 1925) and Nicaragua (occupied by the United States from 1912 until 1933).[17]

In these asymmetric wars, if "protection" was not a cynical euphemism for punishment, then it irrevocably became entangled with it. The simultaneity of these "protection" efforts in colonial contexts is also notable, as is the fact that they were more or less concurrent with the Hague Convention, which codified customs of warfare. At this time, to advocate brutality—and especially against adversaries who were white and of European descent, as the Boers were—was not so easy as it had been before, although of course such violence and brutality was exercised in practice, and certainly on black and brown bodies who were not considered "like us." Thus, incarceration had to be devised as a protective, rather than overtly punitive, measure for it to be acceptable.

As the twentieth century proceeded, and especially with anticolonial struggles, civilians were still concentrated and controlled in vanquished and regulated spaces, but to make this act of discipline palatable, military tactics were wedded to political agendas of development, improvement, and modernization.

"HUMANE" POPULATION CONTROL
PRECEDENTS: MALAYA AND ALGERIA

> [The New Village] is not the final objective, but affords only that measure of protection and concentration which makes good administration possible.
>
> *Sir Harold Briggs, 1951*[18]

By the time Lin Biao wrote his famous 1965 call to arms to Asian and African peoples to follow the Maoist methods of guerrilla warfare, the Maoist idea of rural encirclement had been consolidated as the target of counterinsurgency doctrines in the United States, Britain, and France.[19] Robert Thompson abstracted from peasant insurgencies an allegory of the siege of the free world by the savage peasants of the East and the South, warning that should the Vietnamese domino fall, the "Chinese strategic concept of revolutionary wars, of using the 'countryside of the world' to encircle the 'cities' (North America and Europe), would be several steps nearer fulfilment."[20] The solution on the ground level to such menace was to empty the countryside and to transform the rural areas into free-fire zones (or "black areas," as they were called in Malaya).

Seizing and grouping civilians together—whether to persuade or punish—were most clearly theorized and refined in practice in Malaya and Algeria. After the Second World War had given "concentration camps" a macabre meaning, the concentration of peoples was called by more innocuous names, which in some instances had a ring of progressive intent to them. These resettlements were called *agrovilles* (in Indochina under the French), New Villages (in Malaya), Gikuyu reservations (in Kenya), *centres de regroupement* (in Algeria), and strategic hamlets (in Vietnam). Although techniques of population control are methods of mass incarceration, they are also of social restyling; a conjugation of military tactics, systems of knowledge, and social engineering. In the words of the counterinsurgents, population control is at once "armed social science" and "armed social work."

Malaya

> In order to destroy the enemy [Briggs] is breaking up the nesting places of the pests.
> *Paul Linebarger, 1951*[21]

The Malayan counterinsurgency is often admiringly cited by Anglophone counterinsurgents as a model to be emulated, for it guaranteed the "success" of the British there.[22] The Chinese guerrilla insurrection in Malaya began in 1948 and was finally suppressed by 1960, although many of the guerrillas continued to struggle in the Malaysia-Thailand border for years to come. The guerrillas were logistically supported by Chinese "squatters"—landless peasants farming small plots on state or plantation lands. These squatters provided victuals, intelligence, hiding places, and recruits to the guerrillas who operated there.

The Briggs Plan to suppress the insurgency was devised in 1948 by Lieutenant General Harold Briggs, chief of the Imperial General Staff in Malaya. The plan called for declaration of a state of emergency, which allowed mass detention and deportation of tens—if not hundreds—of thousands of Chinese supporters to China.[23] The plan also established unity of command and placed civilian administration under the control of the military.[24] But perhaps the most important element of the plan, enthusiastically and brutally implemented by Briggs's replacement, Field Marshal Gerald Templer, was the resettlement of Chinese squatters into New Villages, and the "regrouping" of others near tin mines and rubber plantations, under a strict regime of population and food control.[25]

Even before the Malayan Emergency, provincial Malay governments had attempted to resettle squatters in other locations, as they occupied "good accessible forest under intensive management."[26] Regrouping such a large population near tin mines and rubber plantations—which the advent of the Korean War in 1950 made indispensable commodities—provided a solution to labor needs of the planters and mine owners. After resettlement, "the population of wage-earners in the NVs engaged in the rubber and tin industries rose from 25 to 53 per cent."[27] Regroupings also addressed the demands of the plantation owners for the military to deal with the laborer's "state of lawlessness" and support for the guerrillas.[28]

As a result of the emergency measures, 1.2 million people were eventually moved into New Villages and regrouping areas. Not all were Chinese, but so many were; as such, the British mobilized existing ethnic cleavages to ensure quashing of unified support for the guerrillas or for the uprooted and concentrated populations.[29] From the very beginning the main aim of the program was to remedy the "lack of administrative control" and make these populations, incarcerated as they were in their New Villages, "governable."[30] Squatters were thus forcibly uprooted, and their villages and vegetable plots were burned down. In some instances people who did not want to move were shot.[31]

The barrack-like New Villages were built in uniform rows and were surrounded by two barbed-wire fences thirty-five to forty-five feet apart, in whose interstice household vegetables could be grown under the strictest guidelines. These forbade the cultivation of tall plants that could obscure the view of the guards.[32] Villagers were expected to clear the area around the fence, forgoing wage labor to do so, and they were punished collectively if they resisted.[33] The villages were surrounded by watchtowers, had only one gate for entry and exit, and were floodlit at night and subjected to intrusive searches. The resettlement budget was primarily expended on "enough policemen and women to search most of the adult population every morning."[34] All male villagers between the ages of eighteen and fifty-five were conscripted into the security forces.[35] Residents of New Villages were often from different locations and did not know one another, thus allowing the Special Branch to infiltrate informers into the communities.[36]

"Security" and "protection" were the main aims, even as the New Villages suffered from a lack of amenities. By the end of 1952 only 8 percent of the total allocation for resettlement and regroupment was spent on services ($5.41 million).[37] Schools and clinics were added only much later, and the British brought in Christian missionaries to do it. The latter saw their job as not only social service but also evangelizing (complaining that the ethnic Malays were not so amenable to conversion).[38] When childhood education was eventually provided, it was explicitly configured to remake the Chinese into "loyal citizens," but even with schools receiving the highest education grants within the meager budget allocated to the new villages, "it was often only barely enough to meet the teacher's salary."[39] Although the promise of access to better and bigger agricultural plots had been the carrot of persuasion, such land failed to materialize, and the percentage of agriculturalists in the New Villages decreased from 60 percent to 27 percent.[40] Because of the economic devastation, a missionary wrote, "quite a number of people [are] going backwards and forwards between town and country, trying to see if hawking in the towns would make them any better-off than rubber-tapping."[41]

If the villagers failed to provide intelligence to the British, they were severely punished. Templer himself was known to appear in intransigent villages and to thunder instructions for collective punishment. Tanjong Malim was placed under twenty-two-hour curfew for nine days to force residents to inform on the guerrillas.[42] When the residents of Permatang Tinggi refused to provide intelligence, they were all sent to a detention camp.[43]

When Malaysia became independent in 1960, the British declared victory over the insurrection. They had succeeded in installing a friendly government and had prevented Malaya from becoming communist. If the counterinsurgency prevailed, it was because of massive coercion—so many millions detained, deported, resettled. Its most "persuasive" elements were almost afterthoughts: the granting of citizenship and land title to the squatters, aims for which they had been struggling in the first place. The emergency also left in place a repressive security apparatus, consolidation of ethnic boundaries, proletarianized populations, New Villages that came to be part of the landscape, and of course a dubious reputation as a successful counterinsurgency.

The absence of certain sociological and political factors that made the Malayan New Villages a "success" led to the failure of the strategic hamlets in Vietnam in the 1960s. The strategic hamlets had consciously been modeled on the New Villages, and they were enthusiastically advocated by both US academics and former British colonial administrators in Malaya, especially Robert Thompson in his new guise as the head of British Advisory Mission in Vietnam.[44] The differences between New Villages and strategic hamlets were profuse. The British allocation of certain support services to missionaries, however problematic, meant that "persuadable" residents of New Villages had eventual, if minimal, access to education and health services.[45] The Chinese Malayans concentrated in the New Villages were promised title to their land and equal citizenship (the latter of which they received shortly after independence; the former, much later). Strategic hamlets did not secure land title for those incarcerated in them and the nebulous promise of democracy and elections differed from citizenship. In Malaya, the number of the Chinese resettled in New Villages was around 1 million, but the Chinese squatters were still a minority of the population of Malaya. In Vietnam, millions of peasants were displaced into strategic hamlets. In Malaya, the Chinese could be singled out as an intransigent "racial minority" and subjected to strategies of divide and rule; such a policy could not be adopted against the Vietnamese peasants. The British had total imperial control over emergency legislation and administration; in Vietnam, the US policy makers and generals invariably and persistently lamented the inadequacy, incompetence, and ingratitude of their clients as the obstacles to the rational and scientific implementation of the hamlet program. In both, bureaucratic solutions were meant to address fundamental political grievances of the people.

Algeria

A tight, impassable perimeter is created (of barbed-wire, underbrush, various other materials), protected by a few

armed blockhouses, manned with automatic weapons
and capable of covering the whole perimeter. . . . A police
operation is undertaken immediately within the village thus
protected. . . . The inhabitants are allowed to leave the village
only by the gates, and all exits will be controlled. They are
permitted to take neither money nor supplies with them.
No one will be able to leave or enter the village by night. . . .
Inhabitants of the principal town and villages will, as we said
earlier, receive a census card, a copy of which will be sent to
the command post of the sector and district. . . . The census
card will also enable us to control individual ration cards. . . .
Even the animals will be strictly controlled. . . . In this way,
we have in our hands an important mass of people adequately
protected and controlled, and able to be used to block the
enemy offensive on all sides.

Roger Trinquier, 1961[46]

The French idea of carceral villages as a tactic of counterinsurgency had preceded New Villages. In the face of Viet Minh rebellion in Cambodia in 1946,
Captains Jacques Hogard and Andre Souyris inaugurated *agrovilles* whose intent
was first "to organize the people and to force them to side with the government
through conducting auto-defense," and second, "to regroup the population
and locate them where government surveillance would be best facilitated."[47]
The barrack-like design of the *agrovilles* facilitated both surveillance and the
movement of security forces. Half a million Cambodians (of a population of
3.78 million) were moved into these carceral spaces.[48]

The French employed the concept and practice again in 1955 Algeria. There,
in addition to putting into place other offensive measures such as the Morice
Line, walling off the border between Algeria and Tunisia, and the massive siege
and suppression of the Casbah in Algiers, rural populations were "sealed-off,
or encircled" into regroupment centers.[49] The first step of the process was a
total destruction of existing villages and nomadic habitations in areas that the
French military wanted to transform into "forbidden," or less euphemistically,
free-fire, zones.[50] A great percentage of the rural population who had not been
resettled were driven to *bidonvilles* near cities, becoming "city-dwellers without
cities" in slums without water, sewers, electricity, land, and employment.[51] The

devastation was so apparent that in 1957, guidelines were established to better locate and equip the regroupment centers, but as late as 1962, official correspondence indicated that the condition was far from improved.[52] Regroupment centers were administered by officers of the Section Administrative Spécialisée (SAS), whose primary aim was to pacify the rural population through both social and economic administration and coercion (via *harki* proxies). They were ostensibly there to improve the social and moral condition of the regrouped, providing education, "female solidarity committees," and health care, most of which was woefully inadequate.[53] The SAS officers were in charge of tactical intelligence as well as mapping the kind of social knowledge such counter-insurgencies require (many were Arabists or had worked in Morocco or had fought guerrillas in Indochina).[54] They exercised a great deal of authority in the centers, for example in preventing remittance checks received by families from relatives working in France to be cashed in toto, to prevent any money from going to the Front de Libération Nationale (FLN).[55]

By 1961, 3.5 million people, or half the rural population of Algeria, had been displaced. Pierre Bourdieu and Abdelmalek Sayad write of the "morbid geometry of symmetry, planning and logic" of barrack-like regroupment centers.[56] The regrouped population had lost their agricultural land, not only to displacement but also to curfews, military closures, and the encroachment of the expanding forbidden zones. As in Malaya, many were resettled close to European plantations; thus on the one hand they lost access to land they could cultivate for themselves, and on the other hand they became wage laborers for the *pied-noirs*.[57] Much of the grazing land had been destroyed by napalm bombing, decimating the livestock, and as the food rations barely surpassed starvation levels, what farm animals remained were once and for all slaughtered for meat.[58] Because of the proximity of the houses to one another and the constant monitoring by the military, women were forced indoors, thus severely constricting their social space.[59] Children suffered from appalling malnutrition, with one child per population of one thousand dying every two days.[60] *Le Figaro* reported in 1958 that some camps had not had olive oil or chickpeas for nearly a year, and children received one pint of milk per week.[61]

Although perhaps the starvation regime was not intentional, many of the other transformations were apparently planned. Official documents detailed how to ensure the economic viability of the camps and how to organize their collective life, legal order, and administrative requirements. Officers described the centers as "symbole des progress du bled," and their militarist geometry as modern and hygienic.[62] The mass displacement of populations to city slums was lauded as modernizing urbanization. Regroupment was said to allow "civil and military authorities to put in place the necessary structures to renew Algeria."[63] Descriptions of the squalid conditions of the camps were interpreted as enemy propaganda.

By uprooting and resettling half the rural population of Algeria, one aim was to increase the efficiency of the military in interdicting guerrillas or "food, goods, persons, and animals."[64] The concentration of the population also permitted surveillance and severance of their support to guerrillas. The effect, however, was to intensify Algerian bitterness, to redraw the map of the country, to reshape its geography and everyday spaces, and to transform the social lives and relations of its inhabitants. In contrast to the other settler-colonial counterinsurgent, Israel, the expropriation of indigenous Algerian lands had already been under way for more than a century and, like in Israel, was massively accelerated in war. Many of the tactics, punishing and devastating as they were, were repeated in both contexts, and strikingly, in both cases, settler populations would wholeheartedly support even the most drastic measures of mass incarceration. Predictably, although the US *Counterinsurgency Field Manual* refers to the rural pacification processes in Algeria glowingly—via its appropriation of David Galula as its mascot—it is strangely silent about the regroupment centers.[65]

ISRAELI AND US POPULATION CONTROL

> Israeli officials have confirmed . . . on multiple occasions that they intend to keep the Gazan economy on the brink of collapse without quite pushing it over the edge.
> *Cable from the US Embassy in Tel-Aviv, 2008*[66]

> People talk about the concrete caterpillar that grows 500 meters every night in certain parts of Baghdad or the Arizona creeper. All of this is part of efforts to control population and to provide security for people in Baghdad and in other locations.
> *General David Petraeus, 2007*[67]

The mid-twentieth-century idea of a rural menace to civilization was, in the course of time, replaced by the notion of the chaotic city in need of pacification by Military Operations on Urban Terrain.[68] The transformation happened both because of the large-scale migration of populations from the countryside to the cities and concurrent emergence of enormous slums and megacities, and because of the shift in wars that the counterinsurgents were fighting: Israelis in the dense urban fabric of Palestinian life; the Russians in Grozny; the British in the cities of Northern Ireland; the Americans in Panama City and Grenada, and later, in Iraqi towns, cities, and suburbs.[69] In the 1970s, General Kitson, who had served in all the major post–Second World War British counterinsurgencies, was already considering the adaptability of the techniques to British cities in revolt and lamented that war-fighting doctrine had not been sufficiently urbanized.[70] In 2001, the US Army's Strategic Studies Institute published an instructive edited volume to which both generals and academics contributed and that included case studies of urban warfare from Stalingrad, Saigon, Hue, Grozny and Beirut, and rather more intriguingly, Los Angeles.[71] In subsequent writing, and especially because of the media attention to the specific battles, Falluja and Gaza became models of how to do—or not to do— urban warfare.

In both Israeli and US counterinsurgency against civilians in the past few decades, unlike in Malaya or Algeria, populations have not so much been resettled as encircled in situ, through spatial restrictions and technologies of control. Of course, there is a distinct difference between the United States and Israel. Although the ultimate aim of US counterinsurgency is to withdraw the army, leaving behind a chastened and improved population and an allied or proxy regime, expansionism has been the byword of Israeli settler-colonial counterinsurgency. Hence, rather than attempt to win the loyalty of the population, Israeli military tactics have followed the political imperative for more land with fewer indigenous people on it, more expulsion and less population to control. Operationally, the biggest difference between the two is in the character of the civilian extension to the military. Although the Israeli process of counterinsurgency exists in symbiotic relations with settlers (who act as paramilitaries while maintaining their civilian status), the United States uses civilian-led Provincial Reconstruction Teams to circulate the "humanitarian" aspects of the counterinsurgency. This civilianization allows the military plausible deniability, diffuses and broadens techniques of control, and spreads culpability to the greatest number of people.

Although Israeli settler colonialism is predicated on expulsion, carceral methods are used throughout the Occupied Palestinian Territories (OPT) via encirclement and enclavization of vast terrains. These methods have also become familiar from both the kinetic and population-centric phases of US counterinsurgency in Iraq. The carceral regime includes spatial containment through walls and checkpoints, temporal coercion through closures and curfews, and extraordinarily strict and arbitrary administrative processes that at best hamper and at worst completely prohibit movement. The concentration of people within these enclaves also facilitates punitive operations.

Walls

> Someone who lives in Khan Yunis or Rafah and wants to enter Israel to work has to go through all the circles of hell in order to reach the Erez crossing point. He has to leave home at six-seven in the evening, after supper, in order to get to Erez at two-three the next morning and stand in line to wait for the foreman.
>
> *Brigadier General Zvika Fogel, 2007*[72]

Walls have been used both in urban counterinsurgencies and in the countryside not as defensive measures—keeping out the unwanted—but as offensive measures: incarcerating populations and providing a point of contact to engage guerrillas and to solidify boundaries that create or consolidate population categories (ethnicities, communities, nations). Counterinsurgency walls were used in Aden, Belfast, and Cyprus.[73] The French built the Morice Line in Algeria along its border with Tunisia, upon whose minefields and barbed-wire entanglements many FLN guerrillas were slain.[74] The Moroccan government has constructed a three-meter-high and 2,700–kilometer-long sand berm against Polisario in the Sahara.[75]

In Israel-Palestine, the Wall has a prehistory.[76] During the Arab Revolt of 1936–1937, the British mandatory powers introduced the use of security walls and watchtowers to arrest the movement of rebels across the landscape. Charles Tegart, previously of the Calcutta Police, hired Histadrut's construction firm, Solel Boneh, to erect a security fence with imported barbed wire from

Mussolini's Italy, and a substantial body of militarily trained Jewish guards to ensure the safety of the wall-builders.[77] The wall impeded the movements of ordinary civilians and limited Palestinians' access to their own farmlands. When it came to forestalling rebels, however, as one official complained, the fence "proved useless. The Arabs dragged it apart with camels."[78]

After 1967, the use of walls continued. Ariel Sharon built walls around Palestinian refugee camps in Gaza in 1970 to isolate these hubs of revolt and resistance. These were later replicated in other refugees camps in the OPT, with many having a limited number of turnstile gates, both to control the flow of the population and as a punitive measure. A gate can be closed if the refugees inside the camp are too restive or if some unknown person has committed an infraction and intelligence is needed. These early walls, like the double-barbed-wire fence of New Villages, created new geographies and provided a means of military control at the same time.

This process was accelerated on a vaster canvas as time went on. The first berms around Jerusalem were built in 1990 to physically separate it from the West Bank and to consolidate its annexation to Israel. Shortly after the Oslo Accords, the Rabin government began planning for a wall to separate Gaza from Israel. The eventual fifty-one-kilometer electrified perimeter fence had only a few entry and exit points, most famously the Erez crossing, which became a nightmarish space of transit: claustrophobic, filled with workers in an underground tunnel whose process of passing through the multiple checkpoints and entry and exits could take more than twenty-four hours. Other checkpoints, like Tufah near Al-Mawasi village in Gaza, could be closed without warning, thus completely cutting off Mawasi residents outside the enclosed enclave.[79] Thirteen electric turnstiles were constructed in the old city of Hebron in 1998 to protect the most virulent settlers of all, those invading and taking over Palestinian homes in Hebron's old city.[80] With the start of the Second Intifada, the government of Israel began new experiments in encirclement and enclavization. In 2001, the Israeli military dug a deep trench around the whole of the city of Jericho and confirmed that "Jericho was chosen as a test case since it is relatively isolated and surrounded by open territory which allowed the easy digging of the trenches."[81]

In early 2002, the sand berm around Jerusalem was replaced with cement walls and electrified fences.[82] By the end of that year, the plans for the Wall were

slowly implemented, and massive cement barriers started to appear throughout the West Bank.[83] To construct the Wall, expropriation orders were issued,
orchards and olive trees were uprooted, and homes were razed. The Wall complex would eventually consist of a series of electronic sensors, trenches, berms,
and barbed-wire entanglements with patrol roads running alongside it, with
the whole measuring sixty to one hundred meters wide in places.[84] The Wall
zone would also benefit from "special" or less restrictive rules of engagement.[85]

Given that the route of the Wall is designed to go deep inside the West
Bank, it is intended as another method for territorial expansion, but it also serves
specific counterinsurgency functions. Like a New Village, it is a mechanism for
concentration of populations, but on an enormous scale. Its operations includes
a whole series of human and technological elements that monitor the people
inside the enclaves but also allow the occupying military to test its capabilities
and weapons, experiment with new technologies, and constantly revise and
refresh "traditional" methods. For example, the electrified and touch-sensitive
fence around Gaza is monitored both by sensors and by "Bedouin trackers" in
the Israeli military who check

the sandy shoulders for footprints, signs of digging or any other suspicious change
that could indicate terror activity. But the patrols along the fence are only one part
of the system. Behind the patrol road, sometimes out of sight of the closely-guarded
border area, spotters from the IDF's Intelligence Corps keep their eyes glued to
screens monitoring the fence, and the area around it, 24 hours a day. In a task almost
exclusively performed by female soldiers, it is the spotters who are responsible for
most of the sightings along the fence, alerting tanks and infantry when they notice
suspicious movement in the area.[86]

The Wall and its technology make and reproduce gender and civilizational
hierarchies. The women soldiers of the IDF are said to be good at "spotting"
on the monitors—noncombat work suitable to the gentler sex, no doubt—and
the IDF's Bedouin soldiers are recast as the eternal nomadic trackers, with
instincts and abilities to read nature that the "modern" man (read, Israeli soldiers) does not have.

In Iraq, walls have been used to remake the lived environment. In the
earlier phases of the war, before population-centric counterinsurgency
had become fashionable, some carceral elements were already influencing

operations. After an ambush near the town of Abu-Hishma in 2003, the commander of US forces there

began to wrap the entire village in barbed wire, and closed all but one entrance and exit, which was guarded by American soldiers. Every male in the village between the ages of eighteen and sixty-five was given an identification card, and anyone who wished to enter or leave the village was required to present his ID. A curfew was installed, which sometimes conflicted with the agrarian nature of the Iraqi economy. The Iraqi citizens, not surprisingly, found this process degrading and responded with anger and hostility of their own. They compared themselves to Palestinians, who sometimes endured the same sort of indignity.[87]

Later, such carceral methods were reinterpreted as humanitarian. When in 2007, the United States began to construct three- to four-meter-high barriers around neighborhoods in Baghdad, what Petraeus had laconically called a "500 meter caterpillar," the US military spokesman reassured the Iraqis that "it's only coincidence that so many of the enclaves are Sunni."[88] The residents of the Adhamiyya neighborhood in Baghdad furiously protested the walls, and one imam astutely noted that the Wall was "the beginning of a huge plan intended to divide Baghdad ethnically and according to sect."[89] Sadr City, the site of much resistance, was entirely walled in by August 2008. The walls, which were supposed to protect the neighborhoods from sectarian bloodshed and were quaintly called "gated communities," in practice accelerated the sectarian homogenization of each neighborhood. Here, instead of expropriation, the military tactics of population control, encirclement, and enclavization were consolidating difference by dismantling social relations and unraveling the everyday fabric of life across neighborhood boundaries.[90]

Seam Zones, Security Zones, Death Zones

> When you maintain two crossings, you can play them off
> as pressures change: if you're good we will give you both of
> them, if not we will open only one.
> *Brigadier General Zvika Fogel, 2007*[91]

Another Israeli spatial carceral mechanism has been the creation of a variegated landscape of zones, entry to which is unpredictably restricted. These zones have their precedents in the black zones of Malaya, forbidden zones of Algeria, and the free-fire zones of Vietnam. Here I delineate three Israeli zones: the seam zone, special security zones, and a Gazan death zone.

The seam zone is the area of land expropriated for the Wall complex. The seam zone creeps well inside the West Bank, and in fact, several Palestinian villages and/or their farmlands are trapped therein, most significant among these the Qalqilya area villages and nine thousand acres of their farmland. In October 2003 the head of the Central Command, General Moshe Kaplinski, declared, "No person shall enter or stay in the seam area" and "a person found in the seam area shall be obligated to leave it immediately," although these restrictions do not apply to Israeli citizens or the settlers, or "persons entitled to immigrate to Israel pursuant to the Law of Return, even if they are not Israeli citizens (i.e. Jews from elsewhere in the world)."[92] Palestinians, however, are categorized into thirteen clusters: twelve different categories that do receive permits of various sorts—each with its own set of applications and required documentation—and one final category that is denied access.[93] A quarter of all applications are denied, and the appeal process is profoundly complex and differs across different permit regimes. Access is granted only through the sole gate recorded on the permit, and nighttime access requires additional permissions. Permits expire after varying periods. Donkeys, automobiles, and work vehicles may or may not be allowed in the seam zone, depending on specificities, although this is also arbitrary. Some gates allow entry by villagers for farming their lands, whereas other gates allow only merchandise to pass to and from Israel. Some gates open two or three times a day; others are closed randomly and without any previous notice. The hours of operation of the gates are erratic. More recently, privatization of some of these crossing points has meant that "civilian security guards" are in charge of some crossing points alongside or instead of soldiers or border police.[94] The dizzying complexity and arbitrariness of the measures create disorientation, confusion, and uncertainty, excellent techniques for maintaining control over civilians.

Security zones are much more familiar affairs, as wherever the Israeli military goes, security zones follow. Also called buffer zones, these are, more often than not, offensive in nature, granting the Israeli military the ability to train its guns on strategic targets such as Hizbullah strongholds and Palestinian refugee camps in Lebanon.[95] In the OPT, the entirety of the Jordan Valley has been declared a security zone, and Palestinians have been evicted from it.

Settler-only roads in the West Bank are similarly forbidden areas to Palestinians, although only informally rather than through a military edict. Although settlers can travel swiftly and conveniently on these roads from the West Bank to inside the Green Line, the Israeli military establishes checkpoints, roadblocks, and patrols to prevent Palestinians from travelling the roads. Classified "army training zones" cover up to a quarter of all land in the West Bank, which are of course strictly forbidden to Palestinians.[96]

Special security zones have also become another geographic category with their own Byzantine access rules. Special security zones are three-hundred- to four-hundred-meter-wide cordons around settlements, as measured from the outer wall of the outer ring of settlement outward. Given that the settlements are already placed in close proximity to existing Palestinian habitation, the zones often overlap with Palestinian homes, farmlands, and public spaces. These cordons were first established in 1998, but their expansion and consolidation occurred in 2005, concurrent with an uptick in the building of the Wall. The breadth of these zones, according to the Israeli military, is determined by "a balancing of time and space considerations (the need for warning to deploy troops when there is an 'infiltration'), topological consideration, minimization of the infringement on the right of property of the individual and to freedom of movement and the like."[97] The anodyne language of expertise (legal, topological, cartographic, and security) veils how the zones circumscribe Palestinian movement and access in the West Bank. Much of the land so expropriated, and often doubling the surface area of a settlement, is farmland of adjacent Palestinian villages. Because the Israeli military ostensibly claims that the lands are not expropriated but "temporarily seized," the Palestinian owners of the land should be able to access them to farm them. However, unsurprisingly, the labyrinthine permit regime is applicable here as well, with the added inconvenience of having to secure permission from the settlers themselves.[98]

Finally, in addition to the formalized regime of spatial variegation, there are the death zones of Gaza. Brigadier General Zvika Fogel, the former head of Southern Command, explained that after the Second Intifada, the Southern Command unofficially declared death zones in Gaza, where anyone entering could be shot: "We understood that in order to reduce the margin of error, we had to create areas in which anyone who entered was considered a terrorist."[99]

Searches and Sweeps

> I will demolish [houses] if it appears a good thing to do (we did 10 houses in October) but I believe a policy of searching and upsetting one quarter at a time keeps them more in suspense.
> *Brigadier Whetherall, 1939*[100]

> A Phoenix team would take the informant, put a sandbag over his head, poke out two holes so he could see, put commo wire around his neck like a long leash, and walk him through the village and say, "When we go by Nguyen's house scratch your head." Then that night Phoenix would come back, knock on the door, and say, "April Fool, motherfucker." Whoever answered the door would get wasted. As far as they were concerned whoever answered was a Communist, including family members. Sometimes they'd come back to camp with ears to prove that they killed people.
> *Lieutenant Vincent Okamoto, 2008*[101]

Of all the ways in which lives can be disrupted in counterinsurgencies, searches and sweeps are one of the most distressing, as they breach people's intimate spaces and, by using collaborators, drive wedges of suspicion into the heart of communities. In mandatory Palestine a British assistant district commissioner of Gaza wrote that the military and police

hope to terrorise the population by punitive searches and then taking of hostages so that they will help Government by bringing information. They maintain that the population will help the rebel agents rather than the Government forces and think they can change this attitude by demonstrating their power to inconvenience the population.[102]

Palestinians themselves vividly recount cordons and searches that resulted in the destruction of food carefully stored for their annual consumption, of the sale of their furniture in towns, of the expropriation and destruction of harvests and livestock, and especially of the detention of women and children under blazing summer suns for days without the provision of food or water while the searches went on (which in a few instances led to the death of the detainees).[103]

In both Malaya and Kenya such searches became part of the regime of terror in counterinsurgency, at once a method of gathering intelligence and of intimidating the population.[104] The British used hooded informants and gathered vast numbers in a public area, all too frequently in unpleasant weather conditions, while their houses, bodies, and belongings were searched and sometimes damaged. These searches and sweeps were an elementary part of the French regime of terror in Algiers, where each house in the Casbah was adorned with a secret code indicating the status of the house during the search; people were detained and houses destroyed if they were found to contain FLN leaflets, arms caches, or other suspicious materials.[105]

The search-and-destroy sweeps in Vietnam became famous not only for their lethalness but also for their utter futility. One such program was named Cedar Falls, planned and executed in January 1967, in which the village of Ben Suc was ordered "destroyed, thousands of people moved and the whole triangular area was to become a 'free fire zone.'" After the operation ended, intelligence was collected on and from the casualties, some "750 confirmed 'enemy' dead, 280 prisoners captured, 540 'ralliers' and 512 suspects detained—a total of 2082 people." The operation, however, yielded only 590 weapons, indicating the extent to which the people killed and captured had been noncombatants.[106]

For the Palestinian population of Israel under military rule between 1948 and 1966, sweeps and accompanying mass detentions were deployed both to demonstratively keep them in their place and as a means of gathering yet more Palestinians to be expelled.[107] In Gaza after 1967, Ariel Sharon ordered foot patrols throughout the neighborhoods and camps, and ordered that when bunkers and homes were to be searched, the troops were to throw in a hand grenade before entry. During these sweeps, suspect civilians who did not stop when so ordered were shot with the intent to kill.[108] Such sweeps were also the norm when Israel occupied Lebanon in 1982. The Israeli commander in control, who introduced himself as the "consultant" to the municipalities subjected to population control, ordered house-to-house searches, especially in the Palestinian refugee camps, established a pass system, and conducted widespread sweeps of men on no other basis than their demographic profile.[109] A system so perfected could prove very useful as a practice for large-scale military operations in the OPT. There, cities were invaded and encircled, all men were gathered in one location, and all houses and shops were searched.[110] The Israeli military often bans reporters from such operations.[111]

In Iraq, both before and after the regime of population-centric counterinsurgency was put into place, such searches and sweeps had become a terrifying but ordinary part of everyday US military operations. A soldier recounted:

We'd set up a perimeter around the house so nobody could go in or out, and then another team would actually make entry into the house and take everybody down and look for the guy that was supposed to be there. . . . There were a lot of failures where the person wasn't actually there. . . . I think it's kind of a, If you mess with us, we'll come in your house and do something. I think it was kind of like a deterrent.[112]

John Nagl, the guru of population-centric counterinsurgency, conducted such searches, though with that "excruciatingly fine calibration of lethal force" which has become a hallmark of counterinsurgency. Sometimes the effect was comical: Nagl "would always make a point of waving at civilians."[113] Similarly, Colonel H.-R. McMaster's pacification activities in Tal Afar, which became the blueprint for operations in the *Counterinsurgency Field Manual*, consisted of building a high berm around the city, forcing all movement through checkpoints manned with informants, and conducting door-to-door sweeps of a city of two hundred thousand people. One neighborhood was massively bombed and heavily searched because it was suspected of harboring insurgents, but no evidence of this was found.[114] Additionally, a mass sweep of men of a certain age was conducted in which a masked informant gave thumbs up or thumbs down on lines of detainees to indicate their guilt or innocence.[115] As in elsewhere in Iraq, and indeed all counterinsurgencies anywhere, "any male was fair game."[116]

Food Control

> Though Section 17, G.O. [General Order] 100, authorizes the starving of unarmed hostile belligerents, as well as armed ones, provided it leads to a speedier subjection of the enemy, it is considered neither justifiable nor desirable to permit any person to starve who has come into towns under our control seeking protection.
>
> *General Franklin Bell, 1901* [117]

> It's like a meeting with a dietician. We need to make the
> Palestinians lose weight, but not to starve to death.
> *Dov Weissglas, 2006*[118]

One of the most effective disciplinary measures in counterinsurgencies is food control, or more euphemistically, "resource control." Over time, withholding food as punishment has had to be veiled for it to be considered acceptable. In Boer War concentration camps, the use of food as prize or punishment was explicit. Women and children whose male relatives were still fighting were denied meat, fruit, vegetables, and fresh milk in their rations.[119] Starvation had been the primary cause of death of the *reconcentrados* of Cuba and the Philippines.[120]

Food control received its more innocuous name in Malaya, where it became a regular component of the regime of control in the camps, with the properties and bodies of New Villagers searched for food everyday as they left for work outside the wire, to prevent them from supplying guerrillas. One British soldier recounted, "We used to search all the buses that were going in and out, search all the cars, search all the bicycles. . . . So we had to search all the rubber cans that they carried out."[121] The effect was enormous anxiety for anyone leaving the perimeter of the village and even transformations of religious practice, as taking food to the ancestors' graves was banned.[122] Food denial operations prevented the sale of anything but precooked rice (which spoiled quickly) and the movement of hawkers and street-food vendors, often concurrent with intensified intelligence and operations.[123] Templer had on several occasions ordered the reduction of rations of rice as a punitive measure.[124] Malaya was one of the first instances in which chemical defoliation was used to destroy crops and deny food to guerrillas.[125]

Emulating the British in Malaya, but on a much grander scale, in Vietnam between 1962 and 1971, the United States used chemical defoliation to destroy rice paddies and manioc and sweet potato crops, and to deny plant cover to the guerrillas. The chemical agents used for spraying were color coded: orange-purple, blue, and white. Agent Orange was preferred above all because of its low cost and effectiveness, and although it was banned in the United States in 1970 because of its carcinogenic effects, it continued to be used in Vietnam. A RAND Corporation analyst reported that for every ton of rice denied the guerrillas, some five hundred civilians were deprived of their crop.[126] A side effect of the massive defoliation was the proliferation of rats and a commensurate rise in the number of cases of plague to 4,500–5,500 a year at the height of the herbicide spraying.[127]

In Algeria, food control entailed confiscation of entire crops of cereals by the military, which then issued ration cards to distribute the grain. The procedure was intended not only to deny guerrillas victuals but also as "an instrument of economic warfare."[128] In regroupment camps, many of which were far from supply routes, and where many of the inhabitants had lost their crops and cattle, "it was common to see pot-bellied children, young Algerians with rickets, and many others close to starvation. On one occasion, for example, the Red Cross distributed 50 pints of oil to 2,774 people in a camp where no fatty food had been distributed in over a year."[129]

The "humanitarianism" of liberal counterinsurgency should presumably rule out food denial and control. However, both Israeli and US militaries have used some variation of food (and medicine) control as punitive measures. For example, to punish the insurgency in Samarra, that city's water and electricity were cut and deliveries of food and medicine were reduced. During the 2004 Operation Vigilant Resolve, only three of sixty vehicles carrying relief supplies, food, and medicine were allowed into Falluja.[130]

In Israel's case, such food control occurs more subtly. The complete closure of Gaza—supported by Egypt at least until the fall of Husni Mubarak—with its accompanying refusal of food and medicine is intended to compel the civilian population of Gaza to topple Hamas. Food denial is carefully calculated through both bureaucratic measures and reliance on international organizations.[131] The bureaucratic mechanism for calibrating food denial is the "List of Critical Humanitarian Goods for the Population," supplemented with another list, "Foodstuffs Consumption in Gaza—Red Lines," which systematically calculates the minimum caloric intake needed by Gazans, statistically grouped by gender and age, to stay alive. Such luxuries as coriander, ham[sic], chocolate, and dried fruit have at various times been blacklisted.[132]

The complete closure of Gaza would probably have resulted in mass starvation were it not for the handouts from the United Nations and even more so the ingenious smuggling of food and medicine through transborder tunnels. The tunnels, however, have created a black market in food, denying all but the most affluent access to the broad range of goods smuggled from Egypt. An International Committee of the Red Cross report from 2009 stated that children in Gaza suffered from massive deficiencies in vitamins A and D, and iron, and that families without access to fresh food and vegetable had to rely on sugars, cereals, and oils for sustenance.[133] Israel has as a matter of course, and with great indignation, denied that any such food denial operation had been in effect. Amos Gilad, the Israeli military intelligence chief, has claimed that Palestinians did not suffer hunger, as "hunger is when people walk around with a swollen belly, collapse and die."[134]

PARSING POPULATIONS, READING CIVILIANS

> It is imperative that a scout should know the history,
> tradition, religion, social customs, and superstitions of
> whatever country or people he is called on to work in or
> among. This is almost as necessary as to know the physical
> character of the country, its climate and products.
> *Frederick Russell Burnham, 1926*[135]

The co-imbrication of knowledge and power—or intelligence and operations—has always been central to warfare. What is new about counterinsurgency is the explicit emphasis on quotidian knowledge about civilians and not tactical knowledge about combatants. Sociological, geographic, and anthropological methods are called on to lubricate the machinery of warfare, and military intelligence is expanded to incorporate the kind of "data" that is neither tactical (e.g., including the number and equipment of enemies used to shape operations) nor strategic (e.g., broad economic trends, doctrinal changes). The new form of intelligence, pieced together as in a mosaic, includes such prosaic information as the layout of spaces, kinship structures, and everyday needs of civilian populations. Mosaic intelligence, in a sense, utilizes sociological (especially demographic) and anthropological methods to construct a picture of the civilian population who are to be persuaded or coerced to support the counterinsurgent.

Population Profiles and Demography

> When you get below a median age of 20, you're talking
> about places where Islamist radicalization is taking place on a
> massive scale. The biggest radicalizer is fertility hovering at

> 6, 7[%] and masses of economically superfluous young men
> of fighting age between 15–29. . . . If a state can't control these
> young men, then someone else will. . . . Radical Islam is a way
> for the superfluous sons to enter history.
> *Martin Kramer, 2010*[136]

Demographics not only inform tactical counterinsurgency operations but also—and more perniciously—shape justificatory discourses that underpin counterinsurgency's work on civilian populations. Demography has always been a major sociopolitical indicator in settler colonialism, where population statistics are significant to the overall power of a given regime.[137] In nonsettler colonialism, censuses have drawn on demographic knowledge to reproduce colonial hierarchies and power asymmetries.[138] Demography has also become a central explanatory variable in discussions of radicalization in more recent liberal counterinsurgencies.

During the Algerian War of Independence, regroupment was justified on the basis of Algeria's "demographic crisis"; the crisis came about ostensibly because the 50 percent of the population that was younger than age twenty was also "uneducated, undernourished" and susceptible to the "vague hope of well-being" promised in "nationalist slogans."[139] On this basis, French security forces detained 40 percent of the male population of the Casbah at one time or another, regardless of culpability, and entirely according to their demographic profile.[140]

More recently, the idea of a "youth bulge" has been tied to US and European national interests. Such a population "imbalance" is evidently only ever dangerous if it emerges among a population opposed to a Euro-American policy.[141] The idea, propounded by academic demographers, was articulated by the director of the US military's Defense Intelligence Agency in a testimony to Congress, who warned about it being "a key factor in instability" and as a "global threat" and "challenge to the United States and its interests abroad."[142] As "NATO's demographer" Gunnar Heinsohn insists, the problematic populations are young men between the ages of fifteen and thirty, especially in Muslim countries.[143]

Gendered and generationally skewed demographics are often employed in planning military action. As young men are viewed as automatically useful resources for radical recruitment, women's education and job-creation programs are advocated as "necessary antidotes."[144] The counterinsurgency guru David Kilcullen has similarly argued that "coopting neutral or friendly women, through targeted social and economic programs, builds networks of enlightened self-interest that eventually undermine the insurgents. . . . Win the women, and you own the family unit. Own the family, and you take a big step forward in mobilizing the population" on the side of the counterinsurgents.[145] These ideas are operationalized in the Female Engagement Teams in Afghanistan. Their mission is described as "non-lethal targeting of the human terrain" to "enable systemic collection of information from the female population in a culturally respectful manner to facilitate building confidence with the Afghan population."[146] A press release by NATO's International Security Assistance Force (ISAF) in Afghanistan indicates that "the information they've collected has . . . led to the capture or detention of several terrorists in the area."[147] Provision of aid to women becomes a tactical act. A RAND analyst writes that "on repeated occasions, [Afghan] female patients in health clinics, thankful for care received and motivated to support the new order that provided it, have volunteered valuable tactical information to U.S. forces."[148]

If women are potential collaborators, demography becomes the basis of gendered profiling of men, where any man between the ages of fifteen or sixteen and fifty is considered a suspect and the target of this intensive, aggressive, and invasive surveillance. A US military oral history of the war in Falluja explains that "military-aged men, defined as 16 to 55, would not be permitted to leave [Falluja], but children and women certainly could leave."[149] In essence, demographics became the sole basis of the creation of suspect categories of people.

In settler-colonial contexts, demography measures the relative strength of the indigenous population.[150] In Israel, discussions of demographics often describe it as a military instrument. David Ben-Gurion himself has written, "Any Jewish woman who, as far as it depends on her, does not bring into the world at least four healthy children is shirking her duty to the nation, like a soldier who evades military service."[151] In settler-colonial counterinsurgencies, "demographic dilution techniques" define the parameters for expulsion, detention, and encirclement.[152]

After the 1967 War, although Israel did not prevent some forty-five thousand refugees from returning to their homes in the West Bank, it did exclude men between the ages of sixteen and sixty.[153] Such gendered demographic profiling has continued, where as recently as the Second Intifada, the movement of any Palestinian vehicle that contained only male passengers was banned.[154] Gaza in particular has been of grave demographic concern to Israel and its supporters overseas.[155] Martin Kramer, an Israeli scholar at Harvard, has written of the "superfluous young men" of Gaza, and he has called the birth of Palestinian children "extreme demographic armament." He has also suggested that such demographic "imbalances" can be remedied through sanctions that can "break Gaza's runaway population growth," presumably through starvation.[156]

Identity Cards and Permits

> The psychological effect of registration helps to condition
> people to believe that they are known and numbered and
> therefore less likely to get away with illegal activity.
> *Chief of intelligence of Aden Colony, 1965*[157]

To keep track of these growing populations, techniques of surveillance and measurement are needed. The ostensibly innocuous identity card has served this function since it was first used by the French mandatory powers in Syria in the 1920s, and it was borrowed by the British during the Arab Revolt of 1936–1939. On January 31, 1939, the district commissioner for Ramallah wrote:

The best way to deal with these various obligations is to go from village to village with the necessary staff and a photographer. To stay in each village until a reasonable proportion of the taxes have been collected, until every male has been photographed and presented with his identity card and his name, photograph, and history, inscribed in detail in two village registers, one for the Assistant District Commissioner and one, when the situation returns to normal, for retention in the village. The Mukhtars should also be responsible for providing complete lists of absentees from the village and the reasons for their absence.[158]

Palestinian memoirs recount raids by the British police and military and pervasive identity checks, used to discover the presence of suspicious "outsiders" in the village or even more suspicious absent male villagers who might have joined the rebel groups.[159] The British in Malaya used a system of "national" registration, which began with Chinese residents and expanded from there.[160] In Algeria, military authorities used censuses and elaborate identity-card systems to keep track of populations. David Galula recalls:

There were identity controls during every operation in addition to the controls every day on practically every road and means of access to towns. A man without a card was sure to be arrested, investigated, and perhaps kept for several days.[161]

Identity cards, ever more technologically sophisticated, have continued to be used as instruments of surveillance and control in Israel and Palestine. In the years of military administration of the Palestinian population in Israel (1948–1966), temporary residence cards were made compulsory not only to obtain work permits but also to secure one's place of residence and travel passes necessary for leaving that place, thus allowing the Israeli state and military to keep track of all Palestinian "trouble-makers."[162] Israeli identity cards list the "nationality" of the bearer, thus providing a swift and efficient means of determining to which class of citizens a person belongs. In the OPT, identity cards are color coded, and they increasingly contain biometric data used to track population movements.[163] The process of inspection itself is a mode of harassment. For example, military orders clearly delineate the number of hours that Palestinians can be held at checkpoints: four hours in one place, two in another.[164]

An elaborate palimpsest of laws and regulations is the basis of quotas for permits to travel, to build, to repair, to open a business, to graze sheep, to access one's farms, to grow fruits and vegetables. The arcane and labyrinthine process for procuring permits is a bureaucratic means to monitor and harass, with its "colossal inefficiency, unpredictability, unaccountability, conflicting orders, unpublished rules, and what seems to be a chaotic handling of administrative matters."[165]

In the US counterinsurgency in Iraq, identity cards have become the norm. As of 2007, the Automated Fingerprint System managed by US police trainers in Iraq contained 750,000 individual records, with 280,000 of those having been collected by the Ba'ath era criminal justice system. Other records are biometric data collected from the police and Ministry of Interior employees, and the employees of any agency the US "aids." The database also contains "latent" fingerprints found at crime scenes. In addition to the aforementioned database, the Iraqi Ministries of Interior, Defense, and Justice also maintain hundreds of thousands of digital fingerprint records of conscripts, employees, prison guards, detainees, and prisoners.[166]

For several years after Operation Phantom Fury in November 2004, Falluja became another site of collection of biometric data. To enter or exit the city or to move between neighborhoods, electronic identity cards (or badges) were needed. These badges listed the kinship affiliations of the bearer, their place of work and residence, and any detention history, and they contained biometric data including fingerprints and iris scans. People who had lost their badges were prevented entry into Falluja, even if their family members were still there.[167] Although the badges did not include information about religious belonging, they included such extensive mapping of kinship and familial belonging as to facilitate what Allen Feldman has called "telling," the ability to assign a given person to a given ethnic or religious community on the basis of physical markers, or in this instance badge identifiers.[168] The Biometrics Automated Toolset used in Falluja had initially been used in detention centers in Iraq, and it was extended to entire urban populations in places where population control measures were in effect.[169] The entirety of the collected data in the field—the iris-scan and fingerprint data—is eventually deposited in the Biometrics Fusion Center in West Virginia, in the United States.[170] The United States was aware of the Orwellian nature of the program, and in fact, utilized it as a form of intimidation. A poster produced by psychological operations experts in Falluja read: "We know where you are and what you are doing. Who will you trust now?"[171]

Geography and Mapping of Spaces

In addition to mapping people, spaces are also mapped in counterinsurgencies. When the emergency began in Malaya, the Land Office there began recruiting "technical survey staff and Chinese-speaking officers for field investigations" of the terrain, necessary for drawing up control measures.[172] The French used a system of *quadrillage*, of dividing a rural or urban space into a grid that can be "mopped up" and controlled one by one, in both Indochina and Algeria. The sweeps through the Casbah in Algiers were performed on the basis of such gridding.[173]

Writer Mary McCarthy's 1967 account of strategic hamlets in Vietnam also points to the centrality of mapping in the placement of such hamlets:

[Stanford University economist Eugene] Staley *perfected* the *agrovilles*. With a professor's fondness for the diagram, he divided the country into yellow zones, blue zones, red zones, the yellow zones being governmental (available for US aid), the blue dubious, and the red VC [Viet Cong]. His plan was to transfer the population, wherever movable, into Prosperity Zones, which were to contain 15,000 model hamlets, for a starter, all heavily fortified and surrounded by barbed wire. Life in them was diagrammed down to the last detail. Everyone was obliged to purchase and wear a uniform—four different color combinations, according to age and sex—and to carry two identity cards, one for moving about in the hamlet and the other for leaving it.[174]

In Palestine, an early component of the Yishuv's military education was long hikes in the countryside, which were primarily about the reading and recording of spaces, and using such records in future military activities.[175] After the establishment of the state of Israel, under article 124 of the Defence (Emergency) Regulations inherited from the British Mandate, all Palestinian villages throughout the nascent state were "divided into small pockets called 'closed areas,'. . . which no Arab could leave or enter for any reason without first obtaining a written permit from the military governor of that area."[176] Ariel Sharon writes in his memoir that to acquire "a detailed knowledge of everyday life" in Gaza, he divided the entire Strip

into small "squares," sometimes a mile by a mile, sometimes a mile by two miles, laying them out so that they divided along natural boundaries and markers. Each square was given a number, and into each square I put a squad of soldiers. "You only have one problem," I would tell them. "This one single square is your problem. It is your job to know this square inside and out, and it is your job to find and kill every terrorist in it."[177]

In all these "little squares" foliage was trimmed, and some orchards were cut down to improve the soldier's field of vision. Routes through camps were widened to ease the movement of troops and military vehicles. The excruciatingly detailed maps created through these efforts would prove useful whenever the military decided to reinvade or conduct punitive operations throughout.

The maps drawn through this process are constantly updated with geographic and human information. In testimonies collected by Breaking the Silence, "mapping" operations recur that combine the collection of information on persons and places. One soldier describes them thus:

Mapping is when you get an address from above, I don't know why, and you like go, go from house to house. You enter a house, you take IDs. I remember that you do searches in the room afterwards, and then one of the senior guys came, dumped out the closet, so you also dump out the closet. . . . [T]hen you dump-dump-dump and then leave, you move to the next house. When I was a soldier I didn't understand what it was. Afterwards, I became an officer and then I understood that mapping is basically, you collect information in order to . . . afterwards you pass it over to intelligence and the Shin Bet. It's information which, so you know who the people in the house are, how many people, who lives there. Very, very specific details about the house. And then, at some point the Shin Bet has information about the whole city, they know who is in each house, how many rooms are in the house.[178]

The *Counterinsurgency Field Manual* also refers to the utility of property ownership records and census data, used for gathering intelligence and supplemented with door-to-door collection of missing data by the soldiers.[179] That this method of gathering data—by uniformed and heavily armed combatants—is also an excellent means of intimidating the civilians is left unsaid.

Culture and Anthropology

> It is in the realm of gathering useable, real-time intelligence on an elusive enemy that the USA must make some significant headway as fast as it possibly can, and Israeli expertise in fighting Arabs and understanding their culture and motivation could be invaluable.
> *Jane's Foreign Report, 2002*[180]

> In accurately defining the contextual and cultural population of the task force battlespace, it became rapidly apparent that we needed to develop a keen understanding of demographics as well as the cultural intricacies that drive the Iraqi population.
> *Major General Peter W. Chiarelli, 2004–2005*[181]

As in colonial contexts, cultural (or social) anthropology is considered another "useful" form of knowledge in counterinsurgencies.[182] Populations are transformed into human "terrains," and the terrain's cultural and social contours must be apprehended, mapped, and instrumentalized. Because culture is conceptualized as something static, unchanging, monolithic, and hermetically sealed, such knowability is deemed not only desirable but also possible.[183]

French archival material on Algeria abounds with reports and memoranda delineating the cultural, psychological, and sociological characteristics of the Arab population.[184] Arab "personality and culture" could be rescued from inscrutability through the study of psychology and ethnography, even if rather unimaginatively, all psychological lessons essentially converged on one final cliché: that Arabs would respect the strong.[185] The French SAS in Algeria drew on the principles of the Bureaux Arabes of the nineteenth century, which were intended to possess a surplus of cultural knowledge, necessary for "direct military administration" of the population.[186] The military officers who populated the SAS were veritable amateur anthropologists who recorded not only direct military intelligence but also the kind of everyday intimate information that could create a broad ethnographic portrait, however incomplete and distorted.

The British Empire had also long drawn on anthropological knowledge. In the nineteenth century, anthropology had been a useful tool for solving thorny problems of colonial administration, as it allowed the officials to overcome native inscrutability. The International Institute of African Languages and Cultures, established in Britain in 1926, received hearty support from colonial governors, and Lord Lugard became the head of its Executive Council.[187] The Royal Anthropological Institute surveys in Southern Africa were commissioned by Lord Hailey to "provide Government with knowledge which must be the basis of administrative policy" and which would aid in the "government of subject races."[188] Such anthropological knowledge was considered apposite not in Middle East or Asia, where the study of "oriental despotism" was left to Orientalists, but in Africa, and more specifically, in countries subjected to indirect rule. It was thought that anthropology could aid in the improvement and maturation of the native.[189]

The third chapter of the *Counterinsurgency Field Manual*, dedicated to the role of intelligence, specifies the data needed for military operations, and these data include social structures, identities, and cultural norms. The manual states, "intelligence in COIN is about people."[190] The most vociferous advocate of cultural training for military personnel, Montgomery McFate, has explicitly delineated why "understanding adversary culture" matters:

using preexisting indigenous systems creates legitimacy for the actions of the occupying power, indigenous social organization (including tribal and kinship relationships) determines the structure of the insurgency, and avoiding the imposition of foreign norms will generate public cooperation.[191]

In the process, cultural intelligence has become paramount in counterinsurgencies, and anthropology is called on for its superior capacity for reading "adversary cultures."[192] This militarized anthropology is thin, instrumental, and unreflexive, but it provides useful techniques for collecting data about immutable cultures. Montgomery McFate, a founder of the Human Terrain System (HTS) program, wrote her doctoral thesis on the "cultural permanence" of conflict in Northern Ireland.[193] Her 2005 *Military Review* article on the uses of anthropology in counterinsurgency draws on her doctoral dissertation and recounts the history of this marriage of convenience from the colonial era to the present. She insists on the importance of anthropological knowledge needed to exploit sectarian divisions, "tribal" structures, "traditional authority figures," and "the divide between urban and rural."[194] Following on this, HTS couples military officers with social scientists who interview local populations, to understand not only their needs and wants but also their kinship relations, the peculiarities of their gender hierarchies, and their ways of life.[195] The HTS produces papers that make unequivocal statements about tribes and kinship structures in the Middle East and Afghanistan.[196]

Another characteristic of the use of culture in US counterinsurgency is its technologization; quantification; and domestication of vast quantities of complex, incoherent, and inconsistent data into efficient data grids. A report on "culture maps" produced by military and Human Terrain Teams in Afghanistan describes their method:

Human terrain analysts are trained to hone in on cultural facts quickly and fuse them with geospatial data to make maps that traditional analysts wouldn't normally consider. . . . They document attitudes—where a population's beliefs and values are most prevalent—and annotate where certain behaviors tend to occur or not occur. . . . One map might show the locations of all the tribes in a region. A second map of that same region might depict the known locations of all the suspected insurgents. By superimposing one over the other, an analyst might discover that the bad guys are in a single tribe.[197]

Other tools are cultural smart cards issued by the Marine Corps Intelligence Activity. These distill Iraqi "culture" into morsels, including basic linguistic needs (e.g., numbers, commands, questions) and illustration of gestures, explanations of naming, rules of etiquette, exposition of various aspects of Islamic practice, political allegiances, and notions such as honor and shame. Bewilderingly, the smart card reifies social and political attitudes across a broad range of communal groupings, most of which are described as irreconcilably hostile to one another.[198] Here again, the notion of culture is of a static national-personality type so beloved of modernization theorists. This simplistic mapping of a vast complex society is supposed to lubricate the encounter between an occupying military and the occupied.

Parsing the Category of Civilian

> I recommended the establishment of several Jewish
> settlements, Jewish "fingers," as I called them, to divide the
> Gaza district. . . . If in the future we wanted in any way to
> control this area, . . . we would need to establish a Jewish
> presence now.
> *Ariel Sharon, 1967*[199]

The effect of such detailed gathering of knowledge and the transformation of this knowledge into tactical or mosaic intelligence is to transform the category of civilian into something ambiguous, finessed, and parsed. Because this form of knowledge carves people into those who are more or less dangerous, more or less suspect, more or less in need of punishment and protection, it easily exceeds the more definitive categories of combatant and noncombatant that are the subjects of international laws of warfare.

The chief ethicist of the Israeli military rejects "the common conception of noncombatants having preference over combatants," explaining:

Israel should favor the lives of its own soldiers over the lives of the well-warned neighbors of a terrorist when it is operating in a territory that it does not effectively control, because in such territories it does not bear moral responsibility for properly separating between dangerous individuals and harmless ones, beyond warning them in an effective way. . . . The sick can wave white flags; their relatives can do it, too. The person who is afraid his home would be looted does not create by his odd behavior a reason for jeopardizing soldiers' lives. . . . The person who does not know where to go is a myth.[200]

To decide which civilian is considered a legitimate target, new means of identification become necessary. Aside from racial and gender categories, predicting future behavior and intent becomes the basis of rules of engagement. In a coauthored article, Amos Guiora—who has been a judge advocate general in the Israeli military and legal adviser to the military on Gaza—characterizes the distinction between combatants and noncombatants as obsolete and calls for new categories of civilians who are not innocent and therefore can be made objects of violence. These categories include legitimate targets (e.g., a farmer whose land is used by the Taliban to fire missiles at US forces), transitory targets (e.g., someone on his way to an act of bombing), recurrent target (e.g., someone who engages in such acts repeatedly), and permanent targets (e.g., those who are the masterminds of such acts).[201]

This casuistic reasoning vastly expands the civilians who are considered suspect and therefore legitimate targets of military action. This process of categorization parallels not only the creation of the "unlawful combatant" category but also the older continua of civilization that excluded "barbarians" and "savages" from protection and recast them as legitimate subjects of maximal violence.[202] In rejecting the "crude"—if clear—distinction between combatants and noncombatants, counterinsurgents engage with international laws of war on their own terms.[203] In the occupied zone, the practical implication of such broadening of the category of suspect civilian is the extension of a regime of terror, surveillance, and control to all.

Counterinsurgency, however, is also dependent on the militarization of counterinsurgent civilians. Some categories of militarized civilians are only technically so: hired soldiers employed by private military corporations, or paramilitary organizations in hire of civilian intelligence agencies.[204] Others are more ambiguous: the Provincial Reconstruction Teams (PRTs) in Iraq and Afghanistan clearly advertise themselves as civilian-military ventures with "developmental" remits, but their entire raison d'être is to "[work] closely with maneuver units and local government entities to ensure that shaping operations achieve their desired effects."[205] Finally, in Israel, settlers act as militarized civilians in service of Israeli small war-fighting.[206] In the remainder of this section, I focus on the PRTs and on settlers.

As the US *Counterinsurgency Field Manual* indicates, the Provincial Re-construction Teams constituted in Afghanistan first in 2001–2002 and in Iraq in 2005–2006 actually have their roots in a Vietnam War program, the Civil Operations and Revolutionary (and later, Rural) Development Support (CORDS).[207] Although CORDS has justifiably become notorious for its Phoenix Program of detention and "neutralization" of civilian supporters for the Vietnamese guerrillas, it also aimed to implement a developmental agenda, ultimately to lay the groundwork for "village security." The PRTs were devised as similar programs, intended to "pursue security sector reform, build local governance, or execute reconstruction and development."[208] In fact, as an alarmed humanitarian nongovernmental organization reported in rather circumspect language, "PRTs have an ambiguous political identity, which blurs the lines between combat and stabilization forces," and "by undertaking similar work as humanitarian agencies, there is widespread concern in the humanitarian community, and beyond, that the partisan, politically-driven identity of the military as aid-providers will be transferred to humanitarian actors."[209] As important as the "civic action" programs is the public diplomacy component of the PRT. The PRT represents the counterinsurgency war as a humanitarian effort to an outside audience, and it is supposed to show the kinder face of the occupation to the local population.

The settlers, in contrast, have a more kinetic role. From the very start, Yishuv settlements served as military instruments and means of territorial control. The mythology of the *Sabra* settlers with gun in one hand and plow in the other—in tower and stockade settlements—spoke to how the duality of the settlements was openly celebrated as an archetype of Zionism.[210] Towers and stockades were established by fanatical members of the Yishuv, who chose sites in the heart of Arab population as territorial beachheads, also intended to generate friction. They would assemble prefabricated buildings overnight, surround them with barbed wire, and set up a searchlight in a tower to illuminate the perimeter. The most symbolically significant was the settlement of Hanita, established far from any other Jewish settlements in 1938 and defended by Yitzhak Sadeh's paramilitaries and Wingate's Special Night Squads.[211] Yigal Allon, who along with Moshe Dayan was present at the establishment of Hanita, writes:

The settlement by the Yishuv of strategically placed points in areas of Palestine, such as the northern Galilee, the western Galilee and the Jordan Valley, where Jewish settlement was discouraged or prohibited, was the first major expression of the determination of the Jews of Palestine to possess the land.[212]

The process continued after the establishment of the state of Israel. Settlements were built on hilltops overlooking those Palestinian cities and villages that had not been destroyed, depopulated, or expropriated in 1948. Additionally, development towns were emplaced strategically near borders, and often populated by less "civilized" new migrants (e.g., Mizrahis). These acted as territorial buffers in case of a land invasion but also allowed maximal pegging of borders by creating facts on the ground.

In the territories occupied after 1967, the process was consolidated. Yigal Allon enthusiastically put forward his plan for the settlement of the Jordan Valley as "one of the weapons of our national revival movement."[213] As Shlomo Gazit, a former military governor of the West Bank, writes, settlements not only served the military-strategic function of capturing land, fixing borders, occupying strategic hilltops and lookouts and creating facts on the ground (as set out by Allon), their construction was also "based on the desire to punish or deter the local population through the message that acts of violent resistance would be punished by building Israeli settlements, thereby decreasing the amount of land open to discussion or bargaining."[214] Although the former functions were most observable in the West Bank, East Jerusalem, and Golan, the latter principle was primarily put into effect in Gaza. The Israeli Supreme Court has ruled that "the quotidian struggle with the terrorists" is a legitimate function of settlements in the OPT.[215]

The civilian character of settlements is crucial. Allon had astutely argued that "the integration of civilian settlements in the defense plan, especially for outlying locales and the vulnerable regions, will provide the state with permanent advance lookouts that save mobilized manpower and are able not only to warn of the start of a surprise attack from the enemy side but also to try to stop it, or at least to delay the enemy's progress until the army takes control of the situation."[216] This "civilianization" was so significant that Nahal brigades of the Israeli military would expend every effort to transform their original military camps into civilian settlements.[217] As civilian habitations, they received subsidies and support from government ministries in Israel. By the 1990s, the settlements' security function had been so formalized that settlers were forming their own reserve units and "policing" their area.[218]

Not only do the settlements save the military additional costs; they also diffuse military responsibility; remove such minimal military-legal restrictions as Israel adheres to; and in a sense, incorporate a vast apparatus of construction, planning, security—both publicly funded and privately established—into the counterinsurgency plans. Civilian (read, settler) encirclement of Palestinians is a highly effective form of control. The ostensible insecurity of settlements acts as the excuse for increase in troop presence in the Occupied Palestinian Territories. The settlements themselves become significant bargaining chips, but most important, "security settlements" nestled on the east side of the Green Line may be incorporated into Israel proper should there ever be a two-state solution, thus expanding Israel's landmass.

CONCLUSION: THE POLITICS OF SOCIAL ENGINEERING

> I'm not really all that concerned about their hearts right now. . . . We're into the behavior-modification phase. I want their minds right now. Maybe we'll get their hearts later, as we spend $100,000 on their schools and health clinics this week and another $100,000 on their schools and health clinics next week and $100,000 on their schools and health clinics the week after that. . . . Right now I just want them to stop shooting at us, stop planting I.E.D.'s. If they're not involved in these activities, they should start turning in the people who are. Whatever techniques that are legal and moral that I have to use to accomplish that, I will. Counterinsurgency is not always a pretty thing.
> *John Nagl, 2004*[219]

The encirclement, concentration, and mass incarceration of civilians are often presented as a tactical and transient military solution to a problem of (dis)order, but they become a massive project of social engineering. Population control transforms people into legible suspect populations, changes spaces into intensely surveilled battle grids, and securitizes all forms of social solidarity. The mass incarceration of civilian populations in counterinsurgencies is perhaps the most distinctive form of confinement in asymmetric warfare. It is often presented not as the tactically expedient internment of civilians but as "a great field of social experiment," as with the New Villages of Malaya, or as "a truly concentrated effort to help at least some Algerians to jump into the twentieth century."[220] It is precisely the processes of intensive "reform," cultural interventionism, and social engineering that makes these carceral programs such carriers of liberal intent.

Mass incarcerations of civilians in developmental villages have triggered an array of large-scale transformations, from a change in land tenure to acceleration in the scale and rapidity of rural to urban migration. In this process of uprooting, poor peasants have been proletarianized and introduced into a system of production of commodities. What James Scott has written about resettlement in the Malayan Emergency is also applicable to other such efforts elsewhere. He argues that the long-term effect of these efforts has been the creation of "state spaces, suitably modified for the context of a market economy" but also wholly open to long-term "direct control and discipline."[221]

An additional impact of such social engineering is to fix fluid and complex identities in ways that befit the rational order of things. Here, such technologies of knowing as biometrics not only allow for counterinsurgent forces to populate vast databases of information on people but also create crude social maps that pin people within given sectarian and religious categories. In some instances, where populations are divided by religious or ethnic lines of fissure, such methods of control solidify what are often blurry and ambiguous community boundaries, laying the foundation of (or at least exacerbating) long-term intercommunal conflict. In Malaya, the making of New Villages marked out Chinese citizens of Malaya; in Kenya, the Gikuyu population from whom the Mau Mau revolt arose were similarly distinguished. In Falluja, the electronic ID cards have mapped the population's genealogy through the detailed listing of family names. Not only are populations demarcated and circumscribed in this way, but also what is ambiguous and overlapping and complex, like familial loyalties, ends up becoming reified, simplified, problematically fixed in time. In this context, the "tribe" becomes a mode of understanding, of aggregating, groups. That is one reason for tribes emerging as so significant in both knowledge production and policy making in Afghanistan and Falluja and indeed Gaza.

Ultimately, the counterinsurgents' aim is not only to defeat the combatants but also to make the population "surrender psychologically."[222] As in Ze'ev Jabotinsky's famous iron wall, "a living people makes such enormous concessions on such fateful questions only when there is no hope left."[223] The enormity of measures of control and discipline are intended to oblige the occupied people to admit defeat and recognize their own subjugation.

Finally, and perhaps most significant, this focus on civilians erases the already-blurry boundary between tactical military actions and political transactions. In settler-colonial contexts, the erasure of this boundary is often an imperative of the survival of the regime. In other settings, this elision allows the transfer of colonial methods into asymmetric warfare across time, and it conversely becomes a conduit for translating military activity into civilian infrastructures, implicating the largest number of people in the process of domination. Hence the regimes of control that are used to ensure the sustenance of settler colonialism end up being also the same regimes of control that a modern liberal interventionist military uses in the wars in which it unpersuasively claims, "We don't want to stay." The claim is unpersuasive not because it is untrue—yes, the United States probably does not want to establish permanent structures of direct rule overseas—but because in effect, population-centric counterinsurgency produces these structures of rules, through its persistent focus on civilians.

CHAPTER 7

THE FRACTURE OF
GOOD ORDER

The Government of India . . . is patient because among other
things it knows that if the worst comes to the worst, it can
shoot anybody down. Its problem is to avoid such hateful
conclusions. It is a sedate Government tied up by the laws,
tangled about with parleys and many intimate relations; tied
up not only by the House of Commons, but by all sorts of
purely Anglo-Indian restraints varying from the grandest
conceptions of liberal magnanimity down to the most minute
obstructions and inconveniences of red tape.

Winston Churchill, 1930[1]

The purpose of power is not power itself; it is the
fundamentally liberal purpose of sustaining the key
characteristics of an orderly world. Those characteristics
include basic political stability; the idea of liberty,
pragmatically conceived; respect for property; economic
freedom; and representative government, culturally
understood. At this moment in time it is American power,
and American power only, that can serve as an organizing
principle for the worldwide expansion of a liberal civil society.

Robert Kaplan, 2003[2]

Winston Churchill served in three colonial wars at the end of the nineteenth
century and the beginning of the twentieth. These three wars trace an arc
of transformation in the specific tactics of warfare used by the metropolitan
powers to suppress rebellious natives. The Boer War also does another thing:

it shows how racializing the enemy can influence the tactics of warfare on the one hand and, perhaps more significant, the extent of metropolitan mobilization against colonial warfare on the other.

The first of these wars, fought in 1897, was a punitive expedition of the butcher-and-bolt variety in the Northwest Frontier Province of India. Here, the British forces, which included the young Churchill, "proceeded systematically, village by village, and . . . destroyed the houses, filled up the wells, blew down the towers, cut down the great shady trees, burned the crops and broke the reservoirs."[3] Where "surly" Pashtun enemies—"as degraded a race as any on the fringe of humanity: fierce as the tiger, but less cleanly; as dangerous, not so graceful"—were encountered, they were killed.[4]

In contrast, during the suppression of the Mahdiyya revolt in Sudan in 1898, the Sudanese fought frontally and were slaughtered in the tens of thousands. There, Churchill enumerated the characteristics of the enemy as "fanatical frenzy" wedded to "fatalistic apathy," which led to "improvident habits, slovenly systems of agriculture, sluggish methods of commerce, and insecurity of property."[5] Churchill described the Battle of Omdurman as the moment in which "the weapons, the methods and the fanaticism of the Middle Ages were brought by an extraordinary anachronism into dire collision with the organization and inventions of the nineteenth century."[6] The slaughter of thirty thousand rebels there was accompanied by the shooting of the wounded Sudanese combatants and by the opening of the Mahdi's tomb by General Herbert Kitchener, who carried off the Mahdi's head as a trophy.[7] In an article written about the "savage" Sudanese of Omdurman, Churchill argued that "the Laws of war do not admit the right of a beaten enemy to quarter."[8]

Given Churchill's positions in these two wars, his writing about the white Boers of South Africa is startlingly different. When taken captive by the Boers, Churchill offers nothing but praise for them:

The Boers were the most humane people where white men were concerned. Kaffirs [a derogatory name for black Africans] were a different story, but to the Boer mind the destruction of a white man's life, even in war, was a lamentable and shocking event. They were the most good-hearted enemy I have ever fought against in the four continents in which it has been my fortune to see active service.[9]

The triumphal language of conquest in the previous two campaigns is replaced here with a more regretful tone. Fundamental distinctions are made between the Boer who is made familiar and the Kaffir who is represented as indifferent to war-wrought destruction. Churchill writes of "a feeling of irritation that Kaffirs [fighting on the British side] should be allowed to fire on white [Boer] men" in "a white man's war."[10] This clear racial distinction plays a major role in the Boer War becoming a turning point in colonial warfare.

Churchill, of course, is not representative of a humane liberal ideology, even if at the time of writing these three books he was a member of the British Liberal Party and, after returning from South Africa, a parliamentary member. Although sympathetic to the Boers, he did not belong to that wing of the Liberal Party that mobilized against the war, and in fact, he accused the antiwar party of aggravating the war and held "these humanitarian gentlemen . . . responsible for the great loss of life."[11]

Nevertheless, Churchill's frank writing about these wars—he only censored his distaste of Kitchener's excesses in a heavily excised second edition of the account of the Sudanese war—indicates something about the trajectory of asymmetric warfare at the end of the nineteenth century. This transformation was by no means linear—there have been far too many asymmetric wars fought by liberal empires in the twentieth century in which the guerrilla combatants and civilians were slaughtered alike—and it was not universal (racial gradations and considerations saw to that), but it was real enough. In this chapter, I reflect on the social and political pressures that led to the "humanization" of asymmetric warfare. This humanization was reflected in techniques of warfighting itself through the ascendancy of detention—of both combatants and civilians—as an ostensibly more humane form, and as an operationally effective tactic, of warfare.

The nineteenth-century colonial wars are noteworthy for their singular brutality. Illiberal empires slaughtered indiscriminately, but even those imperial powers professing humane and liberal methods of war-fighting did not shy away from bloody suppression of the natives and annihilations of entire populations.[12] Both liberal and illiberal empires had no compunction in allowing famine and starvation, whether in war or in peace.[13] However, with the liberal empires, I argue, the conjunction of three seismic events brings about a rethinking of how war is waged as a social practice and the way the ostensibly insulated tactics of war are transformed by broader social mobilization. These seismic changes were the emergence of ferocious anticolonial struggles, which by the end of the nineteenth century had begun to articulate their demands in terms of nationalism and autonomy (concepts that owed much to the liberal tradition itself). Second, the consolidation of regulations circumscribing warfare in international treaties, laws, and institutions was also important, even if this regulatory system explicitly and self-consciously excluded the people of the periphery. Finally, anticolonial mobilization in times of colonial warfare in the metropolis itself and transnationally was a considerable factor in transforming how wars were fought, even if metropolitan mobilization itself was not always altruistic or egalitarian but rather tinged by the hierarchies of class and anxieties about the cost of imperial ventures and adventures. In most instances, these three factors worked together, mutually influencing and motivating one another: revolt in the periphery would generate solidarity in the metropolis and transnationally, the changing regulatory regime of warfare could be co-opted by those in revolt, and transnational mobilization would motivate increasing inclusion of the colonized and formerly colonized in these regulatory practices.

These factors were significant in liberal empires in particular because of the tensions inherent in liberalism itself. These tensions pitted the notion of autonomy of individuals or states against the idea of improvability of humans, where Europeans sat at the apex of civilization and the "savage" races at the subordinate end and in need of a firm guiding hand toward improvement.[14] My intent here is not to flatten the liberal project across time and space. I do recognize substantial ideological differences between how liberal societies and subjects were imagined in one context (say, France) and in another (say, Britain). Rather, I want to emphasize that regardless of the broader differences, when liberalism became embroiled in the imperial project, and when it was invoked in times of colonial war, it could—and did—affect the method of warfare in peculiar ways, through mobilization and advocacy.[15] And paradoxically, the liberal ethos was ultimately co-opted by the colonial project, providing a "softer," more acceptable patina to relations of domination.

The internal fissures within liberalism as an ideology were exacerbated by the divisions within the ranks of ruling liberals in France, the United States, and Britain. Positions taken toward empire and imperialism could not necessarily be predicted from ideologies to which the metropolitan political elites declared adherence. In the United States, some racist Southern politicians were apprehensive about imperial expansion because of the possibility of incorporation of "lesser races" into the US body politic. The Liberal Party in Britain was divided between the pro-Boers and the imperialists. Gladstone, with his reputation as the overseer of the dismembering of the empire, also supervised the colonization of Egypt in 1882.[16] In France, the liberals opposed the Viet Minh vehemently while a liberal impulse for improvement of the colonized underwrote the socialist and communist positions toward France's colonial holdings.[17]

Other factors also contributed to the move toward a more humane colonial warfare. Suppression was not only financially costly but also had costs in power and prestige; and as such, more consent-based forms of rule were more expedient. Even here, however, caution is warranted. As Wm. Roger Louis reminds us, even while the British Empire was so weak as to be unable to defend the British Isles during the First and Second World Wars, it nevertheless expended treasure and effort in suppressing nationalists in India, Egypt, and Iran. From very early on, the solution to nationalist demand was either a "quick and dirty" suppression—in which there was no intention of long-term rule—or finding administrative and legal solutions and more humane modes of war-fighting, to allow for rule over a rebellious people when the war itself was over. The most successful of these solutions was indirect rule or *politique des races*, and the incorporation of private enterprise into the business of rule, or what Louis has eloquently called "profit-sharing with business and power-sharing with indigenous elite overseas."[18]

The remainder of this chapter sketches the ways in which the emergence of international regulatory bodies, revolt in the periphery, and mobilization in the metropolises all led to the transformation of the micropolitics of asymmetric warfare and the practices of counterinsurgency.

THE REVOLTS IN THE PERIPHERY

> Power concedes nothing without a demand. It never did and
> it never will.
> *Frederick Douglass, 1857*[19]

Colonization has always had to contend with rebellion. Whether represented as economic revolt and channeled through peasant uprisings or union strikes, or explicitly declared as political and increasingly articulated through the combative languages of nationalism and socialism or communism, contestation always has affected the calculus of rule. In so doing, and precisely because all violent responses to revolts could increase the risk and expense of postconflict administration, tactics of war-fighting had to be modified to take into account the popular base of such revolt. I have already written extensively about the prescriptions for policing postconquest societies articulated by people like Gwynn and Gallieni. Here, I sketch the moments of contention in the colonies that were so decisive in shifting the terrain of warfare.

Although resistance to colonization had long made conquest a costly venture for metropolitan powers, these moments of resistance could often be dismissed as a barbarian's visceral (rather than rational) reaction to his "home" (rather than nation) being invaded, with conquest described as the inevitable march of progressive history, with concurrent improvements in agriculture and, later, industry and railways. The emergence of ideological discourses of liberation, and the "common project" of anticolonialism, at the end of the nineteenth and beginning of the twentieth century, transformed the metropolitan understanding and evaluation of the revolt in the colonies.[20]

In Africa, India, Indochina, and the Middle East, the end of the nineteenth century saw the emergence of nationalist and leftist protests.[21] In some places, the movements were anarchist (particularly at the end of the nineteenth century); in others, anticolonial nationalism or transnational "pan-" movements (pan-Arabism, pan-Islamism, pan-Africanism, and negritude) captured the imagination of the revolutionaries; in others still, versions of communism became central to anticolonial struggle.[22] Although the metropolitan policy makers saw insurgencies by "naturally high-spirited martial tribes" as the episodic and naturalized petulance of immature peoples susceptible to being absorbed or co-opted into imperial armies, liberation movements that declared their will to independence through an ideological idiom familiar to Europeans could not be so easily dismissed as so much visceral rebellion.[23] There is broad agreement that the imperialist frenzy of late nineteenth century, combined with the 1905 victory of the Japanese, an "Eastern" power, over Russia, a "Western" one, would act as catalysts for the meteoric rise of anticolonial movements. The prevalence of transnational anarchism and communism and socialism would in many instances provide the framing device for these grievances, alongside pan-Asian, pan-Islamic, and other transnational nationalisms, as well as constitutional or reformist nationalisms.[24]

Ideological revolts in the periphery took a variety of forms, but often a combination of urban protest and armed struggle posed the greatest threat to the empire. In many instances, militant strikes were considered as equally destabilizing to the imperial project as armed resistance, as they were interpreted as harbingers of nationalist anticolonialism.[25] In colonial metropolises, these visible and vocal revolts—clearly articulated in the metropolitan language and a "modern" vocabulary, sometimes invoking the very liberal idiom of the empires themselves—produced an increasing awareness of the costs of repression. A British Liberal Party official's reflection on the nationalist movements in India conveys a sense of how coercion alone could not work in 1929, and invokes the memory of the bloody Irish partition:

Unless we find room for the [Indian] national sentiment we shall start non-cooperation once more in an intensely aggravated form and suffused with the theory and practice of Leninite revolution. We shall be gradually driven towards the position which we finally had to adopt in Ireland of governing the country by a species of Black and Tannery and we shall eventually be defeated, as we were defeated in Ireland.[26]

The end of the Second World War, with the vast toll it took in blood and treasure of the colonial peoples fighting in the wars of the great powers, and with the emergence of two superpowers who sloughed off the imperial holdings of the former powers, accelerated these revolts.

It was this conjunction of armed anticolonial struggle with revolutionary ideologies that produced the modern form of guerrilla warfare. Although Mao Tse-tung's enormous victory in China popularized his systematization of guerrilla warfare, that mode of revolt had become standard long before that, and later—in Che Guevara, Ho Chi Minh, and General Giap—it was to gain a number of practitioners and theoreticians as famous as Mao himself. It was Mao's self-consciously ideological, and revolutionary, embedding of the guerrilla in the population (making the guerrilla dependent on popular support) and his decidedly political expression of military aims that have ultimately forced counterinsurgents to reconsider how to fight. As a disgruntled French officer wrote in the early 1960s (after French defeats in Indochina and Algeria):

Our planes (they have none) have the absolute mastery of the skies; our navy (they have none) controls the sea; our tanks, our armament and technical skills are

unchallenged. All this material— all this military strength— appears to be useless
. . . . What is baffling is the way we civilized people are forced to fight. We are ham-
strung by the rules of war. . . . When we appear, weapons are concealed and we get
smiles. Each village is friendly or inimical, depending on our strength. In the old
times, this too-simple trick would not work with us because the village as a whole
or some hostages were held collectively responsible for any hostile act. But the Communists have noticed that our determination has vanished. Our idealism prevents us
from using these radical remedies, which are the one and only way out unless we use
a fantastic number of soldiers.[27]

The recognition that modern forms of guerrilla warfare are political at
heart is nevertheless deflected through perverting this verity into a technical
problem. As Eqbal Ahmad astutely pointed out several decades ago, this dis-
tortion means that the political problem is immediately transformed into a
military one, and "given this preoccupation with technique, conduct of counterinsurgency is viewed as largely an exercise . . . in managerial and military
experimentation" with the methods and tactics of war-fighting.[28] The basic
political impetus for war is translated into a military problem in need of a solution. When this failure of understanding leads to counterinsurgent political
defeat in asymmetric warfare, they "feel that their particular prescriptions were
never administered in full dosage at the right intervals."[29]

Where rebels and revolutionaries seek support among civilian populations
as a necessary part of their construction of a political base, counterinsurgents
see this interaction as an instrumental move rather than a political one. This
often leads to counterinsurgent strategies that lead to victory on the battlefield and defeat in the political arena.[30] Even Henry Kissinger has conceded
in discussing Vietnam that "We fought a military war; our opponents fought
a political one. We sought physical attrition; our opponents aimed for our
psychological exhaustion. In the process, we lost sight of one of the cardinal
maxims of guerrilla warfare: the guerrilla wins if he does not lose. The conventional army loses if it does not win."[31]

Perhaps most significant, mobilization in the periphery rips open the fissures in the imperial structure itself and encourages the metropolitan powers
to seek out suppler modes of rule and warfare, capable of incorporating, rather
than alienating, the colonial peoples and instituting a form of rule that Frantz

Fanon has perceptively called "technocratic paternalism."[32] The emergence of developmentalist and modernizing discourses in counterinsurgency from Lyautey to Rostow is part of this transformation. These newer discourses introduce a more liberal image of the colonized as amenable to improvement, and in return for the provision of economic goods and Keynesianism (and later, "development"), they require acquiescence to the extant economic, political, and even military arrangements.[33] In this discourse, a limited and local democracy and a developmental program of "improvement" are viewed as sufficient means for containing revolt in the periphery.

METROPOLITAN AND GLOBAL MOBILIZATIONS

> [I write about] the peculiarly barbarous type of warfare which
> civilized Powers wage against tribes of inferior civilization.
> When I contemplate such modern heroes as Gordon, and
> Kitchener, and Roberts, I find them in alliance with slave
> dealers or Mandarins, or cutting down fruit trees, burning
> farms, concentrating women and children, protecting military
> trains with prisoners, bribing other prisoners to fight against
> their fellow countrymen. These are performances which seem
> to take us back to the bad old times. What a terrible tale
> will the recording angel have to note against England and
> Germany in South Africa, against France in Madagascar and
> Tonquin, against the United States in the Philippines, against
> Spain in Cuba, against the Dutch in the East Indies, against
> the Belgians in the Congo State.
> *F. W. Hirst, 1906*[34]

Alongside revolt in the periphery, anticolonial political contestation in the metropolises has also changed the complexion of asymmetric war-fighting.[35] Here, the groups that organized against particular wars, or against colonial wars in general, varied greatly within and across national boundaries and across time. Yet in most instances, shining a spotlight on cruelties against civilians and prisoners became a regular locus around which movements rallied. This began with the pro-Boer movement, which distinguished itself from other nineteenth century liberal anticolonial movements by its specific concentration on tactics of asymmetric warfare; and the phrase "methods of barbarism" was coined by the future Liberal prime minister Henry Campbell-Bannerman specifically to address those tactics.[36] The centrality of the concentration camps of the Boer War to the critiques of the British government were such that Alfred Milner, high commissioner for Southern Africa, lamented, "If we can get over the Concentration Camps, none of the other attacks upon us alarm me in the least."[37] Pro-Boer activism weakened support for Kitchener in the cabinet, which viewed his brutal methods of confinement as an embarrassment.[38]

The pro-Boers included a broad coalition of Liberal Party members (including David Lloyd George), socialists (although prominent Fabians like H. G. Wells and George Bernard Shaw defended the war), intellectuals (most significantly J. A. Hobson, who developed his theory of imperialism on the basis of his reading of the Boer War), and even soldiers.[39] In their work the pro-Boers were aided by philanthropist feminists, foremost among them the Liberal suffragette Emily Hobhouse, who visited the British concentration camps in South Africa and reported the wretched conditions in which incarcerated Boer women and children lived and died.[40] Hobhouse's work did not go unnoticed by the generals and the politicians; Kitchener called her "that bloody woman" and ordered her forcibly deported from South Africa, and the imperialist Joseph Chamberlain, then colonial secretary, saw her as a threat to the whole British Empire.[41] Further, the pro-Boer faction in Britain unusually had the support of many British soldiers, who for a variety of reasons, foremost among them a tory "vision of Boer yeoman culture, squeezed between bankers and blacks," opposed the war.[42]

Many of the supporters of the Boers were themselves imperialists, or at least advocates of softer forms of empire, empires of trade, or indirect rule, whereas others who supported the British assertion of control over South Africa were Fabians, or socialists, or indeed not known for a prior history of defending colonialism. What entered the calculus was not only local politics within the Liberal Party, and in Britain itself, but also considerations of who the Boer were and their designation as "white" or European, at least in the context of arguing against the war. Further, the Hague Conventions of 1899 were significant steps in consolidating international regulation of warfare, and there were voices that challenged the specific methods of fighting on the basis of the Conventions.

I discuss both these elements further below. The overall impact of the pro-Boers was not so much to stop the war but to transform the politics around and after it. Pro-Boer mobilization had the paradoxical effect of paving the way for conciliation with South Africa after the war had ended; "by showing that Englishmen were not incapable of humanitarian impulses, the pro-Boers paved the way for a self-governing South Africa to return to the imperial fold."[43]

Such domestic metropolitan mobilization became de rigueur from the beginning of the twentieth century onward and increasingly focused on specific tactics of war.[44] In Britain after the Second World War, one of the most important anticolonial groups was Fenner Brockway's Movement for Colonial Freedom (1954–1964), which became particularly associated with bringing to light the "pipeline" of detention camps and torture set up by the British to hold Mau Mau insurgents and their supporters in Kenya.[45] Labour member of Parliament Barbara Castle's visit to the detention camps of Cyprus, and her parliamentary questions about the brutality of the Kenyan concentration camps, produced allergic reactions from colonial and military officials there.[46] During the counterinsurgency war in Aden, members of Parliament's request to visit Fort Morbut was denied, and the colonial officials placed the blame for this rejection on their local proxies, who were said to be "bitterly opposed to the four MPs due to arrive here on Friday seeing the detainees. Their reason for this is that they do not consider the four persons in question to be impartial."[47] The activism of these members of Parliament was a matter not only of their own consciences but also of the increasingly anticolonial constituencies of trade unions and other activists they served.

The effect of such mobilization is starkest in Northern Ireland, where Republican exposure of the brutality of internment and torture was combined with both local and international mobilization (whether in the courts or on the streets) and met with especially adverse publicity in the United States. As a result, there was an increasing awareness that tactics of counterinsurgency there, especially as pertaining to confinement, had to be changed. The British approach at the start of the Troubles had been a brutal, wildly indiscriminate mode of internment intended to accrue "tactical advantages" to the military in what it considered a war of attrition.[48] But in response to the extraordinary reaction against internment, the policy changed to criminalization of revolt. From what was in effect a punitive and enemy-centric counterinsurgency, the

British security apparatus shifted to a paramilitary "policing" model. For this to happen, Diplock courts—enhancing powers of arrest and interrogation, shifting the burden of proof to defendants, suspending trial by jury, and broadening the admissibility of evidence—were put into place, political prisoners were stripped of their political status, and the revolt itself was depoliticized and transformed into criminal action.[49]

This transformation eventually culminated in what Kieran McEvoy has perceptively called a "managerial" system of detention, whereby "prison management is increasingly understood as a technical question rather than ideological one," and whereby confinement is "characterized by greater pragmatism in relations with paramilitary prisoners, simultaneous attempts to limit their power and influence, greater autonomy and self-confidence among prison managers and less ministerial [or political] interference."[50] To arrive there, the prisoners had to be made to acquiesce. "The quicker we break the men, the quicker we can bring in a humane system," so the logic went.[51] But the prisoners were not broken, and the humane system emerged only in response to prisoner protest, hunger strikes, and deaths.

Whereas parliamentary anticolonial politics was to some extent important in Britain, mobilization against colonial warfare in France was shaped by the peculiar place of intellectuals and artists in French public discourse. French intellectuals and activists had a history of opposition to colonialism, ranging from liberal and communist mobilization against the Rif War of 1925 to Popular Front opposition to other colonial adventures.[52] But it was the Algerian War of Independence that most starkly divided the intelligentsia and cast a spotlight on the most prevalent French tactic in Algeria: *la torture*.[53] Motivations for French activism around Algeria varied; in some quarters it was inspired by Third-Worldism, and in others by pragmatic liberal considerations about the costliness of the war in blood, treasure, and morality.[54] Some intellectuals' defense of Algerian nationalism went as far as procuring arms illegally for the Front de Libération Nationale (FLN) guerrillas.[55] Toward the end of the war, bloody demonstrations by members of the Algerian diaspora in Paris itself, long since covered up and reexposed, also caused consternation and doubt, if not among the wider public, certainly at the Élysée Palace.[56]

In the United States, domestic mobilization against the colonial conquests of the early twentieth century, and the Philippines in particular, drew together not only those opposed to the idea of empire on principle but also isolationists and even, significantly, racists, who feared that overseas expansion would result in the United States being inundated by the "lesser breeds without the Law."[57] The great majority of Southern senators were opposed to colonizing the Philippines.[58] Anti-imperialists who believed that Filipinos were capable of self-government were scarce but included W. E. B. DuBois, who famously and through the notion of a "global colour line" connected segregation in the United States to "our ownership of Porto Rico, and Hawaii, our protectorate of Cuba, and conquest of the Philippines."[59] The story of the infamous water cure inflicted by US soldiers on captives, of the murder of civilians, and of the *reconcentrados* in the Philippines, exposed by anti-imperialist activists, became the basis of a Senate investigation into the conduct of war in 1902.[60] As in the Boer War, the conduct of war and the racial question were the pivots on which the dispute for and against the war hinged.

It is important, then, to reiterate that many of the metropolitan movements were not necessarily acting through an ideological opposition to colonialism or on the basis of humanitarian principles. Nor was their support for anticolonial movements unconditional. Intra-imperial competition sometimes acted as a trigger, or at least as a context, for such movements. As Stephen Howe drily notes, "Few of those in Britain who celebrated rebels against the empires of other, rival European powers . . . extended similar sentiments to revolts against British rule."[61] E. D. Morel, whose Congo Reform Association exposed the vicious labor conditions in the Belgian Congo, was himself an admirer of Lord Lugard, the theoretician of indirect rule.[62] Many of those who opposed the Boer War were proponents of "civilisation by trade."[63] The post–Second World War French humanists who challenged French atrocities in Indochina sometimes acted on their anxiety about British influence in their spheres of control and attenuated their anticolonial stance accordingly.[64] In France, sensitivity to the French status in the world could move people to oppose French atrocities far more than the moral calculus around torture.[65] Nevertheless, these movements, especially if they had a foot in parliaments or opinion-making media, could weaken the political "will" of the metropolitan government to continue its fight.

More important still were the transnational movements that spoke to a much broader world audience and that, according to Vijay Prashad, bore the

Third World people's hopes "from localities to national capitals and onwards to the world stage. . . . The Third World project (the ideology and institutions) enabled the powerless to hold a dialogue with the powerful, and to try to hold them accountable."[66] The richness and variety of these movements is notable, organized as they were by Africans, Asians, and (North and South) Americans, some in exile in metropolitan cities, and others in world capitals. These movements proved not only places in which hope for the future of Asia and Africa was born but also where trenchant critiques of colonial practice materialized.[67] Some of the cornerstones were the First World War radical scene in New York, which included Indian nationalists in alliance with African-American and socialist American activists such as W. E. B. DuBois and John Reed; London's International African Service Bureau, which was established by such luminaries as George Padmore, C. L. R. James, and Jomo Kenyatta in response to the despoliation of Abyssinia in the 1930s; and the poets and intellectuals of negritude in Paris (who in its early years included Aimé Césaire and Léopold Senghor).[68] In the United States, African-Americans conjugated their civil rights struggle to anticolonial struggles throughout the twentieth century.[69] The 1911 Universal Races Congress was to lead to the 1928 League Against Imperialism, and these were to find their post–Second-World War counterparts in the Bandung Conference, the Tricontinental Congress, the Afro-Asian Solidarity Committee, and the African All-People's Conference.[70] These postwar institutions were vital to the struggles of Algerians for the recognition of their revolt as a War of Independence rather than an internal affair of France.[71]

This global project was crucial in focusing the world's attention on colonial atrocities, to the consternation and anxiety in the metropolitan powers. For example, when in 1950 the London-based *Eastern World* journal published an article by a Chinese author titled "The French Predicament in Vietnam"— which enumerated French atrocities and the demoralization of the French military in Indochina—the response of the Information Department of the Commonwealth Relation Office of Britain was swift and enraged:

We have had to cut down our copies of [*Eastern World*] distributed to our Far Eastern posts because in carrying out his declared policy of opening the paper to articles containing many different and often controversial opinions, [the editor] not infrequently allows the publication of extremely tendentious and biased articles such as this one.[72]

The voice and views of the "Third World" troubled the guardians of the prestige of European empires.

These Third World movements also provided metropolitan conduits to official political parties, which they then influenced to varying degrees.[73] They seismically shifted the language of power, rights, and freedom and provided a parallel channel in which narratives of might and duty spun by imperial centers could be disputed, defied, and displaced. They made spaces to celebrate decolonizing struggles; the end of (formal) empires; and the possibility of dignity, equality, and freedom. More practically, they opened the closed circle of media stories in which the self-righteousness of colonial powers went unchallenged. These transnational movements most directly influenced the methods of war-fighting through mobilizing public opinion. It is not for nothing that so much of today's counterinsurgency doctrine centers on the role of the media or that psychological and information operations are so integral to counterinsurgencies.[74] Military planners and counterinsurgency practitioners have long known that "the game [has] to be played and won rapidly for fear of opinion at home turning against it."[75]

THE EMERGENCE OF INTERNATIONAL LAWS AND TREATIES

> To suppose that the same international customs, and the same rules of international morality, can obtain between one civilized nation and another, and between civilized nations and barbarians, is a grave error, and one which no statesman can fall into.
> *John Stuart Mill, 1859*[76]

> As guerrillas are carrying on a resistance which is illegitimate and do not hold themselves bound by recognized rules of civilized warfare, they are not entitled to all the consideration shown to honourable enemies.
> *Alfred Milner, 1901*[77]

The emergence of institutions and laws that regulate warfare has also been significant in transformations in counterinsurgency practices. Even more important, anticolonial appropriation of human rights law has been a conscious and concerted attempt to make these laws and regulations—originally devised to constitute the colonial subjects and thereafter to maintain their subordinate positions—more capacious, more accountable, more universal.[78] Judith Butler has written perceptively, "The law might . . . be ruptured, forced into a rearticulation that calls into question the monotheistic force of its own unilateral operation."[79]

The outcome of this struggle is perhaps the least predictable, not just because such regulations may be applied unevenly, or because law and "invoking humanity" are as often as not the instrument of the more powerful, but because the metropolitan forces powerful enough not to fear sanction can ignore, discount, or even repudiate these laws and regulations.[80] Nevertheless, it is in the conjuncture of mobilization, revolt, lawmaking, and legal contestation that militaries have to reconsider their tactics, sometimes to facilitate the operation of war itself. As a legal scholar advised soldiers on adherence to law, "only force which can imagine itself to be seen can be enduring. An act of violence one can disclose and be proud of is ultimately stronger, more *legitimate*."[81]

In some ways, the Boer War is again the beginning of the transformation. The first Hague Convention, assembled to address the ravages of intra-European warfare, is the first moment at which attempts were made to regulate tactics of warfare. The Convention, thus, specifically addressed European warfare, but there was an awareness that its jurisdiction could be expanded. As such, the British, for example, reserved their signature on the ban on the use of expanding (or dumdum) bullets, claiming that "experience had shown it was necessary to use expanding bullets against African and Asiatic tribes."[82] The simultaneity of the Boer War and the first Hague Convention resulted in some consideration within the British Government of the "legality" of its methods of fighting. The Liberal imperialist, Herbert Asquith, claimed in the Parliament:

These laws were framed not with a view to any such contest as now going on. They were in the main, and in their normal operation adapted to a state of things where you have a considerable number of men . . . arrayed against each other, acting upon some definite plan of campaign, moving in more or less organised bodies, and subject in greater or less degree to some kind of central control. That description does not in the least correspond with what is now going on in South Africa.[83]

Although various military officers were in agreement, there was dissent in the government ranks. For example, the head of British intelligence, who himself had defended the use of dumdum bullets, wrote:

Although the Boers have not acceded formally to the Hague Conventions and its provisions are not binding technically in a war between a contracting and a non-contracting power . . . [for] practical purposes . . . the Hague Conventions may properly be applied to by both sides.[84]

The debate focused not only on the civilizational status of the enemy but also on the fact that the metropolitan claim to title over the colonies would render the war a police action or civil war and as such outside the jurisdiction of the Hague Conventions.[85]

Many of the same arguments were proffered again during the Geneva Conventions, although, after the Second World War, the language of civilization, though not wholly absent, was no longer broadly accepted as a classificatory mechanism. The actual proceedings of these Conventions reveal the anxiety of the much-weakened metropolitan powers about how the regulatory apparatus of the Conventions could tie their hands in their colonial holdings. The British in particular were cantankerous about the International Committee of the Red Cross (ICRC) monitoring of atrocities committed in internal wars.[86] In the end, despite all the limitations of the Conventions in addressing the rights of the guerrillas or civilians in guerrilla warfare, the European powers and the new superpowers agreed to certain provisions that "would make prospective military occupiers wonder whether they had not given away too much."[87] In the years immediately following the signing of the 1949 Geneva Conventions, the British and the French did not necessarily see them as applicable to the colonial wars being fought in Asia and Africa. Huw Bennet has shown that the British had to be dragged to the 1949 Conventions kicking and screaming, as they were concerned that the Conventions would bind their hands in their counterinsurgency in Malaya. Although in the end they signed the Conventions, they implied that common article 3, which protected noncombatants, would be in effect only should the sovereign so decide.[88] The British did not

ratify the Conventions until 1957, rendering them immaterial to the wars in
Malaya, Cyprus, or Kenya.[89] Similarly, although the French ratified the Conventions in 1951, they did not view the North African revolts of the 1950s as the
kind of conflict that could fall within the jurisdiction of the Conventions, thus
resisting ICRC visits to Tunisia in 1953 and authorizing ICRC prison visits to
Algeria only in 1955.[90] Only in 1961 did France recognize the applicability of
the Conventions to prisoners in the internment camps in response to the Algerian FLN's long legal struggle to be recognized as legitimate belligerents.[91]

Only after nearly all former colonies were already independent, recognition
of guerrillas in the Conventions was mooted. This occurred with the partially
acceded and ratified Additional Protocols of 1977, which at last, and against
massive opposition of the United States in particular, expanded the protection offered civilians under the law, and recognized guerrillas as legitimate
combatants.[92] As I have already written in chapter 3, many in the US establishment circa 1977 saw the Protocols as "pro-terrorist," or as a Soviet plot to
"privilege guerrillas and deprive soldiers."[93] Many of the same people sought
to "modernize" or "update" the Geneva Conventions for a new age of imperial
conquest in the twenty-first century, by essentially gutting it of the hard-won
protections of 1977 and making further allowances for and granting greater
privileges to the imperial militaries of our age.[94]

Aside from the Geneva Conventions, the European Convention on Human Rights could serve as another regulatory mechanism in warfare. This the
British ratified the in 1951 and the French only in 1974, long after France had
been divested of its colonial holdings in Indochina and North Africa.[95] The
French delegates at the drafting committee for the Convention, surprisingly,
had supported the application of the Convention to colonial holdings of the
European powers (perhaps because many future postcolonial officials were
among the delegates, including Léopold Senghor, who later became president
of Senegal). But the fact that France did not ratify the Convention until so
late rendered its application to the colonies moot.[96]

The Colonial Office in Britain had fought over the extent to which the
European Convention could or would apply to the colonies, and the argument
put forward was that the colonies had not yet reached the stage of development to allow them to enjoy the same set of rights as the Europeans.[97] In his
magisterial history of the adoption of the Convention, Brian Simpson argues

that, in this regard, only massive anticolonial mobilization forced Colonial Office bureaucrats to repeatedly claim, "however insincerely, to be wholly in support of the international protection of human rights."[98] To forestall such universalization of rights, a series of maneuvers were suggested by the Colonial Office, including partial acceptance or adaptation of the Convention in the colonies, only allowing contracting states to be complainants under the Convention, and a series of administrative safeguards that could kill any complaints in committee and before it could ever reach adjudication.[99] In October 1953, the British government extended the Convention to forty-two colonies, although it consistently lodged reservations to suspend the law everywhere it fought a counterinsurgency.[100]

In 1956 and 1957, the Greek government used the provision that prevented individuals petitioning the Council of Europe but reserved this right for the states to lodge two cases on behalf of Cypriot Greek detainees.[101] Although in the end the cases were decided in terms favorable to Britain, they left their mark. The fascinating account Simpson gives of the cases (some of the contents of which remain classified even today) indicates the extent to which the British accession to the Convention was transformed into a legal instrument of struggle by the colonized. Colonial officers themselves recognized as much, lamenting that, "however rationally we might present it . . . [the Convention] would expose us to attacks by liberals everywhere. . . . [I]t would certainly be a propaganda gift to the Communists."[102] In another document, they complained:

When we extended the Convention to all our Colonies except Hong Kong, the Aden Protectorate and Brunei, we presumably did not envisage the possibility that we might be opening the way to hostile attacks on our administration in these colonies and even to the intervention in the colonies of investigating commissions.[103]

Despite recognition of their own hypocrisy in this regard, the British derogated the Convention in Aden (1960), Cyprus (1955), British Guiana (1954), Kenya (1954), Malaya (1954), Nyasaland (later Malawi, 1959), Uganda (1954), Northern Rhodesia (later Zambia, 1957), Singapore (1954), Zanzibar (1961), and finally in Northern Ireland (1969, and repeatedly thereafter), precisely because of its potential for appropriation by the colonial rebels.[104] Simpson's circumspect assessment is that the effect of the Convention was far from direct, but "it came to be accepted by a significant sector of British public opinion that the repression of colonial insurrections more or less inevitably led to violations of human rights and illiberal actions by colonial governments."[105]

The 1978 case brought by the Republic of Ireland against the United Kingdom in the European Court of Human Rights perfectly encapsulates the tensions in the utility of international law for struggle against colonial warfare. Here, the Irish subjected to abuse in British detention had recourse to the Convention because the Republic of Ireland—itself a European state—brought the case to court. The ruling in the case was ambiguous. On the one hand, the court ruled that although the "Five Techniques"—wall standing, deprivation of food and drink, deprivation of sleep, hooding, and subjection to noise—do not constitute torture, they do amount "to a practice of inhuman and degrading punishment."[106] Ironically, the court was ruling on the measurability and quantity of pain, declaring a certain amount permissible. On the other hand, the ruling on specific military doctrines and tactics did recognize the claim of insurgents in regard to counterinsurgent practices.

In his powerful polemic on colonial sovereign power, Achilles Mbembe writes, "The sovereign right to kill is not subject to any rule in the colonies. In the colonies, the sovereign might kill at any time or in any manner. Colonial warfare is not subject to legal and institutional rules. It is not a legally codified activity."[107] Although this has been true of many times and places, the evidence presented here demonstrates that Mbembe's totalizing assumption can be challenged—and not always in predictable ways. Although in a great many colonial instances, the law has been nothing but the despoiled handmaiden of power, the very fact that liberal colonial powers have acutely felt the necessity of asserting their lawfulness says something about this malleability of the law.

THE PERSISTENCE OF RACIALIZATION

> How shall they, in the twinkling of an eye, be exalted to the
> heights of self-governing peoples which required a thousand
> years for us to reach, Anglo-Saxon though we are?
> *Senator Albert Beveridge, 1900*[108]

There is no doubt that the lack of adversary cultural knowledge can have grave consequences strategically,

> operationally, and tactically. At a strategic level, certain
> policymakers within the Bush administration apparently
> misunderstood the tribal nature of Iraqi culture and society.
> They assumed that the civilian apparatus of the government
> would remain intact after the regime was decapitated by an
> aerial strike, an internal coup, or a military defeat. In fact,
> when the United States cut off the hydra's Ba'thist head,
> power reverted to its most basic and stable form—the tribe.
> *Montgomery McFate, 2005*[109]

In the transformative process whereby social mobilization and regulatory regimes influence the tactics of war-fighting, another factor is hugely important,
and its effect can be paradoxical, as well as predictable. This factor is the racialization of the enemy in a colonial context.[110] The "hierarchy of races and
civilizations" has been used to justify conquest, to epistemologically construe
some peoples as outside history, to allow for differential application of ostensibly universal laws, to fundamentally produce racial states, and to discipline
the intimate.[111]

This hierarchy of races was always construed as a moral one in which the
dignity of the empire was vested in the education and uplift of the native. In
the nineteenth century racialization was almost always translated into something virtuous and good, a will to protect. The hagiographer of empire, Rudyard Kipling, eulogized the "White Man's burden" to raise the civilizational
status of these "new-caught sullen people, Half devil and half child."[112] A contemporary of Cecil Rhodes argued, "To treat the natives like children, to let
them have what is good for them, and forbid to them what is bad for them, is
Mr. Rhodes's policy, to which is joined legislation . . . the influence of which is
carefully designed to be educative as well as protective."[113] In the French empire,
Saint-Simonian socialists saw their vocation in Algeria as a missionary effort
for the "pacification" of the natives, to lift them out of their savage torpor.[114]

Although the story of race in empire is well told, the paradoxical effect of
racialization on colonial warfare bears further examination. This particular
paradox lies in how the taxonomy of race creates an index of counterinsurgency
practice as applied to different categories of people, racialized in particularly
ways. In this regard, the two major liberal counterinsurgencies that bookend

the twentieth century— the Boer War and the Northern Ireland Troubles—
are instructive for opposite reasons. In both wars, the enemy's whiteness
had a direct effect on the methods used by the British military to counter the
enemy.

Although Kitchener considered the Boers "uncivilized Afrikaner savages
with only a thin white veneer" for the purposes of warfare, the pro-Boers in
the metropolis insisted on the Boer's whiteness.[115] This opinion was reflected
in Callwell's handbook of asymmetric warfare, in which he claimed that the
"Boers presented all the features of rebels in a civilized country except that they
were inured from youth to hardship, and that they were all mounted."[116] As I
mentioned in the opening of this chapter, Churchill himself saw the Boers as
a worthy enemy because of their civilizational status. If the Sudanese or the
Pashtun were irrational remnants of inferior histories or no histories at all, to
be wiped away by civilization and science, the archetypal Boer was a "citizen
soldier, called reluctant, yet not unwilling, from the quiet life of his farm to
fight bravely in defence of the soil on which he lived, which his fathers had
won by all manner of suffering and peril."[117] In the nineteenth-century racializing mind, whereas the barbarian fought on the basis of an unquenchable
natural instinct for war, the Boer battled for political self-determination. In
both instances, Churchill recognized the brutalities of the British invasion and
occupation; but he deemed the suppression of the brown and black people necessary—because they were prepolitical and therefore lesser humans, whereas
the Boers' defeat was an unfortunate by-product of necessary politics.

Callwell and Churchill were not the only British officers to recognize
their Boer enemies as civilized and politically motivated equals. The Boers'
whiteness authorized the support they received from the pro-Boers. The British pro-Boers described the Boers as a "brave race" who, in their manliness
and fidelity to a yeoman culture, were caught between gold-digging British
Jewish financiers in Johannesburg and primitive "Kaffirs."[118] The hero of the
concentration camps, Emily Hobhouse, also adopted a language of racial difference to defend her powerless white charges and warned "that considering
the growing impertinence of the Kaffirs, seeing the white women thus humiliated, every care shall be taken not to put them in places of authority."[119] Her
own ministrations to civilian detainees more or less ignored the black concentration camps, where the rations were half that of the white camps, even

as black internees were forced into heavy manual labor.[120] Other pro-Boers admonished the government that, "by the conflict between the two races of the whites . . . you will have . . . stirred up a spirit of restlessness among the native population of South Africa, and, considering their vast superiority in number and the horrors of war between the white races and these Kaffirs, you cannot exaggerate the mischief of such proceedings as that."[121] In the end, the whiteness of the Boers meant a reconsideration of the strategies and tactics of warfare. While the Boers' land was ravaged and their civilians interned, those civilians were not put to work the way blacks were, they were the focus of antiwar mobilization in London, and they were ultimately conciliated into the British Empire.[122]

In Northern Ireland, the whiteness of the Irish worked in a different way. Here, the treatment meted to "fellow citizens" shocked the conscience in a way that assaults on people in faraway places had not.[123] An officer who had served in both Aden and Borneo complained that counterinsurgency in those places "was easy because they were dealing with a person of a different colour." At the same time, he exoticized the Irish because of their Catholicism and considered them "Mediterranean in their temperament: terribly volatile, a woman-dominated society."[124]

This racial elision becomes even starker in the writings of Brigadier Kitson, who had gained his counterinsurgency experience in so many other colonial contexts. Kitson saw Northern Ireland as a model for policing contention in Britain itself and modes of counterinsurgency as legitimate instruments of control in British cities against strikers, student demonstrators and other nonviolent protesters.[125] In this sense, the Irish become proper colonial subjects rather than citizens, more on par with the peoples of Africa and Asia and less equivalent in rights to other Europeans. The suppression of the Irish colonial subject acted as a laboratory of actions taken on intransigents in Britain itself. Ultimately, as the Irish poet Seamus Deane wrote in 1983, where direct biological race failed to deliver in Northern Ireland, the old dichotomies predicated on civilization were reanimated there:

The language of politics in Ireland and England, especially when the subject is Northern Ireland, is still dominated by the putative division between barbarism and civilization. Civilization still defines itself as a system of law; and it defines barbarism (which by the nature of the distinction cannot be capable of defining itself) as a chaos of arbitrary wills, an Hobbesian state of nature.[126]

The Northern Irish counterinsurgency also displays both the dynamism of the idea of difference and the process of racialization. There, racialization was transformed from a biological method of classification to one based on "culture," "ethnicity" (where religion, be it Catholicism or Islam, is attached thereto), or "stages of development." Recent scholarship has shown that after the Second World War a fear of revolt in the periphery on the one hand, and an embarrassment over the racialized language and practice of Fascists and Nazis on the other hand, led to a restatement of the British colonial policy in nonracial terms. Further, with the Cold War, the rise of Third-Worldist movements, and an awareness of how race could be a factor used to name and shame in international settings, colonialism's justificatory narratives had to be adjusted.[127] As such, the ostensible rightness of British colonialism was made to hinge on ideas of economic and political development in the colonies on the one hand and protection of minority groups on the other hand.[128]

This process in Britain was concurrent with similar processes in the United States—with the emergence of modernization theory—and in France.[129] Everywhere, past intimations of racial inferiority gave way to a language of developmental backwardness. French humanists argued that "overseas people were not sufficiently mature for independence," and even an astute a thinker as Maurice Merleau-Ponty opposed Algerian independence on the basis of Arab "underdevelopment."[130]

Biological notions of difference could also be translated into cultural difference.[131] Cultures were ranked according to an exclusive set of criteria that in a predetermined fashion placed European and American cultures on one end of the spectrum and the colonized on the other end. Cultural difference was used to provide a basis for counterinsurgency action. As early as 1926, a US Army captain wrote about the French bombardment of Damascus:

To a fanatical savage, a bomb dropped out of the sky on the sacred temple of his omnipotent God is a sign and a symbol that that God has withdrawn his favor. A shell smashing into a putative inaccessible village stronghold is an indication of the relentless energy and superior skill of the well-equipped civilized foe. Instead of merely rousing his wrath, these acts are much more likely to make him raise his hands in surrender. If a few "non-combatants"—if there be any such in native folk of this character—are killed, the loss of life is probably far less than might have been sustained in prolonged operations of a more polite character.[132]

The British similarly justified their aerial bombardment of Iraq around the same time by the "moral effect" of such measures on enemies who simply did not care about life.[133] If the enemy does not care about his life, why should the counterinsurgent force? This same logic lies at the heart of Israeli Prime Minister Golda Meir's famous quip, "We can forgive the Arabs for killing our children. We cannot forgive them for forcing us to kill their children."

In chapter 6, I demonstrated how a "culture" discourse permeates the language of counterinsurgency and is fully materialized in the Human Terrain System. But there are other, cruder forms of culture thinking. For example, the unofficial hagiographer of the US Marine Corps, Bing West, who began his career writing about US small-unit counterinsurgency in Vietnam, describes Fallujans as "strange, sullen, wild-eyed," and prone to thievery, thuggery, and brutality.[134] They are imagined as prepolitical and are conveniently compared to "the American Indian tribes in the nineteenth century, sharing a hostility toward the settlers while launching raids at different time for different reasons."[135] These reasons are not legible or logical to counterinsurgents. For ultimately what is on display here is disbelief at the obduracy of a savage people ungrateful for the gift of civilization brought to them by a better breed of men.

CONCLUSION

> Freedom is nothing else but the correlative of the deployment
> of apparatuses of security.
> *Michel Foucault, 2007*[136]

The story I have told in this chapter does not trace an arc of progress from brutal slaughter to gentle confinement. Rather, it is a fitful narrative in which the unruly and unpredictable conjugation of organized protest, reputational concerns, tensions inherent in legal claims, and a liberal will to improve have been translated into practices of incarceration in one place, interrogation in another, executive action in one setting, and a juridical system—however rigged—in another. Even when all factors are present, as they were during

the US War on Terror, mass slaughter in the guise of enemy-centric counterinsurgency or counterterrorism—from the air or on the ground—would
persist. Much of the time, the changes to which the militaries professed were
rhetorical. At other times, they were pragmatic responses necessitated by the
demands for accountability.

The most significant response to this demand for accountability has been
to transform the complexion of power, to make it less dependent on raw,
naked violence and more predicated on some form of acquiescence, secured
through blackmail, bribery, or persuasion. This effect is felt not only in the
way counterinsurgency confinement is reimagined and implemented but also
in the transformation of weapons, and a tilt toward weapons that are (or are
presented as) precision guided and nonlethal, to the use of robotics and unmanned aerial vehicles, and even of the increasing use of special operations
forces whose operations are imagined as less lethal because more precise.[137] And
of course, the effect of this is felt in the desperate claims by political elite that
when the captive body is tortured, mutilated, and destroyed—in Fort Morbut and Long Kesh and Hola Camp, in Ketzi'ot and Khiyam, in Abu Ghraib,
Guantánamo Bay and Bagram, in Côn Són and Ferme Ameziane—that it is
a "few bad apples" at fault rather than a systemic apparatus of coercion whose
functioning rests to a great degree on the extent to which it can be represented
as benign, legal, and legitimate.

CONCLUSION

Once every generation, without fail, there is an episode of
hysteria about the barbarians. . . . In the capital the concern
was that the barbarian tribes of the north and west might
at last be uniting. Officers of the general staff were sent on
tours of the frontier. Some of the garrisons were strengthened.
Traders who requested them were given military escorts. And
officials of the Third Bureau of the Civil Guard were seen for
the first time on the frontier, guardians of the State, specialists
in the obscurer motions of sedition, devotees of truth, doctors
of interrogation.

J. M. Coetzee, 1980[1]

This book has been about confinement in counterinsurgency warfare. The
incarceration of civilians and combatants in warfare most clearly illuminates
the inner workings of asymmetric neo-imperial warfare and its incorporation
of law, administration, and knowledge production. Counterinsurgency confinements are machines of many moving parts: law works with managerialism, culture with economics. The machine works because of the movement of
ideas and of military bodies, because of weapons, and techniques of warfare.
It depends on the making and remaking of conceptual categories: those we
use to understand (e.g., liberalism, colonialism) and those the people we seek
to understand use to explain (e.g., counterinsurgency, human terrain, intelligence, populations, civilians, detainees). And finally, there are the multiple
movements of peoples in opposition to both the broader forms of warfare and
the tactics employed therein; these oppositions can be armed and unarmed,
in the metropolis and in the colony.

I have chosen to focus on confinement because in its breadth, encompassing large civilian populations, and in its negation of the most basic liberal right, the right to liberty, it elucidates the tensions within asymmetric warfare waged by powerful states that profess adherence to liberal rights. I have insisted not simply on the modernity of practices of confinement but also on their rootedness in liberal ideologies and practices. Although the forms of these specific techniques are modern (e.g., processes of categorization, managerial designs), the substance of them is decidedly liberal: law and legality are integral to the self-imagining of such wars; the will to bring about improvement is durable; and notions of autonomy, however despoiled and compromised, are at the center of proxy warfare.

A managerial system of categorization, quantification, and administration is the focus of the incarceration both of civilians and combatants and of counterinsurgency itself more broadly. Militaries are large-scale bureaucratic organizations, subject to the same managerial processes as corporations. Administration and procedure are viewed as standing in for ethics, and the "enterprise form" is generalized to all organizations, "to the conduct of government and to the conduct of individuals themselves."[2] These managerial systems are particularly relevant to the large-scale confinement of civilians and to the mass processing of people suspected of being or of supporting combatants. Both explicitly and implicitly, these managerial procedures are considered safeguards for good behavior, removing the necessity of independent reflection on the ethical dilemmas that are fundamental to asymmetries of power.

The managerial approach also means that all things—even those that should not be calculable—are made subject to measurement and quantitative finessing. All things can be counted: acceptable levels of collateral damage, the degree of pain meted out in interrogations, the number of people detained, the extent of their access to food or water or medical care or to lawyers and the International Committee of the Red Cross (ICRC). This need for quantitative data, for statistics, for an understanding of how to measure death, incarceration, "useful" intelligence, and the like, means that even as the counterinsurgents decry the crude use of metrics (as in the time of Robert McNamara), they try to construct vast databases that capture not only tactical intelligence but also the everyday and the intimate. Everything from the kind and quantity of bread and cilantro people eat to the imprints of their fingers, irises, and DNA are digitized and stored. These knowledge repositories are crucial to managerialism but also, in their quantification of suffering, to the task of defending such confinement in courts of law and public opinion.

In counterinsurgencies a proceduralist interpretation of the law prevails, in which the counterinsurgent power views law as an instrument of legitimation rather than as guidelines converging with ethical principles. Liberal proceduralism leads to the paramountcy of the judicial principle of intent in deciding accountability to such an extent that all wartime brutality can be effaced via claiming a lack of intent. What matters in the end is how virtuous our intent was, how precisely we targeted the guilty, what clean instruments of killing and confinement we used. Along with intent, the legal status of both persons and places of confinement also becomes significant if suspects are to be consigned to interstitial and indeterminate places of confinement.

This insistence on legality of action goes hand in hand with the will to improve that is inherent to liberal imperial invasions, occupations, and confinements. If our intent is to better the condition of living of the "lesser" people (by making a gift of our civilization, or development, or modernisation, or democracy), then what happens in the process matters little, even if what happens in the process is cruelty, torture, or indefinite confinement. A virtuous intent to improve is one of the strongest characteristics of liberal counterinsurgency and is what distinguishes it from its illiberal kin. One can see traces of this improving intent in Marshal Lyautey's declaration that power was "not a matter of destroying [people], but of transforming them," as well as in contemporary counterinsurgents' search for security and order or good governance or democracy.[3] The neo-imperial Robert Kaplan has compared the old-fashioned White man's burden to the work of "post–Cold War humanitarian interventionists" who take seriously their "righteous responsibility to advance the boundaries of free society and good government into zones of sheer chaos, a mission not unlike that of the post-Cold War humanitarian interventionists."[4] Kaplan frankly brings to light the unspoken assumption of liberal counterinsurgency: the essential inequality of peoples—of "races"—which allows a more superior people to uplift an inferior, though improvable, people. Such will to improve could operate on a grand scale or in the more everyday processes of confinement, where prisoners have been subjected to reeducation or behavior modification.

This dovetailing of counterinsurgency with humanitarianism means that military aircrafts drop both bombs and humanitarian aid in the battlefield. The military builds roads, provides community services, and institutes social or economic "reforms" as part of a humanitarian agenda that is an incentive for civilian populations to acquiesce to the rule of the invaders. More often than not, law and humanitarian practices lubricate the operation and administration of confinement.[5] Human rights become as "an aspect of psy-ops."[6]

Liberal counterinsurgencies ultimately require the autonomy of loyal clients. Thus, a central task becomes the training of local proxies who can perform those necessary tasks, both to reduce the costs of rule and to shift the responsibility for the acts of warfare to clients. "CIA experts" suggest that it was important in Afghanistan "to make the war Afghan versus Arab, not some Westerners versus Afghans."[7] Proxies range a broad spectrum, from local collaborator and informants to those engaged in the practices of confinement, policing, and torture. But the use of proxies also applies to the macropolitics of paternalism and tutelary politics, a kind of "benevolent" indirect rule that consolidates the power of local elite, themselves reinvented as "traditional" rulers and arbiters of power. Where counterinsurgency by the imperial power fails, indirect forms of rule and the use of proxies become ever more urgent.

SPECTERS

> A typical example, which can serve as a limiting case, is the relation involved in a State's military oppression of a nation seeking to attain its national independence. The relation is not purely military, but politico-military. . . . The oppressed nation will therefore initially oppose the dominant military force with a force which is only "politico-military," that is to say a form of political action which has the virtue of provoking repercussions of a military character in the sense: 1. That it has the capacity to destroy the war potential of the dominant nation from within; 2. That it compels the dominant military force to thin out and disperse itself over a large territory, thus nullifying a great part of its war potential.
> *Antonio Gramsci, 1971*[8]

Aside from the ghosts of the people murdered, debilitated, and disappeared in confinement, three specters hover over this book: those of Carl Schmitt, Michel Foucault, and Antonio Gramsci. Schmitt appears here not because I agree with his diagnosis but because of his attentiveness, in *The Nomos of the Earth*, to the ways in which colonial spaces become spaces in which international law is made, in breach, and in which violence is permitted. Schmitt also appears here because the decisionism he advocated appeals to powerful liberal democracies in times of emergency—real or concocted—in geographies of invasion and colonization. Schmitt himself saw in this decisionism the real essence of politics, and his vision of fighting the terrorist, the outlaw, the partisan, through martial law is now familiar from not only the War on Terror but also the depredations of Israel in the Occupied Territories, and of France and Britain in their colonies. Schmitt defines martial law as the kind of legal process that creates a designated space "to permit the objective technical execution of a military operation, and in which anything can be done which the situation requires."[9] Schmitt does not recognize that such freedom of operation is circumscribed by the struggles of the conquered peoples and their allies in the metropolis; this is one reason his dystopic vision of politics will always be incomplete and distorted.

Foucault appears throughout the book not only because of how he has altered our understanding of the simultaneous workings of different kinds of power—legal and sovereign, biopolitical, or security-centered—nor only because of his historically detailed and revelatory analysis of discipline in prisons. Foucault's acute diagnosis of why the carceral form is reproduced again and again despite its failure is revealing and highly relevant here. Foucault explains the "reactivation of the penitentiary technique as the only means of overcoming their perpetual failure" by reminding us that penality becomes

a way of handling illegalities . . . of giving free rein to some, of putting pressure on others, of excluding a particular section, of making another useful, of neutralizing certain individuals and of profiting from others. In short, penality does not simply "check" illegalities; it "differentiates" them, it provides them with a general "economy."[10]

Because confinement in counterinsurgencies produces information and informants, allies and enemies, because it makes populations and mobilizes the apparatus of security, and because it justifies disciplinary and legal measures, it is used as expansively as it is. Foucault also tells us that a politics of insurgency that shines a light on slaughter and makes imperial and colonial atrocities the business of the world's population can ultimately best be controlled through a gentler, more disciplinary form of power, not through mass slaughter.

Finally, Gramsci is here not only because he has written about the politics of military violence, or about law and bureaucracy, or about Taylorism, all of which have appeared in these pages. Rather, Gramsci's notions of coercion, consent, and authority are central to the entire project of soft or population-centric counterinsurgencies. On the one hand, confinement as the more humane alternative to mass slaughter is intended to blunt the edge of insurgency, to persuade the public of the virtue and reasonableness of the counterinsurgents. On the other hand, he has exquisitely delineated the crisis of authority in which the balance of coercion and consent is thrown off kilter and which invites— after attempts at imperial hegemony have failed—the military to resolve the crisis: "The military are the permanent reserves of order and conservation; they are a political force which comes into action 'publicly' when 'legality' is in danger."[11] When the mask of consent has slipped, the US imperial forces engage in reinstituting the hegemony. The genius of Gramsci is in his recognition that such moments of crisis emerge politically, are often resolved politically (via the military), and that their emergence is entirely because regimes of rule are challenged from within and without.

WHERE TO FROM HERE?

> Did [the commandant] combine everything in himself, then?
> Was he soldier, judge, mechanic, chemist, and draughtsman?
> *Franz Kafka, 1919*[12]

The official mind itself can be described as the way in which
the bureaucracy perceives its own history, the memory of past
triumphs and past disasters. It possesses its own self-image
and aspirations. It appraises present problems obliquely and
subjectively. It is capable of translating economic interests into

strategic concepts. It is a force in itself. It can be a cause of
imperialism.

Wm. Roger Louis, 2006 [13]

As I write this conclusion, the epistemic community of US military thinkers
is in some turmoil over the sustainability of the counterinsurgency vision put
forward by General Petraeus and his fellow travelers. Some military thinkers
question the viability of a "soft" counterinsurgency in circumstances where
such developmental and "humane" war-fighting will not be effective. Others
question the division between counterinsurgency and counterterrorism (in
which the aim is simply to assassinate or otherwise neutralize combatant enemies and their civilian supporters). Such questions have long been resolved in
places such as Israel, where assassination, "kinetic" action, and enemy-centric
warfare are used enthusiastically, cocooned in a persistent assertion of legality
and ethicality of all their acts. Two contributions by thoughtful students of
counterinsurgency point the way to how such asymmetric wars may be fought
in the future and how military visionaries think they should be understood
and theorized. In a special issue of *Joint Forces Quarterly* titled "Conceptual
and Operational Challenges of COIN," one of the prime thinkers of counterinsurgency, David Kilcullen, and his academic coauthor, Sebastian Gorka,
reflect on the methodology by which US counterinsurgency had chosen its
progenitors and role models. They conclude that the most frequently cited
cases, Malaya and Algeria, were insufficient and inadequate as ancestral role
models. Gorka and Kilcullen insist on the need for "the Counterinsurgency
data set" to be broadened to include revolutions (Russia, Hungarian, Iranian,
Cuban), domestic resistance, and partisan warfare.[14] This widening is revealing. First and foremost, it shows the continuities between today's counterinsurgencies, past (and in the case of Israel, present) colonial counterinsurgencies,
and repressive states that aim to suppress revolutionary movements. In this,
the article is not as innovative as it may seem. Its focus on the modes of suppression of popular revolt (whether offshore or at home) remind us of Rupert
Smith's "war among the peoples," itself an echo of French military theoreticians of revolutionary wars and their delineation of "war in the social milieu."[15]
However, the article also brings to mind General Kitson's vision of British
counterinsurgency in Northern Ireland, which he saw as a modular practice

that could be transported to mainland Britain for suppression of domestic revolt. Such elision of spaces of counterinsurgency is increasingly apparent in the transposition of counterinsurgency and counterterror tactics into domestic and municipal policing in the cities of North America and Europe. The fungibility of asymmetric violence shows most starkly the interconnections between military adventures *there* and policing *here*, at home. Where this matters to confinement in counterinsurgencies is the further criminalization of a politics of insurgency and the expansion of an already-gargantuan prison system in countries that conduct counterinsurgencies to accommodate such rebellions.

The second contribution is by one of the more thoughtful theoreticians and practitioners of counterinsurgency, Andrew Exum. Exum's reflections on the failures of the United States in Afghanistan lead him to suggest two things: first that counterinsurgency in Afghanistan will ultimately fail because although military tactics and techniques have been effective, the absence of coherent strategic thinking and the incompetence and venality of the local clients have led to failure in the political arena. Second, he suggests a reassessment of "civilian strategy" and exertion of pressure by the United States on its local clients to improve their modes of rule.[16]

The implications here are twofold. We are expected to accept that tactics and strategy can be so easily separated, an argument that liberal counterinsurgents make ad nauseam. For a group of thinkers who borrow so much from Clausewitz, their denial that specific tactics are a reflection of particular policies and politics rings hollow. This separation also denies the very political effect of the techniques of war not only on the subject populations but also, in its feedback loop, on the sovereign imperial powers waging war. If a humane, or limited, or circumscribed war is easier and more palatable to wage, then the tactics cannot be so easily insulated from the decision making that shapes strategies. But more directly, the countries whose war-fighting machines I focus on here—the United States, Israel, Britain, and France—have in a sense long perfected the marriage of counterinsurgency warfare and technocratic administration. Although Britain and France had as adjuncts to their militaries and colonial police forces, separate and extensive colonial administration offices, the United States and Israel have administered their colonies, and the territories they have occupied, through their military apparatuses.[17] This effectively means that war making and governance have been married to each other in these contexts. To claim somehow that politics has been absent in the counterinsurgency in Afghanistan is to deny the fundamentally political nature of military activity there.

But Exum also obliquely points to another inevitable result of waging asymmetric warfare in our time. Precisely because the United States does not (and does not want to) claim sovereignty over Afghanistan, its military activity there has to be severely limited to direct counterterror practices conducted with the ostensible approval and agreement of the local regime (an option Exum discusses only briefly and allusively) or alternatively channeled through the proxy regime with the head of Afghan government answering to a local US handler, to ensure that the proxy behaves correctly, that the United States can save on the costs of waging war in Afghanistan, and ultimately to ensure that US interests are met. In other words, indirect rule.

More significant than the writings of counterinsurgent theorists is the official policy of the United States. The January 2012 US Defense Strategic Guidance, announced with some fanfare by President Obama himself, shifted the focus of US military activity to preparation for conventional warfare against China and Iran, and explicitly indicated a shift from population-centric counterinsurgency to a counterterrorism policy of special operations and drone warfare. The document stated,

In the aftermath of the wars in Iraq and Afghanistan, the United States will emphasize non-military means and military-to-military cooperation to address instability and reduce the demand for significant US force commitments to stability operations. US forces will nevertheless be ready to conduct limited counterinsurgency and other stability operations if required, operating alongside coalition forces wherever possible. Accordingly, US forces will retain and continue to refine the lessons learned, expertise and specialized capabilities that have been developed over the past ten years of counterinsurgency and stability operations in Iraq and Afghanistan. *However, US forces will no longer be sized to conduct large-scale, prolonged stability operations* (italics in original).[18]

Although this shift means a turn away from developmental liberal warfare with its "large-scale" and "prolonged" deployment of troops, it certainly does not include a retreat from intervention. Rather, the document indicates a "recalibrated" focus on "a mix of direct action and security force assistance" or a ratcheting of invisible or covert operations conducted without the hindrance of monitoring or accountability combined with a continued and more emphatic dependence on proxies.[19] Indeed, this emphasis on working "by, with, and through" the governments of countries in which the United States intervenes seems to appear with great frequency now in the writings of all counterinsurgents.

In a sense, this reclamation of indirect rule is where a great many supple counterinsurgencies come to rest. The Malayan counterinsurgency was considered an unadulterated success because the government that emerged at the end of the campaign was allied with Britain. The Philippine counterinsurgencies of the United States, both in the early and the mid-twentieth century, similarly left proxy regimes in place. Of course the tension inherent within indirect rule is that the proxy regime will never be as competent, well functioning, honest, trustworthy, or humane as their overlords desire. Having venal clients—who use unrestricted and unrestrained methods of interrogation, or of population control, or various forms of information gathering—can actually be a useful means of diffusing responsibility and of ensuring opacity as regards sensitive and controversial counterinsurgency actions. But the client has to be internationally presentable, and the client's application of force has to act as a measure of suppression of revolt rather than as a catalyst for uprisings. Such a delicate balance is all too frequently impossible to achieve, but in the absence of a wholly acquiescent population, it is nevertheless the desideratum of long-distance counterinsurgency.

CODA

In a wrenching poem rich with the symbolism of Christianity and Islam, the communist Iraqi poet Sa'di Youssef evokes the horrors of Abu Ghraib:

We will go to God
naked
our shroud is our blood
our camphor
the teeth of dogs
turned wolves

The closed cell suddenly swung open
for the female soldier to come
our swollen eyes could not make her out
perhaps because she comes from a mysterious world
she did not say a thing
she was dragging my brother's bloody body behind her
like a worn-out mat[20]

The poem is named "The Wretched of the Heavens," and in its echo of Frantz Fanon's *Wretched of the Earth*, it consciously draws a lineage of brutality from Algiers to Abu Ghraib. In that older book, Fanon wrote of the promise of revolt to "reintroduce mankind into the world, the whole of mankind."[21] The promise also reverberates in Youssef's poem, which ends—after all, after everything—with the possibility of redemption:

But we are on the way to you. We will remain on the way even if you let us down. We are your dead sons and have declared our resurrection. Tell your prophets to open the gates of cells and paradises! Tell them that we are coming! We have wiped our faces and hands with clean earth. The angels know us one by one.

NOTES

INTRODUCTION

1. Alter, "Time to Think About Torture."
2. Begg, *Enemy Combatant*, 204.
3. Begg, *Enemy Combatant*, 230–231.
4. Interview with Abu Samer.
5. Quoted in Al-Haq, "Building Walls," 18.
6. Lenin, *War and Revolution*.
7. Dillon and Reed, *The Liberal Way of War*, 17.
8. Foucault, *Security, Territory, Population*, 65.
9. White House, "Military Commissions."
10. Gorka and Kilcullen, "COIN," 16.
11. Gorka and Kilcullen, "COIN," 16.

CHAPTER I

1. de Vargas Machuca, *The Indian Militia*, 133.
2. Schmitt, *The Theory of the Partisan*, 3.
3. On the Napoleonic army as the first modern army and the first instigator of total war, see Bell, *The First Total War*.
4. This sleight of hand occurs precisely because of the way in which Schmitt himself incorporates the understanding of colonization into his theory of legal ordering of the world. Schmitt, *The Nomos of the Earth*. For a brilliant explanation of Schmitt's position vis-à-vis colonialism, see Toscano, "Carl Schmitt in Beijing."
5. Parker, *Military Revolution*, 119.
6. Parker, *Military Revolution*, 120.
7. Williams, *The American Indian*.

8. de Tocqueville, "Essay on Algeria," 70–71.

9. Quoted in Richter, "Tocqueville on Algeria," 18.

10. Rid, "Nineteenth Century Roots."

11. Kiernan, *Colonial Empires*, 73.

12. Sullivan, *Bugeaud*, 68.

13. Bugeaud, *Oeuvres Militaires*, 268.

14. Bugeaud, *Oeuvres Militaires*, 271.

15. Porch, "Bugeaud, Gallieni, Lyautey," 378.

16. Gottman, "Bugeaud, Gallieni, Lyautey," 236.

17. Sullivan, *Bugeaud*, 123.

18. Rid, "*Razzia*," 620.

19. Quoted in Sullivan, *Bugeaud*, 125.

20. Sullivan, *Bugeaud*, 99–101.

21. Sullivan, *Bugeaud*, 113–115, 102.

22. With the expansion of settler colonialism, the Bureaux Arabes also aided the *colons*. Perkins, *Qaids, Captains, Colons*, 18.

23. This recommendation in particular was taken up after the Algerian revolt of 1871, when the rebels were exiled to Pacific islands, where they encountered similarly exiled Communards. Lallaoui, *Kabyles du Pacifique*.

24. Porch, "Bugeaud, Gallieni, Lyautey," 380–381; Sullivan, *Bugeaud*, 127–132.

25. Colby, "How to Fight Savage Tribes," 285.

26. Wolfe, *Settler Colonialism*, 209.

27. Perdue and Green, *The Cherokee Removal*, 119.

28. Jahoda, *Trail of Tears*; Missal and Missal, *Seminole Wars*.

29. Utley, *Frontiersmen in Blue*, 108–110.

30. Birtle, *US Army Counterinsurgency Doctrine*, 62.

31. Utley, *Frontiersmen in Blue*, 112–126; *Frontier Regulars*, 50–53; Birtle, *US Army Counterinsurgency Doctrine*, 60; Weigley, *American Way of War*, 153–163.

32. Go, "Introduction," 9; Amoroso, "The Moro Problem," 125.

33. Birtle, *US Army Counterinsurgency Doctrine*, 80; Amoroso, "The Moro Problem," 125; Kramer, *Blood of Government*, 266–269.

34. Kramer, *Blood of Government*, 152–154; also Amoroso, "The Moro Problem," 127.

35. Kramer, *Blood of Government*, 113.

36. Bickel, *Mars Learning*.

37. Churchill, *My Early Life*, 146.

38. The "Forward Policy" was occasionally resurrected and added to the mix. This entailed permanently stationing troops among the tribes or "a continuous barbed-wire line with tanks and men standing shoulder to shoulder." Noel, "A Frontier Policy," 74–76.

39. Thornton, *Sandeman*, 302.

40. Bruce, "Sandeman," 48; Baha, *NWFP Administration*, 38.

41. Elliott, *The Frontier*, 112–113.

42. Elliott, *The Frontier*, 115.

43. Bayly, *Empire and Information*, 128–140.

44. Letter from A. F. Perrott (deputy inspector general of the police) from Peshawar to Major General Richard O'Connor (in Palestine), dated October 18, 1938, 3/2/1, O'Connor Papers, LHCMA.

45. Callwell, *Small Wars*, 286–347.

46. Bruce, "Sandeman," 49; Bruce, *Waziristan*, 1.

47. Bruce, *Waziristan*, 2.
48. Quoted in Thornton, *Sandeman*, 294.
49. Thornton, *Sandeman*, 304.
50. Elliott, *The Frontier*, 68.
51. Beattie, *Imperial Frontier*, 155.
52. Tripodi, "The Sandeman System," 796.
53. Quoted in Maurois, *Lyautey*, 61.
54. Hoisington, *Lyautey*, 7; Gottman, "Bugeaud, Gallieni, Lyautey"; Beckett, "Introduction," 15.
55. Rabinow, *French Modern*, 148. As Gwendolyn Wright tells us, both Gallieni and Lyautey admired British imperial ideas of indirect rule. See *Politics of Design*, 76.
56. Rabinow, *French Modern*, 150.
57. Zinoman, *Colonial Bastille*, 109.
58. Cole, *Forget Colonialism?* 45–59.
59. Gallieni, quoted in Cole, *Forget Colonialism?* 58.
60. Gallieni, *Pacification*, 339; the translation is my own.
61. In Madagascar, Senegalese, Algerian, and Hausa troops were used. Gallieni, *Pacification*, 92.
62. Porch, "Bugeaud, Gallieni, Lyautey," 384.
63. Gallieni, *Pacification*, 340.
64. Gallieni, *Pacification*, 76–77.
65. Kilcullen, "Twenty-Eight Articles," 107.
66. Lyautey, quoted in Maurois, *Lyautey*, 63; de Durand, "France," 14.
67. Lyautey, quoted in Maurois, *Lyautey*, 180–181.
68. Lyautey, quoted in Singer and Langdon, *Cultured Force*, 192.
69. Rabinow, *French Modern*, 113; Singer and Langdon, *Cultured Force*, 198.
70. It should not be forgotten that the magnanimous discourse was not reflected in the massively disparate spending on European and native cities. Rabinow, *French Modern*, 280–281.
71. Gottman, "Bugeaud, Galliéni, Lyautey," 252.
72. Singer and Langdon, *Cultured Force*, 205.
73. Lyautey, quoted in Rabinow, *French Modern*, 285.
74. Callwell, *Small Wars*, 40.
75. Gwynn, *Imperial Policing*, 3, 5. Some paragraphs below are adapted from Khalili, "New Classics."
76. Gwynn, *Imperial Policing*, 30, 15.
77. Gwynn, *Imperial Policing*, 397.
78. Gwynn, *Imperial Policing*, 398.
79. Gwynn, *Imperial Policing*, 3.
80. Anglim, "Callwell vs. Graziani," 592.
81. Callwell, *Small Wars*, 25.
82. Callwell, *Small Wars*, 24.
83. Callwell, *Small Wars*, 42.
84. Callwell, *Small Wars*, 42.
85. Callwell, *Small Wars*, 33.
86. Callwell, *Small Wars*, 50, 89, 128.
87. Callwell, *Small Wars*, 49–50.
88. Callwell, *Small Wars*, 85.
89. Callwell, *Small Wars*, 130–149.
90. Callwell, *Small Wars*, 128–129.
91. Sepp, *Resettlement*, 12.

92. Thompson, *No Exit*, 128.

93. Ben-Gurion, "Our Friend"; Bierman and Smith, *Fire in the Night*, 379.

94. Royle, *Wingate*, 105; Bierman and Smith, *Fire in the Night*, 85.

95. On Yitzhak Sadeh, see Ben-Eliezer, *Israeli Militarism*, 23–27; Allon, *Shield of David*, 72–88.

96. "Appreciation by Captain O. C. Wingate of Force H.Q. Intelligence on 5.6.38 at Nazareth of the possibilities of night movements by armed forces of the Crown with the object of putting an end to terrorism in Northern Palestine" and "Impressions of Wingate," in the private papers of Major General H. E. N. Bredin, 81/33/1, IWM Document Archives.

97. Tzion Cohen, quoted in Segev, *One Palestine Complete*, 430.

98. "Some experiences in Palestine: ex the Lorettonian," in the private papers of Lieutenant Colonel R. King-Clark, 83/10/1, IWM Document Archives.

99. Mosley, *Gideon*, 63–64.

100. Nagl, *Learning to Eat Soup with a Knife*, 194.

101. Bloch and Fitzgerald, *British Intelligence*, 74.

102. Thompson, *Make for the Hills*, 71–76, 88–90; Short, *Communist Insurrection*, 132.

103. Thompson, *Make for the Hills*, 93; Short, *Communist Insurrection*, 401.

104. Of course, Thompson goes on to say then that "very tough laws" can be enacted; mass deportations, collective fines, imposition of strict curfews, "preventive detention," mandatory death penalty for carrying arms and life imprisonment for providing supplies to guerrillas were all passed into law. Thompson, *Defeating Communist Insurgency*, 53; Thompson, *Make for the Hills*, 93.

105. Thompson, *Defeating Communist Insurgency*, 50–58.

106. The strategic-hamlet concept in Vietnam had been preceded by the French *agrovilles* and, as such, was not wholly new. The scale of the strategic-hamlet program, however, was unprecedented. Zasloff, "Rural Resettlement."

107. Thompson, *No Exit*, 154.

108. Thompson, *No Exit*, 60, emphasis added.

109. Kitson, *Bunch of Five*, 200. The proceedings of the RAND symposium can be found in Hosmer and Crane, *Counterinsurgency*.

110. Kitson, *Low Intensity Operations*, 15.

111. Hosmer and Crane, *Counterinsurgency*, 125.

112. Kitson, *Bunch of Five*, 58; *Gangs and Counter-gangs*, 2; Ellison and Smyth, *Crowned Harp*, 74–75.

113. Kitson, *Low-Intensity Operations*, 25.

114. However, it is important to note that such cross-fertilization has a much longer history. See Brogden, "The Emergence of the Police"; Khalili "Palestine in Global Counterinsurgency"; Palmer, *Policing and Protest*; Sinclair and Williams, "Home and Away."

115. Fall, "Theory and Practice," emphasis in the original.

116. Lacheroy, quoted in de Durand, "France," 20.

117. Boot, "Key to a Successful Surge"; Petraeus and Nagl, "Preface," xix; de Durand, "France," 23; Valeyre and Guerin, *Du Galula à Petraeus*.

118. Galula, *Pacification*; Galula, *Counterinsurgency*.

119. Galula, *Pacification*, 30–40, 5, 8.

120. Galula, *Pacification*, 20–21.

121. Galula, *Counterinsurgency*, 46.

122. Galula, *Pacification*, 24–45.

123. Galula, *Pacification*, 32.

124. Galula, *Pacification*, 69, 168.

125. Galula, *Pacification*, 143.

126. Galula, *Pacification*, 246–247; see also Galula, *Counterinsurgency*, 52–55.

127. Villatoux, "Hogard et Némo"; Kelly, *Lost Soldiers*.

128. Paret, *French Revolutionary Warfare*; Aussaresses, *The Battle of Casbah*; de Durand, "France"; Robin, *Escadrons de la Mort*, 237–256, and especially 254n.

129. On Trinquier and his Meo and Thai militias, see Windrow, *The Last Valley*, 218–220.

130. Aussaresses, *Casbah*; Robin, *Escadrons*; see also Branche, *La Torture*; Harbi and Stora, *La Guerre d'Algérie*.

131. US Army, *Counterinsurgency Field Manual*, 392.

132. Trinquier, *Modern Warfare*, 17–18; Valeyre and Guerin, *Du Galula à Petraeus*, 17.

133. Trinquier, *Modern Warfare*, 43–51.

134. Aussaresses, *Casbah*, 92–93.

135. Horne, *Savage War*, 198.

136. Horne, *Savage Wars*, 199; Branche, *La Torture*, 167.

137. Paret, *French Revolutionary Warfare*.

138. Paret, *French Revolutionary Warfare*, 26–29.

139. Paret, *French Revolutionary Warfare*, 26.

140. See Bernard Fall's introduction in Trinquier, *Modern Warfare*, xv.

141. Trinquier, *Modern Warfare*, 28.

142. Sorley, *A Better War*.

143. Rostow, "Countering Guerrilla Attack," 25.

144. He was for that reason massively resented by the counterinsurgents, including William Colby, who ran the Phoenix Program and who is said to have screamed in frustration about Rostow's bombing plans: "For God's sake, let them go bomb something, anything, so they can get it out of their system! Then maybe we can get them to turn their attention to fighting the war where it has to be fought!" Colby meant the villages. See Elliott, *Vietnamese War*, 859.

145. Halberstam, *The Best and the Brightest*, 161–162; Milne, *America's Rasputin*.

146. Rostow, *Stages of Economic Growth*.

147. Rostow, *Stages of Growth*, 162; Rostow, "Countering Guerrilla Attack," 22.

148. Rostow, *Stages of Growth*, 107.

149. Halberstam, *The Best and the Brightest*, 125.

150. Rostow, *Stages of Growth*, 121.

151. Sheehan, *Bright Shining Lie*, 90–91.

152. August 1967 letter to Daniel Elsberg, quoted in Sheehan, *Bright Shining Lie*, 668.

153. Bergerud, *Dynamics of Defeat*, 108.

154. Bergerud, *Dynamics of Defeat*, 109.

155. Hunt, *Pacification*, 94–95.

156. Moyar, *Phoenix*; Andrade and Willbanks, "CORDS/Phoenix"; Westerman "Pacifying Afghanistan"; Nagl, *Learning to Eat Soup with a Knife*, 164–166.

157. Sheehan, *Bright Shining Lie*, 317.

158. Sheehan, *Bright Shining Lie*, 734–736; Hunt, *Pacification*.

159. Interestingly, David Elliott tells us that "the disruptions of incessant bombing and shelling linked to the initial 'clearing phase' of successive pacification programs in the following years had much more profound effect on the revolutionary movement than any of the more widely publicized 'counterinsurgency' tactics employed in pacification." Elliott, *The Vietnamese War*, 635.

160. Phillips, *Why Vietnam Matters*, 288.

161. It is worth noting that, although Abrams became the archetypal hero of the transformative narrative, most ardently in the works of Lewis Sorley, he continued Westmoreland's war of attrition.

Sorley, *A Better War*; Sorley, *Thunderbolt*. In his magisterial history of the war Elliott concludes that the Abrams plan of clear and hold had "a devastating consequence for many civilians" in the provinces Elliott studied. Elliott recounts that in program planned by Abrams, the Speedy Express, ten thousand Viet Cong killed in action were reported in six months, but only nine hundred weapons were found, indicating massive civilian casualties and little unconventional "hearts and mind." See Elliott, *The Vietnamese War*, 1134.

CHAPTER 2

1. Petraeus, "Lessons of History," 51.

2. Kiszely, "Learning About Counter-Insurgency," 18.

3. Kilcullen, "Twenty-Eight Articles," 106.

4. US Army, *Army Capstone Document*, 6.

5. US Army, *Army Capstone Document*, 6.

6. Parts of this section are adapted from Khalili, "New Classics."

7. David Petraeus, "Learning Counterinsurgency"; McMaster, "Learning from Contemporary Conflicts"; Crane, "United States"; Mansoor, *Baghdad at Sunrise*; Nagl, *Eating Soup*; Sepp, "Best Practices"; Kilcullen, "Twenty-Eight Articles"; "Counterinsurgency Redux"; *Accidental Guerrilla* and *Counterinsurgency*.

8. Crane, "United States," 68.

9. McFate, "Anthropology and Counterinsurgency"; McFate, "Adversary Culture." McFate's doctoral dissertation can be located under her maiden name; see Carlough, *Pax Britannica*. McFate's involvement in the militarization of anthropology has generated a great deal of controversy. See especially the entries by David Price ("Faking Scholarship") and Greg Feldman ("Radical or Reactionary?") in Network of Concerned Anthropologists, *The Counter-Counterinsurgency Manual*.

10. Corum, "Getting Doctrine Right," 95.

11. Kleinfeld, "Petraeus."

12. Bateman, "How to Make War"; Sewall, "Introduction," xxi–xliii.

13. Kleinfeld, "Petraeus," 111; Sewall, "Introduction," xxxiii.

14. Lawrence, *Seven Pillars*, 194.

15. Wendy Brown criticizes precisely this "boundary breakdowns and erasure of settled jurisdictions" that the manual advocates. See Brown's contribution in the review symposium organized by *Perspectives on Politics*; Biddle et al., "*COIN Manual* as Science and Political Practice."

16. Mao, *On Guerrilla Warfare*, 93.

17. In the aforementioned symposium, Stephen Biddle criticizes the manual for leaving out "coercive bargaining with the host" and for assuming that it is possible for the US military to train a reliable indigenous security force in conditions of sectarian conflict, whereas Kalyvas argues that emphasis on the population-insurgent-counterinsurgent triad ignores the internal cleavages within the population that may matter in the eventual deal counterinsurgent forces make with the elite within the population. See Biddle et al., "*COIN Manual* as Science and Political Practice."

18. Kilcullen, "Twenty-Eight Articles," 105.

19. Kilcullen, "Twenty-Eight Articles," 106–107.

20. Kilcullen, *Accidental Guerrilla*, 30–32. Kilcullen's doctoral dissertation in politics was based on "fieldwork," some of which he conducted as a military officer on duty in Indonesia. Kilcullen, *Military Operations in Indonesia*, ix–x.

21. Kilcullen, *Accidental Guerrilla*, 35.

22. Kilcullen, *Accidental Guerrilla*, 38.

23. Kilcullen, *Accidental Guerrilla*, 66.

24. Galula, *Counterinsurgency Warfare*, 53.

25. Kilcullen himself cites Kalyvas in his analysis; Kilcullen, *Accidental Guerrilla*, 68. Kalyvas's book is much read and much cited on counterinsurgency blogs, even if Kalyvas dissociates himself from the counterinsurgency epistemic community.

26. Shrader, *The Withered Wine*, 225, 254.

27. Kalyvas, *Logic*, 12.

28. Ironically, Kalyvas himself has criticized the manual for precisely stripping counterinsurgency wars of politics beyond what happens on the battlefield. See Kalyvas's contribution to Biddle et al., "*COIN Manual* as Political Science and Political Practice," 351–353.

29. US Army, *Counterinsurgency Field Manual*, chapters 3 and 5.

30. Kilcullen, *Accidental Guerrilla*, 296.

31. Kilcullen, *Accidental Guerrilla*, 299. On sovereign and disciplinary power, see Foucault, *Society Must Be Defended*.

32. *The Daily Show with Jon Stewart*, August 23, 2007, http://www.thedailyshow.com/watch/thu-august-23-2007/lt--col--john-nagl (accessed April 17, 2012).

33. Nagl, *Eating Soup*; Sir Robert Thompson, *Defeating Communist Insurgency*.

34. Short, *Communist Insurrections*, 159, 244; Karl Hack, "The Malayan Emergency," 386.

35. Short, *Communist Insurrections*, 173–205.

36. Short, *Communist Insurrections*, 375–379.

37. Nagl, *Eating Soup*, 71–76.

38. Nagl, *Eating Soup*, 65–111.

39. Nagl, *Eating Soup*, 75.

40. Nagl, *Eating Soup*, 74–75.

41. Gant, *One Tribe at a Time*, 8–14.

42. *Washington Post*, January 17, 2010.

43. Todd et al, *Iraq Tribal Study*.

44. Patriquin, "How to Win in Anbar."

45. Marlowe, *Galula*, 9.

46. Ricks, *Fiasco*, 266.

47. Ricks, *The Gamble*, 219.

48. Ricks, *The Gamble*, 64.

49. US Army, *Counterinsurgency Field Manual*, 33; quoted approvingly in Ricks, *The Gamble*, 30.

50. Gentile, "A Strategy of Tactics," 11.

51. US Army, *Counterinsurgency Field Manual*, para. 5-62.

52. Luttwak, "Dead End," 41–42. Luttwak suggests that "whenever insurgents are believed to be present in a village, small town, or distinct city district—a very common occurrence in Iraq at present, as in other insurgency situations—the local notables can be compelled to surrender them to the authorities, under the threat of escalating punishments, all the way to mass executions."

53. Crane, "United States," 69, emphasis added.

54. Smith, *Utility of Force*, 1.

55. Smith, *Utility of Force*, 3.

56. Smith, *Utility of Force*, 390.

57. Smith, *Utility of Force*, 391.

58. The first generation of warfare begins with the invention of gunpowder and the transition from feudal social systems to modern nation-states. The second generation emerges because of the increased capacity of the states to tax, the *levy en masse*, the emergence of mechanized transportation, and the rise of nationalist sentiment and patriotism among peoples. The third generation, or maneuver

warfare, began during the First World War and was consolidated in the Second World War. A broad industrial base, a democratic polity, and invention of the blitzkrieg are the defining characteristics of third-generation warfare. Lind et al., "Changing Face of War"; see also Hammes, *Sling and Stone*, 2.

59. Hammes, *Sling and Stone*, 195–200.

60. US Army, *Counterinsurgency Field Manual*, para. 5-56.

61. US Army, *Counterinsurgency Field Manual*, paras. 5-67 and 5-70.

62. Jabotinsky, "Iron Wall."

63. Quoted in Catignani, *Israeli Counter-Insurgency*, 73.

64. Exum, "Civilians Caught."

65. The section that follows has been adapted from Khalili, "Location of Palestine."

66. Ben-Eliezer, *Israeli Militarism*; Catignani, *Israeli Counter-Insurgency*; Tira, *Nature of War*.

67. Quoted in Tira, *The Nature of War*, 17.

68. Jabotinsky (1880–1940) opposed the partition of Palestine and was the prime challenger of early Labor Zionism.

69. Jabotinsky, "Iron Wall."

70. Saltman, "Mandatory Emergency Laws"; Moffett, *Perpetual Emergency*.

71. Baker and Matar, *Threat*.

72. Jiryis, *The Arabs in Israel*, 9–74.

73. Jiryis, *The Arabs in Israel*, 19–20.

74. Robinson, *Occupied Citizens*, 97, 117.

75. Robinson, "Local Struggle."

76. Schwarz, *The Arabs in Israel*, 89. For an excellent account of the temporary residence permits, see Robinson, *Occupied Citizens*, 117–193.

77. Frisch, "The Druze Minority"; Kanaaneh, *Surrounded*.

78. Robinson, *Occupied Citizens*, 69n61, 71n65, 100, 205.

79. Jiryis, *The Arabs in Israel*, 66.

80. For an excellent analysis of Israeli policing of the Palestinian "ghetto," see Ron, *Frontiers and Ghettos*. On beatings as collective punishment, see Hunter, *The Palestinian Uprising*, 99–102.

81. Hunter, *The Palestinian Uprising*, 102–104; Rosenfeld, *Confronting the Occupation*, 211–265; Nashif, *Palestinian Political Prisoners*; Cook, Hanieh, and Kay, *Stolen Youth*.

82. The number of regulations is from Hanieh, "The Politics of Curfew," 325. On Israeli occupation law, see Shehadeh, *Occupier's Law*; on military courts, see Hajjar, *Courting Conflict*.

83. Hiltermann, *Israel's Deportation Policy*.

84. Rosenfeld, *Confronting the Occupation*, 236; Hunter, *The Palestinian Uprising*, 95–98; Hanieh, "The Politics of Curfew."

85. Ginbar and Talmor, *House Demolition*.

86. Hanieh "The Politics of Curfew," 329.

87. Stein, *Human Shield*.

88. Pseudo-gangs were groups of white settlers disguised in blackface fighting against Mau Mau rebels in Kenya and ZANU (Zimbabwe African National Union) guerrillas in Rhodesia. Henderson, *Man Hunt*; Kitson, *Gangs and Counter-gangs*; Reid-Daly and Stiff, *Selous Scouts*. On Israeli Duvdovan units, see Vitullo, "Yitzhak Rabin"; Palestine Human Rights Information Center, *Targeting to Kill*. On local collaborators, see Rigby, *The Legacy of the Past*. The same method of "going native" has also been used by US Special Forces in Afghanistan. See Boot, "What Makes Some Soldiers 'Special.'"

89. B'Tselem, "Testimony of Colonel Itai Virob."

90. Peres, *David's Sling*, 24; Ben-Gurion, "Bevin."

91. Weizman, *Hollow Land*, 111–138.

92. Kasher and Yadlin, "Military Ethics," 17.

93. Kasher and Yadlin, "Military Ethics," 18.

94. See Hajjar, *Courting Conflict*; Weizman, "Lawfare"; Gordon, *Israel's Occupation*, 26–29.

CHAPTER 3

1. Kitson, *Low Intensity Operations*, 66.

2. White House, "Military Commissions."

3. Dunlap, "Law," 5; Feith, "Law."

4. US Government, "Counterinsurgency Guide," 14; US Army, *Counterinsurgency Field Manual*, para. 1-4; US Army, *Stability Operations Field Manual*, para. 1-40. A military lawyer defending a Guantánamo detainee recalls that another committed officer had applauded his work by saying, "The rule of law is what I fight for." Mahler, *The Challenge*, 139.

5. Dunlap, "Lawfare," 35.

6. Neuman, "Anomalous Zones."

7. For arguments about lawlessness of extraterritorial spaces, see Cole, *Enemy Alien*; Fletcher and Stover, *Guantanamo Effect*; Greenberg, *Least Worst Place*; Margulies, *Guantánamo*; Ratner, *Guantánamo*; Sands, *Torture Team*; Mayer, *Dark Side*; Stafford Smith, *Bad Men*.

8. Schmitt, *Nomos*; Agamben, *Homo Sacer*; Hussain, *Emergency*.

9. Kitson, *Low Intensity Operations*, 66.

10. Kafka, "In the Penal Colony," 75.

11. Toth, *Beyond Papillon*. For an evocative account of the internal regime of control in a penal colony in French Guiana, see Price, *The Convict and the Colonel*, 79–110.

12. Governor Gipps of Sydney regarding Norfolk Islands, quoted in Benton, *A Search for Sovereignty*, 207.

13. Benton, *A Search for Sovereignty*, 167.

14. Morgan, *New Caledonia*, 154.

15. Lallaoui, *Kabyles du Pacifique*; Mailhé, *Déportation*; Morgan, *New Caledonia*; Pieris, *Invisible Hands*.

16. Zinoman, *Colonial Bastille*, 60–61. Zinoman writes that "between 1867 and 1887, most of the prisoners sent to the South American penal colony (of Guiana) were Vietnamese or Algerians, who, it was argued, could withstand the humid tropical climate better than Frenchmen."

17. Anderson, *Convicts*; Mian, *Prisoners of Malta*. Also see UK National Archives, FO 371/123897 on the quiet deportation of Cypriot insurgents to Seychelles in the 1950s; CO 537/404, CO 537/405, CO 537/406, WO 78/2996 on Boer prisoners in Ceylon; FO 371/132869 on Bahraini detainees exiled to St. Helena.

18. Anderson, *Legible Bodies*; Sen, *Disciplining Punishment*; Sinha, *In Andamans*.

19. Van Schoor, *Die Bannelinge*, quoted in Van Der Merwe, "Boer Prisoner-of-War Camps."

20. Buntman, *Robben Island*.

21. The laws were based on the Collective Responsibility Ordinance of 1924 and formed the basis of Israelis administrative law after the establishment of that state. See Khalili, "Location of Palestine"; Saltman, "Mandatory Emergency Laws."

22. Abu-Gharbiyya, *Fi Khidam*, 113–118.

23. Ordinance No. 12 of 1937, Government of Seychelles, dated October 11, 1937, CO 530/440.

24. Secret letter from Colonial Office to the governor of Seychelles, dated October 14, 1937, CO 530/440.

25. Colonial Office covering note, July 26, 1938, CO 530/473.

26. Secretary of State for Colonies to General Cunningham in Palestine, September 16, 1946, CO 537/1315.

27. From Cairo to Foreign Office, March 2, 1946, CO 537/1315.

28. From Cairo to Foreign Office, March 2, 1946, CO 537/1315.

29. Gong, *Standard of Civilization*; Anghie, *Imperialism*.

30. To Kenya from secretary of state for colonies, February 13, 1946, CO 537/1315. The fear of habeas actions was so strong that the same note concluded, "We are experiencing great difficulty in finding a means of transporting them to the Seychelles without staying long enough on British soil for them to take legal action as described above."

31. Colonial office memo from a Mr. Trafford Smith addressed to Mr. Martin, January 8, 1946, CO 537/1315.

32. Horesh, "To Die," 7.

33. Cunningham to the secretary of state for colonies, February 12, 1946, FO 371/52578. For more on the detainees, see FO 371/23245; FO 371/52578; FO 371/52579; FO 371/61902; FO 371/68640; PREM 8/300.

34. Ironically, at the time of this writing, former Kenyan Mau Mau detainees are attempting to bring a suit against the British government for torture during the emergency in that country in the 1950s. The response of the British government in 2011 was that "it could not be liable because it happened outside of the UK and that Kenya had its own legal colonial government, which was responsible for the camps." BBC, "Mau Mau Kenyans."

35. Meridor, *Road to Freedom*, 21.

36. Section 15b, which continues to be used in the Israeli emergency regulation (adopted wholesale from the British) is the administrative detention provision.

37. Report from Mr. Munier of ICRC, June 12–13, 1946, FO 1015/68.

38. The British used this combination in their counterinsurgency in Aden, where they sent protesters and insurgents to Zanzibar and Jaar, but asserted, "We would prefer not to publicise their whereabouts for security reasons." See telegram from the high commissioner, dated December 12, 1963, Records of the British Administration in Aden, IOR/R/20/D/20.

39. Swift, *Gulliver's Travels*, 325

40. See the majority's opinion in *Boumediene v. Bush*.

41. Cuban excludables, who numbered thirty-two thousand, were those asylum seekers whose entry to the United States was denied in the mid-1990s. The Haitian refugees complained that the Cubans were treated much better than they were. Williams and Suro, "Detention of Cubans."

42. Greenberg, *The Least Worst Place*, 44.

43. Greenberg, *The Least Worst Place*, 64.

44. Johns, "Guantanamo Bay," 614.

45. Blom Hansen, "Legality and Authority," 183.

46. Marks, "Anxieties of Influence," 347; Singha, *Despotism of Law*.

47. Payen, "Lavalas," 759.

48. I borrow the term from Neuman, "Anomalous Zones." Greenberg tells the story of that image in *The Least Worst Place*.

49. See the text of the amendment at the Our Documents website, at http://www.ourdocuments .gov/doc.php?flash=old&doc=55 (accessed October 15, 2010). The Platt Amendment was abrogated in 1934, but the terms of the lease for Guantánamo were extended.

50. Murphy, *The History of Guantanamo Bay*, chapters 11 and 16.

51. Murphy, *The History of Guantanamo Bay*, chapter 21.

52. Lipman, *Guantánamo*, 199.

53. Ratner, "Guantanamo HIV Camp," 201n56.

54. Ratner, "Guantanamo HIV Camp," 201n56.

55. Payen, "Lavalas."

56. Neuman, "Anomalous Zones," 1228. Neuman gives the example of how "in 1971 the Court of Claims assumed that the Takings Clause of the Fifth Amendment applied to a Cuban contractor at

Guantanamo," and how until 1991, "the United States has exercised criminal jurisdiction over both citizens and aliens at Guantánamo, to the exclusion of Cuban law; in practice, civilian criminal defendants [were] brought to the United States for prosecution, and enjoy[ed] full constitutional protection."

57. Ratner, "Guantanamo HIV Camp," 199.

58. Ratner, "Guantanamo HIV Camp," 193.

59. Colby, "How to Fight Savage Tribes," 279.

60. Testimony of Christopher Arendt in Iraq Veterans Against the War and Glantz, *Winter Soldier*, 84.

61. Berman, "Privileging Combat," 7.

62. For a lengthy catalogue of the labels that can be applied to different War on Terror detainees, see Fallon and Metzler, "Habeas Corpus."

63. Posner and Yoo, "International Adjudication"; Sulmasy and Yoo, "Counterintuitive"; Yoo, "War Powers"; Yoo, "Using Force."

64. Yoo, *Powers of War and Peace*; Yoo, "Transferring Terrorists."

65. *Padilla and Lebron v. Yoo.*

66. Greenberg, *The Least Worst Place*, 154–155.

67. DOJ OLC, "Application of Treaties," January 9, 6.

68. DOJ OLC, "Application of Treaties," January 22, 37.

69. White House, "Human Treatment."

70. *Ex parte Quirin.*

71. *Hamdi v. Rumsfeld*, Scalia dissenting.

72. Berman, "Privileging Combat."

73. *Rasul v. Bush*, Kennedy concurring; see also Halliday and White, "Suspension Clause," 645.

74. *Arar v. Ashcroft*, citing *Sanchez-Espinoza v. Reagan*, emphasis added.

75. Human Rights Watch, "Without Status or Protection"; B'Tselem, "Illegal Combatants Law," 2.

76. Benton, *Law and Colonial Cultures*; Hussain, *Emergency*.

77. Singha, *A Despotism of Law.*

78. Benton, *Search for Sovereignty*, 174; Spieler, *Empire and Underworld*. In US legal history, slaves were also a kind of civil dead, whereas "criminal prisoners" in special isolation units are similarly categorized. See Dayan, *Law.*

79. Dörmann, "Combatants."

80. Li, "A Universal Enemy?" 416.

81. Lorimer, *Institutes*, 101.

82. Lorimer, *Institutes*, 161.

83. Nabulsi, *Traditions of War*; Wright, "Bombardment"; Kinsella, "Civilian, Combatant"; Mégret, "From 'Savages' to 'Unlawful Combatants.'"

84. Mégret, "From 'Savages' to 'Unlawful Combatants,'" 270.

85. Mégret, "From 'Savages' to 'Unlawful Combatants,'" 277.

86. Quoted in Bennett, "The Other Side of the COIN," 642.

87. Bennett, "The Other Side of COIN."

88. Bond, *Rules of Riot*, 39.

89. Casey, Rivkin, and Bartram, "Unlawful Belligerency."

90. Feith, "Law"; Solf, "A Response to Feith."

91. Quoted in Chomsky, "Dakota Trials," 43.

92. Chomsky, "Dakota Trials," 64.

93. Adjutant General's Office, *Lieber Instructions.*

94. Chomsky, "Dakota Trials," 14.

95. Chomsky, "Dakota Trials," 62n310.

96. Fisher, "Ex parte Quirin"; Beard, "The Geneva Boomerang." For an argument for the military commission, see Rivkin, Casey, and Bartram, "Bringing Al-Qaeda to Justice," 6.

97. Mayer, *Dark Side*, 81.

98. White House, "Military Order of November 13 2001."

99. Rivkin, Casey, and Bartram, "Bringing Al-Qaeda to Justice," 4.

100. Mahler, *The Challenge*.

101. *Hamdan v. Rumsfeld*, Breyer concurring.

102. Military Commissions Act of 2006.

103. However, in *Boumediene v. Bush*, the Court reserved the right to hear habeas corpus cases of Guantánamo detainees, declaring the denial of the habeas provision in the act unconstitutional.

104. Benjamin, "Critique of Violence," 284.

105. *United States v. Hamdan*.

106. Savage, "Ruling Averts Testimony."

107. Cole, "What to Do About Guantánamo."

108. Cole, "What to Do About Guantánamo."

109. Interviews with Muneer Ahmad, Joshua Colangelo-Bryan, Marc Falkoff, Gita Gutierrez, Jonathan Hafetz, Brent Mickum, Barbara Olshansky, Clive Stafford-Smith, Steven Watt, and Ben Wizner.

110. Swift, *Gulliver's Travels*, 324.

111. A large body of legal theory is precisely concerned with analogy and precedent in legal reasoning. Hunter, "Reason Is Too Large."

112. DOJ OLC, "Authority for Use of Military Force," 3n4, 12n16.

113. DOJ, OLC, "Application of Treaties," January 9, 10.

114. DOJ, OLC, "Application of Treaties," January 22, 29n108.

115. Cleveland, "Powers Inherent in Sovereignty," 278.

116. Blasier, *Hovering Giant*; Calder, *Impact of Intervention*; Renda, *Taking Haiti*; Pérez, *Cuba Under the Platt Amendment*; Lindsay-Poland, *Emperors of the Jungle*; Go, *American Empire*; Murphy, *Hemispheric Imaginings*. On the War on Drugs, see Andreas and Nadelmann, *Policing the Globe*, 37–45; on its relationship with the War on Terror, see Andreas and Nadelmann, *Policing the Globe*, 194–199; Petras, "Geopolitics of Plan Colombia"; Kuzmarov, "From Counter-Insurgency"; Stokes, *America's Other War*.

117. Fisher, *In the Name of National Security*.

118. *Johnson v. Eisentrager*; *Boumediene v. Bush*.

119. Dembitz, "Racial Discrimination," 201.

120. *Korematsu v. United States*.

121. Gressman, "Korematsu," 18.

122. Dembitz, "Racial Discrimination," 193.

123. Dembitz, "Racial Discrimination," 218–219.

124. Mahan, *Sea Power*, 514.

125. Weigley, *American Way of War*, 182–186; Williams, *Empire as a Way of Life*, 127. On the US emergence as an empire, see also Maier, *Among Empires*; Smith, *Roosevelt's Geographer*.

126. Kerr, *The Insular Cases*; Thompson, *American Law*; Rivera Ramos, "Legal Construction of Colonialism"; Torruella, "The Insular Cases."

127. *De Lima v. Bidwell*.

128. Burnett, "Edges of Empire," 206.

129. In *Hawaii v. Mankichi*, for example, the degree of civilization of the island was attributed to the proliferation of white settlers, "who brought with them political ideas and traditions which, about sixty years ago, found expression in the adoption of a code of laws appropriate to their new conditions."

130. Torruella, "The Insular Cases," 285n5; Miller, "Verdugo-Urquidez."

131. Kaplan, "Where Is Guantánamo?" 251–252.

132. Root, *The Military and Colonial Policy*, 9.

133. Department of Defense, "National Defense Strategy," 6.

134. Dershowitz, "Want to Torture?"

135. Hussain, *Emergency*, 20.

136. Weizman, "Lawfare."

137. Comaroff and Comaroff, *Law and Disorder*, 22.

138. Anghie, *Imperialism*.

139. Kennedy, "Primitive"; Anghie, *Imperialism*.

140. Borschberg, "Grotius."

141. Jochnik and Normand, "Legitimation of War," 50; Normand and Jochnik, "Legitimation of Violence."

142. Schmitt, *Nomos*; Schmitt, *Space*; Ford, "Jurisdiction"; Benton, *A Search for Sovereignty*.

143. Ford, "Jurisdiction," 846, quoting a Supreme Court opinion written by William Rehnquist; Ford, "Jurisdiction," 854.

144. Kennedy, "History of an Illusion," 124; Rivera Ramos, "Insular Cases," 292.

145. Cheyfitz, "Savage Law."

146. Halliday and White, "Suspension Clause," 581.

147. Halliday and White, "Suspension Clause," 587; Halliday, *Habeas Corpus*.

148. Halliday and White, "Suspension Clause," 641.

149. Ruskola, "Canton," 289; see also Hussain, *Emergency*, 70: "Thus whether in its origins as a facilitation of sovereign power or in its subsequent and modern guises as a check on the executive, whether used to intern or to free, habeas corpus is a mode of binding subjects to the law and to its economies of power. Even in its widest application, the writ demands clarification not of the correctness or 'justice' of an imprisonment, but only of its lawfulness."

CHAPTER 4

1. The quote is from Delavignette's *Service africain*; see also Curtin, *Imperialism*, 280.

2. Petraeus, "Learning Counterinsurgency," 3.

3. Wikileaks, "Abu Zubayda"; Wikileaks, "Khalid Shaykh Muhammad."

4. Worthington, "New Revelations."

5. Hack and Rettig, *Colonial Armies*; Killingray and Omissi, *Guardians of Empire*; Kelly, *Lost Soldiers*.

6. Omissi, *The Sepoy and the Raj*; Streets, *Martial Races*; Barkawi, *Globalization and War*, 59–90.

7. Page, *King's African Rifles*; Elkins, *Britain's Gulag*, 73; Branch, *Defeating Mau Mau*.

8. Charbit, *Les harkis*; Hamoumou and Moumen, "L'histoire des harkis."

9. Gill, *The School of Americas*; Blakeley, "Still Training to Torture?"; Goldman and Eliason, *Diffusion*; Markel, "Building Partner Security Forces." A proponent of such training writes, "From 1950 to 1975 we trained 488,000 officers and troops from seventy countries, most from Asia, Africa, and Latin America. Three thousand officers attended US command courses alongside their American counterparts. Between 1991 and 1995 we trained 3,400 African military personnel, mostly officers, from forty-seven countries." Lefever, *America's Imperial Burden*, 99.

10. Kaplan, *Imperial Grunts*, 48.

11. Nagl, "Local Security Forces," 160.

12. Lumpe, "US Foreign Military Training."

13. US State Department, "2008 Foreign Military Training: Executive Summary."

14. Wilcke, "A Hard Place"; Dubik, "Building Security Forces." As of 2009, such data are classified, as a footnote in a Department of Defense report to Congress informs its readers: "DoD previously reported on readiness posture of Iraqi Security Forces with accompanying charts. With the expiration of the mandate of UNSCR 1790 [UN Security Council resolution adopted in December 2007, which extended the mandate of US presence in Iraq to December 2008], the data is now included in the classified annex because military operational readiness for a sovereign nation is considered sensitive." See Department of Defense, "Measuring Stability and Security (June 2009)," 71n32.

15. Department of Defense, "Measuring Stability and Security (December 2007)"; Department of Defense, "Measuring Stability and Security (December 2008)."

16. Inspectors General, "Intra-Agency Assessment," 7; Department of Defense, "Progress Towards Security (January 2009)," 39.

17. US Army, *Counterinsurgency Field Manual*, chapter 6; US Army, *Stability Operations Field Manual*, chapter 6; Joint Center for International Security Force Assistance, at https://jcisfa.jcs.mil.

18. One example is the Kandahar Strike Force, about which very little is known except that it is trained by the CIA and US Special Forces and was supported by the late Afghan kingpin Ahmad Wali Karzai. Cavendish, "CIA Trains Covert Units."

19. Priest, "National Security Inc."

20. Scahill, "Blackwater's Black Ops."

21. Quoted in Jiryis, "Diaries of Moshe Sharett," 43; see also Shlaim, *Iron Wall*, 133; Rokach, *Israel's Sacred Terrorism*, 28–29.

22. HaMoked, "1999 Annual Report," 8; Amnesty International, "Suleiman Hassan Ramadan."

23. HaMoked, "1999 Annual Report," 8.

24. *Rabah Abou Faour v. Israel.*

25. Amnesty, "Khiam Detainees," 4. French lawyers representing a detainee had asked for permission from Israel to visit their clients in Khiyam. "The request has been turned down on the usual grounds that the SLA, not Israel, controls the prison. 'It's as if no one has the power to decide anything, as if Al-Khiam doesn't really exist' states Agnes Tricoire, one of the French attorneys in Jerusalem. 'Therefore,' she asks the assembled press in exasperation, 'do my clients not exist?'" See Kershner, "Judgement."

26. Lavie, "Khiam," 34; Bechara, *Resistance*, 76.

27. Lavie, "Khiam," 36.

28. Even here it was not always clear who held and controlled an area. The town of Jezzine, ostensibly outside the "security zone," was nevertheless occupied by the SLA until 1999.

29. Lavie, "Khiam," 34.

30. Amnesty, "Detainees Held in Khiam."

31. Amnesty, "Khiam Detainees," 6; see also Bechara, *Resistance*, 92–93.

32. Amnesty, "Khiam Detainees," 6.

33. Bechara, *Resistance*, 75; Blanford, "Riad's Story"; interviews with Ali Haydar, Fatma, Imad Nahbani, and Hajjeh Rasmiyeh; Lavie, "Khiam," 35.

34. See testimonies in Marmal and Asi, *Kam Murr*; Haddad, "Khiam Cost Me My Baby"; interview with Hajjeh Rasmiyeh; Blanford, "Riad's Story."

35. Bechara, *Resistance*, 93.

36. Testimonies in Marmal and Asi, *Kam Murr*; interviews with Ali Haydar and Hajjeh Rasmiyeh.

37. Bechara, *Resistance*, 90.

38. Interview with Hajjeh Rasmiyeh.

39. Interview with Imad Nahbani.

40. Lavie, "Khiam," 35.

41. Amnesty International, "Detainees Held in Khiam."

42. Bechara recalls the particularly vicious Abu Nabil (the nom de guerre of Jean Homsi, now a Canadian citizen) as wanting to "break" her throughout her detention at Khiam. Bechara, *Resistance*.

43. Amnesty, "Khiam Detainees," 6.

44. Here I am writing not about private or corporate warriors but rather about local proxies of a foreign power. For more on corporatized military proxies, see Khalili, "Tangled Webs of Coercion"; Singer, *Corporate Warriors*; Verkuil, *Outsourcing Sovereignty*. There is also a substantial body of legal argument about precisely how these private military corporations fall in an ambiguous zone vis-à-vis the law. Singer, "War."

45. Alongside Dayan's idea of a proxy, a more enduring plan was that of Ben-Gurion for the Alliance of Minorities with the Maronites (Shlaim, *Iron Wall*, 133–134). Although covert contact had been made between Yishuv and Israeli leaders and various Maronite community leaders from early on, the relationships grew in earnest with the Lebanese civil war (1975–1991), when all actors in the Lebanese theater of conflict sought military, financial, and political support from outside. As such, a spectrum of relationships emerged with alliances and coordination (and often, though not always, mutual interests) at one end and a fully controlled proxy relationship at the other end. The relationship at the former end entailed Israeli delivery of economic aid (before 1982, $50 million per year was given to the Maronite militias led by Bashir Jumayyil and Dani Sham'un) and weapons, joint tactical planning, sharing of intelligence, and provision of training in Israeli bases to the members of the same militias; Hamizrachi, *Haddad*, 67).

46. Hamizrachi, *Haddad*, 130, emphasis in the original.

47. Hamizrachi, *Haddad*, 73.

48. Hamizrachi, *Haddad*, 138.

49. Beydoun, "South Lebanon Border Zone," 41.

50. Quoted in Hamizrachi, *Haddad*, 91.

51. Jabir, *Al-Sharit al-Lubnani al-Muhtall*, 411. In an interview with Aql Hashim, the Israeli journalist Ronen Bergman estimated that Shi'a soldiers "make up 30 percent of the army. In Hashem's western brigade, 50 percent of the soldiers are Christian and 50 percent are Muslim, both Shiite and Sunni. Eastern brigade commander Nabih Rifa is Druze and his troops are comprised of a large number of Druze." Bergman, "Thank You for Your Cooperation."

52. Nisan, *Etienne Sakr*, 77–79.

53. Sachar, *A History of Israel*, 2:240.

54. Those not on the frontline earned $380 per month. Increase in rank and each additional year of service brought an additional $10 per month. Bergman, "Thank You for Your Cooperation."

55. Peterson, "Woman Forges New Life."

56. Immigration and Refugee Board of Canada, "Lebanon," quoting a *Ha'aretz* report from July 5, 1998.

57. Hirst, "South Lebanon," 15. Hashim was assassinated by Hizbullah on January 30, 2000.

58. Arnold, "Command Responsibility," 210. Also see Bergman, "Thank You for Your Cooperation."

59. Black and Morris, *Israel's Secret Wars*, 396.

60. Jones, "Israeli Intelligence," 14.

61. Pedahzur, *Israeli Secret Services*, 72.

62. Before Khiam, Sa'ad Haddad kept PLO and leftist Lebanese prisoners in Tal Nahas, where they were visited by the ICRC (Hamizrachi, *Haddad*, 108–109). After 1985, in addition to Khiyam

and Tal Nahas, SLA and Israeli military operated Center 17 Camp (or Saff al-Hawa) in Bint Jubayl and their barracks in Marjayun and Jezzine. Detainees were also transferred into Israel both before and after 1992, thus allowing Shin Bet to interrogate them in Israeli facilities. See Human Rights Watch, "Without Status or Protection," appendix; Follow-up Committee, "Transcripts"; Amnesty International, "Khiam Detainees," 9.

63. Lavie, "Khiam," 36.

64. Interview with Hajjeh Rasmiyeh.

65. Interview with Imad Nahbani.

66. Amnesty International, "Khiam Detainees," 10. In an interview with Hajjeh Rasmiyeh, the officer named Yaki is mentioned.

67. Interview with Ali Haydar.

68. Jones, "Israeli Intelligence," 10. On salary payments, see also Jabir, *Al-Sharit al-Lubnani al-Muhtall*, 409.

69. Halutz went on to become chief of staff in 2005 and held that position during the July 2006 Israeli assault against Lebanon.

70. Human Rights Watch, "Torture in Khiam Prison."

71. Hajjar, "From Nuremberg to Guantánamo," 14.

72. *Assaf v. State of Israel*. Assaf and Nasrallah were released from Khiyam on November 9, 1999.

73. *Assaf v. State of Israel*.

74. *Boumediene v. Bush*, "Israeli Military Law Experts," 6.

75. Israel Supreme Court, *Judgements*, 1:13.

76. It is worth noting that toward the end of their rule in Aden, the British colonial officials regretted not having allowed the "Arab Authorities" to hold detainees, so as to forestall interference or monitoring by the Parliament and the United Nations. See letter dated March 13, 1967, UK National Archives, FCO 8/217.

77. Pelton, "Transcript of John Walker Interview"; Perry, "Qala-i-Jangi."

78. Amnesty International, "Clean Surrender."

79. Barry and Dehghanpisheh, "Convoy of Death"; Physicians for Human Rights, "Preliminary Assessment"; Physicians for Human Rights and Human Rights First, "Shebarghan Prison"; MacKey, "Did US Kill Taliban Prisoners?"; Worthington, *Guantánamo Files*, 19–25. A US State Department official's conservative estimate in a heavily redacted document dated November 26, 2002 (nearly a year after the massacres) hinted at 1,500–2,000 detainees having been killed and buried in Dasht-e-Leyli. See US State Department, "Mass Graves Investigation," 19.

80. Barry and Dehghanpisheh, "Convoy of Death."

81. Risen, "US Inaction."

82. Quoted in US State Department, "Mass Graves Investigation," 17.

83. See Physicians for Human Rights, "Preliminary Assessment"; Physicians for Human Rights and Human Rights First, "Shebarghan Prison."

84. Wikileaks Iraq, "IZ ON IZ"; Davies, "Secret Order."

85. Wikileaks Iraq, "DET ABUSE SUMMARY."

86. Wikileaks Iraq, "ALLEGED DETAINEE ABUSE IN DIYALA"; "SUSPECTED DETAINEE ABUSE"; Wikileaks Iraq, "NON-COMBAT EVENT"; Wikileaks Iraq, "ALLEGED DETAINEE ABUSE IN FARIS."

87. See interview with Abu Uthman. Interview transcripts with Shaykh Abd al-Karim similarly contain stories of massive torture at the hands of Iraqi forces, with full knowledge of the US military.

88. Priest, "CIA Avoids Scrutiny."

89. Mayer, *Dark Side*, 225.

90. Note by Duncan, December 8, 1938, CO 733 341 4.

91. Porch, *French Secret Service*, 381.

92. Thornton, "Minimum Force," 216.

93. Raghavan, "Peace Through Brute Strength."

94. Quoted in Black and Morris, *Israel's Secret Wars*, 399.

95. Smooha, *Israel*, 88.

96. "'Social Aspects of Israel,' Prepared by the AJC Office in Israel," American Jewish Committee Archives, 7; see also "Special Report from Israel," American Jewish Committee Archives, 6.

97. The account to follow is adapted from Khalili, "Gendered Practices of Counterinsurgency."

98. Rubin and MacManus, "Losing Battle."

99. "Lazy Iraqi Police Get Motivational Speech," YouTube, http://www.youtube.com/watch?v=rIGrdTakvl8 (accessed December 21, 2009).

100. McClintock, *Imperial Leather*, 55; see also Levine, *Prostitution*, 257.

101. Levine, *Prostitution*, 263–264.

102. MacKey and Miller, *The Interrogator's War*, 186.

103. Pyle, "Torture by Proxy."

104. Quoted in Grey, "America's Gulag."

105. Bruce, "Middleman." Cannistraro was the former head of the CIA's counterterrorism section.

106. *United States v. Toscanino*, 500 F.2d at 267.

107. Bassiouni, "Unlawful Seizures." The FBI describes irregular renditions as "fall[ing] into three categories: the abduction of an individual from one nation by agents of another nation, the informal surrender of an individual by one nation to another without formal or legal process, or the use of immigration laws to expel an accused or convicted criminal from a country." See FBI, *Terrorism in the United States*, 15. The same document names the following persons abducted overseas and rendered to the United States: Omar Muhammed Ali Rezaq in 1993, Ramzi Yousef in 1995, Tsutomu Shirosaki in 1996, and Mir Aimal Kansi in 1997.

108. Ostrow, "FBI Gets OK."

109. Isikoff and Tyler, "US Military Given Foreign Arrest Powers."

110. The Supreme Court legal doctrine in question is known as Ker-Frisbie, by which "a court's power to bring a person to trial upon criminal charges is not impaired by the forcible abduction of the defendant into the jurisdiction" (*United States v. Lira*). Ker-Frisbie is named after two Supreme Court decisions, *Ker v. Illinois* (concerning the abduction of a wanted US citizen by a Pinkerton agent from Peru) and *Frisbie v. Collins* (in which the US Supreme Court held that the kidnapping of Frisbie by Michigan state authorities did not violate his constitutional right to due process). Although the appeals court in *Toscanino* ruled that he should not have been extradited to the United States because his treatment "shocked the conscience," it did not divest itself of jurisdiction, although it did release him from prison. Abramovsky, "Extraterritorial Abductions," 158–160. Further, the "Toscanino exception" to the Ker-Frisbie doctrine was never applied by any US court.

111. Lake, "Panetta Faces Rendition Queries."

112. Chandrsekaran and Finn, "U.S. Behind Secret Transfer of Terror Suspects."

113. Grey, *Ghost Plane*, 140.

114. Grey, "America's Gulag"; Human Rights Watch, "Black Hole," 21–24.

115. *9/11 Commission Report*, 176.

116. Grey, *Ghost Plane*, 145.

117. Quoted in Grey, *Ghost Plane*, 140–141; Mayer, *Dark Side*, 115.

118. US Congress, *Joint Inquiry*, 225.

119. US Congress, *Joint Inquiry*, 273.

120. Priest and Gellman, "US Decries Abuse."

121. Shephard and MacCharles, "Arar in Canada When 'Seen' by Khadr."

122. Arar Commission, "Report Submitted by the Human Rights Watch," 2, emphasis added.

123. BBC, "Belhaj to Sue"; Cobain, "Rendition Ordeal."

124. Cobain, "Rendition Ordeal."

125. On Abu Umar, see Grey, *Ghost Plane*, 190–213; Hendricks, *Kidnapping in Milan*; on Agiza and Al-Zeri, see Human Rights Watch, "Black Hole"; Grey, *Ghost Plane*, 29–37.

126. Stafford Smith, *Bad Men*.

127. PACE, *2006 Report*, para. 200.

128. Human Rights Watch, "'Why Am I Still Here?'"

129. See the court rulings in *El-Masri v. United States* and *Mohamed v. Jeppesen Dataplan*. In the case of Arar, the Court reasoned that because the United States had acted under its own law to conspire with Syrian torture, the requirement of the Torture Victims Protection Act for a government to act "under the color of law . . . of *a foreign nation*" was not met. See *Arar v. Ashcroft*. I am grateful to Darryl Li for explaining the twisted logic of this reasoning to me.

130. Yoo, "Transferring Terrorists"; see also Yoo, *War by Other Means*; *Powers of War and Peace*.

131. DOJ OLC, "President's Power," 1.

132. See Aldrich, "Dangerous Liaison."

133. US Congress, *Joint Inquiry*, 92, 225, 270–278, 389–390.

134. Priest, "Foreign Network."

135. Amnesty International, "State of Denial," 4.

136. Priest, "CIA's Assurances." On assurances and their unreliability, see Human Rights Watch, "Still at Risk"; Human Rights Watch, "Cases Involving Diplomatic Assurances."

137. Priest, "CIA's Assurances."

138. Rancière, "Ten Theses," 22, emphases added.

139. On other forms of invisibility, see Khalili, "Palestine and Politics of Invisibility."

140. Interview with Muhammad al-Burdayr.

141. Pozen, "The Mosaic Theory," 630.

142. Interview with Muhammad al-Burdayr.

143. Tsemel, "Personal Status and Rights," 62–63.

144. Reeves, "Barak Forced to Free Hostages."

145. HaMoked, Affidavits of Prisoners BJ, GA, HA, HR, MJ, RB, SA; interview with Muhammad Al-Budayr.

146. Lavie, "Israel's Secret Prison."

147. Human Rights Watch, "Without Status or Protection."

148. *HaMoked v. State of Israel*, HCJ 9733/03, "Petition for Order Nisi," 8.

149. Lavie, "Israel's Secret Prison," 8.

150. Committee Against Torture, 2009 Israel Report, 8–9.

151. Lavie, "Israel's Secret Prison," 10.

152. International Commission of Jurists, "Facility 1391," 8

153. Reinfeld, "Obeid, Dirani"; *Dirani v. Israel*.

154. Human Rights Watch, "Without Status or Protection," appendix; see also Follow-Up Committee for Lebanese Detainees, "Transcripts of Detainee Testimonies."

155. Lavie, "Israel's Secret Prison."

156. Levinson and Kyzer, "Ex-Interrogator."

157. Captain George, later identified as Doron Zahavi, was rehabilitated as the police adviser on Arab affairs in East Jerusalem; see Levinson and Kyzer, "Ex-Interrogator."

158. Lavie, "Israel's Secret Prison."

159. Gross, "Human Rights," 721–722.

160. Gross, "Human Rights," 729. Gross, himself a legal scholar in Israel, believes that holding the detainees as bargaining chips under the Administrative Detention Law was fully legal.

161. Gross, "Human Rights," 730.

162. Katznell, "Two Lebanese Prisoners."

163. For the text of the law, see the Incarceration of Unlawful Combatants Law 5762-2002, available at http://www.jewishvirtuallibrary.org/jsource/Politics/IncarcerationLaw.pdf (accessed October 10, 2010).

164. Drumheller, *On the Brink*, 35.

165. Mayer, *Dark Side*, 147.

166. Rodriguez, *Hard Measures*, 51–53.

167. Mayer, *Dark Side*, 147.

168. Campbell and Norton-Taylor, "Prison Ships." John Walker Lindh, the "American Taliban" and detainee 001, had been held on the USS *Bataan* and USS *Peleliu*. See Human Rights First, "Secret Detentions," 17. David Hicks, the "Australian Taliban" and detainee 002, was held on USS *Peleliu*; see Sales, *Detainee 002*, 51. Detention on navy ships continues at the time of this writing; see Savage and Schmitt, "Somali Suspect."

169. Testimony of Domingo Rosas in Iraq Veterans Against the War and Glantz, *Winter Soldier*, 94.

170. Schmitt and Shanker, "Rumsfeld"; see also Taguba Report, annex 53, 131–133; Li, "A Universal Enemy?" 405–408.

171. Taguba Report, 26–27; Fay Report, 52–53.

172. Department of Justice, Office of Legal Counsel, "Protected Persons"; see also Yoo, "Testimony to the Judiciary Committee," 4, 7.

173. Caslen Report, 17.

174. Schmitt and Shanker, "Rumsfeld."

175. Strobel, "CIA Sacked Baghdad Station Chief." A *Washington Post* report showed that after years of cover-up it was still difficult to determine how Mowhush had died, as "the circumstances are listed as 'classified' on his official autopsy, court records have been censored to hide the CIA's involvement in his questioning, and reporters have been removed from a Fort Carson courtroom when testimony relating to the CIA has surfaced." See White, "Documents Tell." On Jamadi, see McKelvey, *Monstering*, 122–123.

176. Schmitt and Marshall, "Black Room."

177. Dozier, "Afghan Secret Prisons"; Savage and Schmitt, "Somali Suspect"; Scahill, "CIA's Secret Sites in Somalia"; Whitlock, "McRaven."

178. CIA, "Background Paper," 6.

179. Rejali, *Torture and Democracy*, 371–389; McCoy, *A Question of Torture*.

180. Pace, *Second Report*, paras. 258–260.

181. Amnesty International, "Secret Detention," 11–12. For more on black sites, see Amnesty International, "Below the Radar"; Amnesty International, "Off the Record"; Amnesty International, "Law and Executive Disorder"; Amnesty International, "State of Denial."

182. Amnesty International, "Off the Record," 20–21.

183. Suskind, *The One Percent Doctrine*, 94–96.

184. Worthington, "Ibn al-Shaykh al-Libi."

185. *United States v. Khalid Sheikh Mohammed*, "Defense Motion."

186. Central Intelligence Agency, Office of Inspector General, "Counterterrorism," 3–4, 7, 11–12, 16–24, 40, 44, 100–102.

187. Central Intelligence Agency, Office of Inspector General, "Counterterrorism," 11.

188. Central Intelligence Agency, Office of Inspector General, "Counterterrorism," 36.

189. Central Intelligence Agency, Office of Inspector General, "Counterterrorism," 42.

190. Vine, *Island of Shame*. Vine (see 72–76) has uncovered the fascinating history of transfer of Chagos to the United States and has found the fingerprints of the CIA, via the famous Bob Komer, all over the use of US island bases.

191. Stafford Smith, *Bad Men*, 233.

192. Walker and Baxter, "Terror Prison in Morocco"; Amnesty International, "Yemen Black Sites."

193. Parliamentary Assembly of the Council of Europe, *Second Report*, para. 70; Leary, "CIA Air Operations."

194. Amnesty International, "State of Denial," 6; Parliamentary Assembly of the Council of Europe, *Second Report*, para. 138.

195. Parliamentary Assembly of the Council of Europe, *Second Report*, para. 203.

196. Roberts, "NATO," 88–89; Parliamentary Assembly of the Council of Europe, *Second Report*, para. 110.

197. Parliamentary Assembly of the Council of Europe, *Second Report*, para. 129.

198. Parliamentary Assembly of the Council of Europe, *Second Report*, para. 129; US State Department, "Agreement Between USA and Romania," articles 5 and 7.

199. Parliamentary Assembly of the Council of Europe, *Second Report*, paras. 153 and 154.

200. Parliamentary Assembly of the Council of Europe, *Second Report*, paras. 170–172.

201. Parliamentary Assembly of the Council of Europe, *Second Report*, para. 168.

202. Suskind, *The One Percent Doctrine*, 98.

203. White House, "Military Commissions."

204. Khalili, "Tangled Webs of Coercion."

205. Arnold, "Command Responsibility."

CHAPTER 5

1. West, "A Report from Iraq."

2. Stone, "Strategic Communication Plan," 2.

3. Wikileaks, "TIF SOP 701, Detainee Death and Reporting Procedures."

4. Wikileaks Iraq, "TIF SOP 701."

5. Brown, Goepner, and Clark, "Detention Operations."

6. Brown, Goepner, and Clark, "Detention Operations," 47n3.

7. Brown, Goepner, and Clark, "Detention Operations."

8. Brown, Goepner, and Clark, "Detention Operations," 46.

9. Gourevitch and Morris, *Standard Operating Procedure*; Hersh, *Chain of Command*; Karpinski, *One Woman's Army*; Lagouranis, *Fear Up Harsh*; Metsrovic, *Trials of Abu Ghraib*; McKelvey, *Monstering*. For the reports, see ICRC, "Treatment by Coalition Forces"; Taguba Report; Fay Report.

10. Hersh, *Chain of Command*.

11. Woods, "The Business End"; Pincus, "'Deprogramming' Iraqi Detainees."

12. Foucault, *Territory, Security, Population*, 4–6; 55.

13. Berman, "Privileging Combat," 10.

14. US Army, *Counterguerrilla Operations*, paras. 249a and 249b.

15. DoD Joint Chiefs, "Joint Doctrine for Detainee Operations," I11–I13. The 2008 final draft removes the gradations in classifying enemy combatants but retains the category of "unlawful enemy combatant." More important, the category of "high-value detainees" continues to be used.

16. Dale, "Operation Iraqi Freedom," 126.

17. Rubin, "US Remakes Jails." Of this number, around 3,500 juveniles and high-value detainees were held in Camp Cropper, and the remainder were held in Camp Bucca.

18. Eviatar, "Obama's Gitmo"; Eviatar, "US General."

19. DoD Joint Chiefs, "Joint Doctrine for Detainee Operations," 14–15.

20. Kelly, *Lost Soldiers*, 98–99.

21. Service order signed by General Raoul Salan and dated November 24, 1957, ICRC Archives, B AG 225 008-009.01. However, for example, in a 1958 service order, General Raoul Salan writes, "When the 30 day limit for screening expires, application for their transfer to the military internee camps will be sent to the appropriate administrative authorities. Proposals for prisoners to be brought before courts will be systematically avoided." See ICRC Archives, B AG 225 008-009.01 "Prisonniers militaires algériens pris les armes à la main."

22. Kelly, *Lost Soldiers*, 189–190; see also Heggoy, *Insurgency and Counterinsurgency*, 182.

23. "Eyewitness account," ICRC Archives, B AG 225 008-012.

24. ICRC Archives, B AG 225 008-014.

25. Service order signed by General Raoul Salan and dated March 19, 1958, ICRC Archives, B AG 225 008-009.01.

26. Vietnam Center and Archive, US MAC, "Phung Hoang Advisor Handbook" (November 20, 1970), 15.

27. Herrington, *Stalking the Vietcong*, 12, 197. These numbers do not include all those detained for a short period. Vietnam Center and Archive, CIA, "Everything Senators Want to Know" (June 21, 1973), 26; Elliott, *The Vietnamese War*, 1137.

28. Vietnam Center and Archive, CIA, "Everything Senators Want to Know" (June 21, 1973), 19.

29. Vietnam Center and Archive, "Phung Hoang: Current Breakout" (January 1, 1970).

30. Valentine, *The Phoenix Program*, 289.

31. Vietnam Center and Archive, CIA, "Everything Senators Want to Know" (June 21, 1973), 20.

32. Ayres, "'Six Floors' of Detainee Operations." The six categories Ayres suggests (which echoes the 2005 draft "Joint Doctrine on Detainee Operations") are prisoners of war, lawful insurgents, protocol 1 insurgents, unlawful combatants, terrorists, and noncombatants.

33. Mackey, *The Interrogator's War*, 250–251.

34. Feith, *War and Decision*, 162. Philippe Sands writes that, according to Feith and others in the administration, "Geneva didn't apply at all to al-Qaeda fighters, because they weren't part of a state and therefore couldn't claim rights under a treaty that was binding only on states. Geneva did apply to the Taliban, but by Geneva's own terms Taliban fighters weren't entitled to P.O.W. status, because they hadn't worn uniforms or insignia. That would still leave the safety net provided by the rules reflected in Common Article 3—but detainees could not rely on this either, on the theory that its provisions applied only to 'armed conflict not of an international character,' which the administration interpreted to mean civil war. This was new. In reaching this conclusion, the Bush administration simply abandoned all legal and customary precedent that regards Common Article 3 as a minimal bill of rights for everyone." See Sands, "The Green Light."

35. Karpinski, *One Woman's Army*; Lagouranis, *Fear Up Harsh*; Metsrovic, *Trials of Abu Ghraib*; Gourevitch and Morris, *Standard Operating Procedure*; McKelvey, *Monstering*.

36. Giordano, "Abu Ghraib Reformer."

37. Mejía, *Road from Ar Ramadi*, 43–56.

38. Tamari, "Salah Tamari," 52; Gourevitch and Morris, *Standard Operating Procedure*, 35.

39. Gerth and Mills, *From Max Weber*, 215–216.

40. Root, *The Military*, 3.

41. Vandergriff, *Path to Victory*, 40–51. Samuel Huntington dates the professionalization of the military to an earlier period in the nineteenth century and argues that its seeds germinated in the

South, where "three generations of Southerners were troubled by the depredations of the Seminoles and Creeks, and the threat was not finally removed until the end of the exhausting six-year Florida War in 1842. The active Indian threat was also supplemented by the potential danger of a slave revolt, the two not being entirely unrelated since escaped slaves often teamed up with Indian tribes. As a result of these two threats, strong military forces and the widespread dissemination of military knowledge and skill were held necessary to the security of the Plantation system." Huntington, *The Soldier and the State*, 211.

42. Aitken, *Taylorism*; Petersen, "Pioneering Efforts"; Crainer, "One Hundred Years"; Weigley, "Root Reforms."

43. Aitken, *Taylorism*, 16.

44. Aitken, *Taylorism*, 17–18.

45. Taylor, *Principles*, 8–10.

46. Bacevich, "Progressivism," 67.

47. Gerth and Mills, *From Max Weber*, 215, emphasis in the original.

48. McLellan, *Karl Marx*, 30–32; Bauman, *Modernity*, 159–161; Arendt, *Eichmann*.

49. Vidal-Naquet, *Torture*, 52.

50. Interview with Eric Fair; Dobbins, *Occupying Iraq*, 160. On ghost detainees, see chapter 4 and Taguba Report, 26–27; also Fay Report, 52–53.

51. Rhem, "Army Improving Procedures."

52. Fay Report, 37; Dobbins, *Occupying Iraq*, 164–172.

53. Mayer, *Dark Side*, 149.

54. Goldberg, *Prisoners*, 126.

55. O Ansar I, see interviews with Abu Ali, Abu Khalid, Abu Samer, Abu Wael, Abu Wisam, and Ibrahim Khalil; Husayn, *100 Yawman*; Husayn, *Ansar 33*. On Ansar III, see Goldberg, *Prisoners*, 25–26.

56. Khalili, "Ansar."

57. Goldberg, *Prisoners*, 25.

58. Letter from Federation of Malaya to the Colonial Office, dated June 9, 1955, in the wake of a detention camp revolt in Ipoh, UK National Archives, CO 1030/145.

59. Tamari, "Salah Tamari."

60. Goldberg, *Prisoners*, 126.

61. Goldberg, *Prisoners*, 25.

62. B'Tselem, "Interrogation of Palestinians," 102; see also testimonies about the Ansar camp in Lebanon. Interviews with Abu Ali and Abu Wael.

63. Quoted in Federal News Service, "Bloggers' Roundtable."

64. Woods, "The Business End"; Ramakrishna, *Propaganda*, 65.

65. Mitchell, *Having Been a Soldier*, 193.

66. Greenberg, *The Least Worst Place*, 78.

67. Greenberg, *The Least Worst Place*, 81.

68. Greenberg, *The Least Worst Place*, 211.

69. See JTF-GTMO, "Standard Operating Procedures," 2003 and 2004.

70. JTF-GTMO, "Standard Operating Procedures," 2003 and 2004, 17-1. The Israeli military similarly restricted access to the ICRC in visiting the Ansar detention camp in Lebanon. Khalili, "Al-Ansar Mass Detention Camp," 104.

71. JTF-GTMO, "Standard Operating Procedures," 2003 and 2004, 8-1.

72. JTF-GTMO, "Standard Operating Procedures," 2003 and 2004, 4-3.

73. JTF-GTMO, "Standard Operating Procedures," 2003 and 2004, 8-2. The use of food control was also extensive in Israeli counterinsurgency prisons in Lebanon and Palestine. Khalili, *Ansar*, 106–107.

74. Mahler, *The Challenge*, 177. Interviews with Gita Gutierrez, Clive Stafford-Smith, Josh Colangelo-Bryan, Marc Falkoff, Barbara Olshansky, Brent Mickum, and Ben Wizner.

75. DoD, "Navy Brig Norfolk Emails."

76. Arar Commission, "Background Report," 175; see also the extensive discussion of the role of various Canadian agencies in the matter, 139–179.

77. Arar Commission, "Background Report," 191.

78. Dobbins, *Occupying Iraq*, 167; Mackey, *The Interrogator's War*, 250.

79. Pincus, "Battlefield of the Mind"; Federal News Service, "Bloggers' Roundtable."

80. Azarva, "US Detention Policy."

81. Azarva, "US Detention Policy."

82. Mackey, *The Interrogator's War*, xxiii. Mackey is the nom de plume of a US interrogator in Afghanistan.

83. Amidror, "Winning Counterinsurgency Wars," 21.

84. US Army interrogator interviewed by Dominic Streathfield. Also see procedures from British documents in Aden: "At this stage [primary interrogations], the detainee is probably suffering from the shock of arrest, and due advantage must be taken of this by the interrogator." "Joint Directive on Military Interrogations," dated February 17, 1965, UK National Archives, CAB 163/68.

85. DOJ OLC, "CIA's Combined Use of Interrogation Techniques."

86. Cohn, "Sex and Death."

87. Testimonies by John Cloonan and Glenn A. Fine at the congressional hearing on "coercive interrogation techniques."

88. "Malaya": Cabinet memorandum by Mr. Lyttelton, appendix 9, December 21, 1951, CAB 129/48, C(51) 59.

89. Assembly-line interrogations were originally used in Stalinist Russia, which idealized mechanized and Taylorist forms of production. Rejali, *Torture and Democracy*, 82–83.

90. McKelvey, *Monstering*, 160–161. *Monstering* in the interrogator vernacular was the term used to describe relentless questioning of the detainee.

91. McCoy, "Cruel Science"; *Question of Torture*; MacMaster, "Torture"; Rejali, *Torture and Democracy*.

92. Mayer, *Dark Side*, 144.

93. CIA, "KUBARK," 85.

94. CIA, "Human Resource Exploitation," 7. The change was made after Congress began investigating the Honduran military's human rights violations.

95. CIA, "Human Resource Exploitation"; para. L.3.

96. CIA, "Human Resource Exploitation," A-6.

97. Mayer, *Dark Side*, 157–164, 190–196, 245–248; Leopold and Kaye, "Guidebook." Also see Department of Defense, "Pre-Academic Laboratory," a SERE manual that was used by Yoo to draft the memos authorizing torture. Reverse engineering the United Kingdom's own SERE had also been quite frequent at the height of British counterinsurgency campaigns in the mid-twentieth century, where British Army interrogators were being seconded to Special Branches of friendly regimes or colonies and were using the same forms of reverse-engineering resistance. See the correspondence in UK National Archives, WO 208/5572. Further, the experience was not limited to UK military personnel, as one particular memo shows: "The Interrogation Wing of the School of Military Intelligence are very anxious to obtain information concerning the experiences, under captivity and interrogation, of the Indian prisoners captured by the Chinese during the North East Frontier affair in 1962/63." Letter from MoD, dated April 20, 1964, UK National Archives, WO 208/5572.

98. Schmidt and Furlow, "Enclosures," 847.

99. Schmitt and Marshall, "Black Room."

100. Formica Report.

101. DoD, "Interrogation Log." This section draws on Khalili, "On Torture."

102. Asad, *Formations*, 114.

103. Asad, *Formations*, 114. On the Landau Commission, see B'Tselem, "Interrogation of Palestinians." The section of the Landau Commission Report that actually delineates what constitutes moderate pressure has never been declassified.

104. DOJ OLC, "Standard of Conduct for Interrogation," 1.

105. DOJ OLC, "Interrogation of Al-Qaeda Operatives," 10.

106. DOJ OLC, "Interrogation of Al-Qaeda Operatives," 13.

107. DOJ OLC, "Interrogation of Al-Qaeda Operatives," 15.

108. DOJ OLC, "Interrogation of Al-Qaeda Operatives," 17.

109. For example, the CIA inspector general's report distinguishes between a debriefer and an interrogator and states that the latter "is a person who completes a two-week interrogations training program, which is designed to train, qualify, and certify a person to administer EITs [Enhanced Interrogation Techniques]." CIA OIG, "Counterterrorism Detention," 6n.

110. Intelligence Science Board, "Educing Information," xxix.

111. Mill, *On Liberty*, 15–16.

112. Brown, Goepner, and Clark, "Detention Operations," 41.

113. Not all liberal counterinsurgencies are so intent on improvement. The Israeli counterinsurgencies in Lebanon and Palestine, and the US asymmetric warfare—until the advent of population-centric counterinsurgency in 2006—were not concerned with transforming, improving, or reeducating detainees.

114. Foucault, *Security, Territory, Population*, 65–66.

115. Li, *The Will to Improve*, 7–8.

116. Woods, "The Business End."

117. Azarva, "US Detention Policy."

118. Federal News Service, "Bloggers' Roundtable"; Kaplan, "Prison Break"; Brown, Goepner, and Clark, "Detention Operations"; Woods, "The Business End"; Pincus, "'Deprogramming' Iraqi Detainees."

119. Durham, "Can Therapy 'Cure' Terrorism?"

120. Doug Stone, quoted in Pincus, "Battlefield of the Mind."

121. Brooks and Miller, "Inside the Detention Camps," 130–131.

122. Azarva, "US Detention Policy."

123. Rosenfeld, *Confronting Occupation*, 266–298.

124. Azarva, "US Detention Policy."

125. Letter from French "Resident" in Algeria (Robert Lacoste), dated August 23, 1956, ICRC Archives, B AG 225 008-003 1955-1957.

126. A petition from 170 prisoners of Boussuet camp to the ICRC, dated November 30, 1959, ICRC Archives, B AG 225 008-014.

127. See request for "methods adopted by authorities for rehabilitation and re-education of Communists detained in camps in Malaya" and Greece in letter from Field Marshal Harding to the Colonial Office; UK National Archives, FO 371/123863.

128. "Extracts from a report of British Advisory Mission visit to Makronisos," dated January 20, 1950, in UK National Archives, FO 371/123863.

129. Photostat of letter dated February 17, 1950, in UK National Archives, FO 371/123863. Indeed, although the same letter recognizes overcrowding, "abuse," and mistreatment of prisoners, it coolly states, "This does not, I think, mean that we should advise the Greek Government to abolish the

Makronisos scheme." Interestingly the violence practiced on the prison camps of Makronisos is wholly absent from Kalyvas's *Logic of Violence*, whose central case is the Greek counterinsurgency."

130. Hamilakis, "The Other Parthenon," 312.

131. Elkins, *Britain's Gulag*, 103–105.

132. Quoted in Bennett, "Counter-Terror Strategy in Malaya," 432.

133. Khor, "Terrorist Disengagement Program."

134. Elkins, *Britain's Gulag*, 109.

135. Elkins, *Britain's Gulag*, 111.

136. Quoted in Elkins, *Britain's Gulag*, 112.

137. Burchell, "Liberal Government," 275.

138. Boltanski and Chiapello, *The New Spirit of Capitalism*, 65. Also strikingly, they cite one 1960s management text which uses the counterinsurgency language of "hearts and minds" to make its point (see 62n).

139. Boltanski and Chiapello, *The New Spirit of Capitalism*, 71.

140. Quoted in Joiner, "Ubiquity of the Administrative Role," 541.

141. Stewart, *Occupational Hazards*, 362.

142. On Israel, see chapter 7. On France, see Porch, *The French Secret Service*.

143. Shapiro, "Lost in Translation."

144. Handelman, "Bureaucratic Organization."

145. Gerth and Mills, *From Max Weber*, 231–233.

146. Heyman, "Power in Bureaucracy."

147. Mayer, *Dark Side*, 270.

148. Brooks and Miller, "Inside the Detention Camps," 130.

149. Foucault, *Security, Territory, Population*, 45.

CHAPTER 6

1. Quoted in Anonymous (*JPS*), "Counterinsurgency in Gaza," 152.

2. Smith, *The Utility of Force*, 3–6.

3. Grubbs and Forsyth, "Is There a Deep Fight," 29.

4. Quoted in Ramsey, "A Masterpiece of Counterguerrilla Warfare," 8.

5. Weyler had been the Spanish military attaché in Washington, DC, during the US Civil War and had admired General Sherman's method of total war and scorched earth. See Thomas, *Cuba*, 328.

6. Tone, *Cuba*, 193.

7. Tone, *Cuba*, 194.

8. Pakenham, *Boer War*, 493.

9. Quoted in Spies, *Methods of Barbarism*, 149.

10. Pakenham, *Boer War*, 505.

11. Zietsman, "Concentration Camp Schools."

12. Mohlamme, "African Refugee Camps," 121. To deflect the outrage of some British parliamentarians about all concentration camps, the government had falsely claimed that most inmates were "coloured." Pakenham, *Boer War*, 505. The black camps were a source of labor for the British military and its small war apparatus. Kitchener's policy vis-à-vis the black population was straightforward: "work or starve." Warwick, *Black People*, 148–151.

13. Section 6 of act 781 of the Philippine Commission, dated June 1, 1903, quoted in Hurley, *Jungle Patrol*, 155–156.

14. Blount, *American Occupation of Philippines*, 388–389.

15. Circular Order No. 22, on December 24, 1901, quoted in Blount, *American Occupation of Philippines*, 390–391.

16. Welch, "American Atrocities," 238n12.

17. Bickel, *Mars Learning*, 124, 178.

18. Quoted in Mockaitis, *British Counterinsurgency*, 115.

19. Not everyone in the United States was concerned by the "encirclement" of the cities. Samuel Huntington called the process "forced draft urbanization" and a "positive manpower source now denied to the enemy." Elliott, *The Vietnamese War*, 1139.

20. Thompson, "Squaring the Error," 442.

21. Linebarger, "They Call 'Em Bandits," 296, originally published in *US Army Combat Forces Journal*.

22. Nagl, *Learning to Eat Soup with a Knife*.

23. Many of the deportees had been in Malaya for decades. The orders under which they were removed were the draconian orders 17D–F, which gradually increased pressure on the Chinese supporters of the revolt in Malaya. Under those orders alone, tens of thousands of squatters had been detained or deported.

24. Templer's first directive in Malaya was that "any idea that the business of normal civil government and the business of the Emergency are two separate entities must be killed for good and for all. The two activities are completely and utterly interrelated." Quoted in Komer, *Malayan Emergency*, 31.

25. On the Malayan Emergency, see CO 1022/29; CO 1022/30; CO 1022/31; CO 1022/32; CO 1022/33; CO 1022/54; CO 1022/55; Short, *Communist Insurrection*.

26. Loh, *Beyond the Tin Mines*, 104. See also Short's description of how the Mentri Besar of Kedah suggested that the answer to the problem of squatters taking good Malay land was "that the Police and Military take the line which has, I believe, been followed elsewhere, [e.g.,] Palestine and N.W. Frontier, etc., of burning out squatters and leaving them to work out their own salvation, i.e. by going into settled areas, towns, and so on, or into other and temporarily less objectionable squatter areas or, best of all, slipping over the Siamese frontier." See Short, *Communist Insurrection*, 180.

27. Loh, "Chinese New Villages," 260.

28. A letter from the Planting Association of Perak complained, "Managers are appalled at the present general lawlessness. They are no longer able to maintain orderly routine on their estates. They demand that a state of emergency, martial law, or other appropriate action be instituted immediately." Quoted in Coates, *Suppressing Insurgency*, 43n24. See also Short, *Communist Insurrection*, 177–178.

29. Of the 650,000 regrouped people, 32 percent were Malays; 45 percent, Chinese; 18 percent, Indians; and 5 percent, Javanese and other. By contrast, of the nearly 580,000 people moved into New Villages, 85 percent were Chinese. Loh, "Chinese New Villages," 257–258. In addition, many Orang Asli, indigenous jungle dwellers, were resettled into New Villages. Leary, *Violence and the Dream People*, 42–71.

30. Loh, *Beyond the Tin Mines*, 108; Shennan, *Our Man in Malaya*, 190, 188.

31. Chin and Hack, *Dialogues with Chin Peng*, 155; see also testimonies in Khoo, *Life as the River Flows*.

32. "Tapioca, yams, tobacco, cereals, climbing beans and cucumber" were among the forbidden vegetables. Short, *Communist Insurrection*, 173.

33. Loh, *Beyond the Tin Mines*, 152.

34. Short, *Communist Insurrection*, 292, 409. Many of Agnes Khoo's informants (in *Life as the River Flows*) remember this particular aspect of their life in New Villages with particular antipathy.

35. Loh, *Beyond the Tin Mines*, 140.

36. Humphrey, *Resettlement*, 110n1.

37. Loh, *Beyond the Tin Mines*, 136.

38. Correspondence and minutes (series 2, box 8, files 4, 7, and 9; series 2, box 9, file 7) of the Malay Mission Council, Presbyterian Church of England Foreign Missions Committee, SOAS Archives.

39. Loh, *Beyond the Tin Mines*, 138. These schools "were encouraged to avoid traditional Chinese names and curricula" and "daily flag-raising ceremonies were encouraged." Humphrey, *Resettlement*, 144; Short, *Communist Insurrection*, 398.

40. Loh, *Beyond the Tin Mines*, 143.

41. "Appeal on Behalf of the New Villages," in PCE FMC, series 2, box 8, file 9, SOAS Archives.

42. CO 1022/54 (Tanjong Malim); CO 1022/55, UKNA.

43. Humphrey, *Resettlement*, 130n1.

44. FO 371/170100; FO 371/170101; FO 371/170102, UK National Archives. The mission also included former Malayan civil servants who were experts in policing, psychological operations, and intelligence. Busch, "Killing the 'Viet Cong.'"

45. Roger Hilsman coined *persuadable* in his report to President Kennedy. Young, *The Vietnam Wars*, 93.

46. Trinquier, *Modern Warfare*, 74–75.

47. Souyris, "Un procédé éfficace de contre-guérilla." The translation is mine. See also Villatoux, "Hogard et Némo."

48. Kelly, *Lost Soldiers*, 100–104.

49. Trinquier, *Modern Warfare*, 82.

50. Sutton, "Resettlement in Algeria," 285; Heggoy, *Insurgency and Counterinsurgency*, 183.

51. Bourdieu and Sayad, *Déracinement*, 117–159.

52. 1 H2030—(dossier 1), Archives de l'Armée de Terre, Vincennes, France.

53. Mathias, *Les sections adminstratives spécialisées*, 85.

54. Mathias, *Les sections adminstratives spécialisées*, 32–33.

55. Heggoy, *Insurgency and Counterinsurgency in Algeria*, 184.

56. Bourdieu and Sayad, *Déracinement*, 36.

57. Sutton, "Resettlement in Algeria," 286–287; Bourdieu and Sayad, *Déracinement*, 99–115; Cornaton, *Les camps de regroupement*, 91–102.

58. Sutton, "Resettlement in Algeria," 288; Heggoy, *Insurgency and Counterinsurgency in Algeria*, 232.

59. Sutton, "Resettlement in Algeria," 289; Boudieu and Sayad, *Déracinement*, 132–134.

60. Heggoy, *Insurgency and Counterinsurgency in Algeria*, 224.

61. Horne, *Savage War of Peace*, 221.

62. Letter, May 2, 1960, in Archives de l'Armée de Terre, Vincennes, France, 1 H2030 D1.

63. Letter, May 23, 1960, in Archives de l'Armée de Terre, Vincennes, France, 1 H2030 D1.

64. Trinquier, *Modern Warfare*, 86; letter dated May 23, 1960, in Archives de l'Armée de Terre, Vincennes, France, 1 H2030 D1.

65. Galula mentions regroupment only in passing. *Pacification in Algeria*, 221.

66. Wikileaks Diplomatic Cable, "Cashless in Gaza."

67. Department of Defense, "Media Stakeout with General Petraeus."

68. Graham, "Cities as Strategic Sites"; Hills, "Continuity and Discontinuity"; Warren, "City Streets."

69. The US invasion of Afghanistan, however, follows the same formulas as before: massive aerial bombings, displacement of large rural populations, and free-fire zones.

70. Kitson, *Low-Intensity Operations*, 173–174. Also see the same complain decades later. Evans, "Lethal Genes," published in 2009, argues, "Western strategy currently lacks an effective urban lens." Gompert calls for nonlethal weapons to be used in urban environments. See Gompert, "'Underkill.'"

71. Desch, *Soldiers in Cities.*

72. Feldman, "Collision Course."

73. Records of the British Administration in Aden, IOR/R/20/D/339; Boal, "Belfast"; Holland, *Cyprus*, 133.

74. Horne, *Savage War of Peace*, 230.

75. Bhatia, "Western Sahara," 295.

76. Some of the material below has been published in slightly different form in Khalili, "The Location of Palestine."

77. Segev, *One Palestine Complete*, 428; see also CO 733/383/3, UK National Archives; K. F. Tegart, "Charles Tegart: Memoir of an Indian Police Officer," MSS Eur c.235; India Office Records, British Library.

78. Keith-Roach, *Pasha of Jerusalem*, 191. On the fence limiting access, see Norris, *"Repression and Rebellion."*

79. B'Tselem, "Behind the Barrier," 14.

80. Ophir, Gavoni, and Hanafi, *Inclusive Exclusion*, 622.

81. O'Sullivan, "IDF Seals Off Jericho."

82. Michael and Ramon, "A Fence Around Jerusalem"; Al-Haq, "Building Walls"; B'Tselem, "A Wall in Jerusalem."

83. Khalili, "Politics of Invisibility."

84. B'Tselem, "Behind the Barrier," 6.

85. Almog, *The West Bank Fence*, 8.

86. Stoil, "Cat and Mouse."

87. Sassaman, *Warrior King*, 184.

88. Bengali, "US Walls Off Baghdad Neighborhood."

89. Weiner, "Walling Off Your Enemies."

90. Zangana, "Walling in Iraq."

91. Feldman, "Collision Course."

92. B'Tselem, "Not All It Seems," 6.

93. Ophir, Gavoni, and Hanafi, *Inclusive Exclusion*, 89.

94. Braverman, "Civilized Borders," 27.

95. As, for example, the security zone established and reconfigured through the decades in Southern Lebanon. See Beydoun, "South Lebanon Border Zone," 48.

96. B'Tselem, "Access Denied," 10n4. By September 1967, the Israeli military had expropriated nearly twenty-four thousand acres of land in the West Bank to build military bases. See Ophir, Gavoni, and Hanafi, *Inclusive Exclusion*, 605.

97. IDF spokesperson, dated January 11, 2005, quoted in Ophir, Gavoni, and Hanafi, *Inclusive Exclusion*, 227.

98. B'Tselem, "Access Denied."

99. Feldman, "Collision Course."

100. "Response from Wetherall to O'Connor," January 23, 1939, O'Connor files 3/4/21, LHCMA.

101. Okamoto is speaking about the Phoenix Program in Vietnam, quoted in Appy, *Vietnam*, 361.

102. "Letter from Buxton," O'Connor Files, 3/4/44, LHCMA. Hostage taking of this sort was openly advocated by the British as recently as 1963 in Radfan in Yemen. See letter from assistant high commissioner of Aden, dated December 22, 1963, Records of the British Administration in Aden, IOR/R/20/D/63.

103. Al-Ali, *Kwikat*, 63–67; Al-Bash, *Tirat Haifa*, 173–175; Al-Shahabi, *Lubiya*, 49; Munayyir, *Al-Lid*, 26–29; Al-Jishshi, *Qurya al-Kabr*, 217. On the Halhul case in which several Palestinian detainees

died of sunstroke, see CO 733/413/3, UK National Archives. On other atrocities committed against civilians (including detainees), see "Impressions of Wingate" in the private papers of Major General H. E. N. Bredin, CB DSO MC, 81/33/1, IWM Documents Archive; CO 733/371/3; CO 733/371/4; CO 733/387/1; CO 733/413/1; CO 733/413/5; CO 733/434/7; CO 733/434/9; FO 371/21881—all in the UK National; the papers of Dr. Elliot Forster, GB165-0109, MEC; Hughes, "The Banality of Brutality."

104. CO 1030/33, UK National Archives; Elkins, *Britain's Gulag*, 62–90.

105. Horne, *Savage War of Peace*, 189–190, 198; Trinquier, *Modern Warfare*, 58.

106. Dunn, "The American Army," 90–92.

107. Robinson, *Occupied Citizens*, 69n61, 71n65, 100, 205.

108. Benziman, *Sharon*, 115–117.

109. Anonymous (*MERIP*), "South Lebanon," 35.

110. Gorenberg, *Occupied Territories*, 135.

111. When rumors of destruction began to circulate, the Israeli government gave tours of the destroyed areas to defense attachés rather than to journalists; see Rid and Hecker, *War 2.0*, 107.

112. Testimony of Toby Winn, in Wood, *What Was Asked of Us*, 145.

113. Maass, "Professor Nagl's War."

114. US Army, *Counterinsurgency Field Manual*, 182–184.

115. Testimony of Scott Ewing in Iraq Veterans Against the War and Glantz, *Winter Soldier*, 71–73.

116. Jamail, *Beyond the Green Zone*, 74–75.

117. Quoted in Ramsey, "Masterpiece of Counterguerrilla Warfare," 55. General Order 100 is the Lieber Code, discussed in chapter 3. Franklin Bell was a US Army commander in the Philippines, from 1899 to 1902.

118. Quoted in Erlanger, "Hamas Leader."

119. Pakenham, *Boer War*, 494.

120. Tone, *War and Genocide*, 193–194; Welch, "American Atrocities," 238n12.

121. Ron Cassidy, in Allen, *Savage Wars*, 38.

122. Loh, *Beyond the Tin Mines*, 153.

123. Yuen, *Operation Ginger*, 31–42. Residents of these villages however attest to the ways in which the New Villagers circumvented some of the measures by telling shopkeepers "not to enter all their stock into the books as was required by law" to be able to smuggle food. See testimony in Chen Xiu Zhu, in Khoo, *Life as River Flows*, 69.

124. Time, "Collective Punishment."

125. Buckingham, "Operation Ranch Hand."

126. Russo, "Statistical Analysis of US Crop Spraying Program."

127. Neilands, "Chemical War," 212–213; see also Buckingham, "Operation Ranch Hand."

128. Heggoy, *Insurgency and Counterinsurgency*, 186.

129. Heggoy, *Insurgency and Counterinsurgency*, 224.

130. Jamail, *Beyond the Green Zone*, 25, 124.

131. Azoulay, "Hunger in Palestine."

132. Feldman and Blau, "Gaza Bonanza"; Hass, "Why Won't Israel Allow Gazans to Import Coriander?" Feldman and Blau also indicate that the interest of Israeli lobbyists, for example fruit growers, can affect what enters Gaza, with the representative of agricultural associations even being present at the loading and unloading of trucks that take foods into Gaza. One such representative is quoted, "Last year I had a bad situation with onions. A lot of growers were stuck with their stock. We pressed the Agriculture Ministry and then they increased the onion quota [going into Gaza] from five to eight trucks at the end of last year."

133. ICRC, "Gaza," 7.

134. Quoted in Weizman, "Thanato-Tactics," 572n67.

135. Burnham, *Scouting on Two Continents*, 15.

136. Kramer, "Superfluous Young Men."

137. Oren, "Seven Existential Threats."

138. Rafael, "White Love."

139. Report of inspector general for regroupment, dated December 11, 1960, in Archives de l'Armée de Terre, Vincennes, France, 1 H2030 D1.

140. Porch, *French Secret Service*, 384.

141. The youths are celebrated as positive agents of change in Iran, when they are demonstrating against the Islamic Republic.

142. Hughes, "Global Threats."

143. Therborn, "Nato's Demographer."

144. Beehner, "The Battle of the 'Youth Bulge.'"

145. Kilcullen, "Twenty-Eight Articles"; Winn Byrd and Decker, "Why the US Should Gender."

146. Combined Joint Intelligence Operations Center—Afghanistan, "Female Engagement Teams."

147. International Security Assistance Force, "Female Engagement Teams."

148. Bernard et al., *Women and Nation-Building*, 13.

149. Testimony of Colonel Michael Formica, in Gott, *Eyewitness to War*, 1:33.

150. Yuval-Davis, "The Demographic Race."

151. Ben-Gurion, *Israel*, 838.

152. Aditjondro, "Ninjas," 184. Aditjondro recounts how Israeli demographic techniques were exported to other contexts where population settlement was central to counterinsurgency, in this instance Indonesia and Aceh.

153. Ophir, Gavoni, and Hanafi, *Inclusive Exclusion*, 604.

154. Ophir, Gavoni, and Hanafi, *Inclusive Exclusion*, 624.

155. Catignani, *Israeli Counter-Insurgency*, 170–171.

156. Kramer, "Superfluous Young Men."

157. Letter dated October 6, 1965, Records of the British Administration in Aden, IOR/R/20/D/347.

158. "Reports on the District of Ramallah, 31 January 1939 from the District Commissioner, Pirie-Gordon," O'Connor Files, 3/3/8, LHCMA.

159. Al-Bash, *Tirat Haifa*, 173.

160. Short, *Communist Insurrection*, 142.

161. Galula, *Pacification in Algeria*, 86; see also Trinquier, *Modern Warfare*, 31–32.

162. Schwarz, *Arabs in Israel*, 89. For an excellent account of the temporary residence permits see Robinson, *Occupied Citizens*, 117–193.

163. Tawil-Souri, "Orange, Green, and Blue"; Zureik, "Constructing Palestine."

164. Procedural memorandum from Shomron Regional Brigade, dated October 27, 2004, quoted in Ophir, Gavoni, and Hanafi, *Inclusive Exclusion*, 151.

165. Shenhav and Berda, "Colonial Foundations," 355; Hass, *Drinking the Sea*, 233–263.

166. Department of Defense, "The Role of Biometrics."

167. Jamail, *Beyond the Green Zone*, 279–280.

168. Feldman, *Formations of Violence*, 56–59.

169. Abshier, "High-Tech ID Systems."

170. Shachtman, "How Technology Almost Lost the War."

171. Shachtman, "How Technology Almost Lost the War."

172. Loh, *Beyond the Tin Mines*, 111.

173. Horne, *Savage War of Peace*, 190.

174. McCarthy, "Report from Vietnam." Ngo Din Diem reported to his adviser Robert Thompson that "everyone in these remote areas would be given an opportunity to move into strategic hamlets. After this was done the area would be a 'no-man's land' and any villagers who remained would be bombed and strafed." FO 371/170100, UK National Archives. On Staley, see Latham, *Modernization*, 171–173.

175. Sela, "Presence and Absence"; Ben-Eliezer, *Israeli Militarism*, 85; Almog, *The Sabra*, 176–184.

176. Jiryis, *The Arabs in Israel*, 17–18; Schwarz, *The Arabs in Israel*, 84.

177. Sharon, *Warrior*, 252.

178. Breaking the Silence, "Occupation," 273–274; see also B'Tselem, "No Minor Matter," 28–29.

179. US Army, *Counterinsurgency Field Manual*, para. 3-153.

180. Jane's Foreign Report, "Israel Trains US Troops."

181. Chiarelli and Michaelis, "Full Spectrum Operations," 5.

182. Asad, *Anthropology*; Wolfe, *Settler Colonialism*.

183. McFate, "Adversary Culture"; Luft, *Beer, Bacon and Bullets*. For a critique, see Porter, *Military Orientalism*.

184. 1 H2524, Archives de l'Armée de Terre, Vincennes, France.

185. Hour and MacMaster, *Paris 1961*, 50.

186. Heggoy, *Insurgency and Counterinsurgency*, 191.

187. Feuchtwang, "The Discipline and Its Sponsors," 83.

188. Feuchtwang, "The Discipline and Its Sponsors," 85.

189. Feuchtwang, "The Discipline and Its Sponsors," 88–89.

190. US Army, *Counterinsurgency Field Manual*, chapter 3.

191. McFate, "Adversary Culture," 45.

192. For a critique, see Albro, "Writing Culture"; Network of Concerned Anthropologists, *The Counter-Counterinsurgency Manual*; Gregory, "The Rush to the Intimate"; Price, "Soft Power, Hard Power."

193. Carlough, *Pax Britannica*, 11, 183–188. Carlough is McFate's maiden name.

194. McFate, "Anthropology and Counterinsurgency," 37.

195. American Anthropological Association, Commission on the Engagement of Anthropology with the US Security and Intelligence Communities, "Final Report." Rather more alarmingly, it turns out that HTS has been involved in interrogations. Weinberger, "Pentagon." Military men themselves see HTS as a descendant of CORDS in Vietnam. Kipp et al., "Human Terrain System." The HTS is not universally appreciated in the military, where some see it as replicating "organic" knowledge within the military. See Connable, "All Our Eggs." Connable is a major in the Marine Corps, which has acted as a sort of colonial constabulary since its inception.

196. TRADOC G2 HTS, "My Cousin's Enemy," 10.

197. Jean, "Culture Maps."

198. Marine Corps Intelligence Activity, "Iraqi Culture Smart Card." For a critique, see Davis, "Culture as Weapon System."

199. Sharon, *Warrior*, 258.

200. Kasher and Yadlin, "Israeli Military Ethics," 17; Kasher, "A Moral Evaluation"; see also Kasher and Yadlin, "Israeli Military Ethics," 14–15.

201. Blank and Guiora, "Commander's Toolbox."

202. Kinsella, "Civilians, Combatants," 163.

203. Kasher and Yadlin, "Israeli Military Ethics," 15.

204. The CIA's Special Operations Group is one such civilian body.

205. US Army, *Counterinsurgency Field Manual*, para. 2-12.

206. On civilian control, see Gordon, *Israel's Occupation*, 116–146; Braverman, "Civilized Borders."

207. US Army, *Counterinsurgency Field Manual*, paras. 2-12 and 2-13; see also chapters 2 and 5.

208. US Army, *Counterinsurgency Field Manual*.

209. Save the Children, "PRTs," 35–36.

210. Almog, *The Sabra*; Ben-Eliezer, *Israeli Militarism*; Shapira, *Land and Power*.

211. Ben-Eliezer, *Israeli Militarism*, 23–24.

212. Allon, *Shield of David*, 92–93.

213. Quoted in Zertal and Eldar, *Lords of the Land*, 23.

214. Gazit, *Trapped Fools*, 249.

215. Quoted in Weizman, *Hollow Land*, 106.

216. Quoted in Zertal and Eldar, *Lords of the Land*, 278.

217. Gorenberg, *Occupied Territories*, 312–318; B'Tselem, "Ofra."

218. Zertal and Eldar, *Lords of the Land*, 319. On settlers "policing," which invariably includes atrocities and brutality against Palestinians, see B'Tselem reports on settlers: "Settler Attacks"; "Hebron, Area H-2"; "Ghost Town"; "Ofra"; "By Hook and by Crook"; "Hidden Agenda."

219. Quoted in Maass, "Professor Nagl's War." Nagl at the time was a commander in Al-Anbar Province in Iraq.

220. Short, *Communist Insurrection*, 176; Heggoy, *Insurgency and Counterinsurgency*, 224; also see Bourdieu and Sayad, *Déracinement*, 16.

221. Scott, *Seeing Like a State*, 188–189.

222. West, *No True Glory*, 321.

223. Jabotinsky, "The Iron Wall"; see also Catignani, *Israeli Counter-Insurgency*, 103.

CHAPTER 7

1. The title of this chapter comes from a phrase coined by Daniel Berrigan to describe his and his brother's protest. Quoted in Young, *The Vietnam Wars*, 202.

Churchill, *My Early Life*, 131–132.

2. Kaplan, "Supremacy by Stealth."

3. Churchill, *My Early Life*, 146.

4. Churchill, *Malakand Field Force*.

5. Churchill, *The River War*, 2:248–250.

6. Churchill, *My Early Life*, 184.

7. Churchill was critical of this act (although he placed the blame entirely on nonwhite troops), but he excised the story of it from the abridged second edition. Toye, *Churchill's Empire*, 56–57.

8. Toye, *Churchill's Empire*, 56.

9. Churchill, *My Early Life*, 255.

10. Toye, *Churchill's Empire*, 68.

11. Churchill, *London to Ladysmith*.

12. Hull, *Absolute Destruction*; Tone, *War and Genocide*; Taithe, *Killer Trail*; Hernon, *Britain's Forgotten Wars*.

13. Davis, *Late Victorian Holocausts*; Mukerjee, *Churchill's Secret War*; Nguyen-Marshall, "Moral Economy"; Taithe, "La famine."

14. Hindess, "Liberal Government."

15. See, for example, the consistency of liberals across time and space—Locke, de Tocqueville, and others—in dealing with questions of right to territory on the basis of agricultural superiority of the colonizing side. Connolly, "Tocqueville"; Williams, *American Indian*. I am grateful to Nick Touloudis for forcing me to clarify this.

16. Cole, "Empires of Liberty."

17. Sorum, *Intellectuals*, 41.

18. Louis, *Ends of British Empire*, 452–453.

19. Douglass, "West India Emancipation," 367.

20. Young, *Postcolonialism*, 164.

21. Brockway, *Colonial Revolution*; Derrick, *Africa's Agitators*; Newsom, *The Imperial Mantle*; Newsinger, *British Counterinsurgency*; Anderson, *Under Three Flags*; Cole, *Colonialism and Revolution*; Anderson, *Indian Uprising*.

22. On anarchism, see Anderson, *Under Three Flags*, which sketches a dense web of transnational mobilization in Europe, the Americas, and Asia. On the centrality of Marxism to some anticolonial revolts, see Young, *Postcolonialism*, 113–158.

23. Hobsbawm, *Nations and Nationalism*, 151.

24. Abdel-Malek, *Nation and Revolution*, 78–114; Smith, "Decolonization," 82–83.

25. Young, *Postcolonialism*, 173.

26. Quoted in Beloff, *Britain's Liberal Empire*, 315–316.

27. Geneste, "Guerrilla Warfare," 265.

28. Ahmad, "Counterinsurgency," 48.

29. Ahmad, "Counterinsurgency," 37–38.

30. Arreguín-Toft, "The Weak"; Mack, "Big Nations."

31. Kissinger, "Vietnam," 214.

32. Fanon, *African Revolution*, 88.

33. Cooper, "Modernizing Bureaucrats"; see also Wolton, *Lord Hailey*. For the French version, see Sorum, *Intellectuals*, 87; Conklin, *A Mission to Civilize*, 175.

34. Hirst was a classic Liberal and an editor of *The Economist*. Quoted in Wright, "Bombardment," 266.

35. Surridge, *The South African War*.

36. Pakenham, *The Boer War*, 508.

37. Quoted in Krebs, "Women in the Boer War."

38. Pakenham, *Boer War*, 511–515.

39. On the pro-Boers, see Nash, "Boer War."

40. Hobhouse, *Boer War Letters*; Krebs, "Women in the Boer War"; Hasian, "Emily Hobhouse."

41. Nash, "Boer War"; Hasian, "Emily Hobhouse," 151.

42. Kramer, "Empire," 68; Surridge, "Military Critique."

43. Koss, *Pro-Boers*, xxxviii.

44. For example, compare with the Congo Reform Association in Britain, which focused on the condition of colonial labor in Belgian Congo (Louis, *Ends of British Imperialism*, 153–184). On nineteenth-century Liberal attitudes to colonialism, see Pitts, *A Turn to Empire*; Dirks, *Scandal of Empire*; Mehta, *Liberalism and Empire*.

45. Howe, *Anticolonialism*, 231–267; Brockway, *Colonial Revolution*, 42; Porter, *Critics of Empire*.

46. For Castle, See PREM 11/2251, UKNA, as well as Hansard, vols. 575 and 547 (1955), 549 and 562 (1956), 563, 566, 568 (1957), and 580 (1958). For the members of Parliament visiting Aden, see Records of the British Administration in Aden, IOR/R/20/D/23, British Library. Also see Goldsworthy, *Colonial Issues*, 254–271, 351–360.

47. Telegram dated December 24, 1963, Records of the British Administration in Aden, IOR/R/20/D/23, British Library.

48. MoD, "Operation Banner," para. 221. See the extraordinary ethnography of detention, interrogation, and prison protests in Feldman, *Formations*.

49. McEvoy, *Paramilitary Imprisonment*, 183; Feldman, *Formations*, 149–151.

50. McEvoy, *Paramilitary Imprisonment*, 183–184.

51. Feldman, *Formations*, 192.

52. Berman, "Appeals of the Orient"; Slavin, "The French Left"; Chafer and Sackur, *French Colonial Empire*.

53. Sorum, *Intellectuals*, 128; Branche, *La Torture*; Robin, *Escadrons de la Mort*.

54. Le Sueur, *Uncivil War*, 197. For example, Raymond Aron's 1956 book on Algeria, which called for independence, was the most influential both on public opinion and on government officials.

55. Le Sueur, *Uncivil War*, 230–238; Sorum, *Intellectuals*, 173.

56. House and MacMaster, *Paris, 1961*; see also Sorum, *Intellectuals*, 177: "De Gaulle, who was solely responsible for French policy on Algeria, doubtless was much less impressed by protest at home than the perseverance of the FLN and by the dramatic Moslem demonstrations in December 1960 [in Paris] in favour of the FLN."

57. The phrase is Rudyard Kipling's. On anti-imperialism at the turn of the century, see Kramer, *The Blood of Government*; Love, *Race over Empire*; Welsh, *Response to Imperialism*.

58. Lasch, "Anti-Imperialists," 324.

59. Quoted in Kaplan, *Anarchy*, 177. Also see Kaplan, *Anarchy*, 121–143, on how African Americans appropriated the language of empire themselves in search of equal citizenship.

60. Kramer, *Blood of Government*, 145–151.

61. Howe, *Anticolonialism*, 31.

62. Howe, *Anticolonialism*, 34. It is important to note that the other founder of the association was Roger Casement who, after public recognition of his extraordinary reports on Congo and Peru, was hanged in 1916 for smuggling arms to Irish Republicans. Louis, *Ends of British Imperialism*, 127–152.

63. Brockway, *Colonial Revolution*, 28.

64. Sorum, *Intellectuals*, 79.

65. Sorum, *Intellectuals*, 187.

66. Prashad, *Darker Nations*, xviii.

67. Howe, *Anticolonialism*; Prashad, *The Darker Nations*.

68. Ahmad, *Landscapes of Hope*, 170; Howe, *Anticolonialism*, 87; Sorum, *Intellectuals*, 212–223.

69. Von Eschen, *Race Against Empire*.

70. Prashad, *The Darker Nations*; Khalili, *Heroes and Martyrs of Palestine*, 13–21.

71. Connelly, *Diplomatic Revolution*; Greenberg, "Law."

72. Letter from Mr. MacFarlane, dated March 1950, FCO 953/751, UKNA.

73. See, for example, the relationship between leftist and anticolonial movements in the United Kingdom and the Labour Party in Howe, *Anticolonialism*.

74. Rid and Hecker, *War 2.0*; Hammes, *Sling and Stone*; Merom, *Democracies*; Howe, *Anticolonialism*, 318.

75. Kiernan, *Colonial Empires and Armies*, 110.

76. Mill, "Treatment of Barbarous Nations," 252.

77. CAB 37/57/58, UKNA.

78. Simpson, *Human Rights*, 300–305; Anghie, *Imperialism*.

79. Butler, *Bodies That Matter*, 122.

80. Zolo, *Invoking Humanity*.

81. Kennedy, "Reassessing," 140.

82. Wright, "Bombardment," 267.

83. Quoted in Spies, *Methods of Barbarism*, 11.

84. Quoted in Spies, *Methods of Barbarism*, 12.

85. Gong, *Standard of "Civilisation."* For a shocking elucidation of opinions about the difference between civilized and noncivilized, see Colby, "Savage Tribes"; see also Berman, "Appeals of the Orient," 203; "Privileging Combat," 20–21; Mégret, "From 'Savages,'" 270–271; Wright, "Bombardment," 267.

86. Best, *War and Law*, 89–90.

87. Best, *War and Law*, 82–83.

88. Bennett, "Other Side of COIN."

89. Bennett, "Other Side of COIN," 643.

90. Branche, "Torture of Terrorists," 546.

91. Greenberg, "Law."

92. India, Indonesia, Israel, Malaysia, Sri Lanka, and Turkey have not signed the Additional Protocols. Iran, Pakistan, Morocco, and the United States, all engaged in civil or asymmetric warfare, have signed them with reservations but have not ratified them.

93. Feith, "Law in the Service of Terror"; Solf, "A Response to Feith"; Whitson, "Laws of Land Warfare."

94. Feith, *War and Decision*, 162–165.

95. Simpson, *Human Rights*, 808. The Convention entered into force in September 1953.

96. Maran, *Torture*, 9–10. Notably, Belgium and Italy explicitly refused to apply the convention to their overseas holdings. Vasak, "European Convention," 1211n7. The Netherlands also refused to recognize the right of individuals to petition the European Council.

97. Simpson, *Human Rights*, 489.

98. Simpson, *Human Rights*, 490.

99. Simpson, *Human Rights*, 495–499.

100. Vasak, "European Convention," 1210; Simpson, *Human Rights*; Bennett, "Other Side of COIN," 641.

101. Simpson, *Human Rights*, 924–1052. Vasak also recalls that the African National Congress approached Iceland to lodge a case on behalf of Hastings Banda of Nyasaland (Malawi). Vasak speculates that the threat of the case alone was enough to convince the British authorities to release Banda. Vasak, "European Convention," 1212.

102. FO 371/137788/WUC1733/16, quoted in Simpson, *Human Rights*, 983.

103. FO 371/130122/WUC1735/50, quoted in Simpson, *Human Rights*, 983.

104. Vasak, "European Convention," 1213. The number in parentheses is the year the derogation was first entered, and in all instances, it was renewed again thereafter. For a comprehensive treatment of UK derogations during emergencies, see Simpson, *Human Rights*, 874–923.

105. Simpson, *Human Rights*, 1057.

106. *Republic of Ireland v. The United Kingdom*, Case No. 5310/71, European Court of Human Rights, 1978.

107. Mbembe, *Necropolitics*, 25.

108. Quoted in Weston, *Racism*, 49.

109. McFate, "Adversary Culture," 44.

110. Goldberg, "Racial Palestinianization"; Kaplan and Pease, *Cultures of US Imperialism*; Kiernan, *Lords of Human Kind*.

111. Jules Harmand, quoted in Curtin, *Imperialism*, 294; also Lorimer, *The Institutes*. For critiques, see Fogarty, *Race and War*; Goldberg, *The Racial State*.

112. Kipling, "White Man's Burden."

113. Vindex, *Cecil Rhodes*, 371.

114. Abi-Mershed, *Apostles*.

115. Quoted in Hasian, "Emily Hobhouse," 152; Krebs, "Women in the Boer War," 48.

116. Callwell, *Small Wars*, 31.

117. Churchill, *London to Ladysmith*.

118. Michael Davitt, quoted in Koss, *Pro-Boers*, 34; J. A. Hobson's writing in Koss, *Pro-Boers*, 25–29.

119. Pakenham, *Boer War*, 508. On her racial attitudes, see also Krebs, "Women in the Boer War," 49–50.

120. Warwick, *Black People*, 152–153.

121. John Morley of the Liberal Party, and a follower of John Stuart Mill, quoted in Koss, *Pro-Boers*, 14.

122. Jan Smuts, a Boer general, became a very significant figure in advocating the "internationalism" of the British Empire, and he had a hand not only in the constitution of the League of Nations but also in drafting the UN Charter nearly three decades later. Mazower, *No Enchanted Palace*.

123. The phrase "fellow citizens" came from a military report commissioned to study how to deal with what was originally a struggle for civil rights. Benest, "Aden," 128; Ellison and Smyth, *Crowned Harp*, 76.

124. Arthur, *Northern Ireland*, 149.

125. Kitson, *Low-Intensity Operations*, 82–94; Strachan, *Politics*, 187.

126. Quoted in Aretxaga, *Shattering Silence*, 90.

127. Wolton, *Lord Hailey*, 4.

128. Wolton, *Lord Hailey*, 119–148; Cooper, "Modernizing Bureaucrats"; *Decolonization*; Goldsworthy, *Colonial Issues*, 9–13.

129. Latham, *Modernization*; Rabinow, *French Modern*; Cooper, *Decolonization*.

130. Sorum, *Intellectuals*, 80, 129.

131. Fox, *Lions*.

132. Colby, "Savage Tribes," 287.

133. Satia, "Defense of Inhumanity," 33.

134. West, *No True Glory*, 13.

135. West, *No True Glory*, 18.

136. Foucault, *Security, Territory, Population*, 48.

137. Koplow, *Death by Moderation*, ix. See also the careful calibration of various forms of suffering (blindness versus paralysis) listed and evaluated in Gross, *Moral Dilemmas*. Also see Singer, *Wired for War*; Human Rights Watch, "Precisely Wrong"; Denes, "From Tanks to Wheelchairs"; Gordon, "Extra-Judicial Executions"; Mayer, "Predator War"; Weizman, "Thanato-tactics." For a defense, see Etzioni, "Unmanned Aircraft Systems"; Jackson, "Imperial Antecedents"; Sepp, "Special Force."

CONCLUSION

1. Coetzee, *Waiting for the Barbarians*, 8.

2. Burchell, "Liberal Government," 275.

3. Quoted in Wright, *Politics of Design*, 76.

4. Kaplan, *Imperial Grunts*, 10.

5. Karen Greenberg writes about the role of ICRC in Guantánamo Bay that, "far from 'interfering' with a highly sensitive American mission, as the War Council had worried, the humanitarian group [ICRC] was making the detention operation work more smoothly. They were finally getting reliable information about the individuals they had in their custody." See Greenberg, *The Least Worst Place*, 102–103; see also Carvin, *Prisoners*, 131.

6. Kaplan, *Imperial Grunts*, 61.

7. Woodward, *Bush at War*, 114.

8. Gramsci, *Prison Notebooks,* 183.

9. Schmitt, quoted in Anidjar, "Terror Right," 46.

10. Foucault, *Discipline and Punish*, 268, 272.

11. Gramsci, *Prison Notebooks*, 215.

12. Kafka, "In the Penal Colony," 74.

13. Louis, *Ends of British Imperialism*, 910.

14. Gorka and Kilcullen, "COIN," 16.

15. Smith, *Utility of Force*; Nemo, "La guerre dans le milieu social."

16. Exum, "Leverage." Of course, Exum does not use a language of clients and proxies. For him, the United States primarily wages counterinsurgency wars "as a third party acting on behalf of a host nation," even if he recognizes that the interests of the United States are "almost never" aligned with those of the "host nation" elite (never mind the population).

17. The Israeli Civil Administration operates out of the Israeli military; and when the United States colonized Puerto Rico and Philippines, the Department of War under Elihu Root became "the de facto colonial office." See Go, *American Empire*, 9.

18. Department of Defense, "Sustaining US Global Leadership," 6.

19. Department of Defense, "Sustaining US Global Leadership," 4.

20. Youssef, *Al-A'mal al-kamila*, 84–85. I am grateful to Sinan Antoon for his beautiful translation.

21. Fanon, *The Wretched of the Earth*, 106.

BIBLIOGRAPHY

ARCHIVES

Archives de l'Armée de Terre, Service Historique de la Défense, Centre Historique des Archives, Vincennes, France

1 H2030—(dossier 1) Regroupement de Population (1957–1962).

1 H2524—(dossier 1) Conférences sur la Guerre Psychologique Données par le Centre d'Instruction de Pacification et Contre-guérilla sur le Milieu Algérien (1956–1961).

1 H2576—(dossier 1) Bulletin de Renseignements Quotidiens Psychologiques sur la Situation de la Rébellion et l'Action des Forces de l'Ordre (1957–1958).

1 H2576—(dossier 2) Bulletins de Renseignements Quotidiens du 2e Bureau de la 9e Division d'Infanterie (1957).

American Jewish Committee Archives

"'Social Aspects of Israel,' prepared by the AJC Office in Israel." Confidential memorandum for AJC Program Contributors from Simon Segal (May 25, 1962). http://www.ajcar chives.org/AJC_DATA/Files/678.PDF (accessed September 1, 2010).

Follow-Up Committee for the Support of Lebanese Detainees in Israeli Prisons.

"Transcript of Interviews with Former Al-Khiyam Detainees." Beirut. http://www .followupcsld-ip.org.lb/testimonies-frames.html (accessed August 17, 2010).

Imperial War Museum (IWM) Document Archives

"Appreciation by Captain O. C. Wingate of Force H.Q. Intelligence on 5.6.38 at Nazareth of the Possibilities of Night Movements by Armed Forces of the Crown with the Object of Putting an End to Terrorism in Northern Palestine" and "Impression of Wingate." Papers of Maj. Gen. H. E. N. Bredin. 81/33/1.

"Special Night Squad 1st. Bn. The Manchester Regiment. Personal Diary. With Training Notes by Capt. Orde Wingate D.S.O. R.A." Papers of Lt. Col. R. King-Clark. 83/10/1.

India Office Records, British Library, London
K. F. Tegart. "Charles Tegart: Memoir of an Indian Police Officer," MSS Eur c.235. European Manuscripts.
Records of the British Administration in Aden, 1839–1967.
IOR/R/20/D/20—file 830/01A: Detention of Persons Under Emergency Decree, 1963; Complaints by Detainees; Commission of Enquiry.
IOR/R/20/D/21—file 830/01B: Detention of Persons Under Emergency Decree, 1963; Complaints by Detainees; Commission of Enquiry.
IOR/R/20/D/23—file 830/02: Visit of MPs, Dec. 1963 and Jan. 1964: Investigation of Detainees' Complaints; Incident at Zingibar.
IOR/R/20/D/63—file 3209A: Radfan and Alawi Affairs.
IOR/R/20/D/339—file 7367/13: Security-Internal: Control of Movement in Aden State.
IOR/R/20/D/347—file 7368/16: Security Measures: Rushford/Cumming Bruce Report: Registration of Population.
International Committee of the Red Cross (ICRC) Archives, Geneva, Switzerland
Algeria:
B AG 225 008-003 1955–1957, Action du CICR au Cours du Conflit, Généralités.
B AG 225 008-009.01 Prisonniers Militaires Algériens Pris les Armes à la Main.
B AG 225 008-012 1959–1960, Action du CICR au Cours du Conflit, Généralités.
B AG 225 008-014 1959–1960, Plaintes Concernant les Camps et les Prisons 09.02.1959–28.12.1960.
Liddell Hart Centre for Military Archives (LHCMA), Kings College London
Private Papers of Maj. Gen. Richard O'Connor.
St. Antony's College, Oxford. Middle East Centre Archives
Papers of Dr. Elliot Forster, GB165-0109.
School of Oriental and African Studies, Archives, London
Presbyterian Church of England (PCE) Foreign Missions Committee (FMC), Malaya Mission Council, Correspondence and Minutes
PCE FMC, series 2, box 8, files 4, 7, 9.
PCE FMC, series 2, box 9, file 7.
UK National Archives
Aden: CAB 163/68; DEFE 13/529; DEFE 24/252; FCO 8/164; FCO 8/165; FCO 8/166; FCO 8/167; FCO 8/180; WO 32/20987; WO 208/5572.
Bahrain: FO 371/123863; FO 371/132869.
Cyprus: FO 371/123897; PREM 11/2251
Malaya: CO 1022/39; CO 1030/145; CAB 21/1681; CAB 129/48; PREM 8/1406; PREM 8/1406/2.
Palestine: CO 530/440; CO 530/473; CO 537/1315; CO 537/1315; CO 967/96; FO 371/23245; FO 371/52578; FO 371/52579; FO 371/61902; FO 371/68640; FO 1015/68; PREM 8/300.
South Africa (Boer War): CO 537/404; CO 537/405; CO 537/406; WO 78/2996.
Vietnam Center and Archive, Texas Tech University, Lubbock, Texas
CIA, internal memorandum for William E. Colby. "Everything Senators Might Want to Know About Phoenix and You Were Afraid They Would Ask" (June 21, 1973). http://www.vietnam.ttu.edu/star/images/041/04115200001.pdf (accessed March 30, 2011).
US Military Assistance Command (MAC), Vietnam. "Phung Hoang Advisor Handbook" (November 20, 1970). http://www.vietnam.ttu.edu/star/images/137/1370406001.pdf (accessed March 30, 2011).

"Phung Hoang: Current Breakout of VCI Executive and Significant Cadres" (January 1, 1970) (Phoenix Program Green Book). http://www.virtualarchive.vietnam.ttu.edu/starweb/ virtual/virtual/servlet.starweb?path=virtual/virtual/materials%5Fnew.web&search1= ONUMN%3D0440317001 (accessed March 30, 2011).

Wikileaks Leaked Documents
US Department of the Army. "TIF SOP 701, Detainee Death and Reporting Procedures" (February 19, 2007). http://file.wikileaks.info/leak/us-camp-bucca-detainee-death-sop-2007.pdf (accessed March 28, 2011).

Wikileaks Diplomatic Cables
"Cashless in Gaza" (November 3, 2008). Released by *Aften Posten* of Norway. http://www .aftenposten.no/spesial/wikileaksdokumenter/article3972840.ece (accessed January 5, 2011).

Wikileaks Guantánamo Files
"Abdul Ghafour, US9AF-000954DP." http://wikileaks.ch/gitmo/pdf/af/us9af-000954dp.pdf (accessed May 30, 2011).
"Abd Al Rahim Hussein Mohammed Al Nashiri, US9SA-010015DP." http://wikileaks.ch/ gitmo/pdf/sa/us9sa-010015dp.pdf (accessed May 30, 2011).
"Khalid Shaykh Muhammad, US9KU-010024DP." http://wikileaks.ch/gitmo/pdf/ku/us9ku-010024dp.pdf (accessed May 30, 2011).
"Shakir Abd Al Rahim Muhammad Aamer, US9SA-000239DP." http://wikileaks.ch/gitmo/ pdf/sa/us9sa-000239dp.pdf (accessed May 30, 2011).
"Zayn Al Abidin Muhammad Abu Zubaydah Husayn, US9GZ-010016DP." http://wikileaks .ch/gitmo/pdf/gz/us9gz-010016dp.pdf (accessed May 30, 2011).

Wikileaks Iraq War Logs
"DET ABUSE SUMMARY; Al-Musayab, Babylon (MND-C)" (May 16, 2005). http:// english.aljazeera.net/services/xml/mediafiles/tsif/showcase.html#report/MEF LNO-50732334 (accessed October 22, 2010).
"IZ ON IZ DETAINEE ABUSE INCIDENTS IVO ISKANDARIYAH: 4 CIV INJ, 0 CF INJ/DAMAGE; Al-Mahawil, Babylon (MND-C)" (June 19, 2005). http://english .aljazeera.net/services/xml/mediafiles/tsif/showcase.html#report/MEF LNO-22694728 (accessed October 22, 2010).
"ALLEGED DETAINEE ABUSE BY IA AT THE DIYALA JAIL IN BAQUBAH; Al-Muq-dadiya, Diyala (MND-N)" (May 25, 2006). http://english.aljazeera.net/services/xml/ mediafiles/tsif/showcase.html#report/2006-146-044740-0967 (accessed October 23, 2010).
"SUSPECTED DETAINEE ABUSE BY IP IN HUSAYBAH: 0 INJ/DAMAGE; Al-Ka'im, Anbar (MNF-W)" (June 26, 2006). http://english.aljazeera.net/services/xml/mediafiles/ tsif/showcase.html#report/2006-177-151817-0981 (accessed October 23, 2010).
"ALLEGED DETAINEE ABUSE IA IN FARIS (ZONE 98): 0 INJ/DAMAGE; Tarmia, Baghdad (MND-BAGHDAD)" (July 7, 2006). http://english.aljazeera.net/services/xml/ mediafiles/tsif/showcase.html#report/2006-191-201925-0973 (accessed October 23, 2010).
"(NON-COMBAT EVENT) OTHER RPT BDHA FOB WARRIOR : 0 INJ/DAM; Kirkuk, Tameem (MND-N)" (November 17, 2007). http://english.aljazeera.net/services/xml/media files/tsif/showcase.html#report/20071117193038SME40912352 (accessed October 23, 2010).

INTERVIEWS
Abd-al-Jabbar, Shaykh Abd-al-Sattar. Imprisoned 2003–2004. Abu Ghraib. Interview conducted in Amman, Jordan, November 5, 2007.
Abu Ali. Born 1955. Imprisoned 1984–1985. Ansar I camp. Interview conducted in Beirut, November 8, 2006.

Abu Khalid. Born 1940. Imprisoned 1982–1984. Interrogation center inside Israel and Ansar I camp. Interview conducted in Burj al-Shamali camp, Lebanon, November 9, 2006.

Abu Samer. Imprisoned 1982–1983. Safa Factory, Atlit prison, and Ansar I camp. Interview conducted in Ain al-Hilwa camp, Lebanon, April 7, 2007.

Abu Uthman. Imprisoned 2005–2006. Iraqi Interior Ministry Prison. Interview conducted in Amman, Jordan, November 5, 2007.

Abu Wael. Born 1955. Imprisoned 1982–1983. Safa Factory, Afule, and Ansar I camp. Interview conducted in Burj al-Shamali camp, Lebanon, November 9, 2006.

Abu Wisam. Born 1960. Imprisoned 1982–1983. Megido, Atilt, Ansar I camp. Interview conducted in Rashidiyya camp, Lebanon, April 29, 2007.

Ahmad. Born 1966. Imprisoned 1987–2000. Lebanese Forces' Qarantina Detention Center, Facility 1391, and Beersheba, Kfar Yona, and Ramleh prisons. Interview conducted in Beirut, August 16, 2007.

Ahmad, Muneer. Civilian lawyer for War on Terror detainees. Interview conducted in Washington, DC, August 21, 2007.

Ahmed, Ruhal. Born 1981. Imprisoned 2001–2004. Afghanistan and Guantánamo Bay detainee. Interview conducted in Tipton, UK, April 21, 2008.

Begg, Moazzam. Born 1968. Imprisoned 2002–2005. Bagram and Guantánamo Bay detainee. Interview conducted in London, April 24, 2008.

Al-Budayr, Muhammad. Born 1974. Imprisoned 1991–2001. Al-Khiyam, Facility 1391, and Jalamy, Ashkelon, Beersheba, and Nafha prisons. Interview conducted in Beirut, March 7, 2007.

Colangelo-Bryan, Josh. Civilian lawyer for War on Terror detainees. Interview conducted in New York, August 2, 2007.

Fair, Eric T. Contract interrogator in Iraq. Interview conducted in Princeton, NJ, July 31, 2007.

Falkoff, Marc. Civilian lawyer for War on Terror detainees. Interview conducted in New York, July 24, 2007.

Fatma. Born 1966. Imprisoned 1986–1987. Al-Khiyam. Interview conducted in Al-Khiyam, Lebanon, August 5, 2007.

Gutierrez, Gita. Center for Constitutional Rights, lawyer for War on Terror detainees. Interview conducted in New York, August 1, 2007.

Hafetz, Jonathan. Civilian lawyer for War on Terror detainees. Interview conducted in New York, August 17, 2007.

Halbusi, Shaykh Abd al-Razzaq. 2005–2006. Provided aid to families of detainees in Iraq; lost sons and nephews to detention. Interview conducted in Amman, Jordan, November 7, 2007.

Haydar, Ali. Born 1963. Imprisoned 1985–1996. Al-Khiyam. Interview conducted in Beirut, March 7, 2007.

Huq, Aziz. Constitutional lawyer involved with War on Terror cases. Informal interview conducted in New York, July 30, 2007.

Husayn. Born 1969. Imprisoned 1987–2000. Center 17 Camp, Al-Khiyam, Facility 1391, and Jalamy, Ashkelon, Kfar Yona, Beersheba, and Ramleh prisons. Interview conducted in Ayta al-Sha'b, Lebanon, August 20, 2007.

Ibrahim, Shaykh Atallah. Head of Hizbullah's Association of Former Detainees. Interview conducted in Beirut, May 22, 2007.

Jaffer, Jameel. American Civil Liberties Union, lawyer for War on Terror detainees. Interview conducted in New York, August 6, 2007.

Jum'a, Asmahan. Born 1962. Imprisoned 1983. Nabatiyya Women's Detention Camp. Interview conducted in Rashidiyya camp, Lebanon, April 29, 2007.

Kamal. Born 1971. Imprisoned 1988–1993. Al-Khiyam. Interview conducted in Bint Jubayl, Lebanon, March 18, 2007.

Karpinski, Col. Janis. Former commander of Abu Ghraib. Interview conducted in Washington, DC, August 13, 2007.

Khalil, Ibrahim. Imprisoned 1982–1983. Safa Factory, Atlit, and Ansar I camp. Interview conducted in Ain al-Hilwa camp, Lebanon, April 7, 2007.

Kleinman, Col. Steve. Retired military intelligence officer, Survival, Evasion, Resistance, and Escape (SERE) expert. Interview conducted in Palo Alto, CA, October 2, 2007.

Lagouranis, Tony. Former military intelligence interrogator in Iraq. Phone interview, August 2, 2007.

Meeropol, Rachel. Center for Constitutional Rights, lawyer for War on Terror detainees. Interview conducted in New York, August 1, 2007.

Mickum, Brent. Civilian lawyer for War on Terror detainees. Interview conducted in Washington, DC, August 20, 2007.

Mori, Lt. Col. Dan. Judge Advocate General, lawyer for War on Terror detainees. Phone interview, August 21, 2007.

Al-Nahbani, Imad. Born 1971. Imprisoned 1988–1996. Al-Khiyam. Interview conducted in Shatila camp, Lebanon, November 3, 2006.

Olshansky, Barbara. Former Center for Constitutional Rights lawyer for War on Terror detainees. Interview conducted in Palo Alto, CA, October 9, 2007.

Porterfield, Kate. Bellevue–New York University Program for Survivors of Torture. Interview conducted in Washington, DC, August 13, 2006.

Qasim, Hajj Said Khalid. Born 1949. Imprisoned 1970–1985. Ramleh and Ashkelon prisons. Interview conducted in Rashidiyya camp, Lebanon, April 29, 2007.

Qaysi, Hajj Ali. Imprisoned 2003. Abu Ghraib. Founder of Organization of Victims of US Occupation Prisons. Interview conducted in Amman, Jordan, November 6, 2007.

Rasmiyeh, Hajjeh. Born 1965. Al-Khiyam. Imprisoned 1990–1992. Interview conducted in Taybeh, Lebanon, August 15, 2007.

Safa, Muhammad. Born 1953. Imprisoned 1982–1983. Safa Factory and Ansar I camp. Head of Follow-Up Committee for the Support of Lebanese Detainees in Israeli Prisons. Interview conducted in Beirut, November 6, 2006.

Shaykh Abd-al-Karim. Imprisoned 2003. Kazmiyya, Iraq. Imprisoned 2005. Interior Ministry Prisons. Interview conducted in Amman, Jordan, November 5, 2007.

Stafford Smith, Clive. Civilian lawyer for War on Terror detainees. Interview conducted in Bridport, UK, June 19, 2008.

Storr, Lt. Col. Jim. Former UK Army doctrine writer. Interview conducted in Birmingham, October 23, 2007.

US Army interrogator. Interviewed by Dominic Streatfield. http://www.dominicstreatfeild.com/2010/11/17/interview-with-us-army-interrogator/ (accessed February 18, 2011).

Watt, Steven. American Civil Liberties Union, lawyer for War on Terror detainees. Interview conducted in New York, July 27, 2007.

Wizner, Ben. American Civil Liberties Union, lawyer for War on Terror detainees. Interview conducted in New York, July 25, 2007.

GOVERNMENT PUBLICATIONS AND MILITARY MANUALS

Adjutant General's Office. 1898. "Instructions for the Government of Armies of the United States in the Field, prepared by Francis Lieber, LL.D." Washington, DC: Government Printing

Office. Originally published as "General Orders No. 100, Adjutant General's Office, 1863." http://avalon.law.yale.edu/19th_century/lieber.asp (accessed September 2, 2010).

Canadian Commission of Inquiry into the Actions of Canadian Officials in Relation to Maher Arar (Arar Commission). 2005. "Report Submitted by Wendy Patten, US Advocacy Director of Human Rights Watch" (May 17). Ottawa.

Caslen, Brig. Gen. Robert A. 2005. "Detainee Senior Leadership Oversight Council Meeting" (December 8). Released as part of Center for Constitutional Rights Freedom of Information Act on ghost detainees. Washington, DC. http://ccrjustice.org/files/Pages%20from%20 Feb%202009%20DOD%20JS%20Release(2).pdf (accessed October 10, 2010).

Central Intelligence Agency. 1963. "KUBARK Counterintelligence Interrogation." Langley, VA. http://www.gwu.edu/~nsarchiv/NSAEBB/NSAEBB122/#kubark (accessed April 1, 2011).

———. 1983. "Human Resource Exploitation Training Manual." Langley, VA. http://www.gwu .edu/~nsarchiv/NSAEBB/NSAEBB122/CIA%20Human%20Res%20Exploit%20A1-G11.pdf (accessed February 16, 2011).

Central Intelligence Agency, Office of Inspector General. 2004. "Counterterrorism, Detention and Interrogation Activities (September 2001–October 2003)" (May 7). Langley, VA. http://www .aclu.org/human-rights_national-security/cia-office-inspector-generals-may-2004-counterter rorism-detention-and (accessed September 17, 2010).

Cloonan, John. 2008. "Testimony to the Senate Committee on the Judiciary." Hearings: "Coercive Interrogation Techniques: Do They Work, Are They Reliable, and What Did the FBI Know About Them?" (June 10). Washington, DC. http://www.loc.gov/rr/frd/Military_Law/pdf/ Senate-Judiciary-Hearing-June-10-2008.pdf (accessed February 14, 2011).

Combined Joint Intelligence Operations Center—Afghanistan. 2010. "Strategic Intelligence Update: Recommended ISAF Guidance; Female Engagement Teams" (February 23). http:// cryptome.org/dodi/COMISAF.ppt (accessed January 6, 2011).

Dale, Catherine. 2009. "Operation Iraqi Freedom: Strategies, Approaches, Results and Issues for Congress" (April 2). Washington, DC: Congressional Research Service.

Department of Defense. 2002. "Navy Brig Norfolk Emails" (April). http://www.aclu.org/files/ pdfs/natsec/dod_emails_20081006.pdf (accessed January 13, 2011).

———. 2003. "Interrogation Log: Detainee 063." http://www.time.com/time/2006/log/log.pdf (accessed April 4, 2011).

———. 2005. "National Defense Strategy" (March). http://www.defenselink.mil/news/Apr2005/ d20050408strategy.pdf (accessed September 15, 2010).

———. 2007. "Measuring Stability and Security in Iraq: Report to Congress in Accordance with the Department of Defense Supplemental Appropriations Act 2008 (Section 9204, Public Law 110-252)" (December). Washington, DC. http://www.defense.gov/pubs/pdfs/FINAL-SecDef%20Signed-20071214.pdf (accessed October 8, 2010).

———. 2007. "Media Stakeout with Gen. Petraeus after a Closed Briefing with U.S. Senators from the Crypt, the Capitol" (April 25). Washington, DC. http://www.defense.gov/ transcripts/transcript.aspx?transcriptid=3950 (accessed November 2, 2010).

———. 2007. "The Role of Biometrics in the Counterinsurgency. Department of Defense Bloggers Roundtable with Lieutenant Colonel John W. Velliquette Jr., USA, Iraqi Biometrics Manager, Coalition Police Assistance Training Team Mission, Via Teleconference from Iraq" (August 15). Washington, DC. http://www.defense.gov/home/blog/ docs/20070815BloggersRoundtable%20wLTC%20Velliquette_transcript.pdf (accessed November 2, 2010).

———. 2008. "Measuring Stability and Security in Iraq: Report to Congress in Accordance with the Department of Defense Supplemental Appropriations Act 2008 (Section 9204, Public Law

110-252)" (December). Washington, DC. http://www.defense.gov/pubs/pdfs/9010_Report_ to_Congress_Dec_08.pdf (accessed October 8, 2010).

———. 2009. "Measuring Stability and Security in Iraq: Report to Congress in Accordance with the Department of Defense Supplemental Appropriations Act 2008 (Section 9204, Public Law 110-252)" (June). Washington, DC. http://www.defense.gov/pubs/pdfs/9010_Report_to_ CongressJul09.pdf (accessed October 8, 2010).

———. 2009. "Progress Toward Security and Stability in Afghanistan: Report to Congress in Accordance with the 2008 National Defense Authorization Act (Section 1230, Public Law 110-181)" (January). Washington, DC. http://www.defense.gov/pubs/OCTOBER_1230_FINAL .pdf (accessed October 8, 2010).

———. 2012. "Sustaining US Global Leadership: Priorities for 21st Century Defense" (January). Washington, DC. http://www.defense.gov/news/Defense_Strategic_Guidance.pdf (accessed May 7, 2012).

———. N.D. "Pre-Academic Laboratory (PREAL) Operating Instructions." http://www.dod .gov/pubs/foi/operation_and_plans/Detainee/PREAL%20Operating%20Instructions.pdf (accessed May 9, 2012).

Department of Defense, Joint Chiefs of Staff. 2005. "Joint Doctrine for Detainee Operations" (Draft). Washington, DC. http://www.fas.org/irp/doddir/dod/jp3_63.pdf (accessed March 30, 2011).

———. 2008. "Joint Doctrine for Detainee Operations." Washington, DC. http://www.dtic.mil/ doctrine/new_pubs/jp3_63.pdf (accessed March 30, 2011).

Department of Justice, Office of Legal Counsel. 2001. "Authority for Use of Military Force to Combat Terrorist Activity Within the United States" (authored by John Yoo and Albert Delaunty, for Alberto Gonzalez, October 23). Washington, DC.

———. 2002. "Application of Treaties and Laws to al Qaeda and Taliban Detainees" (authored by Jay Bybee, for Alberto Gonzalez and Jim Haynes, January 22). Washington, DC.

———. 2002. "Application of Treaties and Laws to al Qaeda and Taliban Detainees" (draft authored by John Yoo and Albert Delaunty, for Alberto Gonzalez, January 9). Washington, DC.

———. 2002. "Interrogation of Al Qaeda Operatives" ("Second Bybee Memo," for John Rizzo, August 1). Washington, DC. http://www.aclu.org/human-rights_national-security/ cia-office-inspector-generals-may-2004-counterterrorism-detention-and (accessed September 18, 2010).

———. 2002. "The President's Power as Commander in Chief to Transfer Captured Terrorists to the Control and Custody of Foreign Nations" (authored by Jay Bybee, for Jim Haynes, March 13). Washington, DC.

———. 2002. "Standards of Conduct for Interrogation Under 18 USC §§ 2340–2340A" ("First Bybee Memo," for Alberto Gonzalez, August 1). Washington, DC.

———. 2004. "Background Paper on CIA's Combined Use of Interrogation Techniques" (December 30). Washington, DC. http://www.aclu.org/torturefoia/released/082409/ olcremand/2004olc97.pdf (accessed April 1, 2011).

———. 2004. "'Protected Person' Status in the Occupied Iraq Under the Fourth Geneva Convention" (authored by Jack Goldsmith, March 18). Washington, DC.

Detainee Treatment Act of 2005 (H.R. 2863, Division A, Title X of the DOD Act). http://jurist .law.pitt.edu/gazette/2005/12/detainee-treatment-act-of-2005-white.php (accessed September 21, 2010).

Fay, Maj. Gen. George R. 2004. "AR 15-6 Investigation of the Abu Ghraib Detention Facility and 205th Military Intelligence Brigade." Washington, DC. http://news.findlaw.com/hdocs/docs/ dod/fay82504rpt.pdf (accessed October 11, 2010).

Federal Bureau of Investigation. 1997. "Terrorism in the United States. Counterterrorism Threat
    Assessment and Warning Unit: National Security Division." Washington, DC: Department
    of Justice.
————. 2004. "Detainees Positive Responses" (September). Washington, DC. http://foia.fbi.gov/
    guantanamo/detainees.pdf (accessed September 18, 2010).
Fine, Gary A. 2008. "Testimony to the Senate Committee on the Judiciary." Hearings: "Coercive
    Interrogation Techniques: Do They Work, Are They Reliable, and What Did the FBI Know
    About Them?" (June 10). Washington, DC. http://www.loc.gov/rr/frd/Military_Law/pdf/
    Senate-Judiciary-Hearing-June-10-2008.pdf (accessed February 14, 2011).
Formica, Brig. Gen. Richard P. 2004. "Article 15-6 Investigation of CJSOTF-AP and 5th SF Group
    Detention Operations" (November 8; "Formica Report"). Washington, DC. http://action
    .aclu.org/torturefoia/released/061906/FormicaReport.pdf (accessed April 4, 2011).
Hughes, Lt. Gen. Patrick M. 1997. "Global Threats and Challenges to the United States and Its
    Interests Abroad." Statement for the Senate Select Committee on Intelligence (February 5)
    and the Senate Armed Services Committee on Intelligence (February 6). http://www.fas.org/
    irp/congress/1997_hr/s970205d.htm (accessed January 4, 2011).
Inspectors General, US Departments of State and Defense. 2006. "Intra-Agency Assessment of
    Afghanistan Police Training and Readiness" (November). Washington, DC. http://oig.state
    .gov/documents/organization/76103.pdf (accessed October 8, 2010).
Intelligence Science Board. 2006. "Educing Information. Interrogation: Science and Art. Founda-
    tions for the Future" (Phase 1 report). Washington, DC: National Defense Intelligence College.
International Security Assistance Force. 2010. "Female Engagement Team Builds Bridges into
    Afghan Society" (October 25). http://www.isaf.nato.int/article/isaf-releases/female-engage
    ment-team-builds-bridges-into-afghan-society.html (accessed January 6, 2011).
Joint Center for International Security Force Assistance. 2008. "Commander's Handbook for
    Security Force Assistance." Ft. Leavenworth, KS. http://usacac.army.mil/cac2/Repository/
    Materials/SFA.pdf (accessed October 5, 2010).
Joint Task Force—Guantánamo. 2003. "Camp Delta Standard Operating Procedures (SOP)"
    (March 28). Guantánamo Bay, Cuba. Originally released by Wikileaks.org. http://human
    rights.ucdavis.edu/projects/the-guantanamo-testimonials-project/testimonies/testimonies-of-
    standard-operating-procedures/camp_delta_sop.pdf (accessed April 1, 2011).
————. 2004. "Camp Delta Standard Operating Procedures (SOP)" (March 1). Guantánamo Bay,
    Cuba. Originally released by Wikileaks.org. http://humanrights.ucdavis.edu/projects/the-
    guantanamo-testimonials-project/testimonies/testimonies-of-standard-operating-procedures/
    camp_delta_sop_2004.pdf (accessed April 1, 2011).
Marine Corps Intelligence Activity. 2004. "Iraq Culture Smart Card" (April). Marine Corps Intel-
    ligence Activity Quality and Dissemination Branch, Quantico, VA. http://www.armytool
    bag.com/Tools/Culture/ArmyCard.pdf (accessed January 5, 2011. (A 2006 version is available
    at http://www.fas.org/irp/doddir/usmc/iraqsmart-0506.pdf.)
Military Commissions Act of 2006. Pub. L. No. 109-366, 120 Stat. 2600, enacted October 17, 2006.
Military Commissions Act of 2009. Title XVIII of the National Defense Authorization Act for
    Fiscal Year 2010, Pub. L. No. 111-84, 123 Stat. 2190, enacted October 28, 2009.
Ministry of Defence, United Kingdom. 2006. "Operation Banner: An Analysis of Military Opera-
    tions in Northern Ireland." London.
Murphy, Rear Adm. M. E. 1964. The History of Guantanamo Bay 1494–1964, vol. 1. 3rd ed., updated
    by Commander B. D. Varner and Chief Journalist Daniel Koze. https://cnic.navy.mil/Guan
    tanamo/AboutGTMO/gtmohistgeneral/gtmohistgeneral (accessed October 15, 2010).

National Commission on Terrorist Attacks upon the United States. 2004. *The 9/11 Commission Report*. New York: W. W. Norton.

Schmidt, Lt. Gen. Randall and Brig. Gen. John Furlow. 2005. "Army Regulation 15-6: Final Report: Investigation into FBI Allegations of Detainee Abuse at Guantanamo Bay, Cuba Detention Facility" (June 9). Washington, DC. http://www.defense.gov/news/Jul2005/d20050714report.pdf (accessed April 4, 2011).

———. 2005. "Enclosures to Schmidt-Furlow Report." http://action.aclu.org/torturefoia/released/061906/Schmidt_FurlowEnclosures.pdf (accessed April 4, 2011).

Stone, Maj. Gen. Doug. 2008. "Strategic Communication Plan" (April). Multi-National Force Iraq: Detainee Operations. https://docs.google.com/viewer?a=v&pid=explorer&chrome=true&srcid=0B2k5Ww3Ah1I5MjgoZWIyMTEtZjRiYS00OThhLWJiOTAtMmFkYTA2MDdmOTg5&hl=en (accessed January 19, 2011).

Taguba, Maj. Gen. Antonio. 2004. "Annex 53" (interview with Lt. Col. Steve Jordan). http://www.dod.mil/pubs/foi/detainees/taguba/ANNEX_053_AR_15-6_INTERVIEW.pdf (accessed October 10, 2010).

———. 2004. "Article 15-6 Investigation of the 800th Military Police Brigade." Washington, DC. http://www.dod.mil/pubs/foi/detainees/taguba/TAGUBA_REPORT_CERTIFICATIONS.pdf (accessed October 10, 2010).

TRADOC G2 Human Terrain System. 2009. "My Cousin's Enemy Is My Friend: A Study of Pashtun 'Tribes' in Afghanistan." White paper, Afghanistan Research Reachback Center, US Army Training and Doctrine, Ft. Leavenworth, KS.

US Agency for International Development. 2006. "Provincial Reconstruction Teams in Afghanistan: An Interagency Assessment." Washington, DC. http://pdf.usaid.gov/pdf_docs/PNADG252.pdf (accessed May 26, 2011).

US Army. 1967. *Counterguerrilla Operations FM 31-16*. Fort Benning, GA: Infantry School.

———. 2009. *The US Army Stability Operations Field Manual: US Army Field Manual No. 3-07*. Ann Arbor: University of Michigan Press.

———. 2009. *TRADOC Pamphlet 525-3-0: The Army Capstone Concept. Operational Adaptability: Operating Under Conditions of Uncertainty and Complexity in an Era of Persistent Conflict, 2016–2028*. Monroe, VA: US Army, Training and Doctrine Command.

US Army and Marine Corps. 2007. *Counterinsurgency Field Manual: US Army Field Manual No. 3-24: Marine Corps Warfighting Publication No. 3-33.5*. Chicago: University of Chicago Press.

US Congress, Senate Select Committee on Intelligence, and House Permanent Select Committee on Intelligence. 2002. *Joint Inquiry into Intelligence Community Activities Before and After the Terrorist Attacks of September 11, 2001* (December). Washington: US Government Printing Office. http://www.gpoaccess.gov/serialset/creports/pdf/fullreport_errata.pdf (accessed October 9, 2010).

US Government. 2009. "Counterinsurgency Guide" (January). Washington, DC. http://www.state.gov/documents/organization/119629.pdf (accessed September 18, 2010).

US Marine Corps. 1940. *Small Wars Manual*. Washington, DC: Government Printing Office.

US National Security Council. 1974. "National Security Study Memorandum NSSM 200: Implications of Worldwide Population Growth for U.S. Security and Overseas Interests" ("Kissinger Report," April 24). Washington, DC. http://pdf.usaid.gov/pdf_docs/PCAAB500.pdf (accessed December 23, 2010).

US Senate Armed Services Committee. 2008. "Inquiry into the Treatment of Detainees in U.S. Custody, Executive Summary and Conclusions." Washington, DC. http://levin.senate.gov/newsroom/release.cfm?id=305734 (accessed September 18, 2010).

US State Department. 2002. "Afghanistan: Proceeding Cautiously on Mass Graves Investigations" (part of "Assessment Roundup," November 26). Washington, DC. http://physiciansforhu manrights.org/library/documents-2008-12-11.html (accessed September 18, 2010).

———. 2005. "Agreement Between the United States of America and Romania Regarding the Activities of United States Forces Located on the Territory of Romania." Washington, DC. http://www.state.gov/documents/organization/75826.pdf (accessed October 12, 2010).

———. 2008. "2008 Foreign Military Training: Executive Summary". Washington, DC. http:// www.state.gov/t/pm/rls/rpt/fmtrpt/2008/126350.htm (accessed October 5, 2010).

White House. 2001. "Military Order of November 13 2001: Detention, Treatment, and Trial of Certain Non-Citizens in the War Against Terrorism" (November 13). Washington, DC. http://frwebgate.access.gpo.gov/cgi-bin/getdoc.cgi?dbname=2001_register&docid=01-28904-filed.pdf (accessed September 21, 2010).

———. 2002. "Humane Treatment of Al Qaeda and Taliban Detainees" (February 7). Washington, DC.

———. 2006. "President Discusses Creation of Military Commissions to Try Suspected Terrorists" (September 6). Washington, DC. http://georgewbush-whitehouse.archives.gov/news/releases/2006/09/20060906-3.html (accessed September 15, 2010).

Yoo, John. 2008. "Testimony to the Committee on the Judiciary, US House of Representatives, Subcommittee on the Constitution, Civil Rights and Civil Liberty" (June 26). Washington, DC.

REPORTS BY NONGOVERNMENTAL AND
INTERNATIONAL ORGANIZATIONS

American Anthropological Association, Commission on the Engagement of Anthropology with the US Security and Intelligence Communities. 2009. "Final Report on the Army's Human Terrain System Proof of Concept Program" (October 14). http://www.aaanet.org/cmtes/commissions/CEAUSSIC/upload/CEAUSSIC_HTS_Final_Report.pdf (accessed December 21, 2009).

Amnesty International. 1985. "Israel/Lebanon: Detainees Held by the South Lebanon Army in Khiam, South Lebanon" (November 21). London.

———. 1992. "Israel/South Lebanon: The Khiam Detainees: Torture and Ill-Treatment" (May 6). London.

———. 1997. "Israel/South Lebanon: Israel's Forgotten Hostages: Lebanese Detainees in Israel and Khiam Detention Centre" (July 10). London.

———. 1998. "Medical Letter Writing Action: Suleiman Hassan Ramadan" (October 9). London.

———. 2001. "Afghanistan: Clean Surrender Needed" (December 11). London.

———. 2005. "United States of America/Yemen: Secret Detention in CIA 'Black Sites'" (November). London.

———. 2006. "Below the Radar: Secret Flights to Torture and 'Disappearance'" (April 5). London.

———. 2007. "United States of America: Law and Executive Disorder: President Gives Green Light to Secret Detention Program" (August 17). London.

———. 2008. "State of Denial: Europe's Role in Rendition and Secret Detention" (June). London.

Amnesty International, Cageprisoners, the Center for Constitutional Rights, the Center for Human Rights and Global Justice at NYU School of Law, Human Rights Watch, and Reprieve. 2007. "Off the Record: U.S. Responsibility for Enforced Disappearances in the 'War on Terror'" (June). London.

Breaking the Silence. 2010. "Occupation of the Territories: Soldier Testimonies 2001–2010."

B'Tselem. 1991. "The Interrogation of Palestinians During the Intifada: Ill-Treatment, 'Moderate Physical Pressure' or Torture?" (March). Jerusalem.

———. 2000. "Position Paper on the Proposed Law: Imprisonment of Illegal Combatants." Jerusalem.

———. 2001. "No Way Out: Medical Implications of Israel's Siege Policy" (June). Jerusalem.

———. 2002. "The Performance of Law Enforcement Authorities in Responding to Settler Attacks on Olive Harvesters" (November). Jerusalem.

———. 2002. "Policy of Destruction: House Demolitions and Destruction of Agricultural Land in the Gaza Strip" (February). Jerusalem.

———. 2003. "Behind the Barrier: Human Rights Violations as a Result of Israel's Separation Barrier" (April). Jerusalem.

———. 2003. "Hebron, Area H-2: Settlements Cause Mass Departure of Palestinians" (August). Jerusalem.

———. 2004. "Forbidden Roads: Israel's Discriminatory Road Regime in the West Bank" (August). Jerusalem.

———. 2004. "Not All It Seems: Preventing Palestinians Access to Their Lands West of the Separation Barrier in the Tulkarm-Qalqiliya Area" (June). Jerusalem.

———. 2006. "Act of Vengeance: Israel's Bombing of the Gaza Power Plant and Its Effect" (September). Jerusalem.

———. 2006. "A Wall in Jerusalem: Obstacles to Human Rights in the Holy City" (Summer). Jerusalem.

———. 2007. "Ghost Town: Israel's Separation Policy and Forced Eviction of Palestinians from the Center of Hebron" (May). Jerusalem.

———. 2007. "Ground to a Halt: Denial of Palestinians' Freedom of Movement in the West Bank" (August). Jerusalem.

———. 2008. "Access Denied: Israeli Measures to Deny Palestinians Access to Land Around Settlements" (September). Jerusalem.

———. 2008. "The Ofra Settlement: An Unauthorized Outpost" (December). Jerusalem.

———. 2009. "The Hidden Agenda: The Establishment and Expansion Plans of Ma'ale Adummim and Their Human Rights Ramifications" (December). Jerusalem.

———. 2009. "Testimony of Colonel Itai Virob" (May). http://www.btselem.org/english/beating_and_abuse/20090521_investigate_officers_testimonies_on_routine_use_of_violence.asp (accessed July 10, 2009).

———. 2010. "By Hook or By Crook: Israeli Settlement Policy in the West Bank" (July). Jerusalem.

———. 2011. "No Minor Matter: Violation of the Rights of Palestinian Minors Arrested by Israel on Suspicion of Stone-Throwing" (July). http://www.btselem.org/download/201107_no_minor_matter_eng.pdf (accessed July 18, 2011).

B'Tselem and Bimkom. 2005. "Under the Guise of Security: Routing the Separation Barrier to Enable the Expansion of Israeli Settlements in the West Bank" (December). Jerusalem.

Committee Against Torture of the United Nations. 2009. "Consideration of Reports Submitted by States Parties Under Article 19 of the Convention: Concluding observations of the Committee against Torture—Israel" (June 23, 2009). Geneva.

Ginbar, Yuval, and Roni Talmor. 1993. "House Demolition During Operations Against Wanted Persons." B'Tselem, Jerusalem.

HaMoked. 1999. "HaMoked's 1999 Annual Narrative Report." Jerusalem.

———. 2002. "Written Submission for Consideration Regarding Israel's Third Periodic Report to the UN Human Rights Committee." Jerusalem. http://www2.ohchr.org/english/bodies/hrc/docs/ngos/Hamoked_Israel99.pdf (accessed December 21, 2010).

———. 2003. "Secret Prison Affidavit of B.J." Jerusalem. http://www.hamoked.net/Document
.aspx?dID=1042 (accessed October 10, 2010).

———. 2003. "Secret Prison Affidavit of G.A." Jerusalem. http://www.hamoked.net/Document
.aspx?dID=1046 (accessed October 10, 2010).

———. 2003. "Secret Prison Affidavit of G.S." Jerusalem. http://www.hamoked.net/Document
.aspx?dID=1600 (accessed October 10, 2010).

———. 2003. "Secret Prison Affidavit of H.A." Jerusalem. http://www.hamoked.net/Document
.aspx?dID=1049 (accessed October 10, 2010).

———. 2003. "Secret Prison Affidavit of H.R." Jerusalem. http://www.hamoked.net/Document
.aspx?dID=1040 (accessed October 10, 2010).

———. 2003. "Secret Prison Affidavit of M.A." Jerusalem. http://www.hamoked.net/Document
.aspx?dID=1048 (accessed October 10, 2010).

———. 2003. "Secret Prison Affidavit of M.J." Jerusalem. http://www.hamoked.net/Document
.aspx?dID=1041 (accessed October 10, 2010).

———. 2003. "Secret Prison Affidavit of R.B." Jerusalem. http://www.hamoked.net/Document
.aspx?dID=1043 (accessed October 10, 2010).

———. 2003. "Secret Prison Affidavit of S.A." Jerusalem. http://www.hamoked.net/Document
.aspx?dID=1047 (accessed October 10, 2010).

Al-Haq. 2002. "Position Paper on the Forced Transfer of Kifah and Intissar Ajuri." Ramallah.

———. 2005. "Building Walls, Breaking Communities: The Impact of the Annexation Wall on
East Jerusalem Palestinians" (October). Ramallah.

Hiltermann, Joost. 1986. "Israel's Deportation Policy in the Occupied West Bank and Gaza."
Al-Haq, Ramallah.

Human Rights First. 2004. "Ending Secret Detentions" (June). New York.

———. 2009. "Undue Process: An Examination of Detention and Trials of Bagram Detainees in
April 2009." New York.

Human Rights Watch. 1996. "Civilian Pawns: Laws of War Violations and the Use of Weapons on
the Israel-Lebanon Border." New York.

———. 1997. "Without Status or Protection: Lebanese Detainees in Israel." New York.

———. 1999. "Torture in Khiam Prison: Responsibility and Accountability" (October 27). New
York.

———. 2002. "Presumption of Guilt: Human Rights Abuses of Post–September 11 Detainees"
(August 15). New York.

———. 2004. "The United States' 'Disappeared': The CIA's Long-Term 'Ghost Detainees':
A Human Rights Watch Briefing Paper" (October). New York.

———. 2005. "Black Hole: The Fate of Islamists Rendered to Egypt" (May). New York.

———. 2005. "Still at Risk: Diplomatic Assurances No Safeguard Against Torture" (April). New
York.

———. 2006. "No Blood No Foul: Soldiers' Account of Detainee Abuse in Iraq" (July). New York.

———. 2007. "Cases Involving Diplomatic Assurances Against Torture Developments Since May
2005" (January). New York.

———. 2007. "Ghost Prisoner: Two Years in Secret CIA Detention" (February). New York.

———. 2008. "'Why Am I Still Here?' The 2007 Horn of Africa Renditions and the Fate of Those
Still Missing" (October). New York.

Immigration and Refugee Board of Canada. 1998. "Lebanon: Situation of the Officers of the
South Lebanese Army (ALS) and on the Protection Offered to Them and Their Families
by the Israeli Government" (September 1; LBN29991.E). http://www.unhcr.org/refworld/
docid/3ae6aafe5f.html (accessed August 27, 2010).

International Commission of Jurists, Swedish Section. 2004. "Facility 1391: A Secret Prison." Gothenburg.

International Committee of the Red Cross. 2004. "Report of the International Committee of the Red Cross on the Treatment by the Coalition Forces of Prisoners of War and Other Protected Persons by the Geneva Conventions in Iraq During Arrest, Internment and Interrogation" (February). Geneva.

———. 2009. "Gaza: 1.5 Million People Trapped in Despair" (June). Geneva.

International Committee of the Red Cross, Regional Delegation for the United States and Canada. 2007. "Report on the Treatment of Fourteen 'High Value Detainees' in CIA Custody" (February 14). Washington, DC.

Palestine Human Rights Information Center. 1992. "Targeting to Kill: Israel's Undercover Units." Jerusalem.

Parliamentary Assembly of the Council of Europe. 2006. "Alleged Secret Detentions and Unlawful Inter-State Transfers of Detainees Involving Council of Europe Member States: Report" (June 7). Strasbourg.

———. 2007. "Secret Detentions and Illegal Transfers of Detainees Involving Council of Europe Member States: Second Report" (June 7). Strasbourg.

Pearlstein, Deborah. 2004. "Ending Secret Detentions." Human Rights First, New York.

Pearlstein, Deborah, and Priti Patel. 2005. "Behind the Wire: An Updated to 'Ending Secret Detentions'" (March). Human Rights First, New York.

Physicians for Human Rights. 2008. "Preliminary Assessment of Alleged Mass Gravesites in the Area of Mazar-I-Sharif, Afghanistan" (January 16–21 and February 7–14). Washington, DC.

Physicians for Human Rights and Human Rights First. 2002. "A Report on Conditions at Shebarghan Prison, Northern Afghanistan" (January 28). Washington, DC.

Rigby, Andrew. 1997. *The Legacy of the Past: The Problem of Collaborators and the Palestinian Case.* Jerusalem: Passia.

Save the Children. 2004. "Provincial Reconstruction Teams and Humanitarian-Military Relations in Afghanistan." London. http://www.savethechildren.org.uk/en/54_5191.htm (accessed May 26, 2011).

Stein, Yael. 2002. "Human Shield: Use of Palestinian Civilians as Human Shields in Violation of High Court of Justice Order." B'Tselem, Jerusalem.

Yaron, Ron. 2008. "Holding Health to Ransom: GSS Interrogation and Extortion of Palestinian Patients at Erez Crossing." Physicians for Human Rights–Israel, Tel Aviv and Jaffa.

US COURT CASES

Ker v. Illinois, 119 U.S. 436 (1888).

Insular Cases

    De Lima v. Bidwell, 182 U.S. 1 (1901).

    Fourteen Diamond Rings v. United States, 183 U.S. 176 (1901).

    Goetze v. United States, 182 U.S. 221 (1901).

    Dooley v. United States, 182 U.S. 222 (1901).

    Armstrong v. United States, 182 U.S. 243 (1901).

    Downes v. Bidwell, 182 U.S. 244 (1901).

    Huus v. New York and Porto Rico Steamship Co., 182 U.S. 392 (1901).

    Hawaii v. Mankichi, 190 U.S. 197 (1903).

    Gonzales v. Williams, 192 U.S. 1 (1904).

    Kepner v. United States, 195 U.S. 100 (1904).

    Dorr v. United States, 195 U.S. 138 (1904).

Mendozana v. United States, 195 U.S. 158 (1904).

Rasmussen v. United States, 197 U.S. 516 (1905).

Trono v. United States, 199 U.S. 521 (1905).

Grafton v. United States, 206 U.S. 333 (1907).

Kent v. Porto Rico, 207 U.S. 113 (1907).

Kopel v. Bingham, 211 U.S. 468 (1909).

Dowdell v. United States, 221 U.S. 325 (1911).

Ochoa v. Hernandez, 230 U.S. 139 (1913).

Ocampo v. United States, 234 U.S. 91 (1914).

Balzac v. Porto Rico, 258 U.S. 298 (1922).

Ex parte Quirin, 317 U.S. 1 (1942).

Korematsu v. United States, 323 U.S. 214 (1944).

Ex parte Endo, 323 U.S. 283 (1944).

In re Yamashita, 327 U.S. 1 (1946).

Johnson v. Eisentrager, 339 U.S. 763 (1950).

Frisbie v. Collins, 342 U.S. 519 (1952).

Youngstown Sheet & Tube Co. v. Sawyer, 343 U.S. 579, 587 (1952).

United States v. Reynolds, 345 U.S. 1 (1953)

United States v. Toscanino, 500 F.2d 267 (2d Cir. 1974).

United States v. Lira, 515 F.2d 68 (2d Cir. 1975).

Sanchez-Espinoza v. Reagan, 770 F.2d 202, 209 (D.C. Cir. 1985).

United States v. Verdugo-Urquidez, 494 U.S. 259 (1990).

Rasul v. Bush & Al-Odah v. United States, 542 U.S. 466 (2004).

Hamdi v. Rumsfeld, 542 U.S. 507 (2004).

al-Marri v. Rumsfeld, 543 U.S. 809 (2004).

Arar v. Ashcroft, 414 F. Supp. 2d 250 (E.D.N.Y. 2006).

El-Masri v. United States, 479 F.3d 296 (4th Cir. 2007).

Boumediene v. Bush, 553 U.S. 723 (2008)
"Brief of *Amici Curiae* Specialists in Israeli Military Law and Constitutional Law in Support of Petitioners" (Nos. 06-1195 & 06-1196).

Arar v. Ashcroft, 585 F.3d 559 (2d Cir. 2009) (en banc).

Arar v. Ashcroft, 585 F.3d 559 (2d Cir. 2009), *cert. denied*, 130 U.S. 3409 (2010)
"Brief in Opposition of the United States" (No. 09-923).

United States of America v. Khalid Sheikh Mohammed, Walid Muhammad Salih, Mubarak Bin 'Attash, Ramzi Binalshibh, Ali Abdul Aziz Ali, and Mustafa Ahmed Adam al Hawsa (Guantánamo Mil. Comm'n., May 9, 2008).
"Defense Motion for Appropriate Relief: Seeking the Appointment of Defense Expert Consultant Dr. Ruben C. Gur, M.A., Ph.D." (June 25, 2009).

Mohamed v. Jeppesen Dataplan (9th Cir., Sept. 8, 2010) (en banc).

United States v. Salim Ahmed Hamdan, CMCR 09-002 (US Court of Military Commissions Review, 2011) (en banc).

Jose Padilla and Estela Lebron v. John Yoo, No. 09-16478 (9th Cir. May 2, 2012).

ISRAELI COURT CASES

Dirani v. Israel, C.C. 1461/00, District Court, Tel Aviv, December 19, 2005. http://www.icrc.org/ihl-nat.nsf/46707c419d6bdfa24125673e00508145/c9397a00563f74cdc12575c1004eed85!OpenDocument (accessed October 10, 2010).

HaMoked v. State of Israel, (Israel) High Court of Justice 9733/03, December 1, 2003. "Petition for Order Nisi." http://www.hamoked.org.il/items/3610_eng.pdf (accessed October 10, 2010).

HaMoked v. Attorney General, (Israel) High Court of Justice 11447/04 and 1081/05, April 21, 2005.

Rabah Abou Faour v. Israel, Working Group on Arbitrary Detention, U.N. Doc. E/CN.4/2001/14/ Add.1 at 90 (2000). http://www1.umn.edu/humanrts/wgad/16-2000.html (accessed August 23, 2010).

Suleiman Ramadan v. Minister of Defence, (Israel) High Court of Justice 1951/99, April 27, 1999.

Tanyus Assaf v. State of Israel, (Israel) High Court of Justice 4887/98, September 16, 1998 (unpublished) (Hebrew).

Israel Supreme Court. 2005. *Judgements of the Israel Supreme Court: Fighting Terrorism Within the Law*. Vol. 1, *1997–2004*. http://www.mfa.gov.il/MFA/Government/Law/Legal+Issues+and+ Rulings/Fighting+Terrorism+within+the+Law+2-Jan-2005.htm (accessed August 27, 2010).

Israel Supreme Court. 2006. *Judgements of the Israel Supreme Court: Fighting Terrorism Within the Law*. Vol. 1, *2004–2005*. http://www.mfa.gov.il/MFA/Government/Law/ Legal+Issues+and+Rulings/Judgments_Israel_Supreme_Court-Fighting_Terrorism_within_ Law-Vol_2.htm (accessed August 27, 2010).

OTHER COURT CASES

Republic of Ireland v. United Kingdom, Case No. 5310/71, European Court of Human Rights, 1978. http://cmiskp.echr.coe.int/tkp197/view.asp?action=html&documentId=695383&portal= hbkm&source=externalbydocnumber&table=F69A27FD8FB86142BF01C1166DEA398649 (accessed May 15, 2011).

PUBLISHED MATERIALS

Abdel-Malek, Anouar. 1981. *Social Dialectics*. Vol. 2, *Nation and Revolution*. Albany: State University of New York Press.

Abi-Mershed, Osama W. 2010. *Apostles of Modernity: Saint-Simonians and the Civilizing Mission in Algeria*. Stanford, CA: Stanford University Press.

Abramovsky, Abraham. 1990. "Extraterritorial Abductions: America's 'Catch and Snatch' Policy Run Amok." *Virginia Journal of International Law* 31: 151–210.

Abshier, Corporal Joel. 2007. "High-Tech ID Systems Sniff Out Hidden Threats." *Marine Corps News*, July 28. http://www.military.com/features/0,15240,144275,00.html?ESRC=marinenews .RSS (accessed April 15, 2012).

Abu-Gharbiyya, Bahjat. 1993. *Fi Khidam al-Nidal al-Arabi al-Filastini: Mudhakkarat al-Munadil Bahjat Abu-Gharbiyya, 1916–1949* (In Service of Palestinian Struggle: Memoirs of Struggler Bahjat Abu-Gharbiyya). Beirut: Institute for Palestine Studies.

Aditjondro, George J. 2000. "Ninjas, Nanggalas, Monuments, and Mossad Manuals: An Anthropology of Indonesian State Terror in East Timor." In *Death Squad: The Anthropology of State Terror*, ed. Jeffrey Sluka, 158–159. Philadelphia: University of Pennsylvania Press.

Agamben, Giorgio. 1998. *Homo Sacer: Sovereign Power and Bare Life*. Trans. Daniel Heller-Roazen. Stanford, CA: Stanford University Press.

Ahmad, Dohra. 2009. *Landscapes of Hope: Anti-Colonial Utopianism in America*. Oxford: Oxford University Press.

Ahmad, Eqbal. 2006. "Counterinsurgency." In *The Selected Writings of Eqbal Ahmad*, ed. Carrollee Bengelsdoorf, Margaret Cerullo, and Yogesh Chandani, 36–64. New York: Columbia University Press.

Aitken, Hugh G. J. 1960. *Taylorism at Watertown Arsenal: Scientific Management in Action, 1908–1915.* Cambridge, MA: Harvard University Press.

Aldrich, Richard J. 2002. "Dangerous Liaisons: Post–September 11 Intelligence Alliances." *Harvard International Review* 24 (3): 49–54.

Al-Ali, Hajj Abd-al-Majid. 2000. *Kwikat: Ahad al-Sharayin Filastin* (Kwikat: One of Palestine's Arteries). Beirut: N.p.

Allen, Charles. 1990. *The Savage Wars of Peace: Soldiers' Voices, 1945–1989.* London: Michael Joseph.

Allon, Yigal. 1970. *Shield of David: The Story of Israel's Armed Forces.* London: Weidenfeld and Nicolson.

Almog, Maj. Gen. Doron. 2004. "The West Bank Fence: A Vital Component in Israel's Strategy of Defense.: Policy Focus No. 47, Washington Institute for Near East Policy, Washington, DC.

Almog, Oz. 2000. *The Sabra: The Creation of the New Jew.* Trans. Haim Watzman. Berkeley: University of California Press.

Alter, Jonathan. 2001. "Time to Think About Torture." *Newsweek*, November 5, 45.

Amidror, Maj. Gen. Yaakov. 2008. "Winning Counterinsurgency War." Strategic Perspectives No. 2, Jerusalem Center for Public Affairs, Jerusalem.

Amoroso, Donna J. 2003. "Inheriting the 'Moro Problem': Muslim Authority and Colonial Rule in British Malaya and the Philippines." In *The American Colonial State in the Philippines*, ed. Julian Go and Anne L. Foster, 118–147. Durham, NC: Duke University Press.

Anderson, Benedict. 2005. *Under Three Flags: Anarchism and the Anti-Colonial Imagination.* London: Verso.

Anderson, Clare. 2000. *Convicts in the Indian Ocean: Transportation from South Asia to Mauritius, 1815–1853.* Basingstoke, UK: Macmillan.

———. 2004. *Legible Bodies: Race, Criminality and Colonialism in South Asia.* Oxford: Berg Publishers.

———. 2007. *Indian Uprising of 1857–8: Prisons, Prisoners and Rebellion.* New York: Anthem Press.

Andrade, Dale. 1990. *Ashes to Ashes, The Phoenix Program and the Vietnam War.* New York: Lexington Books.

Andrade, Dale, and Lt. Col. James H. Willbanks. 2006. "CORDS/Phoenix: Counterinsurgency Lessons from Vietnam for the Future." *Military Review*, March–April, 9–23.

Anghie, Antony. 1996. "Francisco de Vitoria and the Colonial Origins of International Law." *Social and Legal Studies* 5: 321–336.

———. 2005. *Imperialism, Sovereignty and the Making of International Law.* Cambridge: Cambridge University Press.

Anglim, Simon. 2007. "Orde Wingate and the Special Night Squads: A Feasible Policy for Counterterrorism?" *Contemporary Security Policy* 28 (1): 28–41.

———. 2008. "Callwell Versus Graziani: How the British Army Applied 'Small Wars' Techniques in Major Operations in Africa and the Middle East, 1940–41." *Small Wars and Insurgencies* 19 (4): 588–608.

Anidjar, Gil. 2004. "Terror Right." *CR: The New Centennial Review* 4 (3): 35–69.

Anonymous (*JPS*). 1972. "Counter-Insurgency in Gaza." *Journal of Palestine Studies* 1 (3): 150–152.

Anonymous (*MERIP*). 1982. "South Lebanon Behind the News." *MERIP Reports* 108–109 (September–October): 33–35.

Appy, Christian G. 2003. *Vietnam: The Definitive Oral History, Told from All Sides.* London: Ebury Press.

Arendt, Hannah. 1963. *Eichmann in Jerusalem: A Report on the Banality of Evil.* New York: Viking.

Aretxaga, Begoña. 1997. *Shattering Silence: Women, Nationalism, and Political Subjectivity in Northern Ireland*. Princeton, NJ: Princeton University Press.

Arnold, Roberta. 2002. "Command Responsibility: A Case Study of Alleged Violations of the Laws of War at Khiam Detention Centre." *Journal of Conflict and Security Law* 7 (2): 191–231.

Arreguín-Toft, Ivan. 2001. "How the Weak Win Wars: A Theory of Asymmetric Conflict." *International Security* 26 (1): 93–128.

Arthur, Max. 1988. *Northern Ireland: Soldiers Speak*. London: Sidgwick and Jackson.

Asad, Talal, ed. 1973. *Anthropology and the Colonial Encounter*. Amherst, NY: Humanities Press.

———. 2003. *Formations of the Secular: Christianity, Islam, Modernity*. Stanford, CA: Stanford University Press.

Auld, John W. 1975. "The Liberal Pro-Boers." *Journal of British Studies* 14 (2): 78–101.

Aussaresses, Gen. Paul. 2002. *The Battle of Casbah: Terrorism and Counter-Terrorism in Algeria, 1955–1957*. Trans. Robert L Miller. New York: Enigma Books.

Ayres, Thomas. 2005. "'Six Floors' of Detainee Operations in the Post 9/11 World." *Parameters* 35 (3): 33–53.

Azarva, Jeffrey. 2009. "Is U.S. Detention Policy in Iraq Working?" *Middle East Quarterly* (Winter): 5–14.

Azoulay, Ariella. 2003. "Hunger in Palestine: The Event That Never Was." In *Territories, Islands, Camps, and Other States of Utopia*, ed. Anselm Franke, Rafi Segal, and Eyal Weizman, 154–157. Cologne: Walter Koening.

Bacevich, Andrew. 1975. "Progressivism, Professionalism, and Reform." *Parameters* 9 (1): 66–71.

Baha, Lal. 1978. *NWFP Administration Under British Rule, 1901–1919*. Islamabad: National Commission on Historical and Cultural Research.

Baker, Abeer, and Anat Matar, eds. *Threat: Palestinian Political Prisoners in Israel*. London: Pluto Press.

Barkawi, Tarak. 2006. *Globalization and War*. Oxford: Rowman and Littlefield.

Barry, John, and Babak Dehghanpisheh. 2002. "The Death Convoy of Afghanistan." *Newsweek*, August 26, 20–30.

Al-Bash, Ahmad Mustafa. 2001. *Tirat Haifa: Karmiliyya al-Judhur, Filastiniyya al-Intima'* (Tirat Haifa: Carmelite by Origin, Palestinian by Belonging). Damascus: Dar al-Shajara.

Bassiouni, M. Cherif. 1973. "Unlawful Seizures and Irregular Rendition Devices as Alternatives to Extradition." *Vanderbilt Journal of Transnational Law* 7: 25–70.

Bateman, Robert. 2007. "How to Make War: Unusual U.S. Military Field Manual Had an Unusual Provenance." *Chicago Tribune*, September 8.

Bauman, Zygmunt. 1989. *Modernity and the Holocaust*. Oxford: Polity.

Bayly, C. A. 1996. *Empire and Information: Intelligence Gathering and Social Communication in India, 1780–1870*. Cambridge: Cambridge University Press.

BBC. 2011. "Mau Mau Kenyans Allowed to Sue UK Government." July 21. http://www.bbc.co.uk/news/uk-14232049 (accessed July 21, 2011).

———. 2012. "Abdel Hakim Belhaj to Sue Diego Garcia Commission." April 10. http://www.bbc.co.uk/news/uk-17666645 (accessed May 9, 2012).

Beard, Jack M. 2007. "The Geneva Boomerang: The Military Commissions Act of 2006 and US Counterterror Operations." *American Journal of International Law* 101: 56–73.

Beattie, Hugh. 2002. *Imperial Frontier: Tribe and State in Waziristan*. Richmond, VA: Curzon Press

Bechara, Soha. 2003. *Resistance: My Life for Lebanon*. Trans. Gabriel Levine. Brooklyn, NY: Soft Skull Press.

Beckett, Ian F. W. 1988. Introduction to *The Roots of Counter-Insurgency: Armies and Guerrilla Warfare 1900–1945*, ed. Ian F. W. Beckett, 7–22. London: Blandford Press.

Beehner, Lionel. 2007. 'The Battle of the "Youth Bulge."' New York: Council on Foreign Relations Daily Analysis. April 27. http://www.cfr.org/publication/13094/battle_of_the_youth_bulge .html (accessed January 4, 2011).

Begg, Moazzam, with Victorian Brittain. 2006. *Enemy Combatant: The Terrifying True Story of a Briton in Guantánamo*. London: Pocket Books.

Bell, David A. 2007. *The First Total War: Napoleon's Europe and the Birth of Modern Warfare*. London: Bloomsbury Publishing.

Beloff, Max. 1987. *Britain's Liberal Empire, 1897–1921*. 2nd ed. London: Macmillan.

Ben-Eliezer, Uri. 1998. *The Making of Israeli Militarism*. Bloomington: Indiana University Press.

Benest, David. 2006. "Aden to Northern Ireland, 1966–1976." In *Big Wars and Small Wars: The British Army and the Lessons of War in the 20th Century*, ed. Hew Strachan, 115–144. London: Routledge.

Bengali, Shashank. 2007. "U.S. Walls Off Baghdad Neighbourhoods." *McClatchy Newspapers*, April 7.

Ben-Gurion, David. 1963. "Our Friend: What Wingate Did for Us." *Jewish Observer and Middle East Review* 12: 15–17.

———. 1963. "When Bevin Helped Us." *Jewish Observer and Middle East Review* 12: 18–21.

———. 1971. *Israel: A Personal History*. New York: Funk and Wagnalls.

Benjamin, Walter. 1978. "Critique of Violence." In *Reflections: Essays, Aphorism, Autobiographical Writing*, trans. P. Demetz, 277–300. New York: Houghton-Mifflin.

Bennett, Huw. 2007. "The Other Side of the COIN: Minimum and Exemplary Force in British Army Counterinsurgency in Kenya." *Small Wars and Insurgencies* 18 (4): 638–664.

———. 2009. "'A Very Salutary Effect': The Counter-Terror Strategy in the Early Malayan Emergency, June 1948 to December 1949." *Journal of Strategic Studies* 32 (3): 415–444.

Benton, Lauren. 2002. *Law and Colonial Cultures: Legal Regimes in World History, 1400–1900*. Cambridge: Cambridge University Press.

———. 2010. *A Search for Sovereignty: Law and Geography in European Empires, 1400–1900*. Cambridge: Cambridge University Press.

Benziman, Uzi. 1985. *Sharon: An Israeli Caesar*. Trans. Louis Rousso. New York: Adama Books.

Bergerud, Eric M. 1993. *The Dynamics of Defeat: The Vietnam War in Hau Nghia Province*. Boulder, CO: Westview.

Bergman, Ronen. 1999. "Thank You for Your Cooperation: Interview with Colonel Akel Hashem." *Ha'aretz*, October 29.

Berman, Nathaniel. 2004. "'The Appeals of the Orient': Colonized Desire and the War of the Riff." In *Gender and Human Rights*, ed. Karen Knop, 195–229. Oxford: Oxford University Press.

———. 2004. "Privileging Combat? Contemporary Conflict and the Legal Construction of War." *Columbia Journal of Transnational Law* 43: 1–72.

Bernard, Cheryl, Seth G. Jones, Olga Oliker, Cathryn Quantic Thurston, Brooke K. Stearns, and Kristen Cordell. 2008. *Women and Nation-Building*. Santa Monica, CA: RAND Corporation.

Best, Geoffrey. 1994. *War and Law Since 1945*. Oxford: Oxford University Press.

Beydoun, Ahmad. 1992. "The South Lebanon Border Zone: A Local Perspective." *Journal of Palestine Studies* 21 (3): 35–53.

Bhatia, Michael. 2001. "The Western Sahara Under Polisario Control." *Review of African Political Economy* 88: 291–298.

Bickel, Keith B. 2001. *Mars Learning: The Marine Corps' Development of Small Wars Doctrine, 1915–1940.* Boulder, CO: Westview Press.

Biddle, Stephen, Stathis Kalyvas, Wendy Brown, and Douglas Ollivant. 2008. "*The New US Army/Marine Corps Counterinsurgency Field Manual* as Political Science and Political Practice." *Perspectives on Politics* 6 (2): 347–360.

Bierman, John, and Colin Smith. 1999. *Fire in the Night: Wingate of Burma, Ethiopia and Zion.* London: Pan Books.

Birtle, Andrew J. 1998. *US Army Counterinsurgency and Contingency Operations Doctrine, 1860–1941.* Washington, DC: Center of Military History, US Army.

Black, Ian, and Benny Morris. 1991. *Israel's Secret Wars: A History of Israel's Intelligence Services.* New York: Grove Press.

Blakeley, Ruth. 2006. "Still Training to Torture? US Training of Military Forces from Latin America." *Third World Quarterly* 27 (8): 1439–1461.

Blanford, Nicholas. 2000. "Riad's Story: 14 Years of Horror and Pain in Khiam Hellhole." *Daily Star* (Beirut), May 31.

Blank, Laurie R., and Amos N. Guiora. 2010. "Updating the Commander's Toolbox: New Tools for Operationalizing the Law of Armed Conflict." *Prism* 1 (3): 59–78.

Blasier, Cole. 1976. *The Hovering Giant: U.S. Responses to Revolutionary Change in Latin America.* Pittsburgh, PA: University of Pittsburgh Press.

Bloch, Jonathan, and Patrick Fitzgerald. 1983. *British Intelligence and Covert Action: Africa, Middle East and Europe Since 1945.* Dingle, Ireland: Brandon.

Blom Hansen, Thomas. 2005. "Sovereigns Beyond the State: On Legality and Authority in Urban India." In *Sovereign Bodies: Citizens, Migrants, and States in the Postcolonial World*, ed. Thomas Blom Hansen and Finn Stepputat, 169–191. Princeton, NJ: Princeton University Press.

Blount, James H. 1913. *The American Occupation of the Philippines, 1898–1912.* New York: G. P. Putnam's Sons.

Boal, F. W. 2002. "Belfast: Walls Within." *Political Geography* 21: 687–694.

Boltanski, Luc, and Eve Chiapello. 2007. *The New Spirit of Capitalism.* Trans. Gregory Elliott. London: Verso.

Boot, Max. 2002. "What Makes Some Soldiers 'Special.'" *Washington Post*, November 6.

———. 2007. "Key to a Successful Surge." *Los Angeles Times*, February 7.

Borschberg, Peter. 1999. "Hugo Grotius, East India Trade and the King of Johor." *Journal of Southeast Asian Studies* 30 (2): 225–248.

Bourdieu, Pierre, and Abdelmalek Sayad. 1964. *Le déracinement: La crise de l'agriculture traditionnelle en Algérie.* Paris: Les Éditions de Minuit.

Branch, Daniel. 2005. "Imprisonment and Colonialism in Kenya, c. 1930–1952—Escaping the Carceral Archipelago." *International Journal of African Historical Studies* 38 (2): 239–265.

———. 2009. *Defeating Mau Mau, Creating Kenya: Counterinsurgency, Civil War, and Decolonization.* Cambridge: Cambridge University Press.

———. 2010. "Footprints in the Sand: British Colonial Counterinsurgency and the War in Iraq." *Politics and Society* 38 (1): 15–34.

Branche, Raphaëlle. 2001. *La torture et l'armée: Pendant la guerre d'Algérie, 1954–1962.* Paris: Gallimard.

———. 2007. "Torture of Terrorists? Use of Torture in a 'War Against Terrorism': Justifications, Methods and Effects: The Case of France in Algeria, 1954–1962." *International Review of the Red Cross* 89 (867): 543–560.

Braverman, Irus. 2010. "Civilized Borders: A Study of Israel's New Crossing Administration." *Antipode*, September 22, 1–32.

Brockway, Fenner. 1973. *The Colonial Revolution*. London: Hard-Davis, MacGibbon.

Brogden, Mike. 1987. "The Emergence of the Police: The Colonial Dimension." *British Journal of Criminology* 27: 4–14.

Brooks, Mason, and Drew Miller. 2009. "Inside the Detention Camps: A New Campaign in Iraq." *Joint Forces Quarterly* 52: 129–133.

Brown, Col. James B., Lt. Col. Erik W. Goepner, and Capt. James M. Clark. 2009. "Detention Operations, Behavior Modification and Counterinsurgency." *Military Review*, May–June, 40–47.

Bruce, C. E. 1932. "The Sandeman Policy as Applied to Tribal Problems of Today." *Journal of the Royal Central Asian Society* 19 (1): 45–67.

Bruce, Lt. Col. C. E. 1938. *Waziristan 1937–1937: The Problems of the North-West Frontiers of Indian and Their Solutions*. Aldershot, UK: Gale and Polden.

Bruce, Ian. 2002. "Middleman Reveals al Qaeda secrets: Interrogation Methods Would Be Illegal in US." *Herald* (Glasgow), October 17.

Buckingham, Maj. William A., Jr. 1983. "Operation Ranch Hand: Herbicides in Southeast Asia." *Air University Review*, July–August, 42–53.

Bugeaud, Maréchal Thomas Robert. 1883. *Oeuvres militaires*. Paris: Librarie Militaire de L. Baudoin.

———. 1997. *La guerre des rues et des maisons*. Paris: J.-P. Rocher. Originally published 1849.

Buntman, Fran Lisa. 2003. *Robben Island and Prisoner Resistance to Apartheid*. Cambridge: Cambridge University Press.

Burchell, Graham. 1993. "Liberal Government and Techniques of the Self." *Economy and Society* 22 (3): 267–282.

Burnett, Christina Duffy. 2006. "The Edges of Empire and the Limits of Sovereignty: American Guano Islands." In *Legal Borderlands: Law and the Construction of American Borders*, ed. Mary Dudziak and Leti Volpp, 187–212. Baltimore: Johns Hopkins University Press.

Burnham, Maj. Frederick Russell. 1926. *Scouting on Two Continents*. New York: Doubleday, Page.

Busch, Peter. 2002. "Killing the 'Vietcong': The British Advisory Mission and the Strategic Hamlet Programme." *Journal of Strategic Studies* 25 (1): 135–162.

Butler, Judith. 1993. *Bodies That Matter*. London: Routledge.

Calder, Bruce J. 2006. *Impact of Intervention: The Dominican Republic During the U.S. Occupation of 1916–1924*. Princeton, NJ: Markus Wiener.

Callwell, C. E. 1996. *Small Wars: Their Principles and Practice*. Lincoln: University of Nebraska Press. Originally published 1906.

Campbell, Duncan, and Richard Norton-Taylor. 2008. "US Accused of Holding Terror Suspects on Prison Ships·Report Says 17 Boats Used." *Guardian* (London), June 2.

Carlough, Montgomery. 1994. "Pax Britannica: British Counterinsurgency in Northern Ireland, 1969–1982." PhD diss., Yale University.

Carvin, Stephanie. 2010. *Prisoners of America's Wars: From the Early Republic to Guantanamo*. New York: Columbia University Press.

Casey, Lee A., David B. Rivkin Jr., and Darin R. Bartram. 2005. "Unlawful Belligerency and Its Implications Under International Law." Federalist Society. http://www.fed-soc.org/publica tions/pubID.104/pub_detail.asp (accessed September 1, 2010).

Catignani, Sergio. 2008. *Israeli Counter-Insurgency and the Intifadas: Dilemmas of a Conventional Army*. London: Routledge.

Cavendish, Julius. 2011. "CIA Trains Covert Units of Afghans to Continue the Fight Against Taliban: Shadowy, Unaccountable Forces Accused of Human Rights Abuses." *Independent* (London), July 20.

Chafer, Tony, and Amanda Sackur, eds. 1999. *French Colonial Empire and the Popular Front: Hope and Disillusion.* London: Macmillan.

Charbit, Tom. 2006. *Les harkis.* Paris: La Découverte.

Cheyfitz, Eric. 1993. "Savage Law: The Plot Against American Indians in *Johnson and Graham's Lessee v. M'Intosh and the Pioneers.*" In *Cultures of United States Imperialism,* ed. Amy Kaplan and Donald Pease, 109–128. Durham, NC: Duke University Press.

Chiarelli, Maj. Gen. Peter W., and Maj. Patrick R. Michaelis. 2005. "Winning the Peace: The Requirement for Full-Spectrum Operations." *Military Review,* July–August, 5.

Chomsky, Carol. 1990. "The United States–Dakota War Trials: A Study in Military Injustice." *Stanford Law Review* 43 (1): 13–98.

Churchill, Winston. 1897. *The Story of the Malakand Field Force.* London: Longmans, Green. http://www.gutenberg.org/ebooks/9404 (accessed May 9, 2011).

———. 1899. *The River War: An Historical Account of the Reconquest of the Soudan.* 2 vols. London: Longmans, Green.

———. 1900. *London to Ladysmith via Pretoria.* London: Longmans, Green. http://www .gutenberg.org/ebooks/14426 (accessed May 9, 2011).

———. 1902. *The River War: An Account of the Reconquest of the Sudan.* Abridged 2nd ed. London: Longmans, Green. http://www.gutenberg.org/ebooks/4943 (accessed May 9, 2011).

———. 2000. *My Early Life.* London: Eland Publishing. Originally published 1930.

Cleveland, Sarah. 2002. "Powers Inherent in Sovereignty: Indians, Aliens, Territories, and the Nineteenth Century Origins of Plenary Power over Foreign Affairs." *Texas Law Review* 81 (1): 1–284.

Coates, John. 1992. *Suppressing Insurgency: An Analysis of the Malayan Emergency, 1948–1954.* Boulder, CO: Westview Press.

Cobain, Ian. 2012. "Rendition Ordeal That Raises New Questions About Secret Trials." *Guardian* (London), April 8.

Coetzee, J. M. 1980 [1999]. *Waiting for the Barbarians.* New York: Penguin Books.

Cohn, Carol. 1987. "Sex and Death in the Rational World of Defense Intellectuals." *Signs* 12 (4): 687–718.

Coker, Christopher. 2003. "Empires in Conflict: The Growing Rift Between Europe and the United States." Whitehall Paper No. 58, Royal United Services Institute, London.

Colby, Elbridge. 1927. "How to Fight Savage Tribes." *American Journal of International Law* 21 (2): 279–288.

Cole, David. 2003. *Enemy Aliens: Double Standards and Constitutional Freedoms in the War on Terrorism.* New York: New Press.

———. 2010. "What to Do About Guantánamo?" *New York Review of Books* 57 (15): 48–50.

Cole, Jennifer. 2001. *Forget Colonialism? Sacrifice and the Art of Memory in Madagascar.* Berkeley: University of California Press.

Cole, Juan. 1999. *Colonialism and Revolution in the Middle East: Social and Cultural Origins of Egypt's 'Urabi Movement.* Cairo: American University of Cairo Press.

———. 2006. "Empires of Liberty? Democracy and Conquest in French Egypt, British Egypt, and American Iraq." In *Lessons of Empire: Imperial Histories and American Power,* ed. Craig Calhoun, Frederick Cooper, and Kevin W. Moore, 94–115. New York: New Press.

Conklin, Alice. 1997. *A Mission to Civilize: The Republican Idea of Empire in France and West Africa, 1895–1930.* Stanford, CA: Stanford University Press.

Connable, Maj. Ben. 2009. "All Our Eggs in One Basket: How the Human Terrain System Is Undermining Sustainable Military Cultural Competence." *Military Review*, March–April, 57–64.

Connelly, Matthew. 2002. *A Diplomatic Revolution: Algeria's Fight for Independence and the Origins of the Post–Cold War Era*. Oxford: Oxford University Press.

Connolly, William E. 1994. "Tocqueville, Territory and Violence." *Theory, Culture and Society* 11: 19–40.

Cook, Catherine, Adam Hanieh, and Adah Kay. 2004. *Stolen Youth: The Politics of Israel's Detention of Palestinian Children*. London: Pluto Press.

Cooper, Frederick. 1996. *Decolonization and African Society: The Labor Question in French and British Africa*. Cambridge: Cambridge University Press.

———. 1997. "Modernizing Bureaucrats, Backward Africans, and the Development Concept." In *International Development and the Social Sciences: Essays on the History and Politics of Knowledge*, ed. Frederick Cooper and Randall Packard, 64–92. Berkeley: University of California Press.

———. 2005. *Colonialism in Question: Theory, Knowledge, History*. Berkeley: University of California Press.

Cornaton, Michel. 1998. *Les camps de regroupement de la guerre d'Algérie* (Regroupment Camps in the Algerian War). Paris: L'Harmattan.

Corum, James. 2008. "Getting Doctrine Right: On Air Power, Land Power and Counterinsurgency." *Joint Forces Quarterly* 49: 93–97.

Crainer, Stuart. 2003. "One Hundred Years of Management." *Business Strategy Review* 14 (2): 41–49.

Crane, Conrad. 2010. "United States." In *Understanding Counterinsurgency: Doctrine, Operations and Challenges*, ed. Thomas Rid and Thomas Kearney, 59–72. London: Routledge.

Curtin, Philip D., ed. 1971. *Imperialism*. New York: Harper and Row.

Davies, Nick. 2010. "Iraq War Logs: Secret Order That Let US Ignore Abuse Mistreatment of Helpless Prisoners by Iraqi Security Forces Included Beatings, Burning, Electrocution and Rape." *Guardian* (London), October 22. http://www.guardian.co.uk/world/2010/oct/22/iraq-detainee-abuse-torture-saddam?CMP=twt_gu (accessed October 22, 2010).

Davis, Mike. 2001. *Late Victorian Holocausts: El Niño Famines and the Making of the Third World*. London: Verso.

Davis, Rochelle. 2010. "Culture as a Weapon System." *Middle East Report* 255: 8–13.

Dayan, Colin. 2011. *The Law Is a White Dog: How Legal Rituals Make and Unmake Persons*. Princeton, NJ: Princeton University Press.

de Durand, Étienne. 2010. "France." In *Understanding Counterinsurgency: Doctrine, Operations and Challenges*, ed. Thomas Rid and Thomas Keaney, 11–27. London: Routledge.

Defense Tech. 2004. "Army's Insurgent Manual Author Speaks" (November 17). http://defensetech.org/2004/11/17/armys-insurgent-manual-author-speaks/ (accessed November 6, 2010).

Dembitz, Nanette. 1945. "Racial Discrimination and the Military Judgment: The Supreme Court's *Korematsu* and *Endo* Decisions." *Columbia Law Review* 45 (2): 175–239.

Derrick, Jonathan. 2002 "The Dissenters: Anti-Colonialism in France, c. 1900–40." In *Promoting the Colonial Idea: Propaganda and Visions of Empire in France*, ed. Tony Chafer and Amanda Sackur, 53–68. London: Palgrave.

———. 2008. *Africa's "Agitators": Militant Anti-Colonialism in Africa and the West, 1918–1939*. New York: Columbia University Press.

Dershowitz, Alan. 2002. "Want to Torture? Get a Warrant." *San Francisco Chronicle*, January 22. http://articles.sfgate.com/2002-01-22/opinion/17527284_1_physical-pressure-torture-terrorist (accessed October 26, 2010).

Desch, Michael. 2001. *Soldiers in Cities: Military Operations on Urban Terrain*. Carlisle, PA: Strategic Studies Institute, US Army War College.

de Tocqueville, Alexis. 2000. "Essay on Algeria." In *Writings on Empire and Slavery*, ed. and trans. Jennifer Pitts, 59–116. Baltimore: Johns Hopkins University Press. Originally published 1841.

de Vargas Machuca, Capt. Bernardo. 2008. *The Indian Militia and Description of the Indies*. Ed. Kris Lane. Trans. Timothy F. Johnson. Durham, NC: Duke University Press.

Dillon, Michael, and Julian Reid. 2009. *The Liberal Way of War: Killing to Make Life*. London: Routledge.

Dirks, Nicholas B. 2006. *The Scandal of Empire: India and the Creation of Imperial Britain*. Cambridge, MA: Belknap Press.

Dobbins, James, Seth G. Jones, Benjamin Runkle, Siddharth Mohandas. 2009. *Occupying Iraq: A History of the Coalition Provisional Authority*. Santa Monica, CA: RAND Corporation.

Dörmann, Knut. 2003. "The Legal Situation of 'Unlawful/Unprivileged Combatants.'" *International Review of the Red Cross* 85: 45–75.

Douglass, Frederick. 1857 [1999]. "West India Emancipation." In *Frederick Douglass: Selected Speeches and Writing*, ed. Philip S. Foner. Chicago: Lawrence Hill Books.

Dozier, Kimberly. 2011. "Afghanistan Secret Prisons Confirmed by U.S." *Huffington Post*, April 8. http://www.huffingtonpost.com/2011/04/08/afghanistan-secret-prison_n_846545.html?view=print (accessed April 10, 2011).

Drumheller, Tyler. 2006. *On the Brink: An Insider's Account of How the White House Compromised American Intelligence*. New York: Carroll and Graf.

Dubik, Lt. Gen. James. 2009. "Best Practices in Counterinsurgency: Building Security Forces and Ministerial Capacity: Iraq as a Primer." Washington, DC: Institute for the Study of War.

Dunlap, Charles J. 2009. "Lawfare: A Decisive Element of 21st-Century Conflicts?" *Joint Forces Quarterly* 54: 34–39.

Dunlap, Col. Charles J. 2001. "Law and Military Interventions: Preserving Humanitarian Values in 21st Century Conflicts." Cambridge, MA: Carr Center for Human Rights Policy, Harvard Kennedy School. http://www.hks.harvard.edu/cchrp/Web%20Working%20Papers/Use%20of%20Force/Dunlap2001.pdf (accessed September 21, 2010).

Dunn, Peter. 1985. "The American Army: The Vietnam War, 1965–1973." In *Armed Forces and Modern Counter-Insurgency*, ed. Ian F. W. Beckett and John Pimlott, 77–100. London: Croom Helm.

Durham, Nancy. 2008. "Can Therapy 'Cure' Terrorism? Saudi Arabia Uses Creative Approach to Reform Junior Jihadis." January 14. http://www.cbc.ca/news/reportsfromabroad/durham/20080114.html (accessed January 13, 2011).

Elkins, Caroline. 2005. *Britain's Gulag: The Brutal End of Empire in Kenya*. London: Pimlico.

Elliott, David W. P. 2003. *The Vietnamese War: Revolution and Social Change in the Mekong Delta, 1930–1975*. 2 vols. London: M. E. Sharpe.

Elliott, Maj. Gen. J. G. 1968. *The Frontier, 1839–1947*. London: Cassell.

Ellison, Graham, and Jim Smyth. 2000. *The Crowned Harp: Policing Northern Ireland*. London: Pluto Press.

Erlanger, Steven. 2006. "Hamas Leader Faults Israeli Sanction Plan." *New York Times*, February 18.

Etzioni, Amitai. 2010. "Unmanned Aircraft Systems: The Moral and Legal Case." *Joint Forces Quarterly* 57: 66–71.

Evans, Michael. 2009. "Lethal Genes: The Urban Military Imperative and Western Strategy in the Early Twenty-First Century." *Journal of Strategic Studies* 32 (4): 515–552.

Eviatar, Daphne. 2009. "Obama's Gitmo?" *Washington Independent*, January 7. http://washingtonindependent.com/24052/bagram-detainees (accessed January 13, 2011).

———. 2009. "U.S. General: Most Bagram Detainees Should Be Released." *Washington Independent*, August 20. http://washingtonindependent.com/55715/u-s-general-admits-most-bagram-detainees-should-be-released (accessed January 13, 2011).

Exum, Andrew. 2009. "Civilians Caught in Urban Combat: Interpret the Situation." *New York Times* (online blog), March 19, http://roomfordebate.blogs.nytimes.com/2009/03/19/civilians-caught-in-urban-combat/ (accessed June 17, 2009).

———. 2010. "Leverage: Designing a Political Campaign for Afghanistan" (May). Washington, DC: Center for a New American Security.

Fall, Bernard B. 1963. *Counterinsurgency: The French Experience*. Washington, DC: Industrial College of the Armed Forces.

———. 1965. "The Theory and Practice of Insurgency and Counterinsurgency." *Naval War College Review*, April.

———. 2005. *Street Without Joy: The French Debacle in Indochina*. Barnsley, UK: Pen and Sword Books. Originally published 1961.

Fallon, Richard H., Jr., and Daniel J. Meltzer. 2007. "Habeas Corpus Jurisdiction, Substantive Rights and the War on Terror." *Harvard Law Review* 120: 2029–2112.

Fanon, Frantz. 1963. *The Wretched of the Earth*. Trans. Constance Farrington. New York: Grove Press.

———. 1964. *Towards the African Revolution*. Trans. Haakon Chevalier. New York: Grove Press.

Federal News Service. 2007. "Bloggers' Roundtable with Gen. Douglas M. Stone." September 18. http://www.washingtonpost.com/wp-dyn/content/article/2007/09/18/AR2007091801969.html (accessed January 14, 2011).

Feith, Douglas J. 1985. "Law in the Service of Terror: The Strange Case of the Additional Protocol." *National Interest* 1: 36–47.

———. 2008. *War and Decision: Inside the Pentagon at the Dawn of the War on Terrorism*. New York: Harper.

Feldman, Allen. 1991. *Formations of Violence: The Narrative of the Body and Political Terror in Northern Ireland*. Chicago: University of Chicago Press.

Feldman, Yotam. 2007. "Collision Course: As the IDF Presses for Another Large-Scale Military Operation in Gaza, Zvika Fogel, Who Was Head of Southern Command Headquarters When the Second Intifada Broke Out, Recalls What Happened Then." *Ha'aretz*, December 20.

Feldman, Yotam, and Uri Blau. 2009. "Gaza Bonanza." *Ha'aretz*, June 11.

Feuchtwang, Stephan. 1973. "The Discipline and Its Sponsors: The Colonial Formation of British Social Anthropology." In *Anthropology and the Colonial Encounter*, ed. Talal Asad, 71–100. Amherst, NY: Humanity Books.

Fisher, Louis. 2006. "Detention and Military Trial of Suspected Terrorists: Stretching Presidential Power." *Journal of National Security Law and Policy* 2: 1–51.

———. 2006. *In the Name of National Security: Unchecked Presidential Power and the Reynolds Case*. Lawrence: University Press of Kansas.

Fletcher, Laurel E., and Eric Stover. 2009. *The Guantanamo Effect: Exposing the Consequences of US Detention and Interrogation Practices*. Berkeley: University of California Press.

Fogarty, Richard S. 2008. *Race and War in France: Colonial Subjects in the French Army, 1914–1918*. Baltimore: Johns Hopkins University Press.

Ford, Richard T. 1999. "Law's Territory (A History of Jurisdiction)." *Michigan Law Review* 97: 843–930.

Foucault, Michel. 1995. *Discipline and Punish: The Birth of the Prison*. Trans. Alan Sheridan. New York: Vintage Books.

———. 2003. *Society Must Be Defended: Lectures at the Collège de France, 1975–76*. Trans. David Macey. London: Allen Lane.

———. 2007. *Security, Territory, Population: Lectures at the Collège de France, 1977–1978*. Trans. Graham Burchell. London: Palgrave Macmillan.

Fox, Richard G. 1985. *Lions of the Punjab: Culture in the Making*. Berkeley: University of California Press.

Frisch, Hillel. 1993. "The Druze Minority in the Israeli Military: Traditionalizing an Ethnic Policing Role." *Armed Forces and Society* 20: 51–67.

Gallieni, Gen. Joseph. 1900. *Le pacification de Madagascar (Opération d'Octobre 1896 à Mars 1899)*. Paris: Librarie Militaire R. Chapelot et Cⁱᵉ.

Galula, David. 2006. *Pacification in Algeria: 1956–1958*. Santa Monica: RAND Corporation. Originally published 1963.

———. 2006. *Counterinsurgency Warfare: Theory and Practice*. Westport, CT: Praeger International. Originally published 1964.

Gant, Maj. Jim. 2009. *One Tribe at a Time: A Strategy for Success in Afghanistan*. Los Angeles: Nine Sisters Imports.

Gazit, Shlomo. 2003. *Trapped Fools: Thirty Years of Israeli Policy in the Territories*. Trans. Shoshana London Sappir. London: Frank Cass.

Gellman, Barton. 2007. "The Unseen Path to Cruelty." *Washington Post*, June 25.

Geneste, Lt. Col. Marc E. 1962. "Guerrilla Warfare." In *Modern Guerrilla Warfare: Fighting Communist Guerrilla Movements, 1941–1961*, ed. Franklin Mark Osanka, 264–267. New York: Free Press of Glencoe.

Gentile, Gian. 2009. "A Strategy of Tactics: Population-Centric COIN and the Army." *Parameters* (Autumn): 5–17.

Gerth, H. H., and C. Wright Mills, eds. 1946. *From Max Weber: Essays in Sociology*. New York: Oxford University Press.

Gill, Lesley. 2004. *The School of Americas: Military Training and Political Violence in the Americas*. Durham, NC: Duke University Press.

Giordano, Joseph. 2008. "Abu Ghraib Reformer Stone Hands Over Command of Detainee System in Iraq." *Stars and Stripes*, June 7.

Go, Julian. 2003. "Introduction: Global Perspectives on the US Colonial State in the Philippines." In *The American Colonial State in the Philippines*, ed. Julian Go and Anne L. Foster, 1–42. Durham, NC: Duke University Press.

———. 2008. *American Empire and the Politics of Meaning: Elite Political Cultures in the Philippines and Puerto Rico During US Colonialism*. Durham, NC: Duke University Press.

Goldberg, David Theo. 2002. *The Racial State*. Oxford: Blackwell.

———. 2008. "Racial Palestinianization." In *Thinking Palestine*, ed. Ronit Lentin, 25–45. London: Zed Books.

Goldberg, Jeffrey. 2006. *Prisoners: A Story of Friendship and Terror*. New York: Vintage Books.

Goldman, Emily, and Leslie Eliason, eds. 2003. *The Diffusion of Military Technology and Ideas*. Stanford, CA: Stanford University Press.

Goldsworthy, David. 1971. *Colonial Issues in British Politics, 1945–1961: From "Colonial Development" to "Wind of Change."* Oxford: Clarendon Press.

Gompert, David C. 2009. "'Underkill': Fighting Extremists amid Populations." *Survival* 51 (2): 159–174.

Gong, Gerrit W. 1984. *The Standard of "Civilization" in International Society.* Oxford: Clarendon Press.

Gordon, Neve. 2004. "Rationalizing Extra-Judicial Executions: The Israeli Press and the Legitimation of Abuse." *International Journal of Human Rights* 8 (3): 305–324.

———. 2008. *Israel's Occupation.* Berkeley: University of California Press.

Gorenberg, Gershom. 2006. *Occupied Territories: The Untold Story of Israel's Settlements.* London: I. B. Tauris.

Gorka, Sebastian, and David Kilcullen. 2011. "An Actor-Centric Theory of War: Understanding the Difference Between COIN and Counterinsurgency." *Joint Forces Quarterly* 60: 14–18.

Gott, Kendall D. 2006. *Eyewitness to War: The US Army in Operation Al-Fajr, an Oral History.* 2 vols. Ft. Leavenworth, KS: Combat Studies Institute Press.

Gottman, Jean. 1943. "Bugeaud, Galliéni, Lyautey: The Development of French Colonial Warfare." In *Makers of Modern Strategy: Military Thought from Machiavelli to Hitler,* ed. Edward Mead Earle, 234–259. Princeton, NJ: Princeton University Press.

Gourevitch, Philip, and Errol Morris. 2008. *Standard Operating Procedure: A War Story.* London: Picador.

Graham, Stephen. 2004. "Cities as Strategic Sites: Place Annihilation and Urban Geopolitics." In *Cities, War, and Terrorism: Towards an Urban Geopolitics,* ed. Stephen Graham, 31–53. Cambridge: Blackwell.

Gramsci, Antonio. 1971. *Selections from Prison Notebooks.* Ed. and trans. Quintin Hoare and Geoffrey Nowell Smith. New York: International Publishers.

Greenberg, Eldon Van Cleef. 1970. "Law and the Conduct of the Algerian Revolution." *Harvard International Law Journal* 11: 37–72.

Greenberg, Karen. 2009. *The Least Worst Place: How Guantanamo Became the World's Most Notorious Prison.* Oxford: Oxford University Press.

Gregory, Derek. 2008. "The Rush to the Intimate: Counterinsurgency and the Cultural Turn in Late Modern Warfare." *Radical Philosophy* 150: 8–23.

Gressman, Eugene. 2004. "Korematsu: A Mélange of Military Imperatives." *Law and Contemporary Problems* 68 (15): 15–27.

Grey, Stephen. 2004. "America's Gulag." *New Statesman,* May 17, 22–25.

———. 2006. *Ghost Plane: The True Story of the CIA Torture Program.* New York: St. Martin's Press.

Gross, Emanuel. 2002. "Human Rights, Terrorism, and the Problem of Administrative Detention in Israel: Does a Democracy Have the Right to Hold Terrorists as Bargaining Chip?" *Arizona Journal of International and Comparative Law* 18: 721–791.

Gross, Michael L. 2010. *Moral Dilemmas of Modern War: Torture, Assassination, and Blackmail in an Age of Asymmetric Conflict.* Cambridge: Cambridge University Press.

Grubbs, Maj. Lee K., and Maj. Michael J. Forsyth. 2005. "Is There a Deep Fight in a Counterinsurgency?" *Military Review,* July–August, 28–31.

Gwynn, Sir Charles W. 1939. *Imperial Policing.* London: Macmillan.

Hack, Karl. 2009. "The Malayan Emergency as Counter-Insurgency Paradigm." *Journal of Strategic Studies* 32 (3): 383–414.

Hack, Karl, and Tobias Rettig. 2006. *Colonial Armies in Southeast Asia.* London: Routledge.

Haddad, Reem. 2000. "'Khiam Cost Me My Baby.'" *Daily Star* (Beirut), May 31.

Hajjar, Lisa. 2003. "From Nuremberg to Guantánamo: International Law and American Power Politics." *Middle East Report* 229: 8–15.

————. 2005. *Courting Conflict: The Israeli Military Court System in the West Bank and Gaza*. Berkeley: University of California Press.

Halberstam, David. 1992. *The Best and the Brightest*. New York: Ballantine Books. Originally published 1969.

Halliday, Paul D. 2010. *Habeas Corpus from England to Empire*. Cambridge, MA: Harvard University Press.

Halliday, Paul D., and G. Edward White. 2008. "The Suspension Clause: English Text, Imperial Contexts, and American Implications." *Virginia Law Review* 94: 575–714.

Hamilakis, Yannis. 2002. "'The Other Parthenon': Antiquity and National Memory at Makronisos." *Journal of Modern Greek Studies* 20 (20): 307–338.

Hamizrachi, Beate. 1988. *The Emergence of the South Lebanon Security Zone: Major Saad Haddad and the Ties with Israel, 1975–1978*. New York: Praeger.

Hammes, Thomas X. 2006. *The Sling and the Stone: On War in the 21st Century*. St. Paul, MN: Zenith Press.

Hamoumou, Mohand, and Abderahmen Moumen. 2004. "L'histoire des harkis et français musulmans: La fin d'un tabou?" In *Le guerre D'Algérie*, ed. Mohammed Harbi and Mohammed and Benjamin Stora, 455–495. Paris: Hachette Littératures.

Handelman, Don. 1981. "Introduction: The Idea of Bureaucratic Organization." *Social Analysis* 9: 5–23.

Hanieh, Adam. "The Politics of Curfew in the Occupied Territories." In *The Struggle for Sovereignty: Palestine and Israel, 1993–2005*, ed. Joel Beinin and Rebecca L. Stein, 324–337. Stanford, CA: Stanford University Press.

Harbi, Mohammed, and Benjamin Stora, eds. 2004. *Le guerre D'Algérie*. Paris: Hachette Littératures.

Hasian, Marouf, Jr. 2003. "The 'Hysterical' Emily Hobhouse and Boer War Concentration Camp Controversy." *Western Journal of Communication* 67 (2):138–163.

Hass, Amira. 1996. *Drinking the Sea at Gaza: Days and Nights in a Land Under Siege*. Trans. Elana Wesley and Maxine Kaufman-Lacusta. New York: Henry Holt.

————. 2010. "Why Won't Israel Allow Gazans to Import Coriander?" *Ha'aretz*, July 5.

Heggoy, Alf Andrew. 1972. *Insurgency and Counterinsurgency in Algeria*. Bloomington: Indiana University Press.

Heinsohn, Gunnar. 2003. *Söhne und Weltmacht: Terror im Aufstieg und Fall der Nationen* (Sons and World Power: Terror in the Rise and Fall of Nations). Bern: Orell Füssli.

Henderson, Ian. 1958. *Man Hunt in Kenya*. New York: Doubleday.

Hendricks, Steve. 2010. *A Kidnapping Milan: The CIA on Trial*. London: W. W. Norton.

Hernon, Ian. 2003. *Britain's Forgotten Wars: Colonial Campaigns of the 19th Century*. Gloucestershire: Sutton Publishing.

Herrington, Stuart A. 1982. *Stalking the Vietcong: Inside Operation Phoenix, a Personal Account*. Novato, CA: Presidio Press.

Hersh, Seymour. 2004. *Chain of Command: The Road from 9/11 to Abu Ghraib*. New York: HarperCollins.

Heyman, Josiah McC. 1995. "Putting Power in the Anthropology of Bureaucracy: The Immigration and Naturalization Service at the Mexico–United States Border." *Current Anthropology* 36 (2): 261–287.

Hills, Alice. 2004. "Continuity and Discontinuity: The Grammar of Urban Military Operations." In *Cities, War, and Terrorism: Towards an Urban Geopolitics*, ed. Stephen Graham, 231–247. Cambridge: Blackwell.

Hindess, Barry. 2001. "The Liberal Government of Unfreedom." *Alternatives* 26 (2): 93–111.

Hobhouse, Emily. 1984. *Boer War Letters*. Ed. Rykie Van Reenen. Cape Town: Human and Rousseau.

Hoisington, William A., Jr. 1995. *Lyautey and the French Conquest of Morocco*. New York: St. Martin's Press.

Horesh, Roxanne. 2010. "To Die or Conquer the Hill: Sites of Resistance for Jewish Detainees in British Mandate Prisons in East Africa, 1944–1948." Unpublished MPhil thesis, Oxford University.

Horne, Alastair. 2006. *A Savage War of Peace: Algeria 1954–1962*. New York: NYRB Classics. Originally published 1977.

Hosmer, Stephen T., and Sibylle Crane. 1963. *Counterinsurgency: A Symposium*. Santa Monica, CA: RAND Corporation.

House, Jim, and Neil MacMaster. 2006. *Paris 1961: Algerians, State Terror, and Memory*. Oxford: Oxford University Press.

Howard, Michael. 2008. *War and the Liberal Conscience*. London: Hurst and Co. Originally published 1977.

Howe, Stephen. 1993. *Anticolonialism in British Politics: The Left and the End of Empire, 1918–1964*. Oxford: Clarendon Press.

Hughes, Matthew. 2009. "The Banality of Brutality: British Armed Forces and the Repression of the Arab Revolt in Palestine, 1936–39." *English Historical Review* 124: 313–354.

Hull, Isabel V. 2005. *Absolute Destruction: Military Culture and the Practices of War in Imperial Germany*. Ithaca, NY: Cornell University Press.

Humphrey, John Weldon. 1971. "Population Resettlement in Malaya." PhD diss., Northwestern University.

Hunt, David. 2010. "Dirty Wars: Counterinsurgency in Vietnam and Today." *Politics and Society* 38 (1): 35–66.

Hunt, Richard A. 1995. *Pacification: The American Struggle for Vietnam's Hearts and Minds*. Boulder, CO: Westview Press.

Hunter, Dan. 2001. "Reason Is Too Large: Analogy and Precedent in Law." *Emory Law Journal* 50: 1197–1264.

Hunter, Robert. 1993. *The Palestinian Uprising: A War by Other Means*. Berkeley: University of California Press.

Huntington, Samuel P. 1957. *The Soldier and the State: The Theory and Politics of Civil-Military Relations*. New York: Vintage Books.

Hurley, Vic. 1938. *Jungle Patrol: The Story of the Philippine Constabulary*. New York: E. P. Dutton and Company.

Husayn, Sa'dun. 1983. *100 Yawman fi Mu'taqal Ansar* (100 Days in Ansar Detention Camp). Beirut: Al Mu'assassa al Rawa.

———. 1984. *Ansar 33*. Beirut: Al Mu'assassa al Rawa.

Hussain, Nasser. 2003. *The Jurisprudence of Emergency: Colonialism and the Rule of Law*. Ann Arbor: University of Michigan Press.

Inbar, Efraim. 1991. "Israel's Small War: The Military Response to the Intifada." *Armed Forces and Society* 18 (1): 29–50.

Iraq Veterans Against the War and Aaron Glantz, eds. 2008. *Winter Soldier Iraq and Afghanistan: Eyewitness Accounts of the Occupation*. Chicago: Haymarket Books.

Isikoff, Michael, and Patrick E. Tyler. 1989. "U.S. Military Given Foreign Arrest Powers." *Washington Post*, December 16.

Jabir, Mundhir Mahmud. 1999. *Al-Sharit al-Lubnani al-Muhtall: Masalik al-Ihtilal, Masarat al-Muwajahah, Masa'ir al-Ahali* (The Occupied Lebanese Border Strip: Paths of Occupation, Lines of Confrontation, the Fate of the Population). Beirut: Institute for Palestine Studies.

Jabotinsky, Vladimir Ze'ev. 1923. "The Iron Wall: We and the Arabs." Trans. Lenni Brenner. *Jewish Herald* (South Africa), November 26, 1937. Originally published in Russian as "O Zheleznoi Stene," *Rassvyet*, November 4, 1923. http://www.marxists.de/middleast/ironwall/ironwall.htm (accessed October 26, 2010).

Jackson, Ashley. 2009. "The Imperial Antecedents of British Special Forces." *RUSI Journal* 154 (3): 62–68.

Jahoda, Gloria. 1975. *The Trail of Tears: The American Indian Removals 1813–1855*. London: Book Club Associates.

Jamail, Dahr. 2007. *Beyond the Green Zone: Dispatches from an Unembedded Journalist in Occupied Iraq*. Chicago: Haymarket Books.

Jane's Foreign Report. 2003. "Israel Trains US Troops on Iraq Tactics" (November 27).

Jane's International Defence Review. 2008. "Volatility in the Middle East Drives Israeli Defence Industry Innovation" (June 9).

Jane's Terrorism and Security Monitor. 2000. "The Changing Rules of Conflict in Israel." *Jane's Terrorism and Security Monitor*, December 1.

Jean, Grace V. 2010. "'Culture Maps' Becoming Essential Tools of War." *National Defense Magazine*, February. http://www.nationaldefensemagazine.org/archive/2010/February/Pages/%E2%80%98CultureMaps%E2%80%99BecomingEssentialToolsofWar.aspx (accessed April 16, 2012).

Jiryis, Sabri. 1976. *The Arabs in Israel*. Trans. Inea Bushnaq. New York: Monthly Review Press.

———. 1980. "Secrets of State: An Analysis of the Diaries of Moshe Sharett." *Journal of Palestine Studies* 10 (1): 35–57.

Al-Jishshi, Al-Hajj Badr-al-Din. 2002. *Qurya al-Kabri: Rawda min Riyad Filastin Mubaraka* (The Village of Kabri: A Flower). Beirut: Maktaba Sha'rawi.

Jochnik, Chris af, and Roger Normand. 1994. "The Legitimation of Violence: A Critical History of the Laws of War." *Harvard International Law Journal* 35 (1): 49–95.

Johns, Fleur. 2005. "Guantánamo Bay and the Annihilation of the Exception." *European Journal of International Law* 16 (4): 613–635.

Joiner, Charles A. 1967. "The Ubiquity of the Administrative Role in Counterinsurgency." *Asian Survey* 7 (8): 540–554.

Jones, Clive. 2001. "'A Reach Greater than the Grasp': Israeli Intelligence and the Conflict in South Lebanon 1990–2000." *Intelligence and National Security* 16 (3): 1–26.

Kafka, Franz. 1919 [2009]. "In the Penal Colony." In *The Metamorphosis, A Hunger Artist, In the Penal Colony, and Other Stories*. Trans. Ian Johnston. Arlington, VA: Richer Resources Publications.

Kalyvas, Stathis. 2006. *The Logic of Violence in Civil War*. Cambridge: Cambridge University Press.

Kanaaneh, Rhoda. 2008. *Surrounded: Palestinian Soldiers in the Israeli Military*. Stanford, CA: Stanford University Press.

Kaplan, Amy. 2002. *The Anarchy of Empire in the Making of US Culture*. Cambridge, MA: Harvard University Press.

———. 2006. "Where Is Guantánamo?" In *Legal Borderlands: Law and the Construction of American Borders*, ed. Mary Dudziak and Leti Volpp, 239–266. Baltimore: Johns Hopkins University Press.

Kaplan, Amy, and Donald E. Pease, eds. 1993. *Cultures of United States Imperialism*. Durham, NC: Duke University Press.

Kaplan, Fred. 2008. "Prison Break: Maybe the Army Is Not So Hidebound After All." *Slate*, May 8. http://www.slate.com/id/2191008/ (accessed February 19, 2011).

Kaplan, Robert D. 2003. "Supremacy by Stealth." *Atlantic Monthly* 292 (1): 66–83.

———. 2005. *Imperial Grunts: On the Ground with the American Military, from Mongolia to the Philippines to Iraq and Beyond.* New York: Vintage.

Karpinski, Janis, with Steven Strasser. 2005. *One Woman's Army: The Commanding General of Abu Ghraib Tells Her Story.* New York: Hyperion.

Kasher, Asa. 2010. "Analysis: A Moral Evaluation of the Gaza War." *Jerusalem Post*, July 2.

Kasher, Asa, and Amos Yadlin. 2005. "Military Ethics of Fighting Terror: An Israeli Perspective." *Journal of Military Ethics* 4 (1): 3–32.

Katznell, Jack. 2000. "Israeli Government to Introduce Bill That Would Keep Two Lebanese in Prison." Associated Press, April 18.

Keith-Roach, Edward. 1994. *Pasha of Jerusalem: Memoirs of a District Commissioner under the British Mandate.* London: Radcliffe Press.

Kelly, George Armstrong. 1965. *Lost Soldiers: The French Army and Empire in Crisis 1947–1962.* Cambridge, MA: MIT Press.

Kennedy, David. 1977 "International Law and the Nineteenth Century: The History of an Illusion." *Quarterly Law Review* 17: 99–136.

———. 1986. "Primitive Legal Scholarship." *Harvard International Law Journal* 27 (1): 1–98.

———. 2006. "Reassessing International Humanitarianism: The Dark Side." In *International Law and Its Others*, ed. Anne Orford, 131–155. Cambridge: Cambridge University Press.

Kerr, James. 1982. *The Insular Cases: The Role of the Judiciary in American Expansionism.* Port Washington, NY: Kennikat Press.

Kershner, Isabel. 2000. "A Judgment Overtaken." *Jerusalem Post*, June 19.

Khalili, Laleh. 2007. *Heroes and Martyrs of Palestine: The Politics of National Commemoration.* Cambridge: Cambridge University Press.

———. 2008. "Incarceration and the State of Exception: Al-Ansar Mass Detention Camp in Lebanon." In *Thinking Palestine*, ed. Ronit Lentin, 101–115. London: Zed Books.

———. 2008. "On Torture." *Middle East Report* 248: 32–38.

———. 2010. "The Location of Palestine in Global Counterinsurgencies." *International Journal of Middle East Studies* 42 (3): 413–433.

———. 2010. "The New (and Old) Classics of Counterinsurgency." *Middle East Report* 255: 14–23.

———. 2010. "Palestine and the Politics of Invisibility." In *Manifestations of Identity: The Lived Reality of Palestinian Refugees in Lebanon*, ed. Muhammad Ali Khalidi, 125–145. Beirut: Institute for Palestine Studies.

———. 2010. "Tangled Webs of Coercion: Parastatal Production of Violence in Abu Ghraib." In *Policing and Prisons in the Middle East: Formations of Coercion*, ed. Laleh Khalili and Jillian Schwedler, 77–96. New York: Columbia University Press.

———. 2011. "Gendered Practices of Counterinsurgency." *Review of International Studies* 37 (4): 1471–1491.

Khoo, Agnes. 2007. *Life as the River Flows: Women in the Malayan Anti-Colonial Struggle.* Monmouth, Wales: Merlin Press.

Khor, Laura. 2010. "Malaysia's Terrorist Disengagement Program: COIN Theory into Intelligence Practice." Paper presented at the annual meeting of the International Studies Association, New Orleans, LA, February 17.

Kiernan, V. G. 1969. *The Lords of Human Kind: Black Man, Yellow Man, and White Man in an Age of Empire.* London: Cresset Library.

———. 1998. *Colonial Empires and Armies, 1815–1960.* Phoenix Mill, UK: Sutton Publishing.

Kilcullen, David. 2000. "The Political Consequences of Military Operations in Indonesia, 1945–99: A Fieldwork Analysis of the Political Power-Diffusion Effects of Guerrilla Conflict." PhD diss., University of New South Wales.

———. 2006. "Counterinsurgency Redux." *Survival* 48 (4): 111–130.

———. 2006. "Twenty-Eight Articles: Fundamentals of Company-Level Counterinsurgency." *Military Review*, May–June, 103–108.

———. 2009. *Accidental Guerrilla: Fighting Small Wars in the Midst of a Big One.* London: Hurst and Co.

———. 2010. *Counterinsurgency.* London: Hurst and Co.

Killingray, David, and David Omissi, eds. 1999. *Guardians of Empire: The Armed Forces of the Colonial Powers, 1700–1964.* Manchester, UK: University of Manchester Press.

Kinsella, Helen. 2005. "Discourses of Difference: Civilians, Combatants, and Compliance with the Laws of War." *Review of International Studies* 31: 163–185.

———. 2005. "Securing the Civilian: Sex and Gender in the Laws of War." In *Power in Global Governance*, ed. Michael Barnett and Raymond Duvall, 249–272. Cambridge: Cambridge University Press.

Kipling, Rudyard. 1899. "The White Man's Burden." *McClure's Magazine* 12 (February): 290–291.

Kipp, Jacob, Lester Grau, Karl Prinslow, and Capt. Don Smith. 2006. "The Human Terrain System: A CORDS for the 21st Century." *Military Review*, September–October, 8–15.

Kissinger, Henry A. 1969. "The Vietnam Negotiations." *Foreign Affairs* 47 (2): 211–234.

Kiszely, Lt. Gen. Sir John. 2006. "Learning About Counter-Insurgency." *RUSI Journal* 151 (6): 16–21.

Kitson, Frank. 1960. *Gangs and Counter-Gangs.* London: Barrie and Rockliff.

———. 1971. *Low Intensity Operations: Subversion, Insurgency, Peace-Keeping.* London: Faber and Faber.

———. 1977. *Bunch of Five.* London: Faber and Faber.

Kleinfeld, Rachel. 2009. "Petraeus the Progressive: The Surge in Iraq Is a Success and We Must Claim It as Our Own." *Democracy Journal* (Winter): 108–115.

Komer, R. W. 1972. *The Malayan Emergency in Retrospect: Organization of a Successful Counterinsurgency Effort* (report prepared for Advanced Research Projects Agency). Santa Monica, CA: RAND Corporation.

Koplow, David A. 2010. *Death by Moderation: The US Military's Quest for Usable Weapons.* Cambridge: Cambridge University Press.

Koss, Stephen, ed. 1973. *The Pro-Boers: The Anatomy of an Antiwar Movement.* Chicago: University of Chicago Press.

Kramer, Martin. 2010. "Superfluous Young Men." http://www.martinkramer.org/sandbox/2010/02/superfluous-young-men/ (accessed January 4, 2011).

Kramer, Paul A. 2003. "Empires, Exceptions, and Anglo-Saxons: Race and Rule Between the British and US Empires, 1880–1910." In *The American Colonial State in the Philippines: Global Perspectives*, ed. Julian Go and Anne Foster, 43–91. Durham, NC: Duke University Press.

———. 2006. *The Blood of Government: Race, Empire, and the United States & the Philippines.* Chapel Hill: University of North Carolina Press.

Krebs, Paula M. 1992. "'The Last of the Gentlemen's Wars': Women in the Boer War Concentration Camp Controversy." *History Workshop Journal* 33: 38–56

Kuzmarov, Jeremy. 2008. "From Counter-Insurgency to Narco-Insurgency: Vietnam and the International War on Drugs." *Journal of Policy History* 20 (3): 344–378.

Lagouranis, Tony, with Allen Mikaelian. 2007. *Fear Up Harsh: An Army Interrogator's Dark Journey Through Iraq.* New York: NAL Caliber.

Lake, Eli. 2009. "Panetta Faces Rendition Queries: Panel Eyes CIA Pick's Role in Shaping Policy During the Clinton Era." *Washington Times*, January 15.

Lallaoui, Mehdi. 1994. *Kabyles du Pacifique.* Bezons, France: Au Nom de la Mémoire.

Lamb, Christopher J. 2005. *Review of Psychological Operations Lessons Learned from Recent Operational Experience.* Washington, DC: National Defense University Press.

Lasch, Christopher. 1958. "The Anti-Imperialists, the Philippines, and the Inequality of Man." *Journal of Southern History* 24: 319–331.

Latham, Michael E. 2000. *Modernization as Ideology: American Social Science and "Nation Building" in the Kennedy Era.* Chapel Hill: University of North Carolina Press.

Lavie, Aviv. 1997. "Never, Never Land: On Khiam Prison in Southern Lebanon." *Middle East Report* 203: 34–36.

———. 2003. "Inside Israel's Secret Prison." *Ha'aretz*, August 22. http://web.archive.org/web/20071121052741/http://www.haaretz.com/hasen/pages/ShArt.jhtml?itemNo=331637 (accessed April 16, 2012).

Lawrence, T. E. 1935. *Seven Pillars of Wisdom: A Triumph.* New York: Doubleday.

Leary, John D. 1995. *Violence and the Dream People: The Orang Asli in the Malayan Emergency, 1948–1960.* Athens: Ohio University Center for International Studies.

Leary, William M. 1999. "CIA Air Operations in Laos, 1955–1974: Supporting the 'Secret War.'" *Studies in Intelligence.* https://www.cia.gov/library/center-for-the-study-of-intelligence/csi-publications/csi-studies/studies/winter99-00/art7.html (accessed October 11, 2010).

Lefever, Ernest W. 1999. *America's Imperial Burden: Is the Past Prologue?* Boulder, CO: Westview Press.

Lenin, V. I. 1964. *Lenin's Collected Works.* Vol. 24, *War and Revolution.* Moscow: Progress Publishers. Originally published 1917. http://www.marxists.org/archive/lenin/works/1917/may/14.htm (accessed June 24, 2011).

Leopold, Jason, and Jeffrey Kaye. 2012. "'Guidebook to False Confessions': Key Document John Yoo Used to Draft Torture Memo Released." *Truthout*, April 3. http://truth-out.org/news/item/8278-exclusive-guidebook-to-false-confessions-key-document-john-yoo-used-to-draft-torture-memo-released (accessed May 9, 2012).

Le Sueur, James D. 2005. *Uncivil War: Intellectuals and Identity Politics During the Decolonization of Algeria.* 2nd ed. Lincoln: University of Nebraska Press.

Levine, Philippa. 2003. *Prostitution, Race and Politics: Policing Venereal Disease in the British Empire.* New York: Routledge.

Levinson, Chaim, and Liel Kyzer. 2007. "Ex-Interrogator, Accused of Torture, Tapped to Advise Police on Arab Affairs: As Part of His Duties, 'Captain George' Will Oversee the Sensitive Relationship Between the Police and the Arab Community in Jerusalem." *Ha'aretz*, July 28.

Li, Darryl. 2010. "A Universal Enemy? 'Foreign Fighters' and the Legal Regimes of Exclusion and Exemption Under the 'Global War on Terror.'" *Columbia Human Rights Law Review* 41 (2): 355–428.

Li, Tania Murray. 2007. *The Will to Improve: Governmentality, Development, and the Practice of Politics.* Durham, NC: Duke University Press.

Lin Biao. 1965. "Long Live the Victory of the People's War." Beijing: Foreign Language Press. http://www.marxists.org/reference/archive/lin-biao/1965/09/peoples_war/index.htm (accessed December 25, 2010).

Lind, William S., Keith Nightengale, John F. Schmitt, Joseph W. Sutton, and Gary I. Wilson. 1989. "The Changing Face of War: Into the Fourth Generation." *Marine Corps Gazette*, October, 22–26.

Lindsay-Poland, John. 2003. *Emperors in the Jungle: The Hidden History of the US in Panama.* Durham, NC: Duke University Press.

Linebarger, Paul M. A. 1962. "They Call 'Em Bandits in Malaya." In *Modern Guerrilla Warfare: Fighting Communist Guerrilla Movements, 1941–1961,* ed. Franklin Mark Osanka, 293–297. New York: Free Press of Glencoe. Originally published 1951.

Linn, Brian McAllister. 2000. *The Philippine War: 1899–1902.* Lawrence: University Press of Kansas.

———. 2007. *The Echo of Battle: the Army's Way of War.* Cambridge, MA: Harvard University Press.

Lipman, Jana K. 2009. *Guantánamo: A Working Class History Between Empire and Revolution.* Berkeley: University of California Press.

Loh, Francis Kok Wah. 1988. *Beyond the Tin Mines: Coolies, Squatters and New Villagers in the Kinta Valley, Malaysia, c. 1880–1980.* Singapore: Oxford University Press.

———. 2000. "Chinese New Villages: Ethnic Identity and Politics." In *The Chinese in Malaysia,* ed. Kam Hing Lee and Tan Chee-Beng, 255–281. Oxford: Oxford University Press.

Lorimer, James. 2005. *The Institutes of the Laws of Nations: A Treatise of the Jural Relations of Separate Political Communities.* Clark, NJ: Lawbook Exchange. Originally published 1883.

Louis, Wm. Roger. 1978. *Imperialism at Bay: The United States and the Decolonization of the British Empire, 1941–1945.* New York: Oxford University Press.

———. 2006. *Ends of British Imperialism: The Scramble for Empire, Suez, and Decolonization.* London: I. B. Tauris.

Love, Eric T. L. 2004. *Race over Empire: Racism and U.S. Imperialism, 1865–1900.* Chapel Hill: University of North Carolina Press

Luft, Gal. 2010. *Beer, Bacon and Bullets: Culture in Coalition Warfare from Gallipoli to Iraq.* Charleston, SC: BookSurge Publishing.

Lumpe, Lora. 2002. "U.S. Foreign Military Training: Global Reach, Global Power, and Oversight Issues." *Foreign Policy in Focus Special Report* (May).

Luttwak, Edward. 2007. "Dead End: Counterinsurgency Warfare as Military Malpractice." *Harpers Magazine,* February, 33–42.

Lyautey, Hubert. 1900. *Du rôle colonial de l'armée.* Paris: Armand Colin & Cie.

Lyon, David. 2010. "Identification, Colonialism and Control: Surveillant Sorting in Israel/Palestine." In *Surveillance and Control in Israel/Palestine: Population, Territory and Power,* ed. Elia Zureik, David Lyon, and Yasmeen Abu-Laban, 49–64. London: Routledge.

Maass, Peter. 2004. "Professor Nagl's War." *New York Times Magazine,* January 11.

Mack, Andrew. 1975. "Why Big Nations Lose Small Wars: The Politics of Asymmetric Conflict." *World Politics* 27 (2): 175–200.

Mackey, Chris, with Greg Miller. 2004. *The Interrogator's War: Inside the Secret War Against Al-Qaeda.* London: John Murray.

Mackey, Neil. 2002. "Did the US Massacre Taliban?" *Sunday Herald* (Glasgow), June 16.

MacMaster, Neil. 2004. "Torture: From Algiers to Abu Ghraib." *Race and Class* 46 (2): 1–21.

Mahan, Alfred Thayer. 1890. *The Influence of Sea Power upon History, 1660–1783.* Boston: Little, Brown and Company.

Mahler, Jonathan. 2008. *The Challenge:* Hamdan v. Rumsfeld *and the Fight over Presidential Power.* New York: Farrar, Strauss, and Giroux.

Maier, Charles. 2006. *Among Empires: American Ascendancy and Its Predecessors.* Cambridge, MA: Harvard University Press.

Mailhé, Germaine. 1994. *Déportation en Nouvelle-Calédonie des Communards et des révoltés de la Grande Kabyle (1872–1876).* Paris: L'Harmattan.

Mansoor, Peter R. 2008. *Baghdad at Sunrise: A Brigade Commander's War in Iraq.* New Haven, CT: Yale University Press.

Mao Tse-tung. 2000. *On Guerrilla Warfare.* Trans. Samuel B. Griffith. Champaign: University of Illinois Press. Originally published 1937.

Maran, Rita. 1989. *Torture: The Role of Ideology in the French-Algerian War.* New York: Praeger.

Margulies, Joseph. 2006. *Guantánamo and the Abuse of Presidential Power*. New York: Simon and Schuster.

Markel, Matthew W. 2006. "Building Partner Security Forces: Sometimes War *Is* the Answer." *Joint Forces Quarterly* 42: 76–79.

Marks, Susan. 2006. "State-Centrism, International Law, and the Anxieties of Influence." *Leiden Journal of International Law* 19: 339–347.

Marlowe, Ann. 2010. *David Galula: His Life and Intellectual Context*. Carlisle, PA: US Army War College, Strategic Studies Institute.

Marmal, Imad, and Muhammad 'Asi, eds. 2000. *Kam Murr min al-Waqt: 17 asiran lubnaniyyan yaktubun tajaribihim fi al-mu'taqalat al-israyiliyya* (What a Bitter Time: 17 Lebanese Prisoners Write of Their Experience in Israeli Prisons). Beirut: Al-Masar.

Mathias, Grégor. 1998. *Les sections administratives spécialisées en Algérie: Entre idéal et réalité, 1955–1962*. Paris: Harmattan.

Maurois, André. 1931. *Marshal Lyautey*. Trans. Hamish Miles. London: John Lane.

Mayer, Jane. 2008. *The Dark Side: The Inside Story of How the War on Terror Turned into a War on American Ideals*. New York: Doubleday.

———. 2009. "The Predator War: What Are the Risks of the C.I.A.'s Covert Drone Program?" *New Yorker*, October 26, 36–45.

Mazower, Mark. 2009. *No Enchanted Palace: The End of Empire and the Ideological Origins of the United Nations*. Princeton, NJ: Princeton University Press.

McCarthy, Mary. 1967. "Report from Vietnam III: The Intellectuals." *New York Review of Books*, May 18. http://www.nybooks.com/articles/archives/1967/may/18/report-from-vietnam-iii-intellectuals/?pagination=false (accessed April 16, 2012).

McClintock, Anne. 1995. *Imperial Leather: Race, Gender and Sexuality in the Colonial Contest*. London: Routledge.

McCoy, Alfred W. 2005. "Cruel Science: CIA Torture and U.S. Foreign Policy." *New England Journal of Public Policy* 19: 209–262.

———. 2006. *A Question of Torture: CIA Interrogation, from the Cold War to the War on Terror*. New York: Metropolitan Books.

McEvoy, Kieran. 2001. *Paramilitary Imprisonment in Northern Ireland: Resistance, Management, and Release*. Oxford: Oxford University Press.

McFate, Montgomery. 2005. "Anthropology and Counterinsurgency: The Strange Story of Their Curious Relationship." *Military Review*, March–April, 24–37.

———. 2005. "The Military Utility of Understanding Adversary Culture." *Joint Forces Quarterly* 38: 42–48.

McKelvey, Tara. 2007. *Monstering: Inside America's Policy of Secret Interrogations and Torture in the Terror War*. New York: Carroll and Graf Publishers.

McLellan, David, ed. 1977. *Karl Marx: Selected Writings*. Oxford: Oxford University Press.

McMaster, H. R. 2008. "Learning from Contemporary Conflicts to Prepare for Future War." *Orbis* (Fall): 564–584.

Mégret, Frédéric. 2006. "From 'Savages' to 'Unlawful Combatants': A Postcolonial Look at International Humanitarian Law's 'Other.'" In *International Law and Its Others*, ed. Anne Orford, 265–317. Cambridge: Cambridge University Press.

Mehta, Uday Singh. 1999. *Liberalism and Empire: A Study in Nineteenth-Century British Liberal Thought*. Chicago: University of Chicago Press.

Mejía, Camilo. 2007. *Road from Ar-Ramadi: The Private Rebellion of Staff Sergeant Camilo Mejía*. New York: New Press.

Meridor, Ya'akov. 1985. *Long Is the Road to Freedom*. Trans. Molly Lyons and Jaap Bar-David. New York: Judea Publishing Company.

Merom, Gil. 2003. *How Democracies Lose Small Wars: State, Society, and the Failures of France in Algeria, Israel in Lebanon, and the United States in Vietnam*. Cambridge: Cambridge University Press.

Mian, Maulana Syed Mohammad. 2005. *The Prisoners of Malta: The Heartrending Tale of Muslim Freedom Fighters in British Period*. Trans. Mohammad Anwer Hussein and Hasan Imam. Delhi: Manak Publications.

Michael, Kobi, and Amnon Ramon. 2004. "A Fence Around Jerusalem: The Construction of the Security Fence Around Jerusalem. General Background and Implications for the City and Its Metropolitan Area." Jerusalem: Jerusalem Institute for Israel Studies.

Mill, John Stuart. 1859 [1874]. "On the Treatment of Barbarous Nations." In *Dissertations and Discussions: Political, Philosophical, and Historical*. Vol. 3. New York: Henry Holt.

———. 1975. *On Liberty*. In *Three Essays*. Oxford: Oxford University Press. Originally published 1859.

Miller, Randall K. 1997. "The Limits of US International Law Enforcement After *Verdugo-Urquidez*: Resurrecting *Rochin*." *University of Pittsburgh Law Review* 58: 867–910.

Milne, David. 2008. *America's Rasputin: Walt Rostow and the Vietnam War*. New York: Hill and Wang.

Mitchell, Colin. 1969. *Having Been a Soldier*. London: Mayflower Books.

Mockaitis, Thomas R. 1990. *British Counterinsurgency, 1919–60*. London: Macmillan.

Mohlamme, J. S. 2001. "African Refugee Camps in the Boer Republics." In *Scorched Earth*, ed. Fransjohn Pretorius, 110–131. Cape Town: Human and Rousseau.

Morgan, Marston Hunt. 2009. "New Societies in the South Pacific: An Ethnography of French Sovereignty in New Caledonia." PhD diss., University of Chicago.

Mosley, Leonard. 1955. *Gideon Goes to War*. London: Arthur Barker.

Moyar, Mark. 1997. *Phoenix and the Birds of Prey: The CIA's Secret Campaign to Destroy the Viet Cong*. Annapolis, MD: Naval Institute Press.

Mukerjee, Madhusree. 2010. *Churchill's Secret War: The British Empire and the Ravaging of India During World War II*. New York: Basic Books.

Munayyir, Isbir. 1997. *Al-Lid fi 'Ahdayy al-Intidab wa al-Ihtilal* (Al-Lid in the Ages of Mandate and Occupation). Beirut: Institute for Palestine Studies.

Murphy, Gretchen. 2005. *Hemispheric Imaginings: The Monroe Doctrine and Narratives of U.S. Empire*. Durham, NC: Duke University Press.

Nabulsi, Karma. 2005. *Traditions of War: Occupation, Resistance, and the Law*. Oxford: Oxford University Press.

Nagl, John A. 2005. *Learning to Eat Soup with a Knife: Counterinsurgency Lessons from Malaya and Vietnam*. Chicago: University of Chicago Press.

———. 2010. "Local Security Forces." In *Understanding Counterinsurgency: Doctrine, Operations and Challenges*, ed. Thomas Rid and Thomas Kearney, 160–170. London: Routledge.

Nash, David. 1999. "The Boer War and Its Humanitarian Critics." *History Today* 49 (6): 42–49.

Nashif, Esmail. 2004. *Palestinian Political Prisoners: Identity and Community*. London: Routledge.

Neilands, J. B. 1970. "Vietnam: Progress of the Chemical War." *Asian Survey* 10 (3): 209–229.

Nemo, Col. Jean. 1956. "La guerre dans la foule." *Revue de Défense Nationale* 12 (June): 721–734.

———. 1956. "La guerre dans le milieu social." *Revue de Défense Nationale* 12 (May): 605–626.

Network of Concerned Anthropologists, ed. 2009. *The Counter-Counterinsurgency Manual; or, Notes on Demilitarizing American Society*. Chicago: Prickly Paradigm Press.

Neuman, Gerald L. 1996. "Anomalous Zones." *Stanford Law Review* 48 (5): 1197–1234.

Newsinger, John. 2002. *British Counterinsurgency: From Palestine to Northern Ireland*. London: Palgrave.

Newsom, David D. 2001. *The Imperial Mantle: The United States, Decolonization, and the Third World*. Bloomington: Indiana University Press.

Nguyen-Marshall, Van. 2005. "The Moral Economy of Colonialism: Subsistence and Famine Relief in French Indo-China, 1906–1917." *International History Review* 27 (2): 237–258.

Nisan, Mordechai. 2003. *The Conscience of Lebanon: A Political Biography of Étienne Sakr (Abu-Arz)*. London: Frank Cass Publishers.

Noel, Lt. Col. E. 1944. "Wanted: A Frontier Policy." *Journal of the Royal Central Asian Society* 31 (1): 74–79.

Norman, Roger, and Chris af Jochnik. 1994. "Legitimation of Violence: A Critical Analysis of the Gulf War." *Harvard International Law Journal* 35 (2): 387–416.

Norris, Jacob. 2008. "Repression and Rebellion: Britain's Response to the Arab Revolt in Palestine of 1936–39." *Journal of Imperial and Commonwealth History* 36: 25–45.

Omissi, David. 1994. *The Sepoy and the Raj: The Indian Army, 1860–1940*. Basingstoke, UK: Macmillan.

O'Sullivan, Arieh. 2001. "IDF Seals Off Jericho with Anti-Tank Trench." *Jerusalem Post*, March 2.

Ophir, Adi, Michal Gavoni, and Sari Hanafi, eds. 2009. *The Power of Inclusive Exclusion: Anatomy of Israeli Rule in the Occupied Palestinian Territories*. Brooklyn, NY: Zone Books.

Oren, Michael. 2009. "Seven Existential Threats." *Commentary*, May, 16–20.

Ostrow, Ronald J. 1989. "FBI Gets OK for Overseas Arrests. Law: The Justice Department's Decision Allows U.S. Law Officers to Act Without the Consent of Foreign States. That Ruling Could Apply to Efforts to Bring Panama's Noriega to Trial in Florida." *Los Angeles Times*, October 13.

Page, Malcolm. 1998. *A History of the King's African Rifles and East African Forces*. London: Leo Cooper.

Pakenham, Thomas. 1992. *The Boer War*. London: Abacus. Originally published 1979.

Palmer, Stanley. 1988. *Police and Protest in England and Ireland, 1780–1850*. Cambridge: Cambridge University Press.

Paret, Peter. 1964. *French Revolutionary Warfare from Indochina to Algeria: The Analysis of a Political and Military Doctrine*. London: Pall Mall Press.

Parker, Geoffrey. 1996. *The Military Revolution: Military Innovation and the Rise of the West, 1500–1800*. Cambridge: Cambridge University Press.

Patriquin, Capt. Travis. 2006. "How to Win in Anbar." PowerPoint presentation. http://abcnews .go.com/images/US/how_to_win_in_anbar_v4.pdf (accessed July 24, 2011).

Payen, Nikòl. 2002. "Lavalas: The Flood After the Flood." *Callaloo* 25 (3): 759–771.

Pedahzur, Ami. 2009. *The Israeli Secret Services and the Struggle Against Terrorism*. New York: Columbia University Press.

Pelton, Robert Young. 2002. "Transcript of John Walker interview (originally conducted on 2 December 2001)." *CNN*, July 4. http://archives.cnn.com/2001/WORLD/asiapcf/ central/12/20/ret.walker.transcript/ (accessed September 23, 2010).

Perdue, Theda, and Michael D. Green. 1995. *The Cherokee Removal: A Brief History with Documents*. New York: Bedford Press.

Peres, Shimon. 1970. *David's Sling*. London: Weidenfeld and Nicolson.

Pérez, Louis A., Jr. 1986. *Cuba Under the Platt Amendment: 1902–1934*. Pittsburgh, PA: University of Pittsburgh Press.

Perkins, Kenneth J. 1981. *Qaids, Captains, and Colons: French Military Administration in the Colonial Maghrib, 1844–1934*. New York: Africana Publishing Company.

Perry, Alex. 2001. "Inside the Battle of Qala-i-Jangi." *Time*, December 1, 26–33.

Petersen, Peter B. 1989. "The Pioneering Efforts of Major General William Crozier (1855–1942) in the Field of Management." *Journal of Management* 15 (3): 503–516.

Peterson, Scott. 1997. "Woman Forges New Life After Two Years in Israeli-Run Prison." *Christian Science Monitor*, February 9, 7.

Petraeus, David. 1986. "Lessons of History, Lessons of Vietnam." *Parameters* 16 (3): 43–53.

———. 2006. "Learning Counterinsurgency: Observations from Soldiering in Iraq." *Military Review*, January–February, 2–12.

Petraeus, David, and John Nagl. 2008. Preface to *Contre-insurrection: Théories et Pratique*, by David Galula. Trans. Major de Montenon. Paris: Economica. http://www.cdef.terre.defense .gouv.fr/publications/biblio/contre_insurect/contre_insurect.htm (accessed April 16, 2012).

Petras, James. 2000. "Geopolitics of Plan Colombia." *Economic and Political Weekly* 35 (52–53): 4617–4623.

Phillips, Rufus. 2008. *Why Vietnam Matters: An Eyewitness Account of Lessons Not Learned*. Annapolis, MD: Naval Institute Press.

Pincus, Walter. 2007. "'Deprogramming' Iraqi Detainees." *Washington Post*, December 24.

———. 2007. "Iraq's 'Battlefield of the Mind.'" *Washington Post*, December 10.

Pitts, Jennifer. 2005. *A Turn to Empire: The Rise of Imperial Liberalism in Britain and France*. Princeton, NJ: Princeton University Press.

Porch, Douglas. 1986. "Bugeaud, Galliéni, Lyautey: The Development of French Colonial Warfare." In *Makers of Modern Strategy: From Machiavelli to the Nuclear Age*, ed. Peter Paret, 376–407. Oxford: Clarendon Press.

———. 1995. *The French Secret Services: From the Dreyfus Affair to the Gulf War*. London: Macmillan.

Porter, Bernard. 1968. *Critics of Empire: British Radical Attitudes to Colonialism in Africa, 1895–1914*. London: Macmillan.

Posner, Eric A., and John C. Yoo. 2004. "A Theory of International Adjudication." Boalt Working Papers in Public Law, Boalt Hall, University of California, Berkeley.

Pozen, David E. 2005. "The Mosaic Theory, National Security, and the Freedom of Information Act." *Yale Law Journal* 115: 628–679.

Prashad, Vijay. 2007. *The Darker Nations: A People's History of the Third World*. London: New Press.

———. 2011. "*The Wilsonian Moment*: A Review." *Journal of Global History* 6 (1): 153–155.

Price, David H. 2010. "Hard Power, Soft Power, and the Anthropological 'Leveraging' of Cultural 'Assets': Distilling the Politics and Ethics of Anthropological Counterinsurgency." In *Anthropology and the Global Counterinsurgency*, ed. John D. Kelly, Beatrice Jauregui, Sean Mitchell, and Jeremy Walton, 245–260. Chicago: University of Chicago Press.

Price, Richard. 1998. *The Convict and the Colonel: A Story of Colonialism and Resistance in the Caribbean*. Boston: Beacon Press.

Priest, Dana. 2005. "CIA Avoids Scrutiny of Detainee Treatment: Afghan's Death Took Two Years to Come to Light: Agency Says Abuse Claims Are Probed Fully." *Washington Post*, March 3.

———. 2005. "CIA's Assurances on Transferred Suspects Doubted: Prisoners Say Countries Break No-Torture Pledges." *Washington Post*, March 17.

———. 2005. "Foreign Network at Front of CIA's Terror Fight: Joint Facilities in Two Dozen Countries Account for Bulk of Agency's Post-9/11 Successes." *Washington Post*, November 18.

———. 2010. "National Security Inc." *Washington Post*, July 20.

Priest, Dana, and Barton Gellman. 2002. "U.S. Decries Abuse but Defends Interrogations: 'Stress and Duress' Tactics Used on Terrorism Suspects Held in Secret Overseas Facilities." *Washington Post*, December 26.

Pyle, Christopher. 2004. "Torture by Proxy." *San Francisco Chronicle*, January 4.

Rabinow, Paul. 1989. *French Modern: Norms and Forms of the Social Environment.* Chicago: University of Chicago Press.

Rafael, Vicente L. 1993. "White Love: Surveillance and Nationalist Resistance in the US Colonization of the Philippines." In *Cultures of United States Imperialism*, ed. Amy Kaplan and Donald Pease, 185–218. Durham, NC: Duke University Press.

Raghavan, Sudarsan. 2008. "In Fallujah, Peace Through Brute Strength: Iraqi City's Fragile Security Flows from Hussein-Era Tactics." *Washington Post*, March 24.

Ramakrishna, Kumar. 2002. *Emergency Propaganda: The Winning of Malayan Hearts and Minds, 1948–1958.* Richmond, VA: Curzon Press.

Ramsey, Robert D., III. 2007. "A Masterpiece of Counterguerrilla Warfare: BG J. Franklin Bell in the Philippines, 1901–1902." Long War Series Occasional Paper 25, Combat Studies Institute Press, Ft. Leavenworth, KS.

Rancière, Jacques. 2001. "Ten Theses on Politics." *Theory and Event* 5 (3).

Rao, Rahul. 2010. *Third World Protest: Between Home and the World.* Oxford: Oxford University Press.

Ratner, Michael. 1998. "How We Closed the Guantanamo HIV Camp: The Intersection of Politics and Litigation." *Harvard Human Rights Journal* 11: 187–220.

Ratner, Michael, and Ellen Ray. 2004. *Guantánamo: What the World Should Know.* Gloucestershire, UK: Arris Books.

Reeves, Phil. 2000. "Barak Forced to Release 13 'Hostages' but Demands New Law to Keep Others." *Independent* (London), April 20.

Reid-Daly, Ron, and Peter Stiff. 1982. *Selous Scouts: Top Secret War.* Cape Town: Galago Publishing.

Reinfeld, Moshe. 2001. "Obeid, Dirani to Be Allowed Red Cross Visits." *Ha'aretz*, August 24.

Rejali, Darius. 2007. *Torture and Democracy.* Princeton, NJ: Princeton University Press.

Renda, Mary A. 2001. *Taking Haiti: Military Occupation and the Culture of US Imperialism 1915–1940.* Chapel Hill: University of North Carolina Press.

Rhem, Kathleen T. 2005. "Army Improving Procedures for Handling Detainees." *American Forces Press Service*, February 25. http://www.tradoc.army.mil/pao/tnsarchives/February05/025305.htm (accessed April 1, 2011).

Richter, Melvin. 1963. "Tocqueville on Algeria." *Review of Politics* 25 (3): 362–398.

Ricks, Thomas E. 2006. *Fiasco: The American Military Adventure in Iraq.* London: Allen Lane.

———. 2009. *The Gamble: General Petraeus and the Untold Story of the American Surge in Iraq, 2006–2008.* London: Allen Lane.

Rid, Thomas. 2009. "*Razzia*: A Turning Point in Modern Strategy." *Terrorism and Political Violence* 21 (4): 617–635.

———. 2010. "The Nineteenth Century Origins of Counterinsurgency Doctrine." *Journal of Strategic Studies* 33 (5): 727–758.

Rid, Thomas, and Marc Hecker. 2009. *War 2.0: Irregular Warfare in the Information Age.* Westport, CT: Praeger Security International.

Risen, James. 2009. "U.S. Inaction Seen After Taliban P.O.W.'s Died." *New York Times*, July 11.

Rivera Ramos, Efrén. 1996. "The Legal Construction of American Colonialism: The Insular Cases (1901–1922)." *Revista Jurídica Universidad de Puerto Rico* 65 (2): 225–328.

Rivkin, David B., Jr., Lee A. Casey, and Darin R. Bartram. 2001. "Bringing Al-Qaeda to Justice: The Constitutionality of Trying Al-Qaeda Terrorists in the Military Justice System." Heritage Society Legal Memorandum No. 3 (November 5). http://thf_media.s3.amazonaws.com/2001/pdf/lm3.pdf (accessed October 17, 2010).

Roberts, Alasdair. 2003. "NATO, Secrecy and the Right to Information." *East European Constitutional Review* 12 (1): 86–94.

Robin, Marie-Monique. 2004. *Escadrons de la mort: L'école française*. Paris: La Découverte.

Robinson, J. B. Perry. 1956. *Transformation in Malaya*. London: Secker and Warburg.

Robinson, Shira. 2003. "Local Struggle, National Struggle: Palestinian Responses to the Kafr Qasim Massacre and Its Aftermath: 1956–66." *International Journal of Middle East Studies* 35: 393–416.

———. 2005. "Occupied Citizens in a Liberal State: Palestinians Under Military Rule and the Colonial Formation of Israeli Society, 1948–1966." PhD diss., Stanford University.

Rodriguez, Jose A., Jr., with Bill Harlow. 2012. *Hard Measures: How Aggressive CIA Actions After 9/11 Saved American Lives*. New York: Simon and Schuster.

Rokach, Livia. 1980. *Israel's Sacred Terrorism: A Study Based on Moshe Sharett's Personal Diary and Other Documents*. Belmont, MA: Association of Arab-American University Graduates.

Ron, James. 2003. *Frontiers and Ghettos: State Violence in Serbia and Israel*. Berkeley: University of California Press.

Root, Elihu. 1970. *The Military and the Colonial Policy of the United States: Addresses and Report*. New York: AMS Press. Originally published 1916.

Rosenfeld, Maya. 2004. *Confronting the Occupation: Work, Education and Political Activism of Palestinian Families in a Refugee Camp*. Stanford, CA: Stanford University Press.

Rostow, W. W. 1990. *The Stages of Economic Growth: A Non-Communist Manifesto*. Cambridge: Cambridge University Press. Originally published 1961.

Rostow, Walt W. 1961. "Countering Guerrilla Attack." In *Special Warfare*, by US Army, 21–25. Washington, DC: Chief of Army's Office of Chief of Information.

———. 1962. "Guerrilla Warfare in Underdeveloped Areas." In *The Guerrilla and How to Fight Him: Selections from* The Marine Corps Gazette, ed. T. N. Greene, 54–62. New York: Praeger.

Rostow, W. W., and Richard W. Hatch. 1955. *An American Policy in Asia*. London: Chapman and Hall.

Royle, Trevor. 1995. *Orde Wingate: Irregular Soldier*. London: Weidenfeld and Nicolson.

Rubin, Alissa. 2008. "US Remakes Jails in Iraq, but Gains Are at Risk." *New York Times*, June 2.

Rubin, Alissa, and Doyle McManus. 2004. "Why America Has Waged a Losing Battle on Fallouja." *Los Angeles Times*, October 24.

Ruskola, Teemu. 2006. "Canton Is Not Boston: The Invention of American Imperial Sovereignty." In *Legal Borderlands: Law and the Construction of American Borders*, ed. Mary Dudziak and Leti Volpp, 267–292. Baltimore: Johns Hopkins University Press.

Russo, A. J. 1967 "A Statistical Analysis of the U.S. Crop Spraying Program in South." Santa Monica, CA: RAND Corporation.

Saar, Erik, and Viveka Novak. 2005. *Inside the Wire: A Military Intelligence Soldier's Eyewitness Account of Life at Guantánamo*. New York: Penguin Press.

Sachar, Howard M. 1987. *A History of Israel*. Vol. 2, *From the Aftermath of the Yom Kippur War*. Oxford: Oxford University Press.

Sales, Leigh. 2007. *Detainee 002: The Case of David Hicks*. Melbourne, Australia: Melbourne University Press.

Saltman, Mark. 1982. "The Use of Mandatory Emergency Laws by the Israeli Government." *International Journal of the Sociology of Law* 10: 385–394.

Sands, Philippe. 2008. "The Green Light." *Vanity Fair*, May, 218.

———. 2008. *Torture Team: Deception, Cruelty and the Compromise of the Law*. London: Allen Lane.

Sassaman, Lt. Col. (Ret.) Nathan. 2008. *Warrior King: The Triumph and Betrayal of an American Commander in Iraq*. New York: St. Martin's Press.

Satia, Priya. 2006. "The Defense of Inhumanity: Air Control and the British Idea of Arabia." *American Historical Review* III (1): 16–51.

Savage, Charlie. 2012. "Ruling Averts Testimony by a Detainee, for Now." *New York Times*, April 11.

Savage, Charlie, and Eric Schmitt. 2011. "U.S. to Prosecute a Somali Suspect in Civilian Court." *New York Times*, July 5.

Scahill, Jeremy. 2011. "The CIA's Secret Sites in Somalia." *Nation*, July 12.

Schmitt, Carl. 2003. *The Nomos of the Earth in the International Law of Jus Publicum Europaeum*. Trans. G. L. Ulmen. New York: Telos Press.

———. 2007. *The Theory of the Partisan: Intermediate Commentary on the Concept of the Political*. Trans. G. L. Ulmen. New York: Telos Press.

Schmitt, Eric, and Carolyn Marshall. 2006. "In Secret Unit's 'Black Room,' a Grim Portrait of US Abuse." *New York Times*, March 19.

Schmitt, Eric, and Thom Shanker. 2004 "Rumsfeld Issued an Order to Hide Detainee in Iraq." *New York Times*, June 17.

Schwarz, Walter. 1959. *The Arabs in Israel*. London: Faber.

Scott, James C. 1998. *Seeing Like a State: How Certain Schemes to Improve Human Condition Have Failed*. New Haven, CT: Yale University Press.

Segev, Tom. 2000. *One Palestine Complete: Jews and Arabs Under the British Mandate*. Trans. Haim Watzman. London: Metropolitan Books.

Sela, Rona. 2009. "Presence and Absence in 'Abandoned' Palestinian Villages." *History of Photography* 33 (1): 71–79.

Sen, Satadru. 2000. *Disciplining Punishment: Colonialism and Convict Society in the Andaman Islands*. New Delhi: Oxford University Press.

Sepp, Kalev I. 1992. "Resettlement, Regroupment, Reconcentration: Deliberate Government-Directed Population Relocation in Support of Counter-Insurgency Operations." Master of Military Art and Science thesis, US Army Command and General Staff, College, Ft. Leavenworth, KS.

———. 2005. "Best Practices in Counterinsurgency." *Military Review*, May–June, 8–12.

———. 2007. "From 'Shock and Awe' to 'Hearts and Minds': The Fall and Rise of US Counterinsurgency Capability in Iraq." *Third World Quarterly* 18 (2): 217–230.

———. 2010. "Special Forces." In *Understanding Counterinsurgency: Doctrine, Operations and Challenges*, ed. Thomas Rid and Thomas Keaney, 128–140. London: Routledge.

Sewall, Sarah. 2007. "Introduction to the University of Chicago Press Edition." In *Counterinsurgency Field Manual*, by US Army and Marine Corps, xxi–xliii. Chicago: University of Chicago Press.

Shachtman, Noah. 2007. "How Technology Almost Lost the War: In Iraq, the Critical Networks Are Social—Not Electronic." *Wired.com*, November 27. http://www.wired.com/politics/security/magazine/15-12/ff_futurewar (accessed November 2, 2010).

Al-Shahabi, Muhammad Yahya. 1994. *Lubiya: Shawka fi Khasira al-Mashru' al-Sahyuni* (Lubiya: Anticipating the Loss of Zionist Legitimacy). Damascus: Dar al-Shajara.

Shapira, Anita. 1999. *Land and Power: The Zionist Resort to Force, 1881–1948*. Stanford, CA: Stanford University Press.

Shapiro, Stephanie. 2009. "Lost in Translation: The Trials of Chuck Schmitz, Terrorist Interpreter." *Urbanite Baltimore*, March 1. http://www.urbanitebaltimore.com/baltimore/lost-in-translation/Content?oid=1244680 (accessed September 20, 2010).

Sharon, Ariel, with David Chanoff. 1989. *Warrior: The Autobiography of Ariel Sharon*. London: Macdonald and Co.

Sharpless, John. 1997. "Population Science, Private Foundations, and Development Aid: The Transformation of Demographic Knowledge in the United States, 1945–1965." In *International*

Development and the Social Sciences: Essays on the History and Politics of Knowledge, ed. Frederick Cooper and Randall Packard, 176–200. Berkeley: University of California Press.

Sheehan, Neil. 1988. *A Bright Shining Lie: John Paul Vann and America in Vietnam.* London: Picador.

Shehadeh, Raja. 1988. *Occupier's Law: Israel and the West Bank.* Washington, DC: Institute for Palestine Studies.

Shenhav, Yehouda, and Yael Berda. 2009. "The Colonial Foundations of the State of Exception: Juxtaposing the Israeli Occupation of the Palestinian Territories with the Colonial Bureaucratic History." In *The Power of Inclusive Exclusion: Anatomy of Israeli Rule in the Occupied Palestinian Territories*, ed. Adi Ophir, Michal Gavoni, and Sari Hanafi, 337–374. Brooklyn, NY: Zone Books.

Shennan, Margaret. 2007. *Our Man in Malaya: John Davis CBE, DSO, SOE Force 136 and Postwar Counter-Insurgency.* Stroud, UK: Sutton Publishing.

Shephard, Michelle, and Tonda MacCharles. 2009. "Arar in Canada When 'Seen' by Khadr, Hearing Told." *Toronto Star*, January 20.

Shlaim, Avi. 2000. *The Iron Wall: Israel and the Arab World.* London: Penguin Books.

Short, Anthony. 1975. *The Communist Insurrection in Malaya.* London: Frederick Muller.

Shrader, Charles. 1999. *The Withered Vine: Logistics and the Communist Insurgency in Greece, 1945–1949.* Westport, CT: Praeger.

Simpson, A. W. Brian. 2004. *Human Rights and the End of Empire: Britain and the Genesis of the European Convention.* Oxford: Oxford University Press.

Sinclair, Georgina, and Chris A. Williams. 2007. "'Home and Away': The Cross-Fertilisation Between 'Colonial' and 'British' Policing, 1921–85." *Journal of Imperial and Commonwealth History* 35: 221–238.

Singer, Barnett, and John Langdon. 2004. *Cultured Force: Makers and Defenders of the French Colonial Empire.* Madison: University of Wisconsin Press.

Singer, Peter W. 2003. *Corporate Warriors: The Rise of the Privatized Military Industry.* Ithaca, NY: Cornell University Press.

———. 2004. "War, Profits, and the Vacuum of Law: Privatized Military Firms and International Law." *Columbia Journal of Transnational Law* 42 (2): 521–549.

———. 2009. *Wired for War: The Robotics Revolution and Conflict in the 21st Century.* London: Penguin.

Singha, Radhika. 1998. *A Despotism of Law: Crime and Justice in Early Colonial India.* Delhi: Oxford University Press.

Sinha, Bejoy Kumar. 1988. *In Andamans: The Indian Bastille.* New Delhi: People's Publishing House. Originally published 1939.

Slavin, David H. 1991. "The French Left and the Rif War, 1924–25." *Journal of Contemporary History* 26 (1): 5–32.

Smith, Neil. 2003. *American Empire: Roosevelt's Geographer and the Prelude to Globalization.* Berkeley: University of California Press.

Smith, Rupert. 2005. *The Utility of Force: The Art of War in the Modern World.* London: Penguin.

Smith, Tony. 1978. "A Comparative Study of French and British Decolonization." *Comparative Studies in Society and History* 20 (1): 70–102.

Smooha, Sammy. 1978. *Israel: Pluralism and Conflict.* Berkeley: University of California Press.

Solf, Waldemar. 1986. "A Response to Douglas J. Feith's 'Law in the Service of Terror—The Strange Case of the Additional Protocol.'" *Akron Law Review* 20 (2): 261–289.

Sorley, Lewis. 1999. *A Better War: The Unexamined Victories and Final Tragedy of America's Last Years in Vietnam.* Orlando, FL: Houghton Mifflin.

———. 2008. *Thunderbolt: General Creighton Abrams and the Army of His Times.* 2nd ed. Bloomington: Indiana University Press. Originally published 1992.

Sorum, Paul Clay. 1977. *Intellectuals and Decolonization in France.* Chapel Hill: University of North Carolina Press.

Souyris, Capitaine Andre. 1956. "Un procédé éfficace de contre-guérilla: L'auto-défense des populations." *Revue de Défense National,* June, 686–699.

Spieler, Miranda Frances. 2005. "Empire and Underworld: Guiana in the French Legal Imagination, c. 1789–c. 1870." PhD diss., Columbia University.

Spies, S. B. 1977. *Methods of Barbarism? Roberts and Kitchener and Civilians in the Boer Republics, January 1900–May 1902.* Cape Town: Human and Rousseau.

Stafford Smith, Clive. 2007. *Bad Men: Guantánamo Bay and the Secret Prisons.* London: Weidenfeld and Nicolson.

Stewart, Rory. 2004. *Occupational Hazards: My Time Governing in Iraq.* London: Picador.

Stoil, Rebecca Anna. 2008. "A Deadly Cat-and-Mouse Game Along the Fence." *Jerusalem Post,* March 7.

Stokes, Doug. 2004. *America's Other War: Terrorizing Colombia.* London: Zed Books.

Strachan, Hew. 1997. *The Politics of the British Army.* Oxford: Clarendon Press.

Streets, Heather. 2004. *Martial Races and Masculinity in the British Army, 1857–1914.* Manchester, UK: Manchester University Press.

Strobel, Warren. 2009. "CIA Sacked Baghdad Station Chief After Deaths of 2 Detainees." *McClatchy Newspapers,* August 25.

Sullivan, Antony Thrall. 1983. *Thomas-Robert Bugeaud: France and Algeria, 1784–1849: Politics, Power, and the Good Society.* Hamden, CT: Archon Books.

Sulmasy, Gary, and John C. Yoo. 2007. "Counterintuitive: Intelligence Operations and International Law." *Michigan Journal of International Law* 28: 625–639.

Surridge, Keith. 1997. "'All You Soldiers Are What We Call Pro-Boers': The Military Critique of South African War, 1899–1902." *History* 82: 582–600.

Surridge, Keith T. 1998. *Managing the South African War, 1899–1902: Politicians vs. Generals.* Woodbridge, UK: Boydell Press.

Suskind, Ron. 2006. *The One Percent Doctrine: Deep Inside America's Pursuit of Its Enemies Since 9/11.* London: Simon and Schuster.

Sutton, Keith. 1977. "Population Resettlement—Traumatic Upheavals and the Algerian Experience." *Journal of Modern African Studies* 15 (2): 279–300.

Sutton, Keith, and Richard I. Lawless. 1978. "Population Regrouping in Algeria: Traumatic Change and the Rural Settlement Pattern." *Transactions of the Institute of British Geographers* 3 (3): 331–350.

Swift, Jonathan. 1742 [1996]. *Gulliver's Travels.* New York: Random House Modern Library Edition.

Taithe, Bertrand. 2009. *The Killer Trail: A Colonial Scandal in the Heart of Africa.* Oxford: Oxford University Press.

———. 2010. "La famine de 1866–1868: Anatomie d'une catastrophe et construction médiatique d'un événement." *Revue d'histoire du XIXe Siècle* 41: 113–127.

Tamari, Salah. 1984. "Salah Tamari." *Journal of Palestine Studies* 13 (4): 46–69.

Tawil-Souri, Helga. 2010. "Green, and Blue: Colour-Coded Paperwork for Palestinian Population Control." In *Surveillance and Control in Israel/Palestine: Population, Territory and Power,* ed. Elia Zureik, David Lyon, and Yasmeen Abu-Laban, 219–238. London: Routledge.

Taylor, Frederick Winslow. 1998. *The Principles of Scientific Management.* Mineola, NY: Dover Publications. Originally published 1911.

Therborn, Göran. 2009. "NATO's Demographer." *New Left Review* 56: 136–144.

Thomas, Hugh. 1971. *Cuba: The Pursuit of Freedom*. New Brunswick, NJ: Harper and Row.

Thompson, Robert. 1968. "Squaring the Error." *Foreign Affairs* 46 (3): 442–453.

———. 1969. *No Exit from Vietnam*. London: Chatto and Windus.

———. 1989. *Make for the Hills: Memories of Far Eastern Wars*. London: Leo Cooper.

———. 2005. *Defeating Communist Insurgency*. St. Petersburg, FL: Hailer Publishing. Originally published 1965.

Thompson, Wilfred. 1988. "The Introduction of American Law in the Philippines and Porto Rico, 1898–1905." PhD diss., University of Chicago.

Thornton, Rod. 2009. "'Minimum Force': A Reply to Huw Bennett." *Small Wars and Insurgencies* 20 (1): 215–226.

Thornton, Thomas Henry. 1895. *Colonel Sir Robert Sandeman: His Life and Work on Our Indian Frontier*. London: John Murray.

Tira, Ron. 2010. *The Nature of War: Conflicting Paradigms and Israeli Military Effectiveness*. Eastbourne, UK: Sussex Academic Press.

Todd, Lin, et al. 2006. *Iraq Tribal Study—Al-Anbar Governorate: The Albu Fahd Tribe, The Albu Mahal Tribe and the Albu Issa Tribe*. Washington, DC: Department of Defense.

Tone, John Lawrence. 2006. *War and Genocide in Cuba, 1895–1898*. Chapel Hill: University of North Carolina Press.

Torruella, Juan R. 2007. "The Insular Cases: The Establishment of a Regime of Political Apartheid." *University of Pennsylvania Journal of International Law* 29 (2): 283–327.

Toscano, Alberto. 2008. "Carl Schmitt in Beijing: Partisanship, Geopolitics and the Demolition of the Eurocentric World." *Postcolonial Studies* 11 (4): 417–433.

Toth, Stephen A. 2006. *Beyond* Papillon: *The French Overseas Penal Colonies, 1854–1952*. Lincoln: University of Nebraska Press.

Toye, Richard. 2010. *Churchill's Empire: The World That Made Him and the World He Made*. London: Macmillan.

Trinquier, Roger. 1964. *Modern Warfare: A French View of Counterinsurgency*. London: Pall Mall Press.

Tripodi, Christian. 2009. "'Good for One but Not the Other': The 'Sandeman System' of Pacification as Applied to Baluchistan and the North-West Frontier, 1877–1947." *Journal of Military History* 73: 767–802.

Tsemel, Lea. 1984. "Personal Status and Rights." In *Occupation: Israel over Palestine*, ed. Naseer Aruri, 57–66. London: Zed Books.

Utley, Robert. 1967. *Frontiersmen in Blue: The United States Army and the Indian, 1848–1865*. New York: Macmillan.

———. 1973. *Frontier Regulars: the United States Army and the Indian, 1866–1891*. New York: Macmillan.

Valentine, Douglas. 1990. *The Phoenix Program*. New York: William Morrow.

Valeyre, Bertrand, and Alexandre Guerin. 2009. *De Galula à Petraeus: L'héritage français dans la pensée américaine de la contre-insurrection*. Paris: Centre de Doctrine d'Emploi des Forces.

Van Der Merwe, Floris J. G. 1992. "Sport and Games in Boer Prisoner-of-War Camps During the Anglo-Boer war, 1899–1902." *International Journal of the History of Sport* 9 (3): 439–454.

Van Schoor, M. C. E. (1983). *Die Bannelinge: A. B. O. Boerekrygsgevangenes 1899–1902, 'n Gedenkbrosjure*. Bloemfontein, South Africa: Oorlogsmuseum van die Boere-republieke.

Vasak, Karel. 1963. "The European Convention of Human Rights Beyond the Frontiers of Europe." *International and Comparative Law Quarterly* 12 (4): 1206–1231.

Verkuil, Paul R. 2007. *Outsourcing Sovereignty: Why Privatization of Government Functions Threatens Democracy and What We Can Do About It*. Cambridge: Cambridge University Press.

Vidal-Naquet, Pierre. 1963. *Torture: Cancer of Democracy. France and Algeria, 1954–62*. Trans. Barry Richard. London: Penguin Books.

Villatoux, Marie-Catherine. 2003. "Hogard et Némo: Deux théoriciens de la 'guerre révolutionnaire.'" *Revue Historique des Armées* 232: 20–28.

Vine, David. 2009. *Island of Shame: The Secret History of the US Military Base on Diego Garcia*. Princeton, NJ: Princeton University Press.

Vitullo, Anita. 1992. "Yitzhak Rabin and Israel's Death Squads." *Middle East Report* 178: 40–42.

von Eschen, Penny. 1997. *Race Against Empire: Americans and Anticolonialism, 1937–1957*. Ithaca, NY: Cornell University Press.

Walker, Tom, and Sarah Baxter. 2006. "Revealed: The Terror Prison US Is Helping Build in Morocco." *Sunday Times* (London), February 12.

Warren, Robert. 2004. "City Streets—The War Zones of Globalisation: Democracy and Military Operations in Urban Terrain in the Early 21st Century." In *Cities, War, and Terrorism: Towards an Urban Geopolitics*, ed. Stephen Graham, 214–230. Cambridge: Blackwell.

Warwick, Peter. 1983. *Black People and the South African War, 1899–1902*. Cambridge: Cambridge University Press.

Weigley, Russell F. 1969. "The Elihu Root Reforms and the Progressive Era." In *Command and Commanders in Modern Warfare*, ed. William Geffen, 11–27. Colorado Springs, CO: US Air Force Academy.

———. 1973. *The American Way of War: A History of United States Military Strategy and Policy*. Bloomington: Indiana University Press.

Weinberger, Sharon. 2011. "Pentagon Cultural Analyst Helped with Interrogations: 'Experiment' Raises Alarm Among Social Scientists." *Nature*, October 18. http://www.nature.com/news/2011/111018/full/news.2011.598.html (accessed November 15, 2011).

Weiner, Tim. 2007. "Walling Off Your Enemies: The Long View." *New York Times*, April 29.

Weizman, Eyal. 2007. *Hollow Land: Israel's Architecture of Occupation*. London: Verso.

———. 2009. "Lawfare in Gaza: Legislative Attack." *OpenDemocracy*. http://www.opendemocracy.net/article/legislative-attack (accessed August 18, 2010).

———. 2009. "Thanato-Tactics." In *The Power of Inclusive Exclusion: Anatomy of Israeli Rule in the Occupied Palestinian Territories*, ed. Adi Ophir, Michal Gavoni, and Sari Hanafi, 543–573. Brooklyn, NY: Zone Books.

Welch, Richard E., Jr. 1974. "American Atrocities in the Philippines: The Indictment and the Response." *Pacific Historical Review* 43 (2): 233–253.

West, Bing. 2005. *No True Glory: A Frontline Account of the Battle for Fallujah*. New York: Bantam Books.

———. 2008. "A Report from Iraq." *Atlantic Monthly*, January 30.

Westerman, Ian. 2008. "Pacifying Afghanistan: Enduring Lessons from CORDS in Vietnam." *RUSI Journal* 153 (5): 14–21.

Weston, Rubin Francis. 1972. *Racism in US Imperialism: The Influence of Racial Assumptions on American Foreign Policy, 1893–1946*. Columbia: University of South Carolina Press.

White, Josh. 2005. "Documents Tell of Brutal Improvisation by GIs: Interrogated General's Sleeping-Bag Death, CIA's Use of Secret Iraqi Squad Are Among Details." *Washington Post*, August 3.

Whitlock, Craig. 2011. "Adm. McRaven: Obama Administration Has No Plan for Captured Terrorists." *Washington Post*, June 29.

Whitson, Maj. J. L. 1984. "The Laws of Land Warfare: The Privileged Guerrilla and the Deprived Soldier." Quantico, VA: Marine Corps Command and Staff College. http://www.globalsecurity.org/military/library/report/1984/WJL.htm (accessed May 13, 2011).

Wilcke, Christoph. 2006. "A Hard Place: The United States and the Creation of a New Security Apparatus in Iraq." *Civil Wars* 8 (2): 124–142.

Williams, Daniel, and Roberto Suro. 1994. "Detention of Cubans Poses Variety of Problems; Clinton Must Consider Pending Court Ruling, Havana, Anti-Castro Groups and Human Rights Issues." *Washington Post*, October 28.

Williams, Robert A., Jr. 1990. *The American Indian in Western Legal Thought: The Discourses of Conquest*. New York: Oxford University Press.

Williams, William Appleman. 2007. *Empire as a Way of Life*. New York: Ig Publishing. Originally published 1980.

Windrow, Martin. 2004. *The Last Valley: Dien Bien Phu and the French Defeat in Vietnam*. London: Weidenfeld and Nicolson.

Winn Byrd, Col. Miemie, and Maj. Gretchen Decker. 2008. "Why the US Should Gender Its Counterterrorism Strategy." *Military Review*, July–August, 96–101.

Wolfe, Patrick. 1999. *Settler Colonialism and the Transformation of Anthropology*. New York: Cassell.

Wolton, Suke. 2000. *Lord Hailey, the Colonial Office and the Politics of Race and Empire in the Second World War: The Loss of White Prestige*. Houndmills, UK: Macmillan.

Wood, Trish, ed. 2006. *What Was Asked of Us: An Oral History of the Iraq War by the Soldiers Who Fought It*. New York: Little, Brown, and Company.

Woods, Andrew. 2008. "The Business End." *Financial Times*, June 28.

Woodward, Bob. 2002. *Bush at War*. New York: Pocket Books.

Worthington, Andy. 2007. *The Guantánamo Files: The Stories of the 774 Detainees in America's Illegal Prisons*. London: Pluto Press.

———. 2009. "Ibn al-Shaykh al-Libi Has Died In A Libyan Prison" (May 10). http://www.andy worthington.co.uk/2009/05/10/ibn-al-shaykh-al-libi-has-died-in-a-libyan-prison/ (accessed October 11, 2010).

———. 2009. "New Revelations about the Torture of Ibn al-Shaykh al-Libi" (June 18). http:// www.andyworthington.co.uk/2009/06/18/world-exclusive-new-revelations-about-the-torture-of-ibn-al-shaykh-al-libi/ (accessed May 30, 2011).

Wright, Gwendolyn. 1991. *The Politics of Design in French Colonial Urbanism*. Chicago: University of Chicago Press.

Wright, Quincy. 1926. "The Bombardment of Damascus." *American Journal of International Law* 20 (2): 263–280.

Yoo, John C. 1996. "The Continuation of Politics by Other Means: The Original Understanding of War Powers." *California Law Review* 84: 167–305.

———. 2005. *The Powers of War and Peace: The Constitution and Foreign Affairs After 9/11*. Chicago: University of Chicago Press.

———. 2004. "Transferring Terrorists." *Notre Dame Law Review* 79: 1183–1235.

———. 2004. "Using Force." *University of Chicago Law Review* 71: 729–732.

———. 2006. *War by Other Means: An Insider's Account of the War on Terror*. New York: Atlantic Monthly Press.

Young, Marilyn B. 1991. *The Vietnam Wars, 1945–1990*. New York: HarperCollins.

Young, Robert J. C. 2001. *Postcolonialism: An Historical Introduction*. Oxford: Blackwell.

Youssef, Sa'di. 2009. *Al-A'mal al-kamila: al-juz' al-sadis* (Complete Works, vol. 6). Beirut: Dar al-Jamal.

Yuen, Yuet Leng. 1998. *Operation Ginger*. Kuala Lumpur: Vinpress.

Yuval-Davis, Nira. 1989. "National Reproduction and 'the Demographic Race' in Israel." In *Woman-Nation-State*, ed. Nira Yuval-Davis and Floya Anthias, 92–109. London: Macmillan.

Zangana, Haifa. 2010. "Walls in Iraq: Impact on Baghdadi Women." *International Journal of Contemporary Iraqi Studies* 4 (1–2): 41–58.

Zasloff, Joseph J. 1962–1963. "Rural Resettlement in South Viet Nam: The Agroville Program." *Pacific Affairs* 35 (4): 327–340.

Zertal, Idith, and Akiva Eldar. 2007. *Lords of the Land: The War over Israel's Settlements in the Occupied Territories, 1967–2007.* Trans. Vivian Eden. New York: Nation Books.

Zietsman, Paul. 2001. "The Concentration Camp Schools: Beacons of Light in the Darkness." In *Scorched Earth*, ed. Fransjohn Pretorius, 86–109. Cape Town: Human and Rousseau.

Zinoman, Peter. 2001. *The Colonial Bastille: A History of Imprisonment in Vietnam, 1862–1940.* Berkeley: University of California Press.

Zolo, Danilo. 2002. *Invoking Humanity: War, Law, and Global Order.* Trans. Federico and Gordono Poole. London: Continuum.

Zureik, Elia, David Lyon, and Yasmeen Abu-Laban, eds. 2010. *Surveillance and Control in Israel/Palestine: Population, Territory and Power.* London: Routledge.

———. 2001. "Constructing Palestine Through Surveillance Practices." *British Journal of Middle Eastern Studies* 28: 205–227.

INDEX

Made in the USA
San Bernardino, CA
08 April 2017